BILL HYMAN & GARY ODEN

second edition

LIFETIME Health & Wellness

Kendall Hunt
publishing company

Contents

The Importance of Fitness and Wellness

© Warren Goldswain, 2014. Used under license from Shutterstock, Inc.

Specific Objectives

1. List the pathological and behavioral causes of death of Americans.
2. Explain the concept of "diseases of lifestyle" and the four determinants of health.
3. Name the major benefits of physical fitness.
4. Define and contrast physical fitness and total wellness.
5. List and describe the five components of physical fitness.
6. Differentiate between physical fitness for health and motor fitness.
7. Identify positive and negative personal health behaviors.

Adapted from *Fitness for Life, Fourth Edition* by Bill Hyman, Gary Oden, David Bacharach, Tim Sebesta. Copyright © 2011 by Kendall Hunt Publishing Company. Reprinted by permission.

HEALTH STATUS OF AMERICANS

"You, the individual, can do more for your own well-being than any doctor, any hospital, any drug, any exotic medical device." This quote from former U.S. Secretary of Health, Education, and Welfare Joseph Califano provides a perfect introduction to the study of the wellness lifestyle. Studies strongly support the fact that most of the causes of morbidity (an unhealthy state) and mortality (death) in the United States are highly preventable. Chronic diseases caused by unhealthy behavior dominate the causes of death in the United States (see Figure 1.1). Seven out of every ten deaths among Americans are from chronic diseases, and almost one out of every two Americans have at least one chronic illness. In fact, almost two thirds of the deaths in the United States each year are caused by only five diseases: heart disease, cancer, stroke, chronic lower respiratory disease, and diabetes (National Center for Health Statistics, 2017). In contrast, the leading causes of death in the United States just over a century ago were quite different. In 1900, the leading cause of death in the United States was pneumonia and influenza, followed by tuberculosis and then diarrhea (Box 1.1). The average life expectancy was only 47.3 years (National Center for Health Statistics, 2012). Many people did not live long enough for the effects of chronic diseases like heart disease and cancer to take their toll on health. Today, with an average life expectancy of 78.8 years (76 for men, 81 for women), the chronic lifestyle diseases dominate the health charts (National Center for Health Statistics, 2016). Two specific lifestyle factors—obesity and smoking—reportedly reduce Americans' average life expectancy by three to four years (National Research Council, 2013).

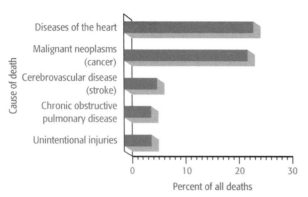

Figure 1.1 • Leading causes of death in the United States in 2016.

Although our national health statistics reveal the leading pathophysiological causes of death, it is important to note that the underlying contributors to these deaths are often controllable lifestyle factors. Heart disease, cancer, and stroke, as well as other chronic diseases, are overwhelmingly caused by smoking and other tobacco use, poor diet and physical inactivity (and accompanying obesity), alcohol consumption, and other poor lifestyle choices (see Figure 1.2). These types of death are called "diseases of lifestyle" and account for the majority of U.S. deaths every year. Despite the increases in average life expectancy that has occurred over recent decades, Americans still trail behind nearly 30 other nations (World Health Organization, 2016) in this category.

Health-compromising behaviors are abundant in our society, and either directly or indirectly we all pay the price for poor health. These behaviors and their consequential

BOX 1.1

Leading Causes of Death—United States—1900

1. Pneumonia and influenza
2. Tuberculosis
3. Diarrhea, enteritis, and ulceration of the intestines
4. Disease of the heart
5. Intracranial lesions of vascular origin

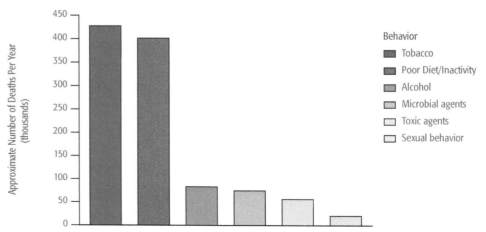

Figure 1.2 • Leading behavioral causes of death.

diseases result in the premature loss of family and friends, mental and emotional burdens that accompany illness, physical pain and suffering, lifelong disabilities, and tremendous stresses on the economy as a result of the high cost of health care. Health care spending in the United States reached an all-time high of 3.3 trillion dollars in 2016, representing 17.9 percent of the gross domestic product (GDP). It is projected to reach nearly 5 trillion dollars and account for 20 percent of the GDP by 2021 (Centers for Medicare and Medicaid Services, 2018). Even though average life expectancy in the United States ranks 27th among countries (Organization for Economic Co-operation and Development – OECD, 2018), per-capita expenditure on health care is almost two and one-half times the average of other developed countries and 25 percent greater than the next highest country (Switzerland) (OECD, 2017). But the most tragic realization is that many of these costly diseases are preventable. The self-exploration opportunities provided throughout this text are designed to create a greater awareness about prevention. Knowledge about nutrition, physical fitness, stress management, and disease risk assessment and reduction provide opportunities for you to set goals and develop strategies for change. The first opportunity for self-assessment provides an overview of personal health behaviors and is found in Personal Growth Opportunity 1.1.

The young adult years are especially critical in developing lifelong wellness habits. Most college students are independent and making their own decisions—including decisions that will shape their health status throughout their lifespan. This new independence is an exciting stage of development, but it is also filled with new risks and responsibilities. Being equipped to handle these challenges during the young adult years and to develop good lifetime health habits is the most important determinate of an individual's health status. The Centers for Disease Control and Prevention (2016) recognizes that the college years present specific health concerns for this population and offer the following general health tips as priorities:

Eat healthy and engage in regular physical activity:

> Follow an eating plan with a variety of nutritious foods.
> Stay active with regular physical activity.

Stay safe:

> Manage stress.
> Get enough sleep.
> Avoid drugs and alcohol.
> Seek help from a mental health professional if you are depressed or experiencing distress.
> Prevent sexual assault before it starts.
> Seek help immediately if you or someone you know is the victim of violence.

Prevent sexually transmitted infections:

> Get tested and know your status.
> Protect yourself and your sexual partners.

Avoid substance abuse:

> Know the dangers of binge drinking and limit alcohol.
> Don't smoke.
> Avoid illicit drugs.

If you or a friend is struggling with a health or safety problem:

> Talk to someone you trust for support.
> Visit your college health center or local clinic or hospital.
> Contact the campus or community police if your or someone else's safety is threatened.

To give an indication of the extent of the health issues in the college student population, the American College Health Association (ACHA) conducts the annual National College

Health Assessment II, which provides the largest known comprehensive data set on the health of college students. The most recent report (ACHA, 2017) provides the following insight:

53 percent (60 percent male and 50 percent female) described their health as very good or excellent. This is down from 61 percent in 2012.

In the area of Exercise and Nutrition:

Only 5 percent reported getting the recommended five or more servings of fruits and vegetables per day (with 7 percent reporting getting zero servings per day).
Just under half (49 percent) reported attaining the recommended amount of exercise.
Only 61 percent (58 percent of males and 63 percent of females) were in the healthy weight category determined through the estimated Body Mass Index (BMI).

In the area of sleep:

Only 12 percent reported that they received enough sleep to feel rested in the morning for at least six of the past seven days.
More than 90 percent reported some degree of problems with sleepiness during daytime activities in the past seven days.

In the area of Alcohol, Tobacco, and Other Drug Use:

67 percent (66 percent for male and 68 percent female) reported using alcohol within the last 30 days.
10 percent (13 percent male and 8 percent female) reported using cigarettes within the last 30 days.
20 (22 percent male and 19 percent female) reported using marijuana within the last 30 days. This is up from 15 percent in 2012.
19 percent reported driving after having any alcohol in the last 30 days.
Of those college students who drank alcohol, 35 percent reported doing something they later regretted, 29 percent reported that they forgot where they were or what they did, and 22 percent reported having unprotected sex and 12 percent reported that they had physically injured themselves within the last 12 months when drinking alcohol.

In the area of Sexual Behavior:

69 percent reported having one or more sexual partners (oral sex, vaginal or anal intercourse) within the last 12 months.
26 percent reported having two or more sexual partners within the last 12 months.
Of sexually active students, only 48 percent reported using a condom or other protective barrier within the last 30 days, and 56 reported using a method of contraception the last time they had vaginal intercourse.

In the area of Mental Health:

61 percent (48 percent of males and 67 percent of females) reported that they felt overwhelming anxiety anytime in the last 12 months. This is up from 50 percent in 2012.
57 percent (78 percent of males and 91 percent of females) reported that they felt overwhelmed by "all you had to do" anytime in the last 12 months.
84 percent (76 percent of males and 88 percent of females) reported that they felt exhausted (not from physical activity) anytime in the last 12 months.

Within the last 12 months, 75 percent reported experiencing an event that was traumatic or very difficult to handle. The most frequently reported issues were academics (48 percent), finances (32 percent), intimate relationships (31 percent), and family problems (27 percent).

INDIVIDUAL CONTROL

Lester Breslow, an American physician who was known for his promotion of chronic disease prevention, once stated, "It's what you do hour by hour, day by day, that largely determines the state of your health; whether you get sick, what you get sick with, and perhaps when you die" (Breslow, 1985). While some uncontrollable life events will undoubtedly occur, most of what happens to us is the result of factors within our control. There are four major determinants of an individual's health at any given time. Shown in Figure 1.3, they are lifestyle, heredity, environment, and available health care services. Note that the number one determinant is behavior or lifestyle, accounting for more than half of health status. The remaining three determinants combined do not match the impact of behaviors. Clearly, those individuals who do not believe that their actions make a difference in their health status have misdirected their quest for well-being. They attempt to blame or rely on other people, the health care system, their environment, and even their parents for their health status. Individuals should recognize personal control over their well-being and take action toward a higher quality of life. This active and deliberate pursuit of the highest level of well-being is known as wellness.

The extent to which an individual believes he or she has control over his or her own health status is known as locus of control. Some understand that their choices and actions are the primary factors that determine health outcomes, whereas others believe that what they do has little effect on their health status. The belief that personal actions determine outcomes, including health status, is known as an internal locus of control. People with this view are much more likely to seek health enhancement actively and deliberately. An external locus of control is the belief that factors outside of one's control determine health status. Those factors include powerful others like doctors, hospitals, the government, the health care system, friends and family members, and even chance, luck, and fate. Individuals with an external locus of control, since they do not believe that their actions make a difference, are less likely to take personal actions that can lead to good health.

Other important factors that determine our ability and willingness to take positive actions toward good health are self-efficacy and health literacy. Self-efficacy is the belief in one's capabilities to organize and execute the course of action required to manage prospective situations (Bandura, 1995). It influences the choices we make, the effort we put forth, and how long we persist when we confront obstacles. In relation to health pursuits, a high degree of self-efficacy will serve as a motivating factor. When one feels capable of making a health behavior change or maintaining good health habits, the likelihood of implementing and continuing healthy lifestyles is enhanced. Health literacy is defined as the capacity to obtain, process, and understand basic health information and services to make appropriate health decisions (CDC, 2014). Nearly 9 out of 10 adults have difficulty using the everyday health information that is routinely available in health care facilities, retail outlets, media, and communities (Kutner, Greenberg, Jin, & Paulsen, 2006). Limited health literacy affects people's ability to search for and use health information, adopt healthy behaviors, and act on important public health alerts and is associated with poorer health outcomes and higher health care costs (Berkman et al., 2004).

One additional influence on health status warrants mention here. It is clear that a significant impact on health is made by ethnicity, race, and culture. Ethnicity typically

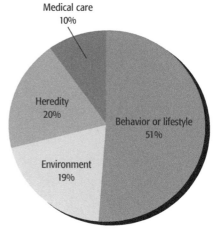

Medical care
10%

Heredity
20%

Behavior or lifestyle
51%

Environment
19%

Figure 1.3 • The four determinants of health status.

refers to ancestry and the commonalities shared among those of like origin. These factors may include country of origin, traditions, learned behavior, and customs. Race is usually used in reference to biological features including skin, eye, and hair color and may even include a tendency toward developing certain diseases. Culture usually indicates a pattern of shared beliefs and values and possibly even geographic location and religious affiliation. A sense of connectedness is often found among individuals from like racial, ethnic, and cultural backgrounds. Certain ethnic, racial, and cultural groups also share health concerns. For example, the advances in the health of the general population in the United States has not been shared among all groups. Morbidity and mortality indicators reveal that certain minority groups have disproportional rates of disease including the leading killers—heart disease, cancer, diabetes, and other health problems including infant mortality and drug and alcohol abuse. These differences are called health disparities and are cause for concern among public health leaders. Often, the disparities stem from poverty, lower educational attainment, geographical location, lack of health literacy, and limited access to health information and health services. The reduction of these disparities through innovative prevention and service strategies is a high public health priority and is a high priority goal for our nation's health.

One of the most critical strategies in addressing the health problems of individuals and communities is the establishment of national health goals and objectives. *Healthy People* is a national agenda that communicates a vision for improving health and achieving health equity. Revised every 10 years, the current strategic framework is *Healthy People 2020*. The overarching goals of *Healthy People 2020* are:

- Attain high-quality, longer lives free of preventable disease
- Achieve health equity; eliminate disparities
- Create social and physical environments that promote good health
- Promote quality of life, healthy development, healthy behaviors across life stages

These major goals are expressed through nearly 600 specific health objectives and 1,200 measures. Strategies are presented to address diabetes, cancer, HIV, injuries and violence, heart disease, stroke, nutrition and weight status, physical activity, substance abuse, tobacco use, sleep, and sexually transmitted diseases. Other strategies include addressing health issues such as access to health services, adolescent health, health communication and health information technology, and the social determinants of health. A few selected topics, goals, and overviews from *Healthy People 2020* can be found in Appendix A.

COMPLETE WELL-BEING

The wellness goal of every individual should be to attain the highest level of well-being possible in every dimension of health. Complete well-being encompasses more than physical fitness. In fact, it is quite possible for an individual to possess a high level of physical fitness, yet experience low levels of health in other areas of life. For decades, health professionals have acknowledged the wisdom of the World Health Organization's definition of health—"Health is a state of complete physical, mental and social well-being and not merely the absence of disease or infirmity" (WHO, 1948). While health knowledge and conditions have certainly changed over the years, the WHO definition has not been amended since 1948, as it still provides a good description of the holistic approach and multidimensionality of health. Many have offered new definitions and descriptions of health and wellness, but all acknowledge that it encompasses many domains, and that problems in one area often have a negative impact in other areas. Therefore, individuals should strive to maintain balance in all areas. Figure 1.4 illustrates the multidimensional quality of wellness.

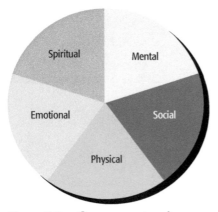

Figure 1.4 • Components of wellness.

BENEFITS OF PHYSICAL FITNESS

As volumes of research continue to emerge about the benefits of healthy lifestyles, perhaps none is more noteworthy than the 2008 Physical Activity Guidelines for Americans (Appendix B). The scientific data cited in this historic report emphasize physical activity as one of the most important steps that Americans of all ages can take to improve health. Strong evidence exists that regular physical activity improves health in the following ways:

- Lower risk of early death
- Lower risk of coronary heart disease and stroke
- Lower risk of high blood pressure and adverse blood lipid profile
- Lower risk of type 2 diabetes
- Lower risk of metabolic syndrome
- Lower risk of colon cancer and breast cancer
- Prevention of weight gain
- Weight loss, when combined with reduced calorie intake
- Improved cardiorespiratory and muscular fitness
- Prevention of falls
- Reduced depression
- Better cognitive function for older adults

Moderate or moderate-to-strong evidence exists that regular physical activity improves health in these additional ways:

- Better functional health for older adults
- Reduced abdominal obesity
- Lower risk of hip fracture
- Lower risk of lung cancer and endometrial cancer
- Weight maintenance after weight loss
- Increased bone density
- Improved sleep quality

HEALTH-RELATED FITNESS

The physical component of health is highly instrumental in determining one's overall well-being. Physical wellness means that the organ systems of the human body (primarily the heart and lungs and their systems as well as muscles and bones) are disease free and capable of functioning at a high level of efficiency. The efficiency of these systems not only enables a person to engage in daily tasks and participate in leisure activities at an enthusiastic and vigorous level, but also helps prevent disease and extend life expectancy. Health-related physical fitness involves the development and maintenance of five primary components. They are:

1. **Cardiovascular Endurance.** This important component of physical fitness is also known by other names, including aerobic capacity, aerobic fitness, cardiorespiratory fitness, and stamina. It is the ability of the heart, circulatory system, lungs, and respiratory system to transport and deliver blood and oxygen to the cells of the body, primarily the working muscles. As muscles are provided with oxygenated blood, they are capable of working more efficiently and sustaining work and activity for longer periods of time. This should be the primary goal of any fitness program, since it provides significant protection against certain chronic diseases, specifically heart disease, stroke, and diabetes. Another desirable effect of cardiorespiratory endurance training is that it provides residual benefits for improving the remaining four components of fitness.

2. **Body Composition.** The percentage of total body weight that is made up of adipose (fat) tissue as opposed to lean body tissue is known as body composition. Disease risk is closely related to body composition. Lean individuals carry lower risk of a number of diseases than those who carry excess fat.

3. **Flexibility.** Defined as the capacity of a joint to move through a full range of motion, this component of fitness provides freedom of movement that enables a person to stretch, bend, twist, and perform other physical tasks with efficiency and a minimal risk of injury to the muscles and connective tissues.

4. **Muscular Endurance.** This term refers to the ability of a muscle or muscle group to sustain the exertion of force over a period of time without fatiguing. Certain daily living tasks and a number of recreational endeavors demand that work be continued for a sustained time period. Muscular endurance allows effective participation in these activities.

5. **Muscular Strength.** This is the ability of a muscle or muscle group to exert a maximum force against a resistance. While similar to muscular endurance, muscular strength involves a one-time exertion as opposed to sustained muscular activity. Applying heavy force and lifting heavy objects demand muscular strength.

MOTOR FITNESS

Motor fitness, as opposed to health-related fitness, refers to skill-related components and is linked more to physical performance than health and wellness. While motor fitness does not directly improve a person's health status, it can indirectly enhance physical fitness by encouraging participation in a variety of physical activities. These components include:

1. **Balance.** The ability to maintain equilibrium while static (stationary) or dynamic (moving) is important in recreational endeavors. It is also important to health maintenance for certain populations, such as the elderly, for whom losing balance and falling is a significant health risk. For this reason, balance is sometimes considered a component of health-related fitness for the older population.

2. **Agility.** This is the ability to change direction while moving and is influenced by body coordination and quickness. It is beneficial in many sports activities.

3. **Coordination.** This neuromuscular skill of using the senses and multiple body movements in unison is fundamental to daily functioning, as well as sports and other physical activity performance. The synchronization of hand–eye movement in racquet sports is an example of coordination.

4. **Quickness.** Also known as reaction time, quickness is the ability to produce a rapid and efficient response to a stimulus. Reacting promptly to hit a moving object such as a baseball or a tennis ball are examples of quickness.

5. **Speed.** The time required to move from one location to another reflects a person's capacity for speed and is probably the greatest skill-related asset for most sports endeavors. Speed may also refer to the performance of a rapid movement, such as generating bat speed while swinging at a ball.

6. **Power.** This is the combination of strength and speed and is a primary skill-related component in many sports.

While genetics play a role in both the development of the components of motor fitness and the components of physical fitness, the role of genetics in the attainment of physical fitness is much smaller. Therefore, most individuals are capable of attaining a high level of physical fitness with the proper program. However, participation in activities requiring motor fitness can work toward the development of physical fitness. Performance in sports and recreational activities is a great motivator to be active. After all, who doesn't like performing well in a competition or setting personal performance goals and attaining them? Motor fitness skills certainly have a place in the pursuit of wellness. Nevertheless, optimal physical fitness can be developed by anyone simply by focusing on the health-related components discussed earlier, and ultimately the pursuit of health holds greater benefits than the pursuit of athletic performance.

FITNESS EDUCATION AND ASSESSMENT

A number of positive changes occur to the human body as a result of wise health choices. Hopefully, you will take control of your own health by adopting a lifestyle of wellness. The chapters of this text will describe the benefits of various activities, identify proper performance guidelines, provide personal growth opportunities to determine your current level of health and help you set goals. Several simple health screenings and assessments maybe available on your campus, and "know your number" campaigns have are popular in health promotion programs. Specifically, individuals are encouraged to know important measures of health risk, including, heart rate, blood pressure, cholesterol levels, body mass index and body composition, waist-to-hip ratio and others. These are opportunites for self-discovery and self-improvement. Important indicators of health status include:

1. **Heart Rate (resting and target rate for exercise).** A low resting pulse rate is a valid indicator of cardiac output, the product of heart rate and stroke volume (amount of blood pumped per beat). Generally, a low resting heart rate indicates a high level of cardiovascular fitness. For aerobic exercise to bestow the greatest benefit, a target heart rate, determined by a simple formula, should be reached.

2. **Body Composition.** A healthy body fat percentage helps protect against back pain, heart disease, stroke, type 2 diabetes, and several other diseases and disorders. A good percentage of body fat is approximately 15 percent for men (with an acceptable range of 6-24 percent) and approximately 23 percent for women (with an acceptable range of 9-31 percent). While some variation is acceptable, a body fat percentage of 25 or above for men and 32 or above for women puts one at very high risk of disease (Nieman, 2011). Waist-to-hip ratio can also provide information on healthy or unhealthy fat storage.

3. **Maximum Oxygen Consumption**. This measurement reflects the fitness level of the cardiovascular and respiratory systems. A good score reflects an energy level that can add greatly to a person's quality of life. Measured in milliliters of oxygen per kilogram of body weight per minute, an oxygen consumption level of about 43 ml/kg/min for young men (ages 20–29) and about 36 ml/kg/min for young women (ages 20–29) would place a person in the upper 50th percentile and is a worthy goal.

4. **Blood Pressure.** Proper blood pressure reduces wear and tear on the heart, correlating with longevity and reducing the chances for cardiovascular disease. High blood pressure (hypertension), known as the "silent killer" because it usually gives no early warning signs, seriously increases the risk for various types of heart disease as well as stroke and kidney failure. The American Heart Association and the American College of Cardiology issued new blood pressure guidelines in 2017. While normal blood

pressure is still categorized as a systolic pressure less than 120 mm Hg (millimeters of mercury) and a diastolic pressure less than 80 mm Hg., blood pressure is considered elevated when systolic pressure is between 120 and 129 mm Hg. and diastolic pressure is less than 80 mm Hg. Stage 1 hypertension is a systolic pressure of 130-139 or a diastolic pressure from 80-89. Stage 2 hypertension is a systolic pressure or 140 or a diastolic pressure of 90. A systolic pressure over 180 or a diastolic pressure over 120 is considered hypertensive crisis (Whelton, et.al., 2017).

5. **Cholesterol.** The American Heart Association recommends all adults age 20 and older have their cholesterol and other risk factors checked every four to six years, and work with their health care provider to determine their risk for cardiovascular disease and stroke. Cholesterol levels are reported in milligrams per deciliter of blood (mg/dL). Cholesterol testing will identify high density lipoproteins (HDL - the good cholesterol), low density lipoproteins (LD - the bad cholesterol), triglyceride levels (a type of fat found in the blood), as well as total blood (serum) cholesterol. Your health care provider can use these numbers to assess your risk for a heart attack or stroke. Other factors, including blood pressure, family history, age, and smoking status are also considered. Until recently, ranges of cholesterol levels were used to evaluate the risk posed by serum cholesterol. Currently this risk evaluation is made in broader terms, using the test results in context with other risk factors.

6. **Flexibility and Abdominal Strength.** High scores on strength and flexibility lower the chances of low-back pain and other joint ailments.

7. **Risk for Cancer, Diabetes, and Osteoporosis.** Internal and external factors contribute to the incidence of these three diseases, and risk assessments present the opportunity to identify and modify factors that increase one's chances of disease.

8. **Caloric Intake and Expenditure.** Appropriate caloric intake and nutritional balance of carbohydrates, fat, and protein are an important measure of health, and moderate physical activity of at least 150 minutes per week or vigorous physical activity of at least 75 minutes per week reduces numerous disease risks and increases longevity (U.S. Department of Health and Human Services, 2008). The diet that is low in fat and high in complex carbohydrate also provides numerous health benefits, and Chapter 6 provides opportunity to identify dietary deficiencies.

9. **Stress Status.** The stressful impact of life events, the value of your social support connections, and even the impact of your outlook and personality will be assessed to help you understand and identify common stressors and the way they affect health. Coping and control strategies are offered.

TAKING ACTION

With so much evidence of the many benefits of physical activity (PA), one would think that all Americans would pursue this lifestyle. Unfortunately, that is not the case as most Americans have adopted a sedentary (inactive) lifestyle and as a result suffer unnecessarily from the many diseases that scientific findings have connected with that lifestyle. Sadly, over 80 percent of adults do not meet the Healthy People objectives for aerobic PA and muscle-strengthening activity (*Healthy People 2020, 2018*). A couple of terms reflect the link between inactivity and disease. "Sitting Disease" brings attention to the connection between prolonged sitting and several health problems, and "Sedentary Death Syndrome" (SeDS), or death due to physical inactivity, is considered a major public health problem in our country. Research has implicated prolonged sitting, even independently of physical activity, in premature death, cardiovascular disease, diabetes, metabolic syndrome, and obesity. Taking periodic breaks from sitting is correlated with positive metabolic profiles and lower risks related to waist circumference, body mass index, triglyceride levels and blood glucose levels. Simply standing in place of sitting triggers beneficial processes in relation to the breaking down of sugars and fats in the body (Mayo Clinic, 2015; Katzmarzyk, 2009).

These dangers of inactivity are easier to combat than one might think. Creating intentional and deliberate plans to avoid prolonged periods of little or no movement is an attainable approach for most people, but a commitment to some level of movement and activity must be made. The pursuit of physical activity is emphasized throughout this text, with the Physical Activity Guidelines for Americans providing the framework for recommendations. The Guidelines state that to attain substantial health benefits, adults should engage in at least 150 minutes per week of moderate intensity aerobic PA or 75 minutes per week of vigorous aerobic PA (or an equivalent mix of moderate and vigorous PA). For even greater health benefits, the aerobic recommendations are doubled (300 minutes moderate, 150 minutes vigorous, or an equivalent combination). For muscle health, all major muscle groups should be worked 2 or more days per week, exercising each muscle group 8-12 times in a set. These recommendations, including how to attain moderate and vigorous PA and how to design a muscle health exercise regimen, as well as the detailed benefits of each, are discussed thoroughly in later chapters (United States Department of Health and Human Services - DHHS, 2008). However, one easily adopted plan to get started with initial activity is simply to start walking, and research clearly points to the benefits of a simple walking/moving plan. While higher intensity activity levels can produce greater fitness gains, and the information needed to design various fitness programs is included in this text, walking is clearly recognized as an efficient and attainable avenue toward health fitness. Because walking is less intensive than running and some other modes of PA, one may need to walk longer or more often to accumulate these benefits. A moderate to vigorous walking program reduces the risk of cardiovascular events and improves cardiac risk factors such as cholesterol, blood pressure, diabetes, obesity, inflammation, and even mental stress. Walking also comes with reduced risk of injury (when compared to higher intensity activities) due to its low impact on the musculoskeletal structures of the body (Harvard Health Publishing, 2009). Several researchers have explored how much walking is needed to meet the PA Guidelines, and some governments, agencies, and professional organizations have made recommendations of how many steps per day are needed in order for healthy adults to meet PA guidelines. As a result, attainment of 10,000 steps per day has become a popular goal, and devices that count steps (pedometers, accelerometers, and step-counting fitness bands and watches) tend to recommend this as a daily goal. The Physical Activity Guidelines state that "some physical activity is better than none", so any reasonable goal beyond a sedentary level would be beneficial. Leading research in this arena has identified 8000-11,000 steps per day as adequate to meet the CDC guidelines of 150 minutes of moderate activity per week. Steps should be taken at a cadence of at least 100 steps/minute to be at least moderate in intensity. Accumulating over 11,000 steps would lead to the attainment of even higher level recommendations and greater health benefits. Conversely, under 5000 steps per day is considered sedentary (Tudor-Locke, et al, 2011).

And what about the time frame of activity sessions? How long must an activity be sustained to confer health benefits? The Guidelines recommend that moderate to vigorous PA occur in bouts of at least ten minutes in duration, and while these guidelines still provide the framework for PA plans and benefits, recent research is pointing to the beneficial health outcomes of accumulating moderate to vigorous PA in periods less than ten minutes in duration, called 'non-bout activity'. Non-bout activity is now recognized as beneficial, with studies showing that it decreases all-cause mortality, and that it contributes to weight loss, and improves health measures including blood pressure, HDL cholesterol levels, waist circumference, and metabolic syndrome. It is an excellent avenue to minimizing prolonged periods of sedentary behavior. Periodically breaking up times of inactivity, by walking, doing light calesthenics, performing some light housework, walking the dog, or performing some active tasks that need to be completed is now recognized as having some health benefits (Pedro, et. al., 2018).

Consideration is given to populations who may not be certain if the Guidelines pertain to them, namely those who have a physical disability or who are pregnant. There is strong evidence that regular physical activity benefits people with disabilities. The benefits include improved muscle health, cardiovascular fitness, mental health, and increased ability to perform daily life activities. The diverse groups that have been studied for the benefits of activity include those with mental illness, intellectual disability or dementia, spinal cord injuries, limb amputations, Parkinson's disease, multiple sclerosis, muscular dystrophy, cerebral palsy, traumatic brain injury, and those who have suffered a stroke. The Guidelines for people with disabilities emphasize the consultation with a health care provider in order to understand and discuss how the disability might affect the ability to do physical activity, any additional safety considerations, and the adaptation of activities to match their abilities. There is also strong evidence that moderate intensity activity for healthy women who are pregnant carries very little risk, and does not increase the risk of low birth weight, preterm delivery, or early pregnancy loss, and that it may reduce the risk of potential complications of pregnancy including preeclampsia and gestational diabetes. It can help maintain healthy weight during the post-partum period. People with disabilities and pregnant women should consult with their health care provider to discuss the amount and type of physical activity that is best for them (United States Department of Health and Human Services – DHHS, 2008). Additional information on physical activity for those who have disabilities or are pregnant is found at the following site: https://health.gov/paguidelines/guidelines/chapter7.aspx

So, the introductory message to set the tone for the pursuit of better health that Lifetime Health and Wellness has as its goal is to get moving. While each individual will have a chance to explore their personal health status and each person will be challenged to develop an effective and efficient wellness plan that works for them, no one need wait a single minute to begin the journey toward health enhancement. Get up, get moving, and enjoy the pursuit of a higher level of health and wellness that can continue to provide benefits for the rest of your life. You can use the Personal Health Profile (Personal Growth Opportunity 1.1) to identify any behaviors that are causing your health to be compromised. Complete the profile and calculate your total health score. Hopefully, the results will affirm the positive things you do and help you establish goals to enhance your health status.

References

American College Health Association. *American College Health Association-National College Health Assessment II: Reference Group Executive Summary Spring 2017*. Hanover, MD: American College Health Association, 2017.

American Heart Association. (2018) *What your cholesterol level means*. Retrieved from: http://www.heart.org/HEARTORG/Conditions/Cholesterol/AboutCholesterol/What-Your-Cholesterol-Levels-Mean_UCM_305562_Article.jsp

Bandura, A. (Ed.) (1995). *Self-efficacy in changing societies*. New York, NY: Cambridge University Press.

Berkman, N. D., DeWalt, D. A., Pignone, M. P., Sheridan, S. L., Lohr, K. N., Lux, L., et al. (2004). *Literacy and Health Outcomes* (AHRQ Publication No. 04-E007-2). Rockville, MD: Agency for Healthcare Research and Quality.

Breslow, L. (1985). *Vision and reality in state health care: Medi-Cal and other public programs, 1946–1975: An interview/conducted by Gabrielle Morris in 1984*. Berkeley, CA: Regional Oral History Office, Brancroft Library, University of California, Government History Documentation Project, Ronald Reagan Gubernatorial Era.

Centers for Disease Control and Prevention. (2009). *National Vital Statistics Data: Historical Data: 1900–1998*. Retrieved from http://www.cdc.gov/nchs/nvss/mortality_historical_data.htm.cdc.gov/nchs/statab/lead1900_1998.pdf

Centers for Disease Control and Prevention. (2016). *Tips for College Health and Safety*. Retrieved from: https://www.cdc.gov/features/collegehealth/.

Centers for Disease Control and Prevention. (2011). Vital signs: prevalence, treatment, and control of hypertension, 1999–2002 and 2005–2008. *MMWR: Morbidity & Mortality Weekly Report, 60*(4), 103–108.

Centers for Disease Control and Prevention. (2014) *Health literacy: Accurate, accessible, and actionable health information for all.* Retrieved from: http://www.cdc.gov/healthliteracy/

Centers for Medicare & Medicaid Services, Office of the Actuary, National Health Statistics Group. (2018). *National health care spending in 2016*. Retrieved from: https://www.cms.gov/Research-Statistics-Data-and-Systems/Statistics-Trends-and-Reports/NationalHealthExpendData/NationalHealthAccountsHistorical.html.

Centers for Medicare and Medicaid Services. (2012). *National Health Expenditures Projections 2011–2021.* Retrieved from www.cms.gov/Research-Statistics-data-and-Systems/Statistics-Trends-and-Reports/NationalHealthExpendData/Downloads/Proj2011PDF.pdf

Hardy, G. E., Jr. (2004, April). The burden of chronic disease: The future is prevention. Introduction to Dr. James Marks' presentation, The Burden of Chronic Disease and the Future of Public Health. *Preventing Chronic Disease.* Retrieved from http://www.cdc.gov/pcd/issues/2004/apr/04_0006.htm

Harvard Medical School. (2009). *Walking: Your steps to health.* Harvard Health Publishing. Retrieved from: https://www.health.harvard.edu/newsletter_article/Walking-Your-steps-to-health.

Katzmarzyk, P.T., Church, T.S., Craig, C.L., Bouchard, C. (2009). Sitting time and mortality from all causes, cardiovascular disease, and cancer. *Medicine and Science in Sports and Exercise*; 41(5): 998–1005.

Kutner, M., Greenberg, E., Jin, Y., & Paulsen, C. (2006). *The health literacy of America's adults: Results from the 2003 National Assessment of Adult Literacy (NCES 2006-483).* Washington, DC: U.S. Department of Education, National Center for Education Statistics.

Mokdad, A. H., Marks, J. S., Stroup, D. F., & Gergerding, J. L. (2004). Actual causes of death in the United States, 2000. *Journal of the American Medical Association, 291*(10).

National Center for Health Statistics. (2013a, May 8). Death: Final data 2010. *National Vital Statistics Reports, 61*(4).

National Center for Health Statistics. (2013b). *Health, United States, 2012: With Special Feature on Emergency Care.* Hyattsville, MD: Author.

National Center for Health Statistics. (2108). Mortality data. Retrieved from: https://www.cdc.gov/nchs/nvss/deaths.html.

National Center for Health Statistics. (2016). *Health, United States, 2016: With Chartbook on Long-term Trends in Health.* Hyattsville, MD. 2017.

National Coalition on Health Care. (2012). *Curbing costs, improving care: The plan to an affordable health care future.* Retrieved from http://www.nchcbeta.org/wp-content/uploads/2012/05/NCHC-Plan-for-Health-and-Fiscal-Policy.pdf

National Heart, Lung, and Blood Institute. (2012). *What is high blood pressure?* Retrieved from http://www.nhlbi.nih.gov/health/health-topics/topics/hbp/

National Heart, Lung, and Blood Institute. (2016). *High blood pressure.* Retrieved from: https://www.nhlbi.nih.gov/health-topics/high-blood-pressure.

Nieman, D. C. (2011). *Exercise testing and prescription: A health-related approach* (7th ed.). New York, NY: McGraw-Hill.

Office of Disease Prevention and Health Promotion. (2018). *Healthy People 2020: Physical Activity.* Retrieved from: www.healthypeople.gov/2020/topics-objectives/topic/physical-activity/objectives#5072.

Organization for Economic Co-operation and Development. (2017). *Health at a Glance 2017: OECD Indicators,* OECD Publishing, Paris. http://dx.doi.org/10.1787/health_glance-2017-en.

Organization for Economic Co-operation and Development. (2018). *Life expectancy at birth.* Retrieved from: https://data.oecd.org/healthstat/life-expectancy-at-birth.htm.

Pedro F. S., Richard P. T., Charles E. M., William E. K. (2018). Moderate-to-Vigorous Physical Activity and All-Cause Mortality: Do Bouts Matter? *Journal of the American Heart Association.* doi.org/10.1161/JAHA.117.007678.

Tudor-Locke, C., Craig, C.L., Brown, W.J., Clemes, S.A., De Cocker, K., Giles-Corti, B., Hatano, Y., Inoue, S., Matsudo, S.M., Mutrie, N., Oppert, J.M., Rowe, D.A., Schmidt, M.D., Schofield, G.M., Spence, J.C., Teixeira, P.J., Tully, M.A., Blair, S.N. (2011). How many steps/day are enough? For adults. *International Journal of Behavioral Nutrition and Physical Activity*. DOI: 10.1186/1479-5868-8-79.

U.S. Department of Health and Human Services. (2008). *2008 Physical Activity Guidelines for Americans* (OPDHP Publication No. U0036). Washington, DC: Author.

United States Department of Health and Human Services. Office of Disease Prevention and Health Promotion. (2018). *Quick Guide to Health Literacy*. Retrieved from: https://health.gov/communication/literacy/quickguide/factsbasic.htm

Whelton, P.K., Carey R.M., Aronow, W.S., Casey, D.E. Jr., Collins, K.J., Himmelfarb, C.D., DePalma, S.M., Gidding, S., Jamerson, K.A., Jones, D.W., MacLaughlin, E.J., Muntner, P., Ovbiagele, B., Smith, S.C. Jr., Spencer, C.C., Stafford,R.S., Taler, S.J., Thomas, R.J., William, K.A. Sr., Williamson, J.D. and Wright, J.T. Jr. (2017). *ACC/AHA/AAPA/ABC/ACPM/AGS/APhA/ASH/ASPC/NMA/PCNA Guideline for the Prevention, Detection, Evaluation, and Management of High Blood Pressure in Adults*. Journal of the American College of Cardiology. DOI: 10.1016/j.jacc.2017.11.006.

World Health Organization. (2018). *Life Expectancy: Life expectancy data by country*. Retrieved from: http://www.who.int/gho/mortality_burden_disease/life_tables/situation_trends/en/.

World Health Organization. (1946). Preamble to the Constitution of the World Health Organization as adopted by the International Health Conference, New York, 19–22 June, 1946; signed on 22 July 1946 by the representatives of 61 States (Official Records of the World Health Organization, no. 2, p. 100) and entered into force on 7 April 1948.

CHAPTER 1

PERSONAL GROWTH OPPORTUNITY 1

Personal Health Profile

Think about your overall health status and specific health behaviors and respond to each item below. Do you generally:

	Column A *Yes*	Column B *No*
1. Engage in moderate physical activity at least 150 minutes per week or vigorous physical activity at least 75 minutes per week.	_____	_____
2. Perform resistance exercises to strengthen your bones and muscles.	_____	_____
3. Always warm up and cool down before and after exercise, respectively.	_____	_____
4. Get 7 to 8 hours of sleep each night.	_____	_____
5. Know the warning signs for cancer, heart attack, and stroke.	_____	_____
6. See your doctor regularly for checkups.	_____	_____
7. Know the appropriate self-examinations and perform them regularly.	_____	_____
8. Maintain body weight within the recommended healthy range.	_____	_____
9. Consistently choose low-fat, high-fiber foods.	_____	_____
10. Consume salt and sugar in moderation.	_____	_____
11. Eat lots of fruits and vegetables.	_____	_____
12. Never use tobacco.	_____	_____
13. Socialize with close friends regularly.	_____	_____
14. Always wear your seatbelt.	_____	_____
15. Drive carefully, within the speed limit, and take no unnecessary risks while driving.	_____	_____
16. Abstain from alcohol or drink lightly (no more than 1 drink per day for women, no more than 2 drinks per day for men).	_____	_____
17. Never drink and drive or ride with a driver who has been drinking.	_____	_____
18. Successfully use several stress-management and coping strategies.	_____	_____
19. Know your blood pressure and maintain it within the desirable range.	_____	_____
20. Know your cholesterol level and maintain it within the desirable range.	_____	_____
21. Have good study habits.	_____	_____
22. Have several leisure-time activities that you enjoy.	_____	_____
23. Have plenty of energy.	_____	_____

	Column A *Yes*	Column B *No*
24. Avoid prolonged periods of inactivity.	_____	_____
25. Regularly prepare healthy and nutritious meals.	_____	_____
26. Consume a diet low in cholesterol and fat.	_____	_____
27. Manage time well.	_____	_____
28. Avoid all forms of tobacco.	_____	_____
29. Believe you have much control over health outcomes.	_____	_____
30. Balance commitments with your time and abilities.	_____	_____
31. Limit sun exposure.	_____	_____
32. Wear sunscreen when outdoors.	_____	_____
33. Know your family history of disease risk.	_____	_____

Add up every check mark made in column A. Determine your relative risk by identifying your health behavior score in one of the categories below:

Your Score	Comment
26 or more	Overall excellent health practices. Few risky behaviors. Nice work. Now use the course to identify a couple of areas that you could adjust to experience even greater overall health.
21–25	Good health behaviors. Where could improvements be made? Use this course to make a few changes that would raise your overall health status into the `excellent' category.
16–20	OK in most areas, but can definitely improve in others. Use this course to prioritize some areas that would make meaningful improvements in some critical areas of your health status.
11–15	Need some help in reducing health risks. Us this course as a motivator to get started with some changes, consistently moving up the scale with more and more healthy behaviors.
10 or fewer	Have few healthy behaviors. Immediate action is needed. Use this course to start a new lifestyle that is likely to result in some long-term changes in health status and greater health experiences through your lifespan.

CHAPTER 2

Cardiovascular Endurance

© Hiper Com, 2014. Used under license from Shutterstock, Inc.

Specific Objectives

1. Explain why cardiovascular endurance is considered the most important component of physical fitness.
2. List the important functions of the cardiovascular system.
3. Describe the function of the heart, blood vessels, and lungs in oxygen transport.
4. Explain the relationship between heart rate, stroke volume, cardiac output, and oxygen consumption.
5. Distinguish between anaerobic and aerobic activities.
6. Define maximal oxygen consumption.
7. List and explain the major benefits of cardiovascular endurance.
8. Explain acute and chronic changes that take place in the circulatory, respiratory, and muscular systems as a result of aerobic activity.
9. Identify the components of an aerobic exercise program.
10. Describe the methods used to assess cardiovascular endurance.
11. Design a personal program for developing and maintaining a healthy level of cardiovascular endurance.

Adapted from *Fitness for Life, Fourth Edition* by Bill Hyman, Gary Oden, David Bacharach, Tim Sebesta. Copyright © 2011 by Kendall Hunt Publishing Company. Reprinted by permission.

OVERVIEW

Cardiovascular endurance, which is often referred to as cardiorespiratory endurance, is ranked the most important component of health-related physical fitness. If we were to rank the order of importance of the chapter topics, cardiovascular endurance would be number one. Moreover, cardiovascular endurance receives universal recognition among fitness experts as the primary component of health-related physical fitness, attaining a superior status to strength, muscular endurance, flexibility, and body composition. Cardiovascular endurance also contributes to greater development or improvement in the other four health-related physical components of fitness, and cardiovascular endurance is the only component that can make that claim.

Commonly used interchangeably with such terms as aerobic capacity and aerobic fitness, the term cardiovascular endurance more accurately describes what is essentially our aerobic energy output, the physical parameter that potentially influences our quality of life more than any other. Furthermore, research from the Center for Disease Control and Prevention (1996) suggests that a proficient cardiovascular system has the potential to promote an increased lifespan. For these reasons alone, it is easy to understand why many people think of aerobic fitness as synonymous with physical fitness.

FUNCTION OF THE CARDIOVASCULAR SYSTEM

Cardiovascular endurance is the ability to extract oxygen from the air, which we breath, and supply this oxygen to working muscles in order to produce energy and sustain body movement over an extended period of time. Two vital organs necessary for survival are involved: the heart and lungs. The cardiovascular endurance combines the cardiovascular and the respiratory systems into one functional unit. While the respiratory system provides a means of exchanging oxygen and carbon dioxide via the lungs, the cardiovascular system pumps oxygen-rich blood to the body's active tissue and returns waste products of normal metabolic function to be exchanged again in the lungs.

Function of the Cardiovascular System in Oxygen Transport

This system of transport has four components: the heart, blood vessels, blood, and lungs (Figure 2.1). The heart works as a pump with the right side of the heart pumping used or deoxygenated blood to the lungs and the left side of the heart pumping fresh oxygen-rich blood to the entire body. The latter function demands more attention with respect to health and fitness. Blood vessels include the arteries, veins, and capillaries. Arteries take oxygen-rich blood away from the heart, delivering oxygen and other nutrients to the

TABLE 2.1   Clinical Benefits of Cardiovascular Endurance

Physiological: Health and Disease	Psychological: Quality of Life
Improved cardiovascular and musculoskeletal fitness	Improved sleep patterns
Improved metabolic, endocrine, and immune function	Reduced depression and anxiety
Reduced overall mortality rate	Improved health behavior
Reduced cardiovascular disease risk	Improved mood levels
Reduced cancer risk (colon, breast)	Overall improved health-related quality of life
Reduced risk of osteoporosis and osteoarthritis	Reduced risk of falling
Reduced risk of non-insulin-dependent diabetes mellitus	Reduced risk of obesity

Adapted from the Surgeon General's Report on Physical Activity and Health (68). American College of Sporto Medicine Standon Resistance Training for Health adult. Med. Sci Sporto Exerc' 34: 364, 380, 2002.

tissues via the capillaries (small vessels). The capillaries in turn connect to veins that transport waste from the tissues back to the heart and ultimately to the lungs for elimination.

REGULATION OF THE CARDIOVASCULAR SYSTEM

Under normal resting conditions for the average adult, the heart pumps about five liters of blood each minute through the cardiovascular system. The amount of blood pumped out of the heart per minute is called cardiac output. Cardiac output is the product of heart rate and stroke volume. Heart rate is simply the number of times the heart beats per minute while stroke volume is the amount of blood pumped out of the heart each beat.

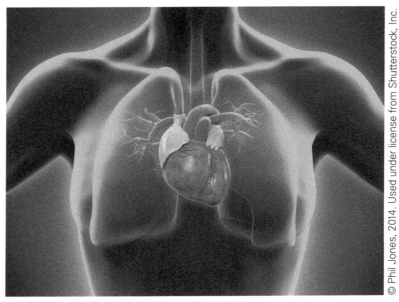

Figure 2.1 • Cardiovascular system.

$$\text{Cardiac Output} = \text{Heart Rate} \times \text{Stroke Volume}$$

During exercise, cardiac output can be increased by speeding up the heart rate or by increasing the stroke volume. Stroke volume increases along with heart rate up to about 40 percent of maximum heart rate (about 100 beats/minute). At maximal levels, the heart pumps 20–25 liters of blood per minute. That represents a four- to fivefold increase from resting conditions. With aerobic training, the heart becomes more efficient by increasing stroke volume, thus allowing resting heart rate to decrease while maintaining the same cardiac output. We hope that the decrease in resting heart rate will reduce the stress placed on the heart and increase the lifespan of the heart.

$$\text{Increased Stroke Volume} \times \text{Decreased Heart Rate} = \text{Cardiac Output}$$

Maximal cardiac output is also influenced by age. After approximately 20 years of age, maximal heart rate declines. The standard formula for estimating maximal heart rate is as follows:

$$\text{Maximal Heart Rate} = 220 - \text{Age (year)}$$

Using the above formula, the average college-age student (20 years) has a maximal heart rate of 200 beats/minute, and a 50-year-old professor has a maximal heart rate of 170 beats/minute.

Pressure inside the blood vessels is what moves blood through the system. When the heart contracts, arterial blood pressure reaches its highest level (systolic pressure). Blood pressure declines slightly when the heart relaxes between beats (diastolic pressure). This change in pressure can be felt as a pulse. Resting blood pressure varies among individuals; however, a systolic pressure above 140 mm Hg and/or a diastolic pressure above 90 mm Hg are the borderline pressures for hypertension (high blood pressure).

ENERGY SYSTEMS

All cellular functions are dependent on energy. Whether you are sleeping, awake but sedentary, or performing exercise, energy is needed to maintain bodily function. The chemical process of converting food into energy is termed *metabolism*. The energy molecule used to produce muscle movement in the body is adenosine triphosphate (ATP). ATP is the only energy source that can cause muscle contraction.

When discussing exercise-related metabolism, the terms *anaerobic* and *aerobic* are often used. Anaerobic processes do not require the presence of oxygen, whereas aerobic energy production depends on oxygen. As outlined in Table 2.1, there are three energy systems in the body that generate ATP, namely, the ATP-PC system, the anaerobic glycolysis or lactic acid system, and the aerobic system. The ATP-PC is stored ATP in the muscle cell. This system is very explosive and very powerful for a short period of time. The ATP-PC system can produce a high volume of energy from 8–12 seconds, dependent on how well it is trained. This system can be very useful for activities that are of high intensity but short duration. The anaerobic glycolysis or lactic acid system is also anaerobic and is very limited in regard to energy supply. This system, if well trained, can supply energy for up to three minutes under current conditions. This system is limited by the accumulation of lactic acid in the blood (this is why we also refer to this system as the lactic acid system). We all produce lactate acid even when we are resting. This small amount of lactate we produce at rest is easily buffered, and lactic acid does not cause fatigue. However, as a person begins to exercise, lactic acid production increase, and with high-intensity exercise lactic acid will accumulate to a point of causing complete muscle fatigue. The term *lactate threshold* is used to describe the point or intensity of exercise when lactic acid production exceeds the buffering ability of the person. When that point or intensity is reached, fatigue will begin to occur. The aerobic energy system cannot supply the body with rapid, explosive energy; however, it has an almost unlimited capacity to produce ATP. In the aerobic energy system, oxygen is used to produce ATP by combining with hydrogen that comes from the breakdown of carbohydrates and fats (proteins can also be used by the aerobic system in extreme conditions).

In most physical activities, a combination of anaerobic and aerobic energy production occurs. A person's maximal level of anaerobic and aerobic energy production is often measured from a standard test. For anaerobic energy measurement, a person can be tested by cycling at maximum effort for 30 seconds, using a stationary cycle. This common test is called the Wingate anaerobic test (Nieman, 2011). The most common cardiovascular or aerobic fitness assessment is the measurement of maximal oxygen consumption (VO$_2$ max). This test measures the body's ability to transport and use oxygen. The test can be submax with the results being predicted from a submaximum workload. Submax tests are common and are accurate enough for most people. A per-

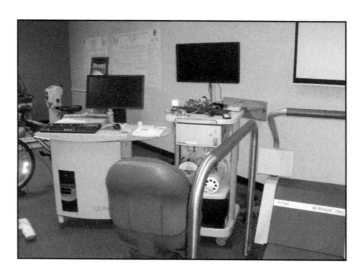

son who wishes very accurate results must perform a maximum effort test measuring oxygen consumption. The maximum effort test requires the subject to exercise to a point of exhaustion. The test results can be predicted on the basis of the amount of work performed or directly measured by having the subject connected to a metabolic cart that measures the oxygen content of the subject's expired air.

As one increases the workload of a task, more oxygen is consumed. The fairly linear relationship of workload to oxygen consumption remains consistent until a person reaches a maximal level of oxygen consumption. Thus, maximal oxygen consumption represents the physiological limit or full capacity of one's cardiovascular system for transporting and utilizing oxygen. While maximum effort tests are performed in a laboratory setting, maximum oxygen consumption can easily be estimated via field tests involving standards of workload and time. Laboratories 2.1, 2.2, and 2.3 at the end of this chapter provide tests that can be used for measurement of VO_2 max.

PHYSIOLOGICAL BENEFITS OF CARDIOVASCULAR ENDURANCE

The physiological benefits of cardiovascular endurance are innumerable. Here are a few major ones to consider:

1. **Greater cardiac output.** Remember that cardiac output is the product of heart rate and stroke volume. During a strenuous effort, a person possessing good cardiovascular endurance is able to deliver far greater quantities of blood to the tissues than an individual who exhibits subpar conditioning of the cardiovascular system. Greater cardiac output at rest can reduce the workload of the heart.

2. **Longevity.** Research by Paffenbarger et al. (1986, 1978) was the first to confirm the link between cardiovascular proficiency and greater life expectancy. Nearly 17,000 Harvard alumni were investigated to determine the effects of physical activity on longevity. Individuals expending 2,000 or more calories during exercise per week, as opposed to the rates of less active participants, extended their life expectancy by more than two years.

3. **Improved maximum oxygen consumption.** By increasing the ability to deliver and process oxygen, an individual enhances his/her capacity to produce more ATP, the universal energy source. It is interesting to note that the world record for maximum oxygen consumption is in the mid-90s for an adult male and high-70s for an adult female, about double the current capacity of the average American college male and female, respectively, suggesting that most adults demonstrate significant room for improvement.

4. **Lowered blood pressure (if high before chronic exercise).** Both diastolic (pressure between heartbeats) and systolic (pressure during heartbeat) pressures tend to go down in hypertensive individuals when they engage in long-term aerobic activity. The result is less strain on the heart.

5. **Reduced body fat content.** Vigorous activity causes a greater hypertrophy in the working muscle groups, plus long bouts of submaximal exercise promote the type of calorie burning that is conducive to reducing body fat percentage. A body fat standard that promotes good health is about 15 percent or less for male adults and roughly 25 percent or less for female adults.

6. **Increased metabolism.** The body simulates a finely tuned engine when the rate of calorie expenditure is high. While it is common knowledge that even two or three hours of weekly aerobic exercise necessitates huge calorie expenditures, it is uncommonly known that the metabolic rate remains elevated for several hours during each recovery period. Since the average person's metabolism slows a few percentage points every decade of life, this particular cardiovascular endurance benefit helps combat the tendency to gain weight as one gets older.

7. **Increased HDL cholesterol and lowered LDL cholesterol levels.** The cholesterol level, measured as the number of milligrams per deciliter (100 milliliters) of blood, includes high-density lipoprotein (HDL) and low-density lipoprotein (LDL) types. The HDL, sometimes labeled "good" cholesterol, is coupled with the LDL or "bad" cholesterol to derive a total cholesterol reading. Staying aerobically active is a factor in a person's ability to keep the total cholesterol amount below 200, considered the

red-flag figure because diseases and other ailments stemming from circulatory problems tend to escalate for persons surpassing the 200 figure.

Persons possessing greater cardiovascular endurance levels also benefit from higher amounts of "good" cholesterol in their blood. The LDL amount, the cholesterol culprit in the bloodstream, is lowered by aerobic exercise, resulting in a healthy ratio for the two types of cholesterol. The proper ratio is kept in check by the HDL's ability to extract portions of the LDL via the liver.

8. **Lower resting heart rate.** With an increase in cardiac output, the resting heart rate will decrease.
9. **Less bone mineral loss.** Strengthened by cardiovascular endurance activity at any age, the bones better retain their capacity to make the body more functional and mobile. Females receive particular benefit in this area as their calcium intake is insufficient to provide adequate protection for the bones. In other words, a lifetime participation in aerobic activities significantly retards the onset of debilities such as osteoporosis.

ACUTE AND CHRONIC ADAPTATIONS TO AEROBIC EXERCISE

Each time a person exercises, the body adapts to the stress of the activity. Some of the adaptations are acute (short lived) whereas others are chronic (long term). Acute changes include an increase in metabolism (energy consumption) as well as increased cardiac output, systolic blood pressure, and ventilation to match the demands of the activity. Working muscles also enlarge because an increased amount of blood is flowing to them. Blood is therefore shunted away from the internal organs, resulting in the slowing of digestion and/or absorption. Each of these adaptations is quick to return to preexercise levels after the activity ends.

Chronic adaptations, on the other hand, do not return to preexercise levels. Such chronic changes include increased metabolism primarily due to an increase in lean body mass, lowered resting heart rate, increased stroke volume, increased aerobic activity at the cellular level (enzyme activity, mitochondrial density, lipid or fat fuel utilization), increased capillarization of muscle tissue, and improved oxygen utilization. How long do these adaptations last? Chronic changes last as long as the body feels a need to meet the exercise stress that is used to produce the adaptations. For example, a person exercises for ten weeks and achieves a 30-percent improvement in his/her aerobic capacity. Then the person stops exercising. In only five weeks the body will lose the aerobic adaptations it took ten weeks to develop. And, the body will revert back to its starting point in all areas within another five weeks. What does this really mean? Simply but impressionistic, it means that a person wanting to possess a strong aerobic capacity must engage in some form of aerobic activity over the entire lifespan to maintain the benefits derived from the training.

COMPONENTS OF AEROBIC EXERCISE PROGRAM

An exercise program is much like a medical prescription. There are things to consider before beginning an exercise program. The aerobic exercise program should consist of dynamic, large muscle activities such as walking, running, cycling (stationary or nonstationary), swimming, elliptical machines, dance, or any other activity that is continuous in movement. The training effect of the program is dependent on the proper frequency, intensity, and duration of the exercise session. The American College of Sports Medicine recommend three to five sessions per week for 20–60 minutes at an intensity of 50–85 percent of heart rate reserve. Heart rate reserve will be discussed later in this chapter.

Aerobic Endurance Training Program Design Variables

1. Exercise Mode (type)
2. Exercise Frequency
3. Exercise Intensity
4. Exercise Duration

Mode

This term identifies the type of exercise being performed. The key here is that the activity should involve large muscles of the body in a slow rhythmical fashion and preferably be weight bearing in nature (Weight-bearing exercise helps prevent osteoporosis). There are several factors to consider when selecting a mode of exercise. First and foremost, it must be enjoyable. A second important element is convenience. If the activity requires too much preparation or is lacking in accessibility, then chances of sticking to the activity are reduced. A third very important factor is the risk of injury. Common sense should prevail. If you are an injury-prone individual, choose low-impact, low-intensity activities until you have a solid foundation of activity without injury. If you rarely get injured, feel free to try higher impact activities. Using a variety of activities (cross-training) with a mixture of low- and high-impact and -intensity can be a good way of keeping your exercise program interesting and fun. Remember that mode of activity is only one part of a well-rounded exercise prescription. Some of the most common modes of aerobic activity include jogging/walking, cycling, swimming, elliptical machines, and dance classes.

Frequency

Frequency of activity is a second aspect of an exercise program. Current epidemiological research suggests that a person can simply accumulate 30 minutes of physical activity each day and reduce his/her risk of cardiovascular disease. The American College of Sports Medicine endorses the concept of cumulative activity, as well as the general claim that engagement in aerobic activity three to five times per week produces gains in cardiovascular fitness. Do not be misled by the old misconception that if a little activity is good, more must be better. Maximum benefits from aerobic activity can be attained by using a frequency of as little as two days per week; however, the intensity and duration necessary during the two days would far exceed recommendations. A three- to five-days-per-week program will produce significant gain without substantially increasing risk of injury. Six or seven days per week is excessive because the body has little time to recover and overuse injuries are virtually guaranteed. One can see from Figure 2.2 that the risk of injury increases dramatically in individuals whose exercise regimen exceeds five days weekly. Also, little or no additional aerobic benefits are acquired by adding the sixth or seventh day.

Intensity

Intensity is another important component of an effective exercise program. Improvement in cardiovascular endurance occurs when intensity is equal to or greater than 50 percent of one's maximal aerobic capacity (maximal oxygen consumption). Since obtaining oxygen consumption during exercise is almost impossible and oxygen consumption is

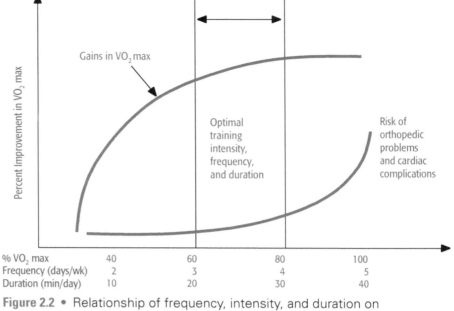

Figure 2.2 • Relationship of frequency, intensity, and duration on improvements and risk of injury.
From *Exercise Physiology: Theory and Application to Fitness and Performance* by Powers and Hawley (2009).

closely related to changes in heart rate during activity, it is quite simple to estimate exercise intensity by monitoring heart rate. However, there is about a 10- to 15-percent difference between oxygen consumption and heart rate at a given submaximal effort. If a 50-percent intensity for oxygen consumption is required, a training heart rate level should then be about 60–65 percent of maximum heart rate. Optimal range for improving cardiovascular endurance is 50–85 percent of oxygen consumption. That relates to a heart rate range of 60–95 percent of maximal heart rate. By knowing how to calculate maximal heart rate, you can quickly find the heart rate training zone for appropriate intensity. For example, a 20-year-old person has a maximal heart rate of 200 beats/ minute (maximal heart rate = 220 − age). At 60 percent, the low end of the training heart rate range is 120 beats/minute, and at the 95-percent end, training heart rate is 190 beats/minute. As you can see, this is a wide range and explains why most experts suggest intensities between 70 and 90 percent maximal heart rate. Intensity is also related to frequency and duration. The greater the frequency or the longer the duration, the lower the intensity can be. For athletes, the greater improvements in cardiovascular endurance come with high intensities, between 80 and 90 percent of maximal heart rate. This would suggest that as a person becomes more fit, intensity must increase to continue gains in cardiovascular endurance. For most college-age individuals, an intensity between 70 and 90 percent of maximal heart rate is a good rule of thumb; however, keep in mind that activity of lower intensity still has cardiovascular benefits.

A more accurate method to determine the appropriate heart rate training zone or target heart rate (THR) is to use the Karvonen formula. The Karvonen formula calculates the training heart rate using a percentage of the heart rate reserve,

Taking one's pulse can help determine proper exercise intensity.

which is the difference between the maximum heart rate and the resting heart rate. The Karvonen formula is as follows:

$$THR = [(MHR - RHR) \times I] + RHR$$
$$THR = \text{target or training heart rate}$$
$$MHR = \text{maximum heart rate}$$
$$RHR = \text{resting heart rate}$$
$$I = \text{intensity (60–90 percent)}$$

In order to use Karvonen, a person will need to know his/her resting heart rate. Resting heart rate should not be measured first thing in the morning as heart rate is depressed until early morning. Accurate resting heart rate can be measured after a person has been up and active for a short period and then sits and relaxes. Resting heart rate can be measured during rest by counting the heart rate at either the radial or carotid artery. Using Karvonen, a 20-year-old person with a resting heart rate of 70, who wished to exercise at an intensity of 60 percent, would have a training heart rate of 148.

$$THR = [(200 - 70) \times 60\%] + 70$$
$$THR = 148$$

A subjective method for measuring exercise intensity is called perceived exertion. Following the scale in Table 2.2, the exerciser estimates his/her rate of perceived exertion [RPE] when asked by a tester in a laboratory situation. The subjective rating becomes more objective once an individual learns to exercise at an RPE level that corresponds well to the aforementioned objective measures of exercise intensity.

Each number on the Borg scale (Table 2.2) multiplied by 10 approximates heart rate. For example, number 19 on the scale is close to a maximum heart rate. Ratings from "fairly light" to "hard" constitute an appropriate heart rate training zone.

Duration

Duration at a training intensity should be between 20 and 60 minutes. As stated before, accumulation of 30 minutes of activity daily produces an adequate level of cardiovascular endurance and is a significant factor in reducing the chance of cardiovascular disease. Duration is best determined by two factors: individual goals for cardiovascular improvement and amount of exercise time available in a daily schedule. Similar individual goals can be accomplished with different durations. An increase in intensity will allow for a shorter duration and will demonstrate similar results. Generally speaking, people were taught that they must exercise for longer durations to achieve higher levels of cardiovascular endurance; however, with a shorter duration but a higher intensity, as discussed under the following heading, a person can also achieve a high level of cardiovascular endurance. Nonetheless, remember our earlier discussion that aerobic energy expenditure beyond 2,000 calories weekly yields minimal additional cardiovascular gains while increasing the risk of overuse injuries. We know from all the wonderful benefits the body derives from participation in aerobic activity that nature clearly intends for it to be part of a universal health prescription. The second part of nature's prescription is that moderate intensity and duration suffice for the development and maintenance of proper cardiovascular health.

HIGH INTENSITY INTERVAL TRAINING

High intensity interval training, commonly called HIIT workouts, is a form of training that uses high intensity exercise bouts with brief recovery periods. HIIT usually involves many repetitions of these high intensity, short duration, exercise bouts with rest between

TABLE 2.2 Rating of Perceived Exertion

Scale	Verbal Rating
6	
7	Very, very light
8	
9	Very light
10	
11	Fairly light
12	
13	Somewhat hard
14	
15	Hard
16	
17	Very hard
18	
19	Very, very hard
20	

From *Med Sci Sports Exercise*, 15:523–528, 1983.

each bout. The short rest period can be complete rest or low intensity exercise rest. For example, running as fast as you can for 1 minute and then walking for 1 minute. The intense exercise bouts can last from 10 seconds up to 5 minutes. Rest between bouts depend on the amount of time spent on the exercise bout. The longer the exercise bout, the longer the recovery time. For exercise bouts lasting less than 30 seconds the usual recovery is a ratio of 1 to 3. This means that if the exercise bout lasted 15 seconds, the recovery period would last 45 seconds. Exercise bouts between 30 seconds and 2 minutes require a 1 to 2 exercise to rest ratio and for exercise bouts longer than 2 minutes a 1 to 1 ratio is recommended. Total exercise time for a normal HIIT training session is usually form 15-30 minutes.

Research has shown HIIT training to be as good as, but not superior to, lower intensity forms of aerobic training (Milanovic, Z, Sporis G, Weston M., 2015). The advantage of HIIT is the efficiency of the workout. HIIT is the ideal workout for a busy schedule. The benefits derived from longer lasting, lower intensity exercise can be achieved in a much shorter training session. The negative of HIIT is safety. Individuals who have been physical inactive may have an increased risk for injury during HIIT training. Prior to beginning a HIIT training program, a person is encouraged to establish a foundational level of fitness. This can be accomplished by performing low intensity aerobic training for several weeks before beginning a HIIT training program.

MEDICAL CLEARANCE

Perhaps the most important decision you must make before engaging in activity is whether or not it is safe to do so. Research is conclusive that aerobic activity is safe for the majority of people. To insure safe entry into an aerobic activity, use the Physical Activity Readiness Questionnaire (PAR-Q) found in Appendix C as a screening tool. Endorsed by the American College of Sports Medicine, the PAR-Q is a useful method for clearing people for participation in exercise programs. One "yes" answer on the questionnaire is all that it takes to warrant medical clearance before proceeding to engage in activity. As a precaution, people above 45 years of age should receive medical clearance regardless of the responses to the questionnaire. We all must remember that for a small number of people, physical activity can be inappropriate.

DESIGNING YOUR OWN PROGRAM

Both specific short- and long-term goals should be addressed when initiating an exercise program. Other issues include concerns for safety, warm-up, type of activity, cooldown, progression, and possible cross-training options.

Safety

Common sense should prevail when questions arise concerning exercise. Proper attire is important. If you plan to walk or run, pay close attention to your shoes. Quality shoes can circumvent many unpleasant injuries of the feet, ankles, and leg muscles. You probably should spend a little extra on a pair of shoes. Wear them around in the store for at least 10–15 minutes. It is worth the extra time to help you determine if they are truly a good fit. Common sense must also supersede your desire to exercise when you are not feeling well. A day off with rest may allow you to return to your regimen both sooner and stronger. Furthermore, the occurrence of pain during activity is a clear sign that something is wrong. Address that pain immediately. Where is it coming from? What could be the cause? Try to answer these questions before you continue with your activity. The old adage of "no pain, no gain" is totally inappropriate in this context, and you need to make sure that your activity program is directed toward reducing health problems instead of creating them.

Target Heart Rate Calculations

Karvonen Method

Formula:

- ❏ Age-predicted maximum heart rate (APMHR) = 220 – age
- ❏ Heart rate reserve (HRR) = APMHR – resting heart rate (RHR)
- ❏ Target heart rate (THR) = (HRR × exercise intensity) + RHR

Do this calculation twice to determine the target heart rate range (THRR).

Example:
A 30-year-old athlete with an RHR of 60 beats/min is assigned an exercise intensity of 60% to 70% of functional capacity:

- ❏ APMHR = 220 – 30 = 190 beats/min
- ❏ RHR = 60 beats/min
- ❏ HRR = 190 – 60 = 130 beats/min
- ❏ Lowest number of the athlete's THRR = (130 × 0.60) + 60 = 78 + 60 = 138 beats/min
- ❏ Highest number of the athlete's THRR = (130 × 0.70) + 60 = 91 + 60 = 151 beats/min

When monitoring heart rate during exercise, divide the THRR by 6 to yield the athlete's THRR in number of beats for a 10-second interval:

138 ÷ 6 = 23   151 ÷ 6 = 25

The athlete's THRR is 23–25 beats per 10 seconds.

Percentage of Maximal Heart Rate Method

Formula:

- ❏ Age-predicted maximum heart rate (APMHR) = 220 – age
- ❏ Target heart rate (THR) = (APMHR × exercise intensity)

Do this calculation twice to determine the target heart rate range (THRR).

Example:
A 20-year-old athlete is assigned an exercise intensity of 70% to 85% of maximal heart rate:

- ❏ APMHR = 220 – 20 = 200 beats/min
- ❏ Lowest number of the athlete's THRR = 200 × 0.70 = 140 beats/min
- ❏ Highest number of the athlete's THRR = 200 × 0.85 = 170 beats/min

When monitoring heart rate during exercise, divide the THRR by 6 to yield the athlete's THRR in number of beats for a 10-second interval:

140 ÷ 6 = 23   170 ÷ 6 = 28

The athlete's THRR is 23–28 beats per 10 seconds.

Reprinted, with permission, from B.H. Reuter and P.S. Hagerman, 2008, Aerobic endurance exercise training. In *Essentials of Strength Training and Conditioning, 3rd ed.*, edited for the National Strength and Conditioning Association by T.R. Baechle and R.W. Earle (Champaign, IL: Human Kinetics), 494

Warm-up

Every workout should begin with a short warm-up which prepares the body for the upcoming stress of activity. Blood is shunted away from internal organs and delivered to the muscles. Muscles are contracted and stretched, causing an increase in their metabolic activity, plus sensory inputs from joints are activated. A good warm-up might include a few minutes of walking, stretching and light calisthenics. During the warm-up session, impulses are sent to the brain, helping to prepare a person psychologically for exercise. Thus, warm-up has both a physiological and psychological influence on the exerciser.

Activity

To improve cardiovascular endurance, one must use large muscles of the body. Typically, this means the hips and legs. Components of activity previously described should be addressed, but remember that any activity that involves a large muscle mass can be used to benefit your endurance. Choose activities that are enjoyable and vary the activity (cross-training) from time to time to prevent boredom. Variety in exercise may be the "spice" you need to maintain an activity program for life.

TABLE 2.3   Potential of Various Activities for Development of Total Fitness

Activity	Calories per Hour (150-lb Person)	Builds Cardiovascular Health and Burns Fat	Builds Muscle Strength
Aerobic dance (vigorous)	474	4	4
Basketball (competitive)	545	4	2
Canoeing or rowing (fast pace)	815	5	4
Cross-country skiing machine	645	5	4
Cycling (fast pace)	680	5	3
Cycling (leisurely pace)	375	3	2
Cycling (stationary, moderate)	475	4	3
Dancing	305	3	2
Gardening	340	3	3
Golf (walking and carrying bag)	375	3	3
Handball (casual)	475	4	3
Lawn mowing (power mower)	305	3	3
Racquetball or squash (casual)	475	4	3
Raking leaves	270	3	3
Rope jumping (moderate to hard)	680	5	3
Running (brisk pace, 8 mph)	920	5	2
Running (moderate pace, 6 mph)	680	5	2
Shoveling dirt or digging	580	4	4
Skating (in-line or ice)	475	4	3
Skiing (cross-country, brisk speed)	610	5	4
Skiing (downhill)	340	3	3
Soccer (casual)	475	4	3
Splitting wood	410	4	4
Stair climbing	610	5	3
Swimming (laps, vigorous)	680	5	4
Swimming (moderate)	545	4	3
Tennis (competitive)	475	4	3
Volleyball (competitive)	270	3	3
Walking (brisk pace, 4 mph)	270	3	2
Walking (slow pace, 2 mph)	170	2	2
Weight training	205	2	5
Yoga	170	1	2

The table shows how well each activity builds cardiovascular health, burns fat, and builds muscle strength (1 = not at all, 2 = a little, 3 = moderately, 4 = strongly, and 5 = very strongly). For muslce strength, the activity is rated high if both upper and lower body muscles are strengthened.

From *Exercise Testing and Prescription: A Health Related Approach*, 7/e by David Nieman. Copyright © 2011 by The McGraw-Hill Education. Reprinted by permission.

Cooldown

After any vigorous activity, you should always try to slow things down gradually. Five minutes of slow walking, light movements, or stretching of the muscles just used aids in the prevention of muscle cramps and even cardiac arrhythmia (abnormal heartbeat) in some extreme cases. Once your body has reached a steady state during exercise, it takes a few minutes for it to return to preexercise conditions. Without a proper cooldown,

TABLE 2.4   Guidelines for Continuous Training

Training Level	Frequency (Sessions per Week)	Duration (Minutes)	Intensity of Exercise (% of VO₂ max or HRR)
Beginner	3	20	40%–50%
Intermediate	4–5	30–45	50%–75%
Advanced	5–6	45–60	75%–85%

From *Fitness for Life* by Prentice, W. et al. Copyright © 1997. Reprinted by permission of The McGraw-Hill Companies.

blood tends to pool in the working muscles (the legs in most instances) and slows your rate of recovery. Some type of mild movement enhances recovery and makes the exercise experience more enjoyable.

Progression

There is no set pattern of exercise progression for everyone, but some general guidelines should be followed to help you increase your aerobic capacity to a desired level. The American College of Sports Medicine recommends that during initial phase of the exercise program, an increase in duration per session of 5–10 minutes every one to two weeks over the first four to six weeks of an exercise training program is reasonable for the average adult (ACSM, 2011). Table 2.4 outlines a progression for an aerobic activity program on the basis of initial levels of fitness. As this information indicates, progression is modified first by frequency, next by duration, and finally by intensity. This is a good rule of thumb for individuals interested in planning a personal progression. One important point to make is that while looking at Table 2.4, the intermediate level is the level recommended for good health.

ASSESSING CARDIOVASCULAR ENDURANCE

The best measurement of cardiovascular fitness is the direct measurement of oxygen consumption (VO₂) during maximal exercise. The exercise is performed using either a treadmill or a stationary bike. During the test, the subject will be instructed to give max effort and all subject's expired air will be collected and measured using a computerized metabolic cart. Maximal oxygen consumption (VO₂ max) is the highest rate at which oxygen can be consumed during this test and is our best measurement of cardiovascular fitness. The higher a person's VO₂ max, the higher his/her cardiovascular fitness level. Other, non-laboratory or field tests have been developed for testing large groups of individuals. These tests are practical, inexpensive, less time-consuming, and easier to administer than laboratory tests. At the end of this chapter are three field tests for assessing cardiovascular endurance. These tests are intended to provide meaningful estimates for students interested in their level of cardiovascular fitness. When completing one of these tests, do your best so the results will give you an accurate picture of your current level of cardiovascular condition.

TABLE 2.5   Equivalent Performances for Various Distances

VO$_2$ max (ml/kg/min)	Performance Time for Various Distances (hours:minutes:seconds)				
	1.5 km	1 mile	5 km	10 km	42.2 km
28	13:30	14:46	56:49	2:39:14	31:41:25
31.5	11:27	12:29	47:04	2:02:00	16:35:05
35	9:56	10:49	40:10	1:38:53	11:13:52
38.5	8:46	9:33	35:02	1:23:08	8:29:26
42	7:51	8:33	31:04	1:11:43	6:49:30
45.5	7:07	7:44	27:54	1:03:03	5:42:21
49	6:30	7:03	25:20	0:56:15	4:54:07
52.5	5:59	6:29	23:11	0:50:47	4:17:48
56	5:32	6:01	21:23	0:46:17	3:49:28
59.5	5:09	5:36	19:50	0:42:30	3:26:44
63	4:50	5:14	18:30	0:39:33	3:08:06
66.5	4:32	4:55	17:20	0:36:33	2:52:34
70	4:17	4:38	16:18	0:34:10	2:39:23
73.5	4:03	4:23	15:23	0:32:12	2:28:05
77	3:50	4:09	14:34	0:30:12	2:18:16
80.5	3:39	3:57	13:50	0:28:33	2:09:41
84	3:29	3:46	13:10	0:27:04	2:02:06
87.5	3:20	3:36	12:34	0:25:44	1:55:21

From *American Journal of Sports Medicine, Volume 27.* Copyright © 1987 by SAGE Publicatons. Reprinted by permission of SAGE Publications.

TABLE 2.6   Norms for the 1.5-Mile Run Test *(for People between the Ages of 17 and 35)*

Fitness Category	Time: Ages 17–25	Time: Ages 26–35
Superior		
Males	<8:30	<9:30
Females	<10:30	<11:30
Excellent		
Males	8:30–9:29	9:30–10:29
Females	10:30–11:49	11:30–12:49
Good		
Males	9:30–10:29	10:30–11:29
Females	11:50–13:09	12:50–14:09
Moderate		
Males	10:30–11:29	11:30–12:29
Females	13:10–14:29	14:10–15:29
Fair		
Males	11:30–12:29	12:30–13:29
Females	14:30–15:49	15:30–16:49
Poor		
Males	>12:20	>13:29
Females	>15:49	>16:49

Note: Before taking this running test, it is highly recommended that the student or individual be "moderately fit." Sedentary people should first start an exercise program and slowly build up to 20 minutes of running, 3 days per week, before taking this test.

From *JOPERD* by DO Draper and GL Jones, American Alliance for Health, Physical Education, Recreation and Dance.

SUMMARY

1. Cardiovascular endurance is the ability to supply oxygen to working muscles for extended periods of body movement.
2. Fitness experts recognize cardiovascular endurance as the primary component of physical fitness because its improvement enhances energy output, promotes longer life, and positively influences the development of strength, muscular endurance, flexibility, and body composition.
3. The heart, blood vessels, blood, and lungs enable oxygen transport in the body.
4. Blood vessels include the arteries, veins, and capillaries.
5. The combination of an increased stroke volume and decreased heart rate improves cardiac output.
6. Maximal heart rate is estimated by subtracting yearly age from 220.
7. A systolic (pressure during heart contraction) blood pressure above 140 mm Hg and/or a diastolic (resting blood pressure) pressure above 90 mm Hg are the borderline indicators for hypertension or high blood pressure.
8. Adenosine triphosphate (ATP), the universal energy source, is accessed by the systems of ATP-PC (one–ten seconds), anaerobic (ten seconds–three minutes), and aerobic (more than three minutes).
9. An exercise program includes recommendations for mode, frequency, and intensity. Performance in one or a variety of aerobic activities for at least 30 minutes daily at moderate intensity is a safe and effective program for developing and maintaining a cardiovascular endurance level that leads to a long and healthy life. The exerciser benefits from 30 minutes of cumulative aerobic movement as well as continuous.
10. Perceived exertion is a subjective method for measuring exercise intensity.
11. Due to the numerous positive changes the body experiences when cardiovascular endurance is improved, it is clear that nature intends for the human body to be active.
12. Warm-up activities enable the body to receive physiological and psychological preparation for movement.
13. Cross-training in aerobic activities allays boredom in the exercise routine.
14. Proper cooldown hastens recovery from strenuous exercise.

References

ACSM. (2011) Position Statement on Exercise. *Med Sci Sports Exerc 43*(7) 1334–1359.

Center for Disease Control and Prevention (1996). Physical Activity and Health a Surgeon General Report.

Milanovic, Z, Sporis G, Weston M. (2015). Effectiveness of high-intensity interval training (HIT) and continuous endurance training for VO2mas improvements. *Sports Med.* 2015; 45:1469–1481

Nieman, D. (2011). *Exercise Testing and Prescription a Health Related Approach* (7th ed.). McGraw-Hill, New York.

Paffenbarger, R. S., Jr., et al. (1978). Physical activity as an index of heart attack risk in college alumni. *American Journal of Epidemiology, 108,* 161–175.

Paffenbarger, R. S., Jr., et al. (1986). Physical activity, all cause mortality and longevity of college alumni. *New England Journal of Medicine, 314,* 606–613.

Powers, S. K., & Howley, E. T. (2009). *Exercise physiology theory and application to fitness and performance* (7th ed.). New York, NY: McGraw-Hill.

CHAPTER 2

PERSONAL GROWTH OPPORTUNITY 1

Cooper's 12-Minute Walking/Running Test

Purpose

To determine the level of cardiovascular endurance of college students during a 12-minute running or walking activity.

Equipment

1. Measured running course, preferably a track.
2. Stopwatch

Procedure

1. During a 12-minute period the subject attempts to cover as much distance as possible by either running or walking.

Treatment of Data

1. Distance covered should be rounded off to the nearest ⅛ mile.
2. Consult table below. Locate the distance covered for either men or women under the appropriate age classification, and determine the level of fitness.

12-Minute Walking/Running Test Distance (Miles) Covered in 12 Minutes

Fitness Category		Distance by Age (Years)					
		13–19	20–29	30–39	40–49	50–59	60+
Superior	(males)	>1.87	>1.77	>1.70	>1.66	>1.59	>1.56
	(females)	>1.52	>1.46	>1.40	>1.35	>1.31	>1.19
Excellent	(males)	1.73–1.86	1.65–1.76	1.57–1.69	1.54–1.65	1.45–1.58	1.33–1.55
	(females)	1.44–1.51	1.35–1.45	1.30–1.39	1.25–1.34	1.19–1.30	1.10–1.18
Good	(males)	1.57–1.72	1.50–1.64	1.46–1.56	1.40–1.53	1.31–1.44	1.21–1.32
	(females)	1.30–1.43	1.23–1.34	1.19–1.29	1.12–1.24	1.06–1.18	.99–1.09
Fair	(males)	1.38–1.56	1.32–1.49	1.31–1.45	1.25–1.39	1.17–1.30	1.03–1.20
	(females)	1.19–1.29	1.12–1.22	1.06–1.18	.99–1.11	.94–1.05	.87–.98
Poor	(males)	1.30–1.37	1.22–1.31	1.18–1.30	1.14–1.24	1.03–1.16	.87–1.02
	(females)	1.00–1.18	.96–1.11	.95–1.05	.88–.98	.84–.93	.78–.86
Very poor	(males)	<1.30	<1.22	<1.18	<1.14	<1.03	<.87
	(females)	<1.0	<.96	<.94	<.88	<.84	<.78

CHAPTER 2

PERSONAL GROWTH OPPORTUNITY 2

1.0-Mile Walk Test

Purpose

To determine the level of cardiovascular endurance of individuals unable to run because of injury or poor fitness. This test is recommended for unconditioned people, men above age 40 and women above age 50. One must merely be able to walk briskly while generating a heart rate (HR) of 120 bpm by the completion of the test.

Equipment

1. Measured one-mile course, preferably a track.
2. Scale to determine body weight before the walk and a stopwatch.

Procedures

1. Walk the measured one-mile course as fast as possible.
2. Record your walking time and immediately take your pulse for 10 sec.
3. Multiply your pulse by 6 to obtain your exercise HR (bpm).
4. Convert your time from minutes and seconds to minutes and fractions of minutes by dividing the seconds by 60 (i.e., if walking time is 13:30, then 30 seconds divided by 60 seconds = 0.5 minutes, yielding a total of 13.5 min.).
5. Use the following formula to estimate your maximal oxygen consumption in relative terms as VO₂ max in ml/kg/min.

   $$VO_2 \text{ max} = 88.768 - (0.0957 \times Wt) + (8.892 \times G) - (1.4537 \times Tt) - (0.1194 \times HR)$$

   where Wt = body weight (lbs), G = gender (0 = female, 1 = male), Tt = total time to walk one mile, and HR = heart rate at the end of the test.
6. Then find and circle your level of fitness on the basis of gender and age using the fitness chart.

Example

A 20-year-old female weighing 150 lbs completes the one-mile walk in 13:30 minutes with an ending HR of 144 bpm. The predicted VO₂ max would be 37.6 ml/kg/min (average fitness level).
   Information needed:

   Wt = 150 lbs, gender = 0, Tt = 13 min + (30 sec/60 sec) = 13.5 min, HR = 144 bpm

   VO₂ max = 88.768 − (0.0957 × 150) + (8.892 × 0) − (1.4537 × 13.5) − (0.1194 × 144)

        = 88.768 −   14.355   +   0   −   19.62   −   17.19

        = 37.6 ml/kg/min

FITNESS CHART—WOMEN					
Age	**Low**	**Fair**	**Avg.**	**Good**	**High**
20–29	<24	24–30	31–37	38–48	49+
30–39	<20	20–27	28–33	34–44	45+
40–49	<17	17–23	24–30	31–42	42+
50–59	<15	15–20	21–27	28–37	38+
60–69	<13	13–17	18–23	24–34	35+

FITNESS CHART—MEN					
Age	**Low**	**Fair**	**Avg.**	**Good**	**High**
20–29	<25	25–33	34–42	43–52	53+
30–39	<23	23–30	31–38	39–48	49+
40–49	<20	20–26	27–35	36–44	45+
50–59	<18	18–24	25–33	34–42	43+
60–69	<16	16–22	23–30	31–41	41+

CHAPTER 2

PERSONAL GROWTH OPPORTUNITY 3

1.5-Mile Run Test

Purpose

To determine the level of cardiovascular endurance of healthy, well-conditioned individuals who have been cleared for exercise. This test is *NOT* recommended for unconditioned people, men above age 40, or women above age 50 without proper medical approval, or people with known risk factors of heart disease.

Equipment

1. Measured running course, preferably a track.
2. Stopwatch

Procedures

1. Complete a warm-up that includes some walking, light jogging, some stretches, and perhaps a few calisthenics.
2. Complete the measured 1.5-mile course as fast as possible.
3. Cool down by jogging/walking slowly for another 4–6 minutes. Do NOT sit or lie down immediately after finishing the test.
4. Consult the Estimated Maximal Oxygen Consumption table below to find and circle your relative VO_2 max in ml/kg/min. Then find and circle your level of fitness on the basis of gender and age using the fitness chart (p. 34).

Time	VO_2	Time	VO_2	Time	VO_2	Time	VO_2	Time	VO_2
6:10	80.0	8:50	59.1	11:30	44.4	14:10	35.5	16:40	29.5
6:20	79.0	9:00	58.1	11:40	43.7	14:20	35.1	16:50	29.1
6:30	77.9	9:10	56.9	11:50	43.2	14:30	34.7	17:00	28.9
6:40	76.7	9:20	55.9	12:00	42.3	14:40	34.3	17:10	28.5
6:50	75.5	9:30	54.7	12:10	41.7	14:50	34.0	17:20	28.3
7:00	74.0	9:40	53.5	12:20	41.0	15:00	33.6	17:30	28.0
7:10	72.6	9:50	52.3	12:30	40.4	15:10	33.1	17:40	27.7
7:20	71.3	10:00	51.1	12:40	39.8	15:20	32.7	17:50	27.4
7:30	69.9	10:10	50.4	12:50	39.2	15:30	32.2	18:00	27.1
7:40	68.3	10:20	49.5	13:00	38.6	15:40	31.8	18:10	26.8
7:50	66.8	10:30	48.6	13:10	38.1	15:50	31.4	18:20	26.6
8:00	65.2	10:40	48.0	13:20	37.8	16:00	30.9	18:30	26.3
8:10	63.9	10:50	47.4	13:30	37.2	16:10	30.5	18:40	26.0
8:20	62.5	11:00	46.0	13:40	36.8	16:20	30.2	18:50	25.7
8:30	61.2	11:10	45.8	13:50	36.3	16:30	29.8	19:00	25.4
8:40	60.2	11:20	45.1	14:00	35.9				

Source: Adapted from "A Means of Assessing Maximal Oxygen Intake," by K. H. Cooper, in *Journal of the American Medical Association,* 203 (1968), 201–204; *Health and Fitness Through Physical Activity*, by M. L. Pollock, J. H. Wilmore and S. M. Fox III (New York: John Wiley & Sons, 1978); and *Training for Sport and Activity*, by J. H. Wilmore and D. L. Costill (Dubuque, IA: Wm C. Brown Publishers, 1988).

Body Composition

© Aleutie, 2014. Used under license from Shutterstock, Inc.

Specific Objectives

1. Differentiate between various types of body tissue and their physiological functions.
2. Differentiate between the terms overweight, overfat, and obese.
3. Explain the importance of a desirable ratio of lean to fat body tissue.
4. List the problems that accompany an overweight condition.
5. Describe the various methods available for the assessment of body composition.
6. Understand the relationship of fat distribution to health.
7. Calculate body mass index and waist-to-hip ratio.

OVERVIEW

Bodies come in all shapes and sizes, and while no perfect body exists, there does seem to be a point at which certain shapes and sizes of bodies present health risks. The composition of our bodies is significant because certain tissues, such as muscles and bones, are highly functional, while too much fat tissue has negative consequences on health and well-being. Americans seem to be carrying more and more of this fat tissue, which can compromise health. In fact, the National Institute of Diabetes and Digestive and Kidney Diseases (NID-DKD, 2017) reports that more than two out of three adults in the United States are overweight or obese (70 percent, 74 percent of males and 67 percent of females). Thirty-three percent fall into the category of overweight (39 percent of men and 27 percent of women) and another 38 percent are obese (35 percent of men and 40 percent of women). Obesity is estimated to account for over seven percent of the health care costs in the United States, with the direct and indirect costs exceeding $190 billion each year (Cawley, Meyerhoefer, 2012). Relationships between high levels of fat and certain chronic diseases and other unwanted conditions have become more evident over recent years as body weights have increased. For these reasons, the composition of our bodies is a critical issue in the pursuit of overall health.

Body composition refers to the fat versus nonfat makeup of the human body. Everyone carries a certain amount of adipose, or fat, tissue. This tissue is referred to as fat mass. Everything which is not adipose tissue is referred to as fat-free mass or lean mass. This lean mass includes muscles, bones, blood, organs, and other tissues, or in other words, everything except the fat mass.

Fat mass consists of the fat found just beneath the surface of the skin, called subcutaneous fat, as well as fat distributed in other parts of the body, specifically that surrounding vital organs. About half of the fat in the body is subcutaneous, where it provides cushion and helps regulate body temperature. It is also the fat which sometimes causes dissatisfaction when one looks into the mirror. While some of this fat is necessary, many individuals carry considerably more than is needed. The fat that is necessary for good health is called essential fat. The body cannot function normally without a certain amount of fat in the heart, brain, liver, lungs, nerves, and a few other body parts. About 3 percent of the total weight in men and about 12 percent of the total weight in women is considered essential body fat. It is important for females to have more essential body fat because some of it is sex specific. This extra essential fat is found primarily in the breasts and the uterus and is attributed to the energy requirements of pregnancy and lactation. Table 3.1 shows the typical body composition of male and female young adults.

Fat in excess of essential fat is called, as you might guess, nonessential fat. It is also referred to as storage fat. The amount of storage fat varies a great deal from person to person and is determined by factors such as heredity, age, and metabolism, but is primarily influenced by diet and activity level. This variation in the amount of storage fat carried by individuals sometimes results in the potentially dangerous conditions known as overweight, overfat, and obese. While these terms are sometimes used interchangeably, there are distinct differences among them.

TABLE 3.1 Typical Body Composition of Male and Female Young Adults

	Men	Women
Muscle	45%	36%
Essential fat	3%	12%
Nonessential	12%	15%
Bone	15%	12%
Other	25%	25%

Adapted from: Fahey, T.D., Insel, P.M., and Roth, W.T. (1997). *Fit & Well* (2nd ed.). Mountain View, CA: Mayfield Publishing Company, p. 132.

OVERFAT VERSUS OVERWEIGHT

The term *overweight* takes into consideration only a person's total body weight in relationship to height and frame size. It does not take into account the relationship of fat mass to lean mass. Height–weight charts are used for this assessment and are sometimes used to determine health status, but they are actually a very poor measure of health because there is so much variation in body makeup from person to person. For example, a very muscular and athletic individual may measure their height, then step on the scales, and, according to a height–weight chart, be assessed as overweight. This is probably not the case because the weight comes from the accumulation of muscle tissue, which is highly functional and useful, and not detrimental to health. Another person may step on the scales and determine, again according to a height–weight chart, that their weight is appropriate for their height and receive a false sense of security about their health status, while actually carrying extra body fat which places them at risk. It is possible to be within the correct weight range for one's height, yet still be overfat. Since muscle tissue is denser and heavier than fat, these two scenarios are highly possible. A height–weight chart is shown in Table 3.2 for comparison purposes.

The term overfat refers to the actual percentage of body mass made up of adipose tissue. When the percentage of fat reaches a level that compromises health, a person is referred to as overfat. Fatness is a much more meaningful indicator of health status and cannot be measured with a height–weight chart. As stated earlier, this relationship of fat to lean tissue is called body composition, and there are several assessment tools that can be used to determine this important component of fitness. When the percentage of body fat reaches a level that causes the health risks to become critical, the person is obese. For men, obesity is identified at a body fat percentage of 25 percent or greater. For women, obesity is 32 percent body fat or greater (Neiman, 2011). Table 3.3 shows healthy and unhealthy body fat percentages for men and women.

TABLE 3.2 Metropolitan Height–Weight Tables (In Pounds by Height and Frame in indoor Clothing: Men—5 lb, 1-Inch Heel; Women—3 lb, 1-Inch Heel)

Men				Women			
Height (inches)	Frame			Height (inches)	Frame		
	small	medium	large		small	medium	large
62	128–134	131–141	138–150	58	102–111	109–121	118–131
63	130–136	133–143	140–153	59	103–113	111–123	120–134
64	132–138	135–145	142–156	60	104–115	113–126	122–137
65	134–140	137–148	144–160	61	106–118	115–129	125–140
66	136–142	139–151	146–164	62	108–121	118–132	128–143
67	138–145	142–154	149–168	63	111–124	121–135	131–147
68	140–148	145–157	152–172	64	114–127	124–138	135–151
69	142–151	148–160	155–176	65	117–130	127–141	137–155
70	144–154	151–163	158–180	66	120–133	130–144	140–159
71	146–157	154–166	161–184	67	123–136	133–147	143–163
72	149–160	157–170	164–188	68	126–139	136–150	146–167
73	152–164	160–174	168–192	69	129–142	139–153	149–170
74	155–168	164–178	172–197	70	132–145	142–156	152–173
75	158–172	167–182	176–202	71	135–148	145–159	155–176
76	162–176	171–187	181–207	72	138–151	148–162	158–179

Source: Metropolitan Life Insurance Company, New York.

TABLE 3.3 Percent Body Fat Classifications

Classification	Male	Female
Unhealthy range	5% and below	8% and below
Acceptable range (lower end)	6–15%	9–23%
Acceptable range (higher end)	16–24%	24–31%
Unhealthy range	25% and above	32% and above

Source: Neiman, D.C. (2011). *Exercise Testing and Prescription: A Health Related Approach* (7th ed.). New York: McGraw Hill.

PROBLEMS WITH OVERWEIGHT AND OBESITY

The health risks of obesity and being overfat are well documented. The NIDDKD (2015) includes type 2 diabetes, high blood pressure, heart disease and stroke, certain types of cancer, sleep apnea, osteoarthritis, fatty liver disease, kidney disease and pregnancy problems including high blood sugar and high blood pressure during pregnancy, and increased risk of cesarean delivery, as the health problems associated with obesity. Several of the negative health consequences of obesity are discussed more thoroughly in the chapter on weight control.

Not only does the overfat or obese person compromise his/her health, but additional problems result. Overfat individuals are likely to have problems sustaining any type of regular exercise, activity, or recreation program. In addition to missing the health benefits of regular recreational pursuits, the overfat person also misses out on the social interaction and enjoyment of participation.

Daily physical demands of a job or physical activities may also create a problem. Jobs that require a great deal of walking or other type of physical movement, which on one hand could be very beneficial for the overfat person, might on the other hand be perceived as exceptionally challenging. Walking a flight of stairs without feeling exhausted or a walking tour of a park, zoo, or other attraction may be a burden for the overfat. Trekking across a college campus may even be difficult for some.

ASSESSSING BODY COMPOSITION

The determination of body composition can be a valuable tool in developing an overall plan for good health, and there are several methods available for the measurement of body composition. While some of these measures are more accurate than others, each has certain advantages and is considerably more valuable than the use of total body weight or height–weight charts. Each of the methods described here is considered an indirect measure of body composition. Direct measurement would consist of actually dissecting a cadaver, separating the fat and lean tissue, weighing both, and calculating the ratio of lean tissue to fat tissue.

Hydrodensitometry

Hydrodensitometry is considered the criterion method for the measurement of body composition because all other methods were compared and formulas written based on this method. This method, also called hydrostatic or underwater weighing, involves total submersion of an individual in a specially designed water tank and the use of a scale to measure the person's weight in the water (shown in Figure 3.1).

Muscle tissue has a higher density than water and tends to sink. Bone and muscle are more dense than water, while fat tissue has a lower density than water and tends to float. Therefore, the heavier the weight of the person in the water, the more muscle and less fat the person possesses. To perform this measurement accurately, not only does there need to be access to the special tank and scale apparatus, but the subject must be quite cooperative as well. Accurate measurements are possible only when the subject can forcefully exhale as much air from the lungs as possible, then sit very still while completely submerged so the technician can gather an accurate reading from the scales. Several trials are required to gain an accurate measure of water weight. This submersion is not an easy task and can contribute to error in the test.

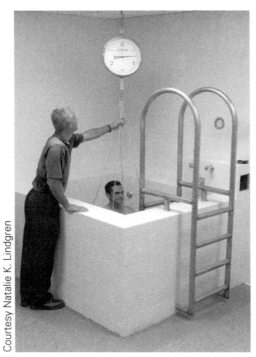

Courtesy Natalie K. Lindgren

Figure 3.1 • Body composition measurement using hydrostatic weighing tank.

A trained and experienced technician is also a must for accuracy. Finally, measurement of residual air volume is needed to determine how much air the subject leaves in their lungs following the forceful exhalation. When all measures have been made, a computer program uses the factors of dry weight, water weight, water density, and residual volume to determine body density. Since few settings have the technical equipment, trained technicians, and time needed to perform this test, it is found only in specialized settings. Sports medicine laboratories, university exercise physiology programs, and some medical settings may have this method of measurement available.

Skinfold Measurements

A more practical and widely used approach for measuring fat mass is called the skinfold measure. This assessment uses a special tool called a skinfold caliper to measure the thickness of the layer of fat just beneath the surface of the skin (the subcutaneous fat) at several sites on the body. Knowing that approximately half of the body's fat is subcutaneous fat and knowing what sites on the body typically hold that fat, researchers have been able to generate equations that predict the percentage of body fat on the basis of these measurements.

Skinfold measurements have a very high correlation with hydrostatic weighing and are considerably more accurate than other measures that utilize only weight, height, or circumference measures of the body.

Calipers are relatively inexpensive and simple to use, but great care must be taken in order to attain accurate results. Calipers should be durable and of good quality and must be properly calibrated. Inexpensive plastic calipers may at times give accurate results, but are less reliable than metal calipers. Various types of calipers are shown in Figure 3.2. Technicians should be trained in a professional setting, and as with any laboratory skill, the more experience they have gained, the more capable they will be. Even an experienced technician should take several measures at each recommended site to reduce the error of the test. Location of the skinfold is also important, as a slight deviation in the area of the pinch of skin taken can

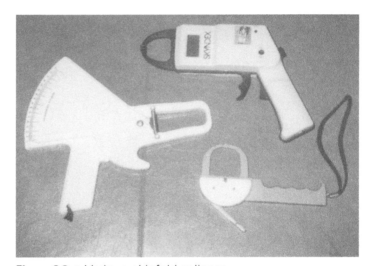

Figure 3.2 • Various skinfold calipers.

produce erroneous readings. Less experienced technicians may even prefer to measure and mark the location on the subject's body. Good lab technicians who know how to locate the site, pinch the skin, place the calipers, and measure properly can attain very accurate results.

Various sites may be used in a skinfold measurement, but a simple three-site test yields accurate results. Those locations are the triceps, suprailiac, and abdomen for men and the triceps, suprailiac, and thigh for women (see Figure 3.3). The sum of the three skinfolds can then be entered into a prediction equation to determine the percentage of body fat. The equations can be found along with instructions for skinfold measurement in Personal Growth Opportunity 3.1.

Bioelectrical Impedance Analysis

Another method for the assessment of body composition is called bioelectrical impedance analysis, or BIA. A specialized piece of equipment is needed to conduct this test. Several different BIA devices are available, but all work on the same principle. For this procedure, small electrodes transmit and measure a small (50 kHz) undetectable electrical current as it passes through the body. Since muscle tissue contains a considerable

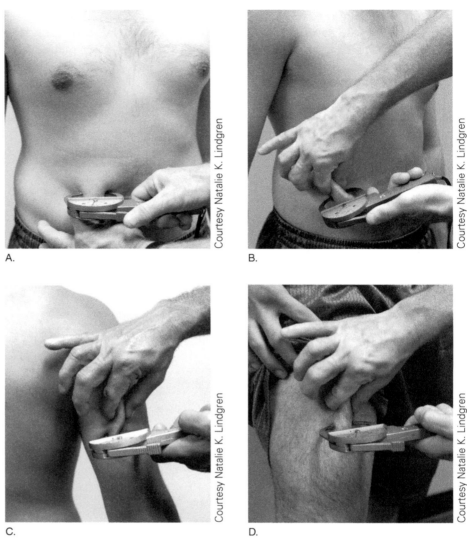

Courtesy Natalie K. Lindgren

Figure 3.3 • Anatomical sites for skinfold measures. A. Abdominal skinfold, B. Suprailiac skinfold, C. Triceps skinfold, D. Thigh skinfold.

amount of water and fat tissue contains little water, and since water is a good conductor of electricity, the leaner individual will more readily conduct the electrical current. The more fat tissue the person has, the more impedance, or resistance, there is to the electrical current. Figure 3.4 shows a special scale that uses BIA to measure body composition.

This technique has the advantages of being portable and noninvasive, plus it takes very little time compared with hydrostatic weighing. The test is also very easy to administer, so the possibility of technician error is greatly reduced. Its major limitation is revealed when used for very lean or obese individuals. Although it correlates highly to other criterion methods, it tends to overestimate body fat in very lean individuals and underestimate body fat in the obese (American College of Sports Medicine, 2014).

Air Displacement Plethysmography

The use of air displacement plethysmography (ADP) is gaining popularity as a method for measuring body composition in some settings. It works on a similar principle to underwater weighing, but instead of measuring water displacement, it measures air displacement. The Bod-Pod® is a fiberglass unit designed to measure changes in pressure within the closed chamber of the unit (see Figure 3.5). It measures the subject's mass and volume and calculates whole body density. From these measures, body composition is determined. This measure is noninvasive and there is little technical expertise needed to attain accurate results, but the minimization of isothermal air by using tight clothing and a lycra swim cap is important to obtaining accurate results of this test. ADP is considered a reliable and valid measure of body composition in comparison to criterion methods and may reduce the anxiety that can come with the water submersion required for hydrodensiometry (American College of Sports Medicine, 2014). However, the expense of the equipment makes it a method that is not yet widely available.

DEXA

The dual energy x-ray absorptiometry (DEXA) technology is another relatively new method for assessing body composition. It measures body fat, muscle, and bone using x-ray energies. It is considered to be a highly accurate measure of assessing body composition (American College of Sports Medicine, 2014) but, again, is a costly procedure, so it is not widely available.

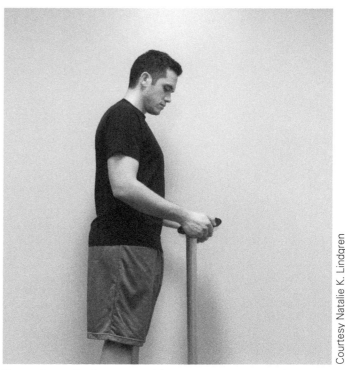

Figure 3.4 • Body composition measurement using bioelectrical impedance analysis.

Body Mass Index

Another technique useful for measuring body mass, although not a true measure of body composition, is called body mass index, or BMI. Like height–weight charts, BMI uses only the measures of height and weight. However, BMI is superior to the use of a height–weight chart in that it calculates a ratio of weight to height, and makes comparison to a desired ratio on the basis of population studies of mortality rates. While BMI does not distinguish between body fat and muscle mass or bone, research does show a correlation to other measures of body fat including dual x-ray absorptiometry and hydrostatic weighing. However, the accuracy of BMI is highly questionable in athletes and regular exercisers. Like body composition, BMI is used to project disease risk on the basis of relative mortality rates. Research indicates that a high BMI carries an increased risk of heart disease, high blood pressure, type 2 diabetes, gallstones, breathing problems, and certain cancers (American College of Sports Medicine, 2014; National Heart, Lung, and Blood Institute, 2013). Additionally, Berrington de Gonzalez and colleagues (2010) report that higher BMIs are linked to a higher risk of death.

BMI is determined by dividing body weight (in kilograms) by height in meters squared. Therefore, BMI = wt (kg)/ht (m)^2. Divide body weight in pounds by 2.2 to convert

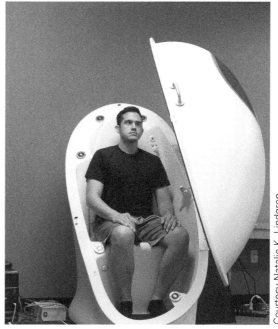

Figure 3.5 • The BodPod®—air displacement plethysmography, is another product that measures body composition.

TABLE 3.4 Body Mass Index

Height (in.)	49	51	53	55	57	59	61	63	65	67	69	71	73	75	77	79	81	83
Weight (lb.)																		
66	19	18	16	15	14	13	12	12	11	10	10	9	9	8	8	8	7	7
70	20	19	18	16	15	14	13	13	12	11	10	10	9	9	8	8	8	7
75	22	20	19	17	16	15	14	13	12	12	11	10	10	9	9	9	8	8
79	23	21	20	18	17	16	15	14	13	12	12	11	11	10	9	9	9	8
84	24	22	21	19	18	17	16	15	14	13	12	12	11	11	10	10	9	9
88	26	24	22	20	19	18	17	16	15	14	13	12	12	11	11	10	10	9
92	27	25	23	21	20	19	17	16	15	15	14	13	12	12	11	11	10	10
97	28	26	24	22	21	20	18	17	16	15	14	14	13	12	12	11	10	10
101	29	27	25	23	22	20	19	18	17	16	15	14	13	13	12	12	11	10
106	31	28	26	24	23	21	20	19	18	17	16	15	14	13	13	12	11	11
110	32	30	27	26	24	22	21	20	18	17	16	15	15	14	13	13	11	11
114	33	31	29	27	25	23	22	20	19	18	17	16	15	14	14	13	12	12
119	35	32	30	28	26	24	22	21	20	19	18	17	16	15	14	14	13	12
123	36	33	31	29	27	25	23	22	21	19	18	17	16	16	15	14	13	13
128	37	34	32	30	28	26	24	23	21	20	19	18	17	16	15	15	14	13
132	38	36	33	31	29	27	25	23	22	21	20	19	18	17	16	15	14	14
136	40	37	34	32	29	28	26	24	23	21	20	19	18	17	16	16	15	14
141	41	38	35	33	30	28	27	25	24	22	21	20	19	18	17	16	15	15
145	42	39	36	34	31	29	27	26	24	23	22	20	19	18	17	17	16	15
150	44	40	37	35	32	30	28	27	25	24	22	21	20	19	18	17	16	15
154	45	41	38	36	33	31	29	27	26	24	23	22	20	19	18	18	17	16
158	46	43	40	37	34	32	30	28	26	25	24	22	21	20	19	18	17	16
163	47	44	41	38	35	33	31	29	27	26	24	23	22	20	19	19	18	17
167	49	45	42	39	36	34	32	30	28	26	25	23	22	21	20	19	18	17
172	50	46	43	40	37	35	32	30	29	27	25	24	23	22	21	20	19	18
176	51	47	44	41	38	36	33	31	29	28	26	25	23	22	21	20	19	18
180	52	49	45	42	39	36	34	32	30	28	27	25	24	23	22	21	20	19
185	54	50	46	43	40	37	35	33	31	29	27	26	25	23	22	21	20	19
189	55	51	47	44	41	38	36	34	32	30	28	27	25	24	23	22	20	20
194	56	52	48	45	42	39	37	34	32	30	29	27	26	24	23	22	21	20
198	58	53	49	46	43	40	37	35	33	31	29	28	26	25	24	23	21	20
202	59	54	50	47	44	41	38	36	34	32	30	28	27	25	24	23	22	21
207	60	56	52	48	45	42	39	37	35	33	31	29	27	26	25	24	22	21
211	61	57	53	49	46	43	40	38	35	33	31	30	28	27	25	24	23	22
216	63	58	54	50	47	44	41	38	36	34	32	30	29	27	26	25	23	22
220	64	59	55	51	48	44	42	39	37	35	33	31	29	28	26	25	24	23
224	65	60	56	52	49	45	42	40	37	35	33	31	30	28	27	26	24	23
229	67	62	57	53	49	46	43	41	38	36	34	32	30	29	27	26	25	24
233	68	63	58	54	50	47	44	41	39	37	35	33	31	29	28	27	25	24
238	69	64	59	55	51	48	45	42	40	37	35	33	32	30	28	27	26	24
242	70	65	60	56	52	49	46	43	40	38	36	34	32	30	29	28	26	25
246	72	66	61	57	53	50	47	44	41	39	37	35	33	31	29	28	27	25
251	73	67	63	58	54	51	47	45	42	39	37	35	33	32	30	29	27	26
255	74	69	64	59	55	52	48	45	43	40	38	36	34	32	31	29	28	26
260	76	70	65	60	56	52	49	46	43	41	39	36	34	33	31	30	28	27
264	77	71	66	61	57	53	50	47	44	42	39	37	35	33	32	30	29	27
268	78	72	67	62	58	54	51	48	45	42	40	38	36	34	32	31	29	28
273	79	73	68	63	59	55	52	48	46	43	40	38	36	34	33	31	30	28
277	81	75	69	64	60	56	52	49	46	44	41	39	37	35	33	32	30	29
282	82	76	70	65	61	57	53	50	47	44	42	40	37	35	34	32	30	29
286	83	77	71	66	62	58	54	51	48	45	42	40	38	36	34	33	31	29
290	84	78	72	67	63	59	55	52	48	46	43	41	39	37	35	33	31	30
295	86	79	74	68	64	60	56	52	49	46	44	41	39	37	35	34	32	30
299	87	80	75	69	65	60	57	53	50	47	44	42	40	38	36	34	32	31
304	88	82	76	70	66	61	57	54	51	48	45	43	40	38	36	35	33	31
308	90	83	77	71	67	62	58	55	51	48	46	43	41	39	37	35	33	32
312	91	84	78	72	68	63	59	55	52	49	46	44	41	39	37	36	34	32

▨ = Underweight;
☐ = Desirable;
▨ = Increased health risks;
▨ = Obese;
■ = Extremely obese

From American College of Sports Medicine, 2003, ACSM Fitness Book, 3rd ed., page 81. © 2003 by American College of Sports Medicine. Reprinted with permission of Human Kinetics (Champaign, IL). Based on values published by the Panel on Energy, Obesity and Body Weight Standards, 1987, American Journal of Clinical Nutrition, 15, p. 1035.

Reprinted, with permission, from American College of Sports Medicine, 2003, *ACSM Fitness Book*, 3rd ed. (Champaign, IL: Human Kinetics), 81.

TABLE 3.5 Disease Risk Associated with Body Mass Index and Waist Cirumference

Classification	Obesity Class	BMI (kg/m^2)	Disease Risk Relative to Normal Weight and Waist Cirumference*	
			Men ≤ 40 in. **Women ≤ 35 in.**	**> 40 in.** **> 35 in.**
Underweight		<18.5		
Normal		18.5–24.9		
Overweight		25.0–29.9	Increased	High
Obesity	I	30.0–34.9	High	Very high
	II	35.0–39.9	Very high	Very high
Extreme obesity	III	≥40	Extremely high	Extremely high

*Disease risk of type 2 diabetes, hypertension, and cardiovascular disease.

Source: NHLBI Obesity Education Initiative Expert panel (1998). *Clinical Guidelines on the Identification, Evaluation, and Treatment of Overweight and Obesity in Adults*. National Heart, Lung, and Blood Institute: www.nhlbi.nih.gov/nhlbi/.

to kilograms. Height in inches can be converted to meters by multiplying by 0.0254. For example, if a person weighs 180 pounds and stands six feet tall, BMI would be calculated as shown:

$$\text{Weight} = 82 \text{ kg } (180/2.2)$$
$$\text{Height} = 1.83 \text{ meters } (72 \text{ inches} \times 0.0254)$$
$$\text{BMI} = 82/1.832^2 = 82/3.35 = 24.47$$

You can also use the BMI calculator offered by the Centers for Disease Control and Prevention by simply entering your height and weight at the following website: https://www.cdc.gov/healthyweight/assessing/bmi/adult_bmi/english_bmi_calculator/bmi_calculator.html

According to current standards, a BMI less than 18.5 is considered underweight; a BMI of 18.5–24.9 is considered normal; a BMI of 25–29.9 is considered overweight; a BMI of 30 or greater is obese, with three grades of obesity and three levels of health risks. Table 3.4 provides a simple chart to identify BMI, and Table 3.5 provides a guide to identifying obesity class and disease risk relative to waist circumference.

Waist-to-Hip Ratio

In addition to how much body fat a person carries, the distribution of that fat is an important factor in its effect on health. In fact, some research indicates that waist-to-hip ratio (WHR) is a stronger predictor of diabetes, coronary artery disease, and overall death risk than are body weight, BMI, or percentage of body fat (Brownell et al., 1987; Folsom et al., 1993). Individuals have a tendency to carry body fat in different locations, with the major difference in location of stored fat being between men and women. Men generally store fat in the upper half of the body, specifically in the abdominal area. This is called the android form of obesity and has been referred to as the apple-shaped body. Women generally store fat in the lower half of their body, specifically in the hips and thighs. This is called the gynoid form of obesity and has been referred to as the pear-shaped body. A third type of obesity is found in individuals who carry fat in both the upper and lower body and is known as intermediate obesity. All three forms of obesity can be found in both sexes.

The location of the fat storage is very important from a health perspective. Android obesity is the type of fat storage that creates the most significant health risk. This pattern of body fat storage is positively correlated with an increased risk of hypertension, type 2

A.

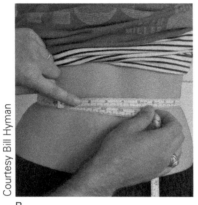

B.

Figure 3.6 • Anatomical locations for circumference measures. A. Hip circumference, B. Waist circumference.

diabetes, metabolic syndrome, dyslipidemia, coronary artery disease, and premature death when compared with gynoid obesity (ACSM, 2014). Additionally, those with high levels of visceral fat, or fat found on and around internal organs, are at greater risk than those with mostly subcutaneous fat, or fat just beneath the surface of the skin.

Since the location of the stored fat is a health concern, measures that help to identify the primary site of fat storage can be valuable. Many researchers prefer the ratio of the waist-to-hip circumference as an assessment for this identification. Measurement of WHR is quite simple and very informative as to fat location.

Measurement of the waist is taken with a soft, flexible tape measure at the point of smallest circumference between the bottom of the rib cage and the umbilicus. Measurement of the hip is taken at the point of greatest circumference of the hip area. Both measures should be taken while the subject is in a relaxed, standing position, with the tape positioned on a horizontal plane around the measurement site. Clothing around the site should be minimal, so it does not interfere with an accurate reading (Figure 3.6).

When waist circumference is divided by hip circumference, the WHR is the result. For example, if a person has a 34-inch waist circumference and a 36-inch hip circumference, their WHR would be .94 (34 divided by 36). The average WHR in males between the ages of 17 and 39 is .90, and in females of this same age group, the average WHR is .80. Increased disease risks accompany greater WHR measurements for both sexes. Table 3.6 shows the relative disease risk for WHR. Use Personal Growth Opportunity 3.2 to determine your WHR.

IDEAL BODY WEIGHT

Once a body composition assessment reveals the percentage of body fat an individual possesses, that person's ideal body weight can be determined. If the percentage of body fat is already within a desirable range, no changes would be recommended in body weight. If, however, as with many Americans, excessive body fat is present, a new body weight can be recommended. This recommendation is made with the assumption that the individual will pursue the weight loss in the correct way—by exercising and following a prudent eating plan as discussed in the chapter on nutrition. This will result in the maintenance of the lean body mass, with the weight loss coming from the reduction in fat tissue.

A target percentage of body fat should be identified using Table 3.3 found earlier in this chapter. Remember that there is not a specifically recommended percent body fat, but everyone should strive for the acceptable range and that moderate reductions in body fat can provide great health benefits. Consultation with a health care provider can help determine a target for percentage of body fat. Once that goal is determined,

TABLE 3.6 Relative Disease Risk for Waist-to-Hip Ratio

	Men		Women	
	Age 20–39	40 and over	Age 20–39	40 and over
Very high risk	>.95	>1.0	>.85	>.85
High risk	.9–.95	.95–1.0	.79–.85	.8–.85
Moderate risk	.85–.9	.9–.95	.72–.79	.75–.8
Low risk	<.85	<.9	<.72	<.75

Adapted from: Bray, G.A. and Gray, D.S. (1988). Obesity: Part I—Pathogenesis, *Western Journal of Medicine*, 149:429–441 and American College of Sports Medicine. (1995). *Guidelines for Testing and Exercise Prescription*. Baltimore: Williams & Wilkins, p. 59.

the following formula and the use of Personal Growth Opportunity 3.3 can assist in determining what that means in terms of body weight.

1. Identify your fat weight (FW). This is done by multiplying your total body weight (BW) by the percent body fat (%F) from your body composition assessment. The equation is:

$$FW = BW \times \%F$$

2. Identify how much lean weight (LW) you have by subtracting your fat weight (FW) from your total body weight (BW).

$$LW = BW - FW$$

3. Determine the fat percentage that you desire to attain (something in the acceptable range) using Table 3.3. Using your target fat percentage (TFP), calculate your ideal body weight (IBW) using the following formula:

$$IBW = LW / (1 - TFP)$$

Once ideal body weight is determined, proper weight loss techniques are critically important. Unfortunately, many people turn to fraudulent, ineffective, and sometimes dangerous attempts to lose weight. It is important to stick to the basics and remember:

1. Safe and effective weight loss is not a rapid process. It is recommended that the weight loss goal be set at a maximum of two pounds per week.

Example

A skinfold measurement for Sam finds that he has 23 percent body fat. He weighs 200 pounds and is 25 years old. He decides that he wants to set a target goal of 18 percent body fat. Therefore, his determination of ideal body weight would be as follows:

1. FW = BW × %F
   FW = 200 × 0.23
   FW = 46   Sam has 46 pounds of fat.

2. LW = BW − FW
   LW = 200 − 46
   LW = 154   Sam has 154 pounds of lean mass.

3. IBW = LW/(1 − TFP)
   IBW = 154/(1 − 0.18)
   IBW = 154/0.82
   IBW = 189   If Sam uses proper reduction techniques to reduce to 18 percent body fat, his target weight is 189 pounds.

---

2. It takes a combination of caloric intake reduction and increase in caloric expenditure through exercise to attain healthy weight loss.
3. While heredity is a factor in a person's body shape and weight, everyone can improve their health status through the attainment of a more desirable body composition.
4. Periodic reassessment of body composition is recommended. Body composition changes with the normal aging process. As we age, fat accumulates and muscle mass is lost—this age-related loss of muscle mass is called sarcopenia. About 10 percent of muscle mass is lost between ages 25 and 50, with an additional 40 percent lost between ages 50 and 80 (Powers & Howley, 2012). In addition, lifestyle changes such as diet and exercise habits will also result in body composition changes. Remember, simply weighing on a scale is not a good way to assess health status, so periodic assessment of body composition can keep up with the ratio of fat mass to lean body mass.

References

American College of Sports Medicine. (2014). *ACSM's resource manual for guidelines for exercise testing and prescription* (7th ed.). Baltimore, MD: Lippincott, Williams & Wilkins.

American College of Sports Medicine. (2018). *ACSM's Guidelines for exercise testing and prescription, 10th edition.* Philadelphia: Wolters Kluwer.

Anspaugh, D.J., Hamrick, M.H., & Rosato, F.D. (2011). *Wellness: Concepts and Applications* (8th ed.). New York: McGraw Hill.

Berrington de Gonzalez, B., Hartge, P., Cerhan, J. R., Flint, A. J., Hannan, L., MacInnis, R. J., et al. (2010). Body-mass index and mortality—Prospective analysis of 1.46 million white adults. *New England Journal of Medicine, 362,* 23.

Brownell, K. D., Steen, S. N., & Wilmore, J. H. (1987). Weight regulation practices in athletics: Analysis of metabolic and health effects. *Medicine and Science in Sports and Exercise, 19*(6), 546–556.

Cawley, J, Meyerhoefer, C. (2012). The medical care costs of obesity: an instrumental variables approach. Journal of Health Economics. (31) pp. 219–230.

Fahey, T.D., Insel, M.I., & Roth, W.T. (2019). *Fit & Well: Core Concepts and Labs in Physical Fitness and Wellness* (13th ed.). New York: McGraw Hill.

Folsom, A. R., Kaye, S. A., Sellers, T. A., Hong, C. P., Cerhan, J. R., Potter, J. D., et al. (1993). Body fat distribution and five year risk of death in older women. *Journal of the American Medical Association, 269*(4).

Frisard, M.I., Greenway, F.L., & Delaney, J.P. (2005). Comparison of methods to assess body composition changes during a period of weight loss. *Obesity Research* 13(5).

Hoeger, W.K., Hoeger, S.A., Hoeger, C.I., and Fawson, A.L. (2017). *Lifetime Physical Fitness and Wellness* (14th ed.). Boston: Cengage.

Maddalozzo, G.F., Cardinal, B.J., & Snow, C.A. (2002). Current validity of the BOD POD and dual energy x-ray absorptiometry techniques for assessing body composition in young women. *Journal of the American Dietetic Association.* 102(11).

National Institute of Diabetes and Digestive and Kidney Diseases (2015). Health Risks of Being Overweight. Retrieved from: https://www.niddk.nih.gov/health-information/weight-management/health-risks-overweight

National Institute of Diabetes and Digestive and Kidney Diseases (2017). Overweight and Obesity Statistics. Retrieved from: https://www.niddk.nih.gov/health-information/health-statistics/overweight-obesity

Neiman, D. C. (2011). *Exercise testing and prescription: A health-related approach.* New York, NY: McGraw-Hill.

Plowman, S. A., & Smith, D. L. (2003). *Exercise physiology for health, fitness, and performance* (2nd ed.). Boston: Pearson Addison-Wesley.

Powers, S. K., and Howley, E. T. (2017). *Exercise physiology: Theory and application to fitness and performance* (10th ed.). New York: McGraw-Hill.

Revick, D. A., & Israel, R. G. (1986). Relationship between body mass indices and measures of body adiposity. *American Journal of Public Health,* 76:992–997.

Rogers, M. A., & Evans, W. Y. (1993). Changes in skeletal muscle with aging: Effects of exercise training. *Exercise and Sports Science Reviews,* 21:65–102.

Stamford, B. (1991). Apples and pears: Where you wear your fat can affect your health. *The Physician and Sportsmedicine,* 19:123–124.

Van Itallie, T. B. (1988). Topography of body fat: Relationship to risk of cardiovascular and other diseases. In: Anthropometric standardization reference manual. Edited by T.G. Lohman, A. F. Roche, and R. Martorelli. Champaign, IL: Human Kinetics Publishers, Inc.

CHAPTER 3

PERSONAL GROWTH OPPORTUNITY 1

Skinfold Lab and Worksheet

In preparation for this assessment, the subject should wear clothing that will allow the technician access to the appropriate sites. A quiet room that promotes modesty and is free from distractions is best. Subjects should be standing for the test, and all skinfolds should be taken on the right side of the body.

Step I

The technician locates the proper anatomical sites for the three-site skinfold assessment. The sites for men are the suprailiac, abdomen, and triceps. The sites for women are the triceps, suprailiac, and thigh. It is important that the sites for the skinfold be accurate. Figure 3.3 assists you in locating the correct sites. The technician may choose to mark them as follows:

Thigh—Use a vertical fold in the front of the thigh, halfway between the knee and the hip.
Suprailiac—Use a diagonal fold just above the crest of the ilium or hip bone.
Triceps—Use a vertical fold on the back of the upper arm, halfway between the shoulder and the elbow.
Abdomen—Use a vertical fold one inch to the right of the umbilicus or navel.

Step II

The technician will grasp the site with his/her index finger and thumb. Lightly pinch the skin and adipose tissue, but do not grasp muscle. Do not pinch too hard or you may compress the fat and get an inaccurate reading. Take a vertical or diagonal measurement (depending on the site) about one-quarter of an inch from the fingertips. After allowing the tips of the calipers to settle, read the dial to the nearest half millimeter. Take at least two measures at each site to ensure consistency. If the two readings are not the same, conduct further tests until consistent readings are attained. Be sure the skin is released and regrasped between readings. If tests are going to be repeated at a later date for comparison purposes, conduct them at the same time of day. Also, do not conduct this test soon after exercise, as normal skinfold size will be inflated due to body fluid shifting to the skin.

Step III

Have someone record the three readings on the chart below.

Women		*Men*	
Thigh	_____	Triceps	_____
Suprailiac	_____	Suprailiac	_____
Triceps	_____	Abdomen	_____

Step IV

Add the measurements of the three skinfolds. Use the sum of skinfolds to calculate percent body fat using the following prediction equations.

Sum of three skinfolds = _____

Females Percent Body Fat = 0.41563 (sum of skinfolds) − 0.00112 (sum of skinfolds)^2
+ 0.03661 (age) + 4.03653
Males Percent Body Fat = 0.39287 (sum of skinfolds) − 0.00105 (sum of skinfolds)^2
+ 0.15772 (age) − 5.18845

Refer back to Table 3.3 to determine your health classification according to your sum of skinfolds.

Example

Eddie is a 22-year-old male whose skinfold measurements yield the following readings:

Suprailiac = 15 mm
Triceps = 8 mm
Abdomen = 21 mm
Sum of skinfolds = 44 mm
Percent body fat = 12.5
Fitness category according to body fat = Acceptable range (lower end)

Sources of Prediction Equations: Jackson, A.S., and Pollock M.L. (1985) Practical Assessment of body composition. *Physician and sports Medicine* 13: 76 − 90; Golding, L.A., Myers, C.R., and Sinning W.E. (1989) *The Y's Way to Physical Fitness* (3rd. ed). Champaign, IL: Human Kinetics.

CHAPTER 3

PERSONAL GROWTH OPPORTUNITY 2

Waist-to-Hip Ratio Lab and Worksheet

Step I

Using a flexible tape measure, measure hip circumference at the largest point and waist circumference at the smallest point.

Step II

Determine the ratio of those measures using the following:

Waist circumference _____ / Hip circumference _____ = _____ Waist-to-hip ratio.

Step III

Using Table 3.6, compare your waist-to-hip ratio with your relative disease risk. Your relative waist-to-hip disease risk ratio is _____.

CHAPTER 3

PERSONAL GROWTH OPPORTUNITY 3

Ideal Body Weight Lab and Worksheet

Step I

After having your percent body fat accurately measured using a valid and reliable method, and after weighing on a physician's scale, calculate your fat weight:

Body weight _____ × percent body fat _____ = _____ fat weight.

Step II

Identify how much lean weight you possess:

Body weight _____ − fat weight _____ = _____ lean weight.

Step III

Select a target fat percentage that you would desire to attain through proper combination of exercise and healthy diet. Use that target fat percentage to determine ideal body weight:

Lean weight _____ / (1 − _____ selected fat percentage) = _____ ideal body weight.

Step IV

Calculate your weight loss goal by subtracting your ideal body weight from your current body weight:

Body weight _____ − ideal body weight _____ = _____ weight loss goal.

In order to attain your ideal body weight, your goal will be to lose _____ pounds of adipose tissue.

Flexibility

© wavebreakmedia, 2014. Used under license from Shutterstock, Inc.

Specific Objectives

1. Define flexibility and its importance as a component of health-related physical fitness.
2. Identify the factors that affect flexibility.
3. Describe the relationship between abdominal, back, hip, and thigh muscles for reducing low back pain.
4. Identify how ballistic, static, PNF, and AIS methods are used to develop and maintain flexibility.
5. Determine your flexibility via modified sit-and-reach, trunk extension, body rotation, and shoulder flexibility tests.
6. Identify several strategies for improving/maintaining flexibility.
7. Discuss Pilates and yoga as ways of maintaining a healthy level of flexibility.
8. Understand the value of warm-up before stretching.

OVERVIEW

The degree of movement that occurs at a joint is called the range of motion (ROM). The ROM of a joint is determined by several factors including connective tissue structure, activity level, age, and gender. ROM is specific to each joints anatomy and the movement required by the joint.

Flexibility is the measure of ROM and has two components: static and dynamic. Static flexibility addresses ROM without regard to how rapidly the ROM can be achieved. Static flexibility requires no voluntary muscular activity; an external force such as gravity, a partner, or a machine provides the force for the stretch. Dynamic flexibility, on the other hand, is the resistance to motion that affects how easily a joint can move through its ROM. In daily living, we often must make rapid, strenuous movements, which may cause injury if a joint cannot move through its full ROM. According to the U.S. Institute of Medicine, 100 million Americans are affected by chronic low back pain. Health economists from Johns Hopkins University reported this chronic condition has an estimated financial cost of between 261 and 300 billion dollars (Gaskin & Richard, 2012). According to the National Institute of Neurological Disorders and Stroke (2012), most low back pain is the result of many factors, with most being controllable. Box 4.1 gives quick tips for a healthier back. More information reported by the National Institute of Neurological Disorder and Stroke suggest 80 percent of all low back problems in the United States result from improper alignment of the spine and pelvic girdle due to inflexibility and weak abdominal muscle. Although flexibility varies from person to person because of body structure, it is important to understand that having adequate flexibility is an acquired state and various forms of stretching are the mechanisms by which we can achieve an appropriate level of flexibility. Without attention being paid to maintaining flexibility, ROM decreases, and although there is little research to document this, most experts feel the potential for musculotendinous injury increases.

WHY FLEXIBILITY IS IMPORTANT FOR HEALTH AND FITNESS

There are several reasons why medical personnel endorse stretching exercises to attain a desirable level of flexibility. Of primary importance is the need to maintain a balanced relationship in the muscles crossing the hips or pelvis. On the front or anterior side of the body, the abdominal muscles and the hip flexors act to stabilize the pelvis. On the back or posterior side of the body, your buttocks, back muscles, and hamstrings (posterior thigh)

BOX 4.1

Tips for a Healthy Back

1. Maintain a healthy body weight. Excess weight takes a toll on the whole body and the back is no exception.
2. Maintain good posture. Improper body alignment places pressure on the back's discs, muscles, and ligaments.
3. Remain flexible. Tight hamstring muscles can increase risk of back injury and pain.
4. Lift correctly. If lifting heavy objects stand close to the object with your feet spread apart. Squat down keeping your back in proper alignment as you lift.
5. Strengthen your core muscles. A strong core will protect your back.
6. Sleep on a good mattress. A poor mattress can cause back pain.
7. If you smoke, stop. Smoking increases risk of back pain.
8. Wear proper shoes. High heels can cause back pain.
9. Exercise smart. Chronic high-impact exercises increase risk of back pain. Consider low-impact activities when exercising.
10. Practice good ergonomics. When standing for long periods, put one foot forward and bend your knees slightly. Be sure your chair is appropriate for your task and supports your back.

work together to stabilize the pelvis. When combined, these muscle groups control how much or how little the pelvis can tilt. Tilting of the pelvis directly affects the lower lumbar vertebrae of the spinal column. If the abdominal muscles are weak, the hip flexors often pull hard enough to cause a person's back to curve inward too much. This places undue pressure on the vertebral discs of the lower back and places the affected person at greater risk of a low back injury. Conversely, if the hamstring muscles are too tight, they may tilt the pelvis in the opposite direction resulting in little or no curve of the lower back. This too can place undue stress on vertebral discs and put the person at greater risk of injury to his/her lower back. One must visualize "long/strong" muscles controlling the pelvis. With this image in mind, it is easy to appreciate good postural alignment for the back.

Concerns for flexibility are not confined to the lower back and/or pelvis, however. Many older adults get caught in a vicious cycle of inactivity and declining health and lose flexibility. If a person loses flexibility, he/she can no longer participate in certain physical activities. Worse yet is when a person's daily activities are limited by his/her inability to bend, turn, or reach. Oftentimes, pain becomes associated with activity and the person further reduces activity, thereby worsening the situation. Of all age groups, older individuals have the most to gain through regular flexibility exercise with several studies showing improved ROM and capacity for daily activities of living (Swank, Funk, Durham, & Roberts, 2003). A simple stretching routine can help those individuals regain their lost ROM and oftentimes return to an active lifestyle. A commitment of five minutes per day for those people with a normal ROM can most often prevent this dilemma.

If you find it difficult or boring to just stretch, then consider doing a strength routine that emphasizes a maximal allowable ROM with each exercise. A study by Jim Whitehead reported at the National ACSM meeting in June 2010 that a strength training program incorporating full ROM exercises was equally as effective in establishing normal flexibility ranges as a program specifically designed to improve flexibility. The resistance-trained group, in fact, produced more improvements in flexibility in several cases, while at the same time, improving strength.

Here are some questions asked about flexibility and how it can vary within a normal range:

1. **Is warm-up the same as stretching?** No. Warm-up is typically light exercises that mimic the movements and ROM used during the activity. A proper warm-up will increase blood flow to the working muscles to allow them to be as efficient as possible in the activity. Stretching is intended to establish a functional ROM needed for either the activity or proper skeletal alignment. Warm-up should always precede stretching.

2. **How much flexibility or ROM does a person need?** It varies with the demands of the activity. For a diver, gymnast, dancer, or sport aerialist, maximizing ROM of major joints is optimal. For the average person, however, being that flexible could make joints unstable. Without very strong muscles crossing these joints, one would have to rely on ligaments to maintain joint and skeletal alignment. Therefore, it would be better to have a little less ROM and allow tendonous structures of muscles crossing each joint to help reduce the risk of a joint injury during activity.

3. **Does physical activity affect flexibility?** Yes. The most important issue for determining how activity will affect flexibility is asking how much ROM is used during the activity. For example, joggers or distance runners often find themselves having tight hamstring and gluteal muscles. They are accustomed to going through a shorter-than-normal ROM at the hip and, consequently, those muscles cause a reduced ROM at that joint. If this doesn't affect spinal alignment, then it is okay to be a little less flexible. In fact, this reduced ROM often makes a runner's performance more economical. So perhaps marathoners would not want to try and stretch these

muscles too much; otherwise, they risk becoming less economical in their running. On the other hand, if ROM is reduced too much, then it can alter skeletal alignment and result in accelerated osteoarthritis, low back problems, and, in some cases, neck pain. A good rule of thumb is to establish and then maintain a ROM that matches your activities and prevents you from having pain due to skeletal misalignment.

BENEFITS OF FLEXIBILITY

The many benefits of appropriate flexibility include
1. maintaining normal joint motion,
2. greater resistance to lower back and spinal column problems,
3. maintenance of good posture,
4. improved personal appearance/self-image,
5. maintenance of motor skills, allowing one to remain active throughout life,
6. reduced muscle tension and/or stress,
7. improvement of spinal mobility in older adults,
8. reduced muscle spasm and soreness,
9. reduction or prevention of muscle trigger points that may produce muscle stiffness, and localized or referred pain,
10. prevention or reduction of some cases of dysmenorrhea (painful menstruation) in women, and
11. improved athletic performance.

FACTORS AFFECTING FLEXIBILITY

A number of major structural factors contribute to the limits of movement: bone, cartilage, ligaments, muscles, tendons, and connective tissue, which make up the joint capsule. Since bones have a fixed shape, they cannot be changed. Nor do we care to alter the state of cartilage, which cushions the bone ends, or ligaments which connect bone to bone and maintain the integrity of the joint itself. With this in mind, it is easy to understand how ROM about a joint is highly specific to the individual and that it can vary from one joint to another.

With the exclusion of bones, cartilage, and most ligaments, we are left with the primary components of muscles, tendons, and joint capsule to target when stretching to improve flexibility. The combination of the three can account for 98 percent of the resistance to flexibility. Of these three, tendons and joint capsule tissue are nonelastic. Even though they are nonelastic, they can undergo plastic elongation (permanent lengthening of soft tissue).

This phenomenon can be explained by the muscles being slightly longer after stretching, therefore, the muscle will move through a greater ROM before it contracts and this will reduce the force of contraction. When subjects were tested on vertical jump after slow static stretching, they actually lost jump height. This phenomenon can be explained by the leg muscles being ever so slightly longer after stretching can go through a greater ROM before they want to contract and return to their resting length. This small change in muscle length has a large influence on the mechanical characteristics of the muscle, reducing the force it produces thereby reducing vertical jump performance. Although not everyone is an athlete, this same reaction takes place in almost every movement we perform. So, does this mean we should not stretch? No, but it could mean we should not use slow static stretching before competitive activities if we are concerned with explosive muscle power needed for jumping and/or running.

So when is it important to stretch? Most experts would agree that stretching is best done after an active warm-up or exercise where the muscles planning to be stretched have good blood flow and are physically warmer because of it. The type of stretch can then vary from slow, sustained stretches to mild, dynamic stretches. The key to improving ROM is changing the tendons and connective tissue that link the muscles to the bones without injuring the bones, ligaments, or joints themselves. For a more comprehensive review of the research on stretching and sports injury risk, one should read Thacker et al. (2004).

There are two forms of stretching or elongation that the muscle experiences: elastic and plastic. Elastic elongation is temporary lengthening of the muscle during stretching activities. Plastic elongation is a permanent lengthening of soft tissue. By performing elastic elongation activities we hope to develop plastic elongation. Muscle actively resists elongation and has intrinsic neural properties that actually cause it to contract in response to being overstretched. This principle is the same one that is represented by a simple reflex or tendon tap (knee jerk) test. The muscle is stretched beyond a point of comfort, and the spinal cord signals the muscle to contract, enabling it to regain its normal resting length. Taking advantage of this same response is what allows athletes to develop greater power for jumping and running. But when the interest is in improving ROM, it makes good sense then to address stretching in such a manner as to not involve the activation of the stretch reflex. Three good options for this are using slow, static stretching where only mild tension is applied to the muscles crossing the joint being stretched, active isolated stretching (AIS) where opposing muscles are contracted to reduce the reflexive action, and proprioceptive neuromuscular facilitation (PNF) where the muscle being stretched is activated and then relaxed just before stretching. Each of these techniques is discussed in further detail later in this chapter.

COMMON METHODS OF STRETCHING

To maintain flexibility, a person simply moves the desired joint through its full ROM. Improving flexibility requires a stretching of the muscles and soft tissue crossing the joint. Four fairly common methods are effective for improving flexibility: ballistic (rapid) stretching, static (slow, sustained) stretching, AIS, and PNF, a combination of contracting and relaxing muscles crossing the joint(s) and being manipulated.

Ballistic

Ballistic actions promoting increased ROM are effective and often used in specific sports training, but they invariably induce muscle damage and delayed muscle soreness. Ballistic stretching of tissue can also loosen ligaments, which increases the risk of partial or full joint dislocation. Certain forms of plyometric training can be considered ballistic stretching as well. Box or depth jumps, bounding drills, and platform shoes used by many basketball programs are good examples of ballistic stretching. For the purpose of improving overall ROM, however, ballistic stretching is not recommended. Faster, safer methods include static, AIS, or PNF stretching.

Static (Slow, Sustained)

With a slow, sustained stretching technique, muscles and joint tissue are gradually lengthened and held in their final position for a short time and then slowly returned to the muscle's resting length. There is, however, considerable variation as to the ideal technique and time allotted to each step in this action. The most current literature on effective stretching suggests that ROM of each stretching exercise should be determined near the point whereby a sensation of tightness, but not discomfort, is developed. The optimal time to hold a stretch is unknown; however, most research suggests that the exerciser should hold it to the point of tightness for 15–30 seconds. Each stretching exercise should be repeated two to four times at a frequency of three times per week.

Active Isolated Stretching

AIS has been presented best by Jim and Phil Wharton in their book *The Wharton's Stretch Book*. The principles of this method are simple, with the following steps as a guide: (1) The person should prepare to stretch one isolated muscle or muscle group. (2) Actively contract the muscle opposite the muscle being stretched. (3) Stretch the targeted muscle gently and quickly holding for no more than two seconds. (4) Release the stretch before the muscle reacts to being stretched. (5) Repeat two to three times. For some stretches assistance from a partner is helpful; however, a rope or flexible tubing can be used for most muscles. The Whartons also propose that AIS should be part of a warm-up routine and if done correctly will not diminish the reflex reaction of the muscle that may often occur with slow static stretching.

Proprioceptive Neuromuscular Facilitation

The concept of alternating the contraction and stretching of a relaxed muscle is not new, but along with AIS it has gained renewed popularity in recent years. Traditionally done with a partner, some pieces of exercise equipment are now being sold for the expressed use of assisting a person in PNF stretching. No matter how it is accomplished, the basis remains the same. Using a partner, a person is assisted in obtaining a moderate stretch in the muscle. At that point, the partner braces the limb to prevent movement, and the person isometrically (no movement) contracts the stretched muscle for four to five seconds. After contracting, the person once again relaxes, and the partner assists by increasing the stretch to a greater angle. The isometric contraction is repeated again, followed by relaxed and assisted stretching. This sequence continues four to five times with the final stretched position being held several seconds.

A modified version of PNF stretching, whereby an active contraction of opposing muscles occurs, has recently become popularized by several professional athletes. Essentially, it includes one additional step in the standard PNF sequence previously described. In a normal PNF stretch, the person stretching relaxes all muscles and passively allows his/her partner to move the limb through a progressively greater ROM. In this modified PNF stretch, the person stretching actively contracts muscles that assist his/her partner in moving the limb to a greater angle. It is also thought that an active contraction of opposing muscles causes the central nervous system to send inhibitory signals to the muscle being stretched, thereby further enhancing the stretching process. This technique has been supported anecdotally and may hold merit for the future, but as of yet, its value has not been verified by research.

POPULAR ACTIVITIES THAT CAN AFFECT FLEXIBILITY

Three popular and proven activities have surfaced that integrate elements of stretching into their philosophies of mind–body control. They are Pilates, yoga, and tai chi. Pilates focuses on core strength while restoring normal body alignment and ROM. Yoga, regardless of discipline, uses various poses that require a normal and/or, in some cases, an extreme ROM. Therefore, yoga can be used to increase ROM in an attempt to achieve and hold desired yoga positions. Tai chi has specific positions, too; however, most of these positions are achievable using less than maximal joint ROM than Pilates or yoga requires. Other combative forms of martial arts can also influence ROM; however, we will limit our focus to only tai chi.

Pilates

Pilates gets its name from its inventor Joseph Pilates, a German-born innovator who combined pieces of yoga, martial arts, and calisthenics to produce an activity that he claimed helped him and his fellow internees resist an influenza epidemic when he was in England during the First World War. Also during that time he engineered a way to rig springs on hospital beds to offer light resistance exercises to bedridden patients, thereby enhancing their recoveries. His combined muscle control, coordination, and stretching activities where efficiency of movement is paramount is still evident in the more modern-day variations of his original Pilates routine. Some of the movements devised from hospital beds are still evident today in the use of Pilates machines that resemble a bed and use springs or shock cords to offer mild resistance to whole-body movements.

The basic idea of Pilates is that all energy and movement starts at the body's center. Four concentric circles start with the abdomen and hip girdle, or "core," expanding to the trunk, then the limbs, and finally, the hands and feet. Workouts include 10-movement principles: becoming aware of your body, breathing properly, developing a focused concentration, finding one's body center, establishing balance, controlling all movement, moving efficiently, and developing flow to moving while moving precisely and harmoniously.

There are two common types of Pilates: mat work, performed on the floor, and apparatus work. Mat work uses one's body weight for resistance. Apparatus work usually involves the wunda and/or arm chairs, a ladder and step barrels, and stability and Bosu balls, as well as a host of other equipment. Most of this equipment uses pulleys, cords, or springs for resistance; but, both types use similar exercises and stretches that begin from a prone position, face up or face down.

Reported benefits of Pilates include improved flexibility, strength, endurance, speed, agility, and coordination. Pilates has the potential to provide most individuals with a way to effectively cross-train without increasing one's risk of injury.

The following information entitled "Pilates Exercises Explanation" from eHow.com on the elements of Pilates may help you decide whether or not you want to give it a try.

© Michael C. Gray, 2014. Used under license from Shutterstock, Inc.

Concentration

- Our mind controls our body; therefore, to do the movements properly, you must concentrate fully. When working on concentration, focus deeply and inwardly. Be aware of every body part while performing the exercises. If with an instructor, listen to the cues and incorporate them into the practice.

Centering

- The powerhouse (the core) is the focal point of all Pilates exercises, especially within the principle of centering. The powerhouse, which consists of the abdominals, pelvic floor, inner thighs, lower back, and buttocks, is considered the center of the body. From this center, all movement should originate by "scooping" the lower abdominals in and up. Be aware of alignment, and always activate the powerhouse before moving the limbs.

Control

- The Pilates method brings together all parts of the mind and body into a physical movement experience. In Pilates, every movement matters and is coordinated, efficient, and smooth. To reach mastery in Pilates, you must control every part of the body at all times. When working on control, perform each movement in a rhythmical, controlled manner. Move with control, not momentum. Coordinate and control the body, mind, and breath to allow physical changes to take place.

Breathing

- The natural rhythm of the breath enhances fluidity of movement and sets the rhythm of an exercise. The breath also helps to keep the mind focused and the body energized; it also facilitates core support. When working on breathing, inhale and exhale through the nose and focus on exhaling completely.

Precision

- In its ideal form, Pilates is practiced with precision and attention to detail. Every movement of every exercise has a purpose, and every cue or instruction is exact. Classical Pilates uses few repetitions and a variety of movements so that precision can be practiced without fatigue. When working with precision, perform each exercise exactly as instructed and coordinate the movements from beginning to end.

Flowing Movement

- When Pilates is performed properly, it is light and fluid. The ultimate goal is to move with greater grace and ease within each exercise and also from exercise to exercise. Transitions are seamless, smooth, and almost dance-like. When working with flowing movement, link the breath and transition of every exercise. Perform each movement smoothly and without rushing or jerking. Work without stress or strain, and allow the natural flow of movement to occur.

Below are a couple of videos resources that can be used for learning the basics of pilates and view pilates workouts. There are numerous video resources available for someone interested in learning more about the benefits of pilates.

Video 1. Free pilates exercises.
www.verywellfit.com/free-pilates-exercises-videos-online-2704368
Video 2. Greatest pilates videos.
http://greatist.com/move/pilates-workout-video

Yoga

Originating in India more than 6,000 years ago, yoga has been practiced by many adhering to the basic philosophy that most illness is associated with poor posture, diet, and mental attitude. People practicing various forms of yoga often report reduced stress, improved self-control over poor habits such as overeating and smoking, and overall enhanced well-being. Yoga's main premise is to unite the mind and body. This is accomplished by using various body positions to improve body alignment and breathing techniques to optimize blood flow and energy to body tissues. Research has demonstrated reduced blood pressure and heart rate while releasing more endorphins (body's own morphine-like painkiller) with deep controlled breathing practiced during a yoga session. Caution should be executed in some cases where extreme yoga positions may be contraindicated for some individuals.

The physical poses, often called "asana" in Sanskrit, attempt to create a balance between the body and the mind. To accomplish this balance, yoga makes use of different asana, breathing exercises (called pranayams), relaxation techniques, and meditation. Each asana tries to stack bones of the skeleton to minimize muscle involvement. If one is out of balance, then certain asanas are more difficult to establish and hold. Finding muscles that are weak or inflexible can then help a person strengthen or lengthen those muscles to create a proper skeletal alignment. Once an asana can be established, it is thought to bring stability to the body and the mind.

Yoga has been promoted as a practice that, when done regularly, can create a positive peaceful harmony to one's life. Even a skeptic would have to agree that yoga has its place. Yoga has been studied as an intervention for many conditions, including pain, stress, and depression. Both meditative and exercise components of yoga have shown promise for general health benefits. Yoga has been reported to be the sixth most commonly used alternative therapy in the United States, with 6.1 percent of the population participating (Barnes et al., 2007).

Yoga classes typically range from 60–90 minutes, and almost all of them will include different asanas, pranayams, and some element of relaxation (savasanas). The practice of yoga is intended to make the body strong and flexible. Additionally, it aims to improve respiratory, circulatory, digestive, and hormonal functions. If truly successful, yoga brings about emotional stability and clarity of mind through a strong mind–body connection.

What is not so well known about yoga is its wide choice of asanas. Depending upon a person's health and/or abilities, specific attainable asanas and pranayams can be performed. All you need to know is the most appropriate exercises meant for the structure of your body, while choosing the asanas of the activity. In addition, you need to know the right way of performing the asanas because any wrong attempt can cause sprains and injuries. This chapter provides several links to beginning yoga sessions. Now you have the luxury of watching before participating and doing it all in the privacy of your own space.

Video 1. Beginner yoga.
https://www.bing.com/videos/search?q=yoga+video&view=detail&mid=1F8E926E7F744FE7F1B11F8E926E7F744FE7F1B1&FORM=VIRE
Vdeo 2. Simple yoga demo.
https://www.youtube.com/watch?v=oX6I6vs1EFs
Vdeo 3. Full body yoga.
greatist.com/move/free-yoga-videos

Tai Chi

Tai chi is a form of martial art involving slow flowing movements. The person most people acknowledge as the founder of modern tai chi was a monk named Chang San-feng. Some debate has surfaced as to his actual existence versus a literary construct while other research and records from the Ming dynasty seem to indicate that he lived in the period from 1391 to 1459 AD. Regardless of real or construct, tai chi exercises stress suppleness and elasticity as opposed to hardness and force demonstrated by other martial art forms. San-feng is credited with creating the fundamental "thirteen postures" of tai chi corresponding to the eight basic trigrams of the I-Ching and the five elements. The eight "postures" are ward-off, rollback, press, push, pull, split, elbow strike, and shoulder strike and the five "attitudes" are advance, retreat, look left, gaze right, and central equilibrium. The fundamental philosophy of tai chi can be summed up in the following verse:

Yield and overcome;
Bend and be straight.
And,
He who stands of tiptoe is not steady.
He who strides cannot maintain the pace.

There are many types of tai chi, but it is tai chi chuan that has been westernized the most. This form involves similar postures or "elements": response drills known as nei gung or tui shou, self-defense techniques, weapons, and solo hand routines called forms (taolu). While the image of tai chi chuan in popular culture is typified by exceedingly slow movement, other styles (including the three popular ones, Yang, Wu, and Chen) have secondary forms of a faster pace. The slow form represents the "yin," while the faster forms reflect the "yang." The combination of the two provides a holistic approach to overall health and well-being.

Since the first widespread promotion of tai chi's health benefits in the early twentieth century, it has developed a following purely for its health benefits. It has been suggested that focusing the mind exclusively on movements of the form helps to create a state of mental calm and clarity. Many martial arts require a uniform or special dress during practice. Tai chi chuan, however, normally does not require a uniform, but merely comfortable loose-fitting clothes and flat-soled shoes.

The physical techniques of tai chi chuan are characterized by using skeletal leverage through each joint. It is based on coordination and relaxation versus muscular tension. The slow, repetitive forms used in learning how leverage is generated gently and measurably without muscular tension has the ability to improve circulation since the muscles are not restricting blood flow.

The study of tai chi chuan primarily involves three aspects:

- Health: An unhealthy person will find it hard to achieve to a state of calmness. Tai chi's health training concentrates on relieving the physical effects of stress.
- Meditation: The focus and calmness generated by a meditative state is a necessary part of maintaining health in the sense of stress relief and doing it using a noncombative form of martial art.
- Martial art: The ability to use tai chi in self-defense is the true test of one's understanding of this art form. It is the holistic study of change in response to various outside forces.

With a reputation as having low physical stress and a natural health emphasis, tai chi classes have become popular in hospitals and clinics, as well as community and senior centers. As a result of this popularity, there has been a separation of groups that practice tai chi for benefits to physical and mental health, meditation, or self-defense.

Researchers report that intensive tai chi practice can burn as many calories as surfing or downhill skiing (Nutristrategy, 2007). It can also have a positive influence on balance control, flexibility, cardiovascular fitness, and a reduced risk of falls in elderly populations (Au-Yeung et al., 2009). Other work has shown tai chi to be effective in treating patients recovering from stroke, heart failure, high blood pressure, heart attacks, multiple sclerosis, Parkinson's tremors, and fibromyalgia (Wang et al., 2004; McAlindon et al., 2010). These studies, among others, have demonstrated a tangible benefit of tai chi as an alternative form of medicine; however, more in-depth studies are needed to determine the most beneficial style, frequency, and duration of practice to show optimal results.

Video 1. Dr. Paul Lamb, MD, demonstrates basics and offers optional DVDs for purchase.
http://www.youtube.com/watch?v=nNWPk6tYoUM
Video 2. Tai chi for beginners. Includes 24 steps in chuan demonstrated by M. Thomas.
http://www.youtube.com/watch?v=P5hvODK2zW4
Video 3. Beginner tai chi segment (with commercial at beginning). Good slow demo with narrative explanation.
http://www.5min.com/Video/Step-by-Step-Tai-Chi—Segment-1-68732873
Video 4. Learn tai chi free. Demonstration of Yang Cheng-fu tai chi. It is a bit cheesy, but it demonstrates how the fast form of tai chi can be used for self-defense or combat. Check out time ~2:55–3:30 on this clip to appreciate the concepts of yin and yang.
http://www.youtube.com/watch?v=w6NdsyK8zPE

DETERMINING YOUR FLEXIBILITY

An important step in establishing optimal flexibility is completing an assessment of one's current ROM of major joints and muscles. Most flexibility tests developed over the years are sport specific and offer little insight into health- or fitness-related status for the average person. There are, however, several simple tests that apply to all people. One must first realize that flexibility is joint specific. This means that the presence of one flexible joint does not indicate the same for all joints in the body. Therefore, several tests are needed to measure flexibility of the major joints. The three tests that follow are the modified sit-and-reach, total body rotation, and shoulder flexibility.

Modified Sit-and-Reach

This test is helpful in assessing ROM of the hamstrings and, to some degree, muscles of the lower back. To perform the modified sit-and-reach, one simply needs a box about 12 inches (30 cm) square and a yard or meter stick. The steps are as follows:

1. Warm-up properly before beginning (brisk walk, light calisthenics, static stretches, etc.).
2. Remove your shoes and sit on the floor with your back, shoulders, and head touching a vertical wall; extend your legs with your feet touching the box.
3. Place one hand on top of the other and extend your arms forward toward the box without removing your head or back from the wall behind you. Your shoulders may move away slightly as you reach as far as possible. A partner or assistant should then match the yard or meter stick to the tip of your longest finger.
4. Gradually reach forward as far as possible, allowing your head, shoulders, and back to flex forward as you stretch. Repeat this action three times, making sure the back of your knees do not come off the floor.
5. Record the maximum distance reached, either in inches to the nearest half inch or to the nearest centimeter.

Health fitness standards for men and women are shown in Table 4.1. An age-specific range of 11.5–15 inches (29–38.5 cm) for males and 12–16 inches (31–40.5 cm) for females is necessary for a person to meet the health fitness standards for adequate trunk flexibility. Ranges for the 99th percentile are 16–20 inches (41–53 cm) for males and 17–22.5 inches (43.5–57.5 cm) for females. Conversely, the lowest one percent range for males is 4–7 inches (10–18 cm) and for females 1.5–6.5 inches (4–16.5 cm).

Total Body Rotation

Three lines are required for this test: a vertical line on a wall six feet from the floor, a three-foot line on the floor perpendicular to the vertical line, and a yard or meter stick for measuring rotation. The steps are as follows:

1. Stand arm's length from the wall with toes of both feet touching the line on the floor.
2. Tape a yardstick to the wall at shoulder height so that one can measure 15 inches in either direction from the vertical line on the wall.
3. Rotate the body so the arm and shoulder farthest from the wall moves backward while keeping the shoulders horizontal. Reaching with the outside arm, rotate as far as possible. Keep the fingers and wrist straight, reaching as far for the yardstick as possible.
4. Repeat the rotation in the other direction and record the highest score in either inches or centimeters.

TABLE 4.1 Percentile Ranks for Modified Sit-and-Reach Test

		Age Category						Age Category		
Rank	≤18	19–35	36–49	≥50		Rank	≤18	19–35	36–49	≥50
		MEN						WOMEN		
99	20.8	20.1	18.9	16.2	High fitness standard	99	22.6	21.0	19.8	17.2
95	19.6	18.9	18.2	15.8		95	19.5	19.3	19.2	15.7
90 (4 pts.)	18.2	17.2	16.1	15.0		90	18.7	17.9	17.4	15.0 (4 pts.)
80	17.8	17.0	14.6	13.3		80	17.8	16.7	16.2	14.2
70	16.0	15.8	13.9	12.3		70	16.5	16.2	15.2	13.6
60 (3 pts.)	15.2	15.0	13.4	11.5	Health fitness standard	60	16.0	15.8	14.5	12.3 (3 pts.)
50	14.5	14.4	12.6	10.2		50	15.2	14.8	13.5	11.1
40 (2 pts.)	14.0	13.5	11.6	9.7		40	14.5	14.5	12.8	10.1 (2 pts.)
30	13.4	13.0	10.8	9.3		30	13.7	13.7	12.2	9.2
20	11.8	11.6	9.9	8.8		20	12.6	12.6	11.0	8.3
10 (1 pt.)	9.5	9.2	8.3	7.8		10	11.4	10.1	9.7	7.5 (1 pt.)
05	8.4	7.9	7.0	7.2		05	9.4	8.1	8.5	3.7
01	7.2	7.0	5.1	4.0		01	6.5	2.6	2.0	1.5

Health fitness standards for total body rotation in women and men are found in Tables 4.2A and 4.2B, respectively. For basic health fitness standards to be achieved, a specific range of 15.5–21 inches (39.5–53 cm) is necessary for females with 14–20 inches (35–50.5 cm) needed for males. For the 99th percentile, the female range is 21.5–29.5 inches (55–75 cm), while the male range is 21–29 inches (53–74 cm). Conversely, the lowest one percent range for females is 0–9 inches (0–23 cm), and for males 0–3.5 inches (0–8.5 cm).

Shoulder Flexibility

No specific equipment is needed to conduct this test. Steps are as follows:

1. While standing, raise your left arm and reach down your back as far as possible.
2. Move your right arm behind your back and upward as high as possible.
3. Try to overlap your fingers and/or hands as much as possible. Estimate the overlap of fingers in inches or centimeters.
4. Repeat with the right arm up and left arm down.

Scores for this test apply to men and women alike. If you cannot touch your hands together, your shoulder flexibility is poor. A score of +1 inches (2.5 cm) is average while a score of +3 inches (7.5 cm) is excellent.

How Do You Rate?

For a global estimate of flexibility, first derive a point total for each test. For the sit-and-reach test, three points are awarded for meeting the minimum health fitness score. The same is true for the body rotation test. If you exceeded the minimum, give yourself four points. If you were barely under the minimum score, two points should be given. One

TABLE 4.2A Female Percentile Ranks for Total Body Rotation Test

Percentile Rank	Left Rotation					Right Rotation			
	≤18	19–35	36–49	≥50		≤18	19–35	36–49	≥50
4 pts. 99	29.3	28.6	27.1	23.0		29.6	29.4	27.1	21.7
95	26.8	24.8	25.3	21.4	High fitness standard	27.6	25.3	25.9	19.7
90	25.5	23.0	23.4	20.5		25.8	23.0	21.3	19.0
80	23.8	21.5	20.2	19.1		23.7	20.8	19.6	17.9
70	21.8	20.5	18.6	17.3		22.0	19.3	17.3	16.8
3 pts. 60	20.5	19.3	17.7	16.0	Health fitness standard	20.8	18.0	16.5	15.6
50	19.5	18.0	16.4	14.8		19.5	17.3	14.6	14.0
2 pts. 40	18.5	17.2	14.8	13.7		18.3	16.0	13.1	12.8
30	17.1	15.7	13.6	10.0		16.3	15.2	11.7	8.5
1 pt. 20	16.0	15.2	11.6	6.3		14.5	14.0	9.8	3.9
10	12.8	13.6	8.5	3.0		12.4	11.1	6.1	2.2
05	11.1	7.3	6.8	0.7		10.2	8.8	4.0	1.1
01	8.9	5.3	4.3	0.0		8.9	3.2	2.8	0.0

TABLE 4.2B Male Percentile Ranks for Total Body Rotation Test

Percentile Rank	Left Rotation					Right Rotation			
	≤18	19–35	36–49	≥50		≤18	19–35	36–49	≥50
4 pts. 99	29.1	28.0	26.6	21.0		28.2	27.8	25.2	22.2
95	26.6	24.8	24.5	20.0	High fitness standard	25.5	25.6	23.8	20.7
90	25.0	23.6	23.0	17.7		24.3	24.1	22.5	19.3
80	22.0	22.0	21.2	15.5		22.7	22.3	21.0	16.3
70	20.9	20.3	20.4	14.7		21.3	20.7	18.7	15.7
3 pts. 60	19.9	19.3	18.7	13.9	Health fitness standard	19.8	19.0	17.3	14.7
50	18.6	18.0	16.7	12.7		19.0	17.2	16.3	12.3
2 pts. 40	17.0	16.8	15.3	11.7		17.3	16.3	14.7	11.5
30	14.9	15.0	14.8	10.3		15.1	15.0	13.3	10.7
1 pt. 20	13.8	13.3	13.7	9.5		12.9	13.3	11.2	8.7
10	10.8	10.5	10.8	4.3		10.8	11.3	8.0	2.7
05	8.5	8.9	8.8	0.3		8.1	8.3	5.5	0.3
01	3.4	1.7	5.1	0.0		6.6	2.9	2.0	0.0

point is the proper score if you are not very close to the minimum health fitness score, regardless of the distance away. Now, add your points from the sit-and-reach test, the total body rotation test, and the shoulder flexibility test (see Table 4.3) for a grand total. Use Table 4.4 to establish your current overall flexibility category.

It is not uncommon for all people, active and inactive, to be classified as average or even below average for any of these tests. Research has shown that only people who routinely engage in stretching exercises are likely to score above average in these tests.

TABLE 4.3 Shoulder Flexibility Fitness Level

Percent Rank	Distance	Fitness Level	Points
⩾90	+3″ (7.5 cm)	Excellent	5
70−89	1−2″ (2.5–5 cm)	Good	4
50−69	0″ (2.5 cm)	Average	3
30−49	−1″ (−2.5 cm)	Fair	2
<30	>−1″ (>−2.5 cm)	Need work	1

From E. Fox, T. Kirby and A. Fox, *Bases of Fitness.* Copyright © 1987 by Allyn & Bacon.

TABLE 4.4 Overall Flexibility Score

Total Score	Category
13	Superior
10–12	
7–9	Typical
4–6	
3	Room for improvement

Adapted from W. Hoeger & S. Hoeger, "Overall Flexibility Score," *Lifetime Physical Fitness & Wellness.*

However, that does not excuse any of us from setting a goal of achieving an average to above-average level in all of these tests.

CONTRAINDICATED EXERCISES

A discussion of flexibility is not complete without including some information about contraindicated stretches. As the name implies, contraindicated stretches are not recommended because they require certain body parts to be placed in positions that greatly increase the chance of injury. Unfortunately, a number of these type of stretches still persist in today's society, despite much research and published information advising against their use.

The stretch exercises in Figure 4.1 should head a list of contraindicated stretches. They are serious violations of the principles of proper stretching.

Figure 4.1 A–F •

A. *Plow—Pressure on the cervical vertebrae can cause paralysis.*

B1. *Bridge—Causes undue stress on the lower lumbar vertebrae.*

B2. Double Leg Lift—Causes undue stress on the lower lumbar vertebrae.

B3. Fire Hydrant—Causes undue stress on the lower lumbar vertebrae.

C. Deep Knee Bend—Bending knees beyond 90 degrees endangers the ligaments and cartilage of the knees.

D1. Hurdler's Stretch—Makes the inside or medial area of the knee vulnerable to ligament and cartilage damage.

D2. Hero Stretch—Makes the inside or medial area of the knee vulnerable to ligament and cartilage damage.

E. Quadriceps Stretch—Hyperflexing the knee 120 degrees or more increases the possibility of injury to the cartilage and/or ligaments.

F. Ballistic Bar Stretch—Hyperextension of the knee predisposes the knee to ligament damage, sciatica, and pyriformis syndrome.

References

Au-Yeung, S. S. Y., Hui-Chan, C. W. Y., & Tang, J. C. S. (2009, January 7). Short-form tai chi improves standing balance of people with chronic stroke. *Neurorehabilitation and Neural Repair, 23*(5), 515. doi:10.1177/1545968308326425. Retrieved from http://nnr.sagepub.com/cgi/content/abstract/1545968308326425v1

Barnes, P. M., Bloom, B., & Nahin, R. (2007). *Complementary and alternative medicine use among adults and children* (CDC National Health Statistics Report No. 12). Retrieved from http://nccam.nih.gov/news/2008/nhsr12.pdf

Gaskin, D.J., and Richard, P. (2012). The Economic Costs of Pain in the United States. *The Journal of Pain*, 2012; 13 (8) DOI:10.1016/j.pain.2012.03.009

McAlindon, T., Wang, C., Schmid, C. H., Rones, R., Kalish, R., Yinh, J., … McAlindon, T. (2010, August 19). A randomized trial of tai chi for fibromyalgia. *New England Journal of Medicine, 363*(8), 743–754. doi:10.1056/NEJMoa0912611

National Institute of Neurological Disorders and Stroke. (2012). Bethesda, MD: National Institute of Health.

NutriStrategy. (2007). *Calories burned during exercise.* Retrieved from http://www.nutristrategy.com/activitylist3.htm

Swank, A. M., Funk, D. C., Durham, M. P., & Roberts, S. (2003). Adding weights to stretching exercise increases passive range of motion for healthy elderly. *Journal of Strength and Conditional Research, 17,* 374–378.

Thacker, S. B., Gilchrist, J., Stroup, D. F., & Kimsey, C. D. (2004). The impact of stretching on sports injury risk: A systematic review of the literature. *Medicine and Science in Sports and Exercise, 36*(3), 371–378.

Wang, C., Collet, J. P., & Lau, J. (2004). The effect of tai chi on health outcomes in patients with chronic conditions: A systematic review. *Archives of Internal Medicine, 164*(5), 493–501. doi:10.1001/archinte.164.5.493

Wang, C., Bannuru, R., Ramel, J., Kupelnick, B., Scott, T., & Schmid, C. H. (2010). *Tai chi on psychological well-being: Systematic review and meta-analysis.* Retrieved from http://www.ncbi.nlm.nih.gov/pubmed/20492638

Wharton, J., & Wharton, P. (1996). *The Wharton's stretch book.* New York, NY: Three Rivers Press, Random House.

CHAPTER 4

PERSONAL GROWTH OPPORTUNITY 1

Flexibility Lab and Worksheet

Step I

For the modified sit-and-reach, use the procedures found in Chapter 4 and record the maximum distance achieved in the "Actual Value" column below. To determine whether you meet the health standard, refer to Table 4.1.

Step II

For the total body rotation, use the procedures found in Chapter 4 and record the greatest distance achieved in the "Actual Value" column below. To determine whether you meet the health standard, refer to Table 4.2.

Step III

For shoulder flexibility, use the procedures found in Chapter 4 and record the greatest distance achieved in the "Actual Value" column below. To meet the health standard, you must be above the 30-percent rank (Table 4.3), which is a minimum distance of a negative one inch (−1"). You can also record points earned for this test using Table 4.3 as well.

Step IV

Your overall flexibility score can be calculated by giving yourself:

From sit-and-reach and total body rotations tests

4 points Exceed the health standard
3 points Meet the standard
2 points Barely under minimum standard
1 point   Not very close to minimum standard

Be sure to use the proper age category!

Add those points from the shoulder flexibility test (Table 4.3) to those received for the sit-and-reach and total body rotation. Table 4.4 can be used to rate your overall flexibility.

Tests	Actual Value	Meet Health Standard? (Y/S)	Points
Modified Sit-and-Reach			
Total Body Rotation			+
Shoulder Flexibility		(≥ −1″ = minimum standard)	+
		Overall Flexibility Score	=

Question

1. Can a person be flexible in some joints and not in others? Why/why not?

_____

_____

_____

_____

_____

_____

Muscular Strength and Endurance

© apiguide, 2014. Used under license from Shutterstock, Inc.

Specific Objectives

1. Explain the functions of the musculoskeletal system.
2. Understand the role strength plays in maintenance of good health.
3. Understand the importance of nutrition in gaining muscle strength and endurance.
4. Explain how muscular strength, endurance, and muscle power are related.
5. Understand the effect of muscle fiber type on strength and endurance gains.
6. Identify what is responsible for strength differences between sexes.
7. Understand the basic principles for strength development.
8. Identify the components of a sound strength-training program.
9. Identify methods for assessing muscular strength/endurance.
10. Design your own program to develop and maintain a healthy level of muscular strength/endurance.
11. Describe how functional strength training differs from traditional methods of strength training.

OVERVIEW

The development and maintenance of muscular strength and endurance is an essential component of anyone's activity program. Strength is simply a measure of force generated by a person's muscles. Strength for the most part is something one obtains through daily living. From the day an individual is born, he/she gains strength through movement and growth. As adults, we only alter strength levels through movement. In essence, individual levels of strength are reflected by the lifestyle each of us has. How important is developing or maintaining strength? Vitally important! A certain level of muscular strength is necessary for daily activities such as sitting, standing, walking, lifting, carrying, and it appears that muscular strength is the most important factor of physical fitness for elderly populations. While heart disease is the number one killer of adults in the United States, it is the loss of strength that compromises independent living for most elderly. Over more than a decade, research has demonstrated elderly people, both men and women, benefit greatly by strength training. The most dramatic demonstration of this fact was a study where older individuals, resigned to full-care nursing facilities, were able to return to an unassisted living arrangement after 6–12 months of basic strength training (Wescott & Baechle, 1998). Discussed in more detail in the section on osteoporosis in chapter 9, weight training can help prevent the loss of bone density which leads to osteoporosis late in life. Strength training is also important for children. In addition to increasing muscular endurance and strength, participation in a resistance-training program can influence other health- and fitness-related measures. Resistant training may favorably alter psychosocial parameters, reduce injury in sport and recreational activities, and improve motor skills. Resistant training has also been shown to reduce fatness among children (Watts, Jones, Davis, & Green, 2005). What is important, however, is to clearly define strength training. By definition, strength training is any activity aimed at increasing the muscle's ability to generate force against a resistance. That resistance can be body weight as in push-ups, picking rocks from a garden, painting a house, or lifting dumbbells in a gym. Regardless of the method of strength training, current literature suggests people of all ages benefit from increasing or maintaining their muscular strength. That makes the following phrase appropriate for everyone:

> *We lose what we do not use, but we can regain what is lost at a simple cost: Strength train.*

The American College of Sports Medicine (ACSM) has initiated a program entitled *Exercise Is Medicine;* the program is worldwide, not just for the United States. The recommendations for strength from the ACSM and American Heart Association (AHA) are:

> *Do 8–10 strength-training exercises, using 8–12 repetitions of each exercise, twice a week.*

This parallels the *2008 Physical Activity Guidelines for Americans*, which suggests, "Adults should also do muscle-strengthening activities that are moderate or high intensity and involve all major muscle groups on 2 or more days a week, as these activities provide additional health benefits" (Key Guidelines for Adults, at http://www.health.gov/PAGuidelines/).

This is a relatively new recommendation. There has always been an emphasis on physical activity that is aerobic in nature; however, we are now beginning to truly understand the implications of strength loss as young adults and how it affects our quality of life long before we reach retirement age. With that in mind, let's look at muscle function from a health perspective.

FUNCTIONS OF MUSCULOSKELETAL SYSTEM

Muscle makes up a fairly large portion of our bodies. On average, there are 600 different muscles that make up some 40 percent of our total body weight. Beyond the most obvious role of movement, muscle performs several key functions. Muscles work constantly to maintain posture and to generate heat needed to stabilize body temperature. Contracting muscle also helps return blood to the heart during lower intensity activity. Another important role muscle has, albeit indirect, is its relationship to metabolism. Metabolism is a measure of energy expended (calories) to maintain normal cellular function (life).

ROLE OF STRENGTH IN GOOD HEALTH

Strength is rarely an issue for children since they are usually quite active, and that activity is enough to maintain functional strength. However, it is well documented that substantial declines in strength occur in both males and females, starting somewhere between 20 and 30 years of age and continuing to old age. The rate of this decline is quite varied (25–40 percent reduction) and is dependent on several factors: (1) loss of muscle mass, (2) changes in the muscle fiber, and (3) reduced nerve activation to the muscles.

Declines in muscle mass affects its ability to contract with the same force. This may be the largest contributor to the decline in strength. The size of muscle fibers also declines with age and this too contributes to the inability of the same muscle to exert force. Finally, the motor nerves that activate the muscles reduce the frequency in which they stimulate the muscles. This reduction in the rate of signaling the muscles results in physiological changes in the muscles that make them smaller, which further reduces mass.

Of greater concern is not so much the exact amount of strength we lose, but how that strength loss affects our lifestyle and/or health. Reduced strength is a direct result of weakened muscles. Weak muscles can lead to instability of joints. Unstable joints can lead to musculoskeletal injuries that may limit activity for life. Poor respiratory muscle function will reduce ability for aerobic activity. The loss in aerobic capacity leads to less activity, further reducing strength. Insufficient strength can make daily tasks such as rising from a chair, carrying packages, or opening jars a real challenge. This is the path that many young adults, like you, are on, and it leads right to a nursing home. Activities of daily living become tasks that depend on others. Thus, muscular strength is important for maintaining a healthy life. Aging of any tissue, including muscle, cannot be prevented; however, muscle is special in that it can and will respond to exercise training in the same way at any adult age; it gets stronger. Simply put, strong muscles produce more force and allow people of all ages to do more.

MUSCULAR STRENGTH, ENDURANCE, AND POWER

As indicated earlier, muscular strength is defined as a muscle's ability to exert effort against a resistance. It is clear that maintenance of at least a minimum level of strength is important. Muscular endurance, although closely related to strength, is a measure of sustained muscle activity. Usually, if one's maximal effort is high, then a sustained submaximal effort will also be good. Dynamic endurance for repeated activities such as raking or shoveling is one form of muscular endurance. More static activities such as postural control or even digestion time through the intestine is dependent more on a muscle's endurance than a percentage of a muscle's absolute maximal strength. In fact, adequate abdominal muscle endurance, for example, is important to control the pelvis and subsequent lower back stability. All things considered to this point, it appears that for most people muscular endurance is of greater interest than strength since it has a stronger influence on one's health. But, one must remember that muscular strength and endurance are closely linked. No matter how we name them, good working muscles are essential pieces of good health and fitness.

Comparatively, muscular power is a combination of strength and speed. Most experts would place power in a skill-related category of fitness because it is a measure of the amount of force being exerted over a given period of time. As soon as speed becomes an issue, genetics plays a larger role. On the other hand, power is related to strength and strength is clearly a health-related category of fitness. Garnica (1986), studying muscle power in young women, suggested that humans operate most effectively for daily tasks when using optimal muscle power. Optimal muscle power is thought to be produced when force and speed are about one-third of their respective greatest efforts.

In sports, power is probably the most important factor for performance. The stronger person is not always the more powerful person. Since power is a function of force and time, it becomes specific to the task requirements. Namely, if time is of the essence, the resistance to be overcome must be relatively low. In order to throw a ball very fast, the ball must be relatively light (i.e., a baseball versus a shot-put). Whereas in the shot-put, time is not critical, only distance is important. So, with a heavier resistance to overcome, the task is performed at a slower speed. Power-type activities have been shown to positively influence muscular strength and endurance. Power training that emphasizes speed tends to positively affect muscular endurance more so than strength. Conversely, power training that emphasizes heavy resistance and slower speeds has a greater positive influence on muscular strength. Knowing the desired task can help determine what type of training can best be utilized to enhance performance. This same concept holds true for all activities, so keep this in mind as we address specific issues regarding muscle tissue itself.

MUSCLE FIBER TYPES

Although there are more than three distinct muscle fiber types, for simplicity we can separate fibers into three types: (1) fast-twitch fibers, (2) intermediate fibers, and (3) slow-twitch fibers. Each fiber type has specific characteristics that make it more suitable for certain tasks than the other two. Table 5.1 outlines the properties of each fiber type. All humans have a mixture of each, but people do vary as to the amount of each type they possess. Most people have near-equal portions of fast-, intermediate, and slow-twitch fibers; however, some successful athletes have been shown to have a greater portion of fibers most appropriate for their sport.

Sprinters have more fast-twitch fibers, while marathoners have many more slow-twitch fibers. A simple way to estimate your own fiber type is to assess your ability for sprinting/jumping and/or endurance-type events. If you excel in neither, then you are like

TABLE 5.1 Characteristics of the Three Muscle Fiber Types

Fiber Type	Slow-Twitch	Intermediate	Fast-Twitch
Contraction tine	Slow	Fast	Very fast
Size of motor neuron	Small	Large	Very large
Resistance to fatigue	High	Intermediate	Low
Activity used for	Aerobic	Long term anaerobic	Short term anaerobic
Force production	Low	High	Very high
Mitochondrial density	High	High	Low
Capillary density	High	Intermediate	Low
Oxidative capacity	High	High	Low

Source: Mark Wagner, Gary Oden, Tim Sebesta, and Ronnie Nespeca, *Strength Training for Total Health and Wellness,* (c) 2013.

most people, somewhere in the middle with a similar number of each fiber type. This notion of fiber type has given rise to the comment that elite international athletes are born, not trained.

This may be true; however, it does not prevent any of us from enjoying activity while getting the most out of the body we own. What is important to remember about muscle and fiber types is that muscles are activated by the demands of the task. Walking, for example, may require 25–30 percent of the muscles in a person's legs. When looking at Table 5.1, one can see that an individual typically uses slow-twitch fibers for walking. That is great exercise for slow-twitch fibers, but what about the other fiber types? If you do not use those fibers, they will decrease in size (atrophy) and total muscular strength will decrease. This suggests that walking, although great for general fitness, would not be enough to sustain muscle mass. A person needs to engage in other physically demanding tasks throughout the day that require muscular strength, endurance, and/or power.

TYPES OF MUSCLE CONTRACTIONS

Muscle contractions can be isometric, isotonic, or isokinetic. Isometric muscle contraction is a static contraction with the muscle contracting with no movement taking place. An example of an isometric contraction would be pushing against a wall. A person can push against the wall with maximum force, however, the wall will not move. Isotonic muscle contractions is what people think about when thinking about resistance training. Isotonic training is by far the most common type of muscular strength and endurance training. Isotonic contractions are performed when using barbells, dumbbells, any type of free weight, and most machine weight equipment. There are two phases of an isotonic contraction; concentric, and eccentric. During the concentric phase of the movement the muscle is contracting while it shortens. During the eccentric phase the muscle is lengthening. For example, while performing a bicep curl the weight is curled from the waist area to the chest and then the weight is lowered back to the starting position. The curling of the weight upward toward the chest causes a shortening of the bicep or a concentric contraction of the bicep. As the weight is lowered the bicep lengthens which is the eccentric phase of the contraction. Most training programs concentrate on concentric contracts because most movement people perform is concentric. Isokinetic muscle contractions is defined as a muscle contracting against a constant resistance at a constant speed. Examples of isokinetic contractions are typically found in rehabilitation facilities. During isokinetic contraction a machine controls the resistance and speed of movement. Isokinetic training is rarely used because of the lack of availability and the extreme expense of the equipment.

GENDER DIFFERENCES IN STRENGTH

Strength development in humans is clear from birth to maturity. Boys and girls from age 3–12 exhibit nearly identical patterns of strength. Upon puberty, overall strength in boys

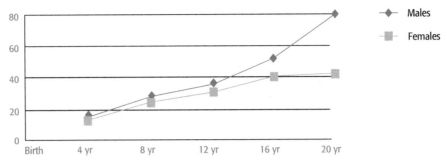

Figure 5.1 • Strength development in males and females.

continues to increase, while overall strength in girls begins to plateau (Figure 5.1). Often women will stay away from resistance training programs due to the mistaken belief that they will dramatically increase their muscle size. However, women will generally not develop large muscles from resistance training due to the lack of testosterone production in women. Male and female hormones, testosterone and estrogen, respectively, are primarily responsible for the difference in muscle size increase. Even though the quality of the muscle between males and females is identical, hormone-wise, they are very different. The notion that a female engaging in strength training will develop large bulging muscles is a misconception. Some female body builders are able to give this appearance during a contest via specific training that creates an acute muscle hypertrophy or "pumped up" look that lasts for a few hours.

Under normal resting conditions, however, a woman's muscles will not appear the same as a man's. Women can achieve excellent results with a well-designed resistance training program leading to loss of body fat and improved muscle tone without fear of dramatically increasing their muscle size. There are of course alternative means of generating muscle mass, namely, anabolic steroids. Anabolic steroids add to or take the place of existing testosterone. The action is the same since it stimulates the development of the muscle. For women who have little endogenous testosterone, adding additional "artificial" testosterone can have significant effects. To achieve more muscle some women bodybuilders resort to using anabolic steroids. Anabolic steroids use has major negative health consequences including damage to the kidneys and liver, and an increase in risk of cardiovascular disease.

Even without modifying substances, females can achieve the same relative strength as males. Pound for pound, female athletes are as strong as male athletes. Many top-level female gymnasts are considered to be some of the strongest athletes in the world.

Role of Nutrition in Muscular Strength and Endurance

Many people mistakenly believe that supplements, along with proper diet, are necessary if they lift weights. Sports supplements have become a multibillion dollar industry based on this misconception perpetuated by false advertising from uninformed individuals and media sources. In fact, individuals who lift weights for strength gains can meet all of their body's needs by consuming a healthy diet. As energy expenditure increases due to lifting weights, energy needs also increase, so the athletic individual commonly consumes a greater number of calories of fuel compared with the less-active person. The percentage of nutrients in the total diet, however, should remain the same, with carbohydrates comprising about 55-65 percent of total calories. Fat should still be kept to about 20-30 percent of the total calories, with protein remaining at 10-15 percent of calories. Many individuals in training are concerned that they are not getting enough protein from their diets. However, while protein requirements are higher for individuals participating in resistance training, they are not high enough to automatically require protein supplements, since the increase in total caloric consumption more than compensates for any additional needs. The recommended daily protein intake is .8 grams per kilogram of body weight. This recommendation includes a margin of safety high enough to cover almost all individuals. Eating more protein will not build muscle faster, in fact, it may contribute to an increase in body fat.

Overload and Specificity

Several fundamental principles must be addressed before any effective strength-development program can be understood. The first two are overload and specificity. For strength gains to be made, we must place demands on muscles we are not accustomed to placing demands on. These demands in effect are the "overload"; hence, the overload principle. By providing a systematic overloading progression to the muscle, it responds by changing its structure. Next is the notion of specificity. Not only is overload necessary, specificity is equally important in that a given increase in the strength or endurance of a muscle is specific to that muscle and does not carry over to other muscles not involved in the movement.

Periodization

In practical terms, periodization involves manipulating the frequency, intensity, and volume of training. This necessitates regular variations in training, which will enhance strength gains and minimize training monotony and staleness.

Reversibility and Individual Differences

Two additional principles to consider include reversibility and a lesser known one of individual differences. Reversibility implies that any gains in muscular strength and/or endurance will be lost if one reduces the overload it experiences. In simple terms, we lose what we fail to use. The concept of individual differences suggests people with different genetic make-ups (that is, muscle fiber types) may do the exact same strength training program and achieve very different results. Both people will get stronger; however, to what degree and how much change occurs is dependent on the individual.

COMPONENTS OF A SOUND STRENGTH-TRAINING PROGRAM

Many professional groups such as the National Strength and Conditioning Association (NSCA), the National Academy of Sports Medicine (NASM), and the ACSM have dedicated journal issues to strength training or established position papers outlining what they believe to be sound components of a strength-training program. Each of these groups agree that the specifics of strength training are addressed by mode, volume of resistance, and frequency. That, however, is where the agreement ends. In a lengthy paper by Carpinelli et al. (2004), the authors critically examine the ACSM's position and argue that much of the recommendations are unsubstantiated. Alternatively, Carpinelli et al. suggest simple, low-volume, time-efficient, resistance training is just as effective as complex, high-volume, time-consuming protocols. This is great news for most of us who are only interested in generating a healthy level of strength and then maintaining that level as we age. Therefore, the three pieces of the strength-training puzzle include mode, volume, and frequency. Tables 5.2 and 5.3 show recommendations for strength-training programs.

TABLE 5.2 Recommendations for Improving Muscular Strength and Endurance (for the General Adult Population*)

	Number of Sets	Number of Reps[†]	Sessions/ Week	Number of Exercises	Overall Purpose
ACSM[12] 1998	1	3–20	2–3	8–10[‡]	Basic development and maintenance of the fat-free mass
ACSM 2010[2]	2–4	8–12	2–3	8–10	
Surgeon general	1–2	8–12	2–3	8–10	Basic muscular strength and endurance
HHS, 2008[5]	1–3	8–12	2	10–12	
Cooper Institute for Aerobics Research					
Minimum	1	8–12	2	10	Strength maintenance
Recommended	2	8–12	2	10	Strength improvement
Optimal	3	8–12	2	10	Noticeable gains in strength

*Recommendations for older people (50–60 years of age and above) and cardiac patients are similar, except that lighter weights and more repetitions (10–15) at a reduced intensity (RPE of 12–13) are recommended,

[†]In all examples listed, repetitions represent maximal weight lifted to fatigue, but not failure.

[‡]Minimum of one exercise per major muscle group (e.g., chest press, shoulder press, triceps extension, biceps curl, pull-down, lower-back extension, abdominal crunch/curl-up, quadriceps extension, leg curls, calf raise).

Recommended for all major muscle groups.

From *Fundamentals of Weight Training* by Matthew C. Wagner, William E. Nix and Gary L. Oden. Copyright © 2011 by Kendall Hunt Publishing Company. Reprinted by permission.

TABLE 5.3 Achievement Objectives

	Strength	Power	Hypertrophy	Endurance
Sets	4–6	3–5	5–8	2–4
Reps	4–8	1–5	8–12	>12
Resistance	80–90%	90–100	60–80	40–60

Mode

Mode is the type of activity used to strengthen the muscle. Muscle strength and endurance can be improved with several modalities. Free weights using plates and bar or barbells are the most common form of resistance training; however, the use of machines will increase the safety of training. Other forms of resistance training include rubber bands, rubber tubing, and individual body weight, and even stationary objects can be used to perform isometric resistance training. Each mode of resistance training has advantages and disadvantages. The predominant factor in choosing the modality should be individual goals and preference, and maybe even availability.

Volume

Volume of resistance refers to the total amount of weight lifted during a training session. Volume is a combination of sets, repetitions, and amount of weight (resistance) lifted per repetition. For example, if a person performed 2 sets of 6 repetitions using 100 lbs, the volume for the training session would be 1,200 lbs. When performing a muscular strength and endurance program, the appropriate combination of sets, reps, and resistance is a must. For muscle endurance, a person can work with as little as 50 percent of maximal strength level. For muscle strength, a minimum of 60 percent of max strength is needed and for max strength gains, a minimum of 80 percent of max is necessary (ACSM, 2010). The number of sets and repetitions will vary on the goals of the individual and the genetic differences between people. Table 5.2 gives a good guideline to follow when developing your program.

Frequency

Frequency of strength training is very important in proper muscle development. To achieve a total body workout, a training schedule of two to three bouts per week is recommended, while alternating days of training with days of rest. People who want to train more often may choose to split the body into halves, working the upper body one day and the lower body the next. To obtain marked strength improvement, one needs to train a minimum of eight consecutive weeks. Once a desired level of strength is achieved, training once each week is usually enough to maintain the newly established strength level. Table on the next page outlines particular achievement objectives using various strength-training routines. These guidelines constitute a basis for establishing the foundation of a sound program. Once the goals of the program are set, selection of exercises for specific muscle groups can be made.

BUILDING YOUR STRENGTH AND ENDURANCE PROGRAM

The first thing to consider when developing your strength and endurance program is to determine your primary goal. Do you wish to gain muscle size (muscle hypertrophy) and get bigger? Do you wish to enhance your strength level? Or, do you wish to improve your muscle endurance? One very good thing about any strength and endurance training program is the fact that you will also accomplish secondary goals while working on primary goals. Meaning, that if your primary goal is to gain muscle strength, and you set up your program to accomplish your primary goal, you will also gain some muscle size and endurance. The number of reps, sets, and the amount of resistance needed to increase muscle size, strength, and endurance differ. Table 5.4 shows the necessary training stimulus and rest needed to maximize your training and accomplish your training goals.

TABLE 5.4 Muscular Endurance, Growth, and Strength Variables

Training Variable	Endurance	Hypertrophy	Strength
Sets	2–4	4–8	4–6
Reps	>12	10–15	Less than 8
Resistance	50–60%	60–80%	>80%
Rest between sets	30–60 seconds	60–90 seconds	120 seconds
Frequency per week	2–3 times per week	3–5 times per week	4–6 times per week
Rest between workouts	1–2 days	1–2 days	1–2 days
Duration of workout	30–60 min	30–60 min	30–60 min

From *Fundamentals of Weight Training* by Matthew C. Wagner, William E. Nix and Gary L. Oden. Copyright © 2011 by Kendall Hunt Publishing Company. Reprinted by permission.

PROGRAM DESIGN

Program design for a beginner is crucial in order to achieve results. The reason why most individuals do not achieve results is because they do not have a solid and accurate program design for strength training. Not having a detailed program design will not allow the body to physiologically adapt to the stress placed upon the muscles. Too many times an individual will randomly select exercises, weight, sets, and reps only to be disappointed in not achieving results. An individual must systematically follow a detailed program design in order to achieve results.

ORDER OF EXERCISES

The order of exercises is very important in the success of a strength training program. There are three fundamental rules to follow for the order of exercises.

1. Train large muscles before small - Small muscles fatigue before larger muscles. If you exercise your smaller muscles before larger muscles they would fatigue first, making it more difficult to perform exercises using large muscles.
   For example, chest or back before arms
2. Perform multijoint exercises before single joint exercises.
   For example, squat before leg extension
3. Alternating between push and pull exercises is fundamental.
   For example, chest press followed by seated row

Starting Resistance

It is important to select a correct starting resistance or weight for any beginning strength trainer. One of the biggest mistakes an individual can make is to select too heavy of a resistance at the start of his/her program. If an individual selects too heavy of a weight, then he/she risks the chance of injury, or more likely suffering from delayed-onset muscle soreness, or **DOMS. DOMS** is an overuse muscle injury resulting in micro-tears in the muscle fibers, which cause muscle damage. The soreness that an individual feels after a day or two of training is the result of **DOMS**. If a person follows a strict program design and selects the correct starting weight, then he/she will reduce the chances of encountering **DOMS**. The best recommendation for a starting weight is to select a weight that you can easily perform. The starting weight an individual selects should almost feel effortless. The reason for selecting a light resistance is to be able to learn to perform each exercise correctly. Also, this allows your body to gradually adapt to this new type of stress placed upon the body. An individual should also progress slowly to keep the risk of injury and the muscle soreness to a minimum.

   Week 1 The goal for Week 1 of the program design is to learn the exercises and to determine a starting weight. If an individual does not know what weight to start with, then he/she should always choose the lightest weight; this will reduce the chances of DOMS. The focus for Week 1 is to **Perform 1 set of 15 repetitions** of the lightest weight for each of the exercise; this will allow for the muscles to slowly adapt to the stress placed upon them.

   Week 2 The goal for Week 2 is to slowly and gradually increase the sets performed. An individual will add a second set for Week 2, keeping the resistance the same as Week 1. The focus for Week 2 is to **perform 2 sets of 15 repetitions of light weight for each exercise**.

   Week 3 The objective for Week 3 is to develop a solid foundation for an individual to build upon. The primary goal for Week 3 is to develop muscular endurance. Muscular endurance is the ability to perform repeated repetitions over an extended period of time and resist fatigue. The program design for Week 3 will increase the sets to 3, increase weight, and decrease reps; hence an individual will **perform 3 sets of 8 repetitions of a moderate weight for each exercise**. After Week 3 the program design will focus on progressive overload along with periodization.

Week 4 Week 4 will maintain 3 sets of the same resistance of each exercise but will increase the repetitions to 10.

Week 5 Week 5 will maintain 3 sets of the same resistance of each exercise but will increase the repetitions to 12.

Week 6 Week 6 will maintain 3 sets of the same resistance of each exercise but will increase the repetitions to 15.

Week 7 After Week 7, the program design starts over, which is incorporating periodization (cycles). For Week 7 an individual will continue with 3 sets, but will increase the weight from Week 6, and reduce the repetitions to 8.

COMMON QUESTIONS ABOUT STRENGTH TRAINING

1. **Will I gain weight if I strength train?** Probably not. With a general strength-training program as suggested by ACSM or the Guidelines for Adults consisting of 8–10 exercises, performing 8–12 repetitions, 2–3 times per week, you may increase your lean mass while decreasing your fat mass, resulting in no change in body weight. Additional benefits are realized by an improvement in body composition and a higher basic metabolic rate.

2. **If I stop strength training, will my muscle turn to fat?** No. Muscle and fat are two very different types of tissue. Muscles will decrease in size if they are not being used much. If you don't reduce your calorie intake to match energy expenditure, the extra calories you consume will often be stored as fat. Since these two processes occur over the same time, it gives the appearance that muscle has "turned to fat"; however, they are two distinct and very separate processes.

3. **Do I need to change my diet or eat more protein if I strength train?** Not if you have a balanced diet. Some research shows that ingesting a carbohydrate–protein mix immediately after strength training can help recovery and, in some instances, increase muscle hypertrophy; but, additional calories or extra protein in one's diet is not typically needed.

4. **How do I keep from getting muscle soreness after strength training?** There are two common types of muscle soreness. There is an acute soreness that one feels right after a workout, which is most often caused by metabolic waste in the muscle. That type of soreness is short lived and can be eliminated with a good cooldown. The soreness one feels a day or two later is thought to be the result of microdamage to the muscle. The inflammatory response that accompanies the damage causes the pain. Once your muscles are repeatedly exposed to such a training stress, they produce protective proteins to prevent or minimize the inflammatory reaction, and thus, the soreness doesn't return. If soreness does occur, repeating the same activity only using a lower intensity or mild stretching can help alleviate the pain.

5. **Why can't I strength train every day?** You can, just don't focus on the same muscle groups every single day. Your muscles need 1–2 days to repair or rebuild after a strength-training session. If you worked the same muscles very intensely every day, they wouldn't be able to adapt fast enough and you would eventually experience a plateau or, in some cases of overtraining, a performance decline. If you want to train every day, chose to work different parts of your body each day. Many people choose to focus on upper body one day and the lower body the next. This provides adequate rest for the muscles, but allows you to train every day.

6. **Will I lose my flexibility if I strength train?** Not if you exercise through the joint's full range of motion. In fact, Whitehead et al. (2010) reported improved flexibility with carefully constructed movements covering a full range of motion during resistance exercises.

TABLE 5.5   Percent Body Weights Used to Assess Combined Strength and Endurance Utilizing Free Weights or a Multi-Station Machine

	Percent Body Weight	
Lift	**Males**	**Females**
Leg Extension	65% BW	50% BW
Leg Curl	32% BW	25% BW
Bench Press	75% BW	45% BW
Lat Pull-down	70% BW	45% BW
Arm Curl	35% BW	18% BW

From *Fundamentals of Weight Training* by Matthew C. Wagner, William E. Nix and Gary L. Oden. Copyright © 2011 by Kendall Hunt Publishing Company. Reprinted by permission.

ASSESSING STRENGTH AND ENDURANCE

Although muscular strength and endurance are related, they are assessed with different procedures. Muscular strength is determined by a person's ability to complete one repetition at his or her maximal resistance (1RM). However, finding a true 1RM is problematic since it requires the person to perform several single repetitions to determine the amount of weight that he/she can actually lift. Add the factors of learning, technique, and endurance, and the tester has a difficult task at hand.

Endurance is typically measured by the number of completed repetitions of a submaximal resistance and is much easier to assess. With either strength or endurance, it is important to assess several different muscle groups. More than two tests are needed to properly assess strength since strength tends to be very specific. Five basic lifts are effective for assessing most large muscles of the body. As outlined by Hoeger and Hoeger (1997), Table 5.5 shows the five lifts and the percent body weights used for determining a combined muscular strength and endurance ranking.

Finally a simple test called the "plank" for core strength is presented. Stuart McGill (2002) has several additional assessments for core strength that he uses in his laboratory in Canada to assess back pain problems in his patients. He has found that by reestablishing a minimal level of core strength in his patients, they can delay and/or even prevent expensive and often less effective surgeries.

Muscular Strength and Endurance Assessment

On the following page are two examples on how to determine the resistance (weight) for each lift. Using the appropriate percentage of weight, complete as many repetitions of each lift as possible and record the number of repetitions. Table 5.6 outlines a healthy standard for the repetitions completed on each lift. Any level above these standards places a person in a high fitness category. Values below the healthy standards suggest a need for improvement.

TABLE 5.6   Number of Repetitions to Meet Healthy Standards

Gender	Bench Jumps	Push-ups	Modified Push-ups	Crunches	Modified Dips
Females	39–42	N/A	30–33	31–34	N/A
Males	54–56	30–33	N/A	33–38	25–27

From *Fundamentals of Weight Training* by Matthew C. Wagner, William E. Nix and Gary L. Oden. Copyright © 2011 by Kendall Hunt Publishing Company. Reprinted by permission.

Several simple field tests exist for measuring upper and lower body muscular endurance. Abdominal crunches, modified push-ups and/or traditional push-ups, as well as modified dips, work well for assessing trunk and upper-body muscle endurance. A one-minute bench jump with the use of a bleacher step or a 16¼ inch box is an excellent test of lower body muscular endurance. Specific instructions to complete each of these assessments are provided in the section below.

Four muscular endurance tests are used for men and three for women. Each test should be done with a partner. The proper procedure for each test is as follows:

Bench Jump (both males and females). Using a bench or box that is 16¼ inches high, jump up and down with a two-foot jump as many times as possible in one minute. One repetition is counted every time both feet touch the floor.

Push-ups (modified push-ups may be done by females). Lie face down on the floor while placing the hands by the shoulders and pointing the fingers forward. The arms must fully extend and support the body on the hands and feet. Lower the body toward the floor and allow only the chest to touch it. Each chest touch counts as one repetition. A modified push-up allows females to support the lower body by the knees instead of the feet. Employing a two-second, down-up cadence, complete as many continuous repetitions as possible. Stop counting when repetitions fail to be performed while adhering to the aforementioned cadence.

Example 1

Female, weighing 130 lbs

Lift	% of BW	Amount to lift
Leg Extension	.50 × 130 =	(65) 65 lbs
Leg Curl	.25 × 130 =	(32.5) 30 lbs
Bench Press	.45 × 130 =	(58.5) 60 lbs
Lat Pull-down	.45 × 130 =	(58.5) 60 lbs
Arm Curl	.18 × 130 =	(23.4) 25 lbs

Example 2

Male, weighing 180 lbs.

Lift	% of BW	Amount to lift
Leg Extension	.65 × 180 =	(117) 120 lbs
Leg Curl	.32 × 180 =	(57.6) 60 lbs
Bench Press	.75 × 180 =	(135) 135 lbs
Lat Pull-down	.70 × 180 =	(126) 125 lbs
Arm Curl	.35 × 180 =	(63) 65 lbs

Abdominal Crunch (both males and females). Although the abdominal crunch has come under scrutiny for administrative feasibility (Hall et al., 1992; Knudson & Johnston, 1995), it still remains the safest test to assess muscular endurance of the trunk. A modified crunch test developed at St. Cloud State University (Figure 5.2) is a way to assess initial strength prior to completing the standard crunch test. Start at level four and move up or down to reach the highest level possible. If a level of four or greater is achieved, then the crunch test can be completed. If a level of three or less is achieved, then repetitions at the level of modified crunches achieved should be done on a routine basis until a level of four can be reached.

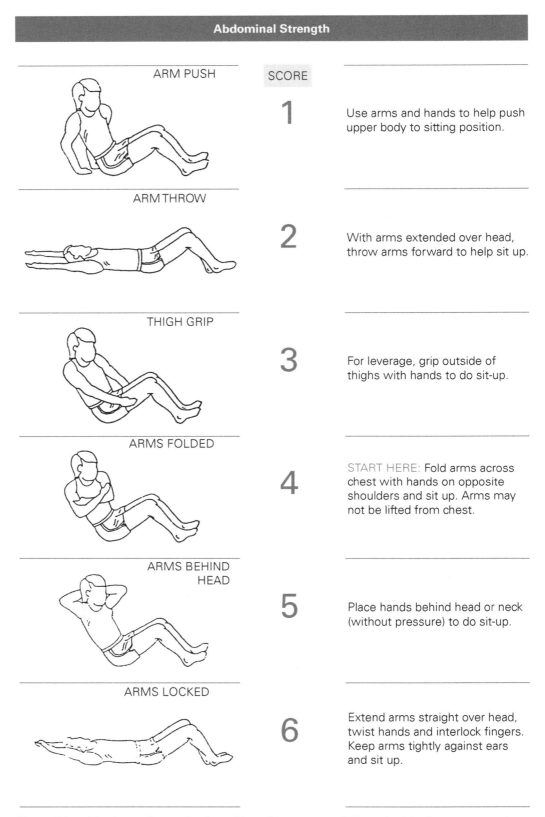

Abdominal Strength

	SCORE	
ARM PUSH	1	Use arms and hands to help push upper body to sitting position.
ARM THROW	2	With arms extended over head, throw arms forward to help sit up.
THIGH GRIP	3	For leverage, grip outside of thighs with hands to do sit-up.
ARMS FOLDED	4	START HERE: Fold arms across chest with hands on opposite shoulders and sit up. Arms may not be lifted from chest.
ARMS BEHIND HEAD	5	Place hands behind head or neck (without pressure) to do sit-up.
ARMS LOCKED	6	Extend arms straight over head, twist hands and interlock fingers. Keep arms tightly against ears and sit up.

Figure 5.2 • Lie down flat on back and bend knees at a 60° angle. Heels must remain on floor at all times. Start with #4: If completed, go on to #5; if unable to complete, go back to #3.

Upon reaching a level of four or more, one can complete the crunch test. While lying in a supine position, cross the arms over the chest. Bend the knees at a near right angle, with legs slightly apart and soles of the feet on the floor. The feet are not held during the test, and the starting position begins when the head is held slightly off the floor. Then, using a two-second cadence, curl up until the shoulders are clearly off the floor and return to the starting position. Count the number of repetitions completed without losing the correct cadence, or until 100 repetitions are completed.

Modified Dip (men only). Using a bench or bleacher step and a box or three chairs, place the hands on the bench or each hand on a chair; the fingers should be forward and the feet up on the box or the third chair. The starting position calls for the arms to be extended, and the trunk bent at the hips approximately 90 degrees. Lower the body so that you achieve a 90-degree angle at the elbow (upper arm should be about parallel to the floor). Using a two-second cadence, complete as many repetitions as possible.

Table 5.5 shows the number of repetitions needed to achieve a normal health-related fitness standard for each of these muscular endurance tests.

Core Strength Assessment—The Plank

Although the standard abdominal crunch is in part a measure of core strength, the plank will give you a true test of overall core strength that involves almost all of your trunk muscles. There are several components of a complete plank test. They include the prone plank, the supine plank, and the side plank. We will start with the simplest one: the prone plank. Similar to the up position of a push-up, the plank starts with a straight body supporting your weight on your toes and your forearms. Your elbows should be beneath your shoulders, and your hands should be under your forehead. Your arms should look like two sides of a triangle coming together at your hands. The test starts in a modified push-up position: supporting your weight on your toes and forearms. If any part of your body, other than the specified limbs, touches the ground, the test is over.

The second plank test starts from a supine position and follows the same order of movements as the prone plank test. Start the test by holding this position for 30 seconds. After 30 seconds, try to lift your left arm straight out in the air, balancing your body on your other three limbs. After 15 seconds, put your left hand down and your right hand up. After another 15 seconds, put your right hand down and lift your left leg up. Then after 15 more seconds, put the left leg down and lift the right leg up. This next part is tricky. Pick your left hand up and your right leg up. Now hold this for 15 seconds. Switch to your right hand and left leg for 15 seconds. Last, come back to the original plank position and hold it for 30 more seconds. If you can complete this test, you have a very strong core. If any part of your body, other than the specified limbs, touches the ground, the test is over.

The third plank test involves a combination of prone and side plank positions. Starting in the prone position on your toes and forearms, hold for 30 seconds; then rotate your trunk 90 degrees so you are now balancing on one forearm and both legs, and hold for 30 seconds; rotate back to the prone position, and hold for 30 seconds; and, finally, rotate your trunk in the opposite direction as before another 90 degrees, balancing on the other forearm and both legs, and hold for 30 seconds. A more challenging variation of this test is to start in a push-up position and raise the top leg each time you complete a side plank, putting you in a spread eagle while holding your trunk in a straight neutral position.

Note: *It is important to focus on form and not just on completing the task. If at any time you are unable to maintain your good starting position, stop the exercise. As you practice these movements, you will get stronger. As your strength develops, so will your success on these exercises, as well as your resistance to muscular injuries related to a weak core.*

The test starts in a modified push-up position, hence its name "the plank."

DESIGNING YOUR OWN STRENGTH PROGRAM

When planning your own program, give consideration to several issues. Of primary importance is the establishment of specific strength goals. Next are the types of equipment available to you. First and foremost, however, is being safety conscious. For a safe weight-training regimen, use this simple template and follow these steps to ensure success.

Plan and Template for a Strength-Training Program

Step 1: Goals: Specific goals:

Goals: Long-term goal(s):

Step 2: Choose your exercises: 8–10 exercises, 8–12 reps/exercise, 1–3 sets, 2–3 times per week.

Step 3: Allow one full day of rest between workouts for the same muscles. Monitor your progress, and vary the intensity, reps, and/or sets relatively often (such as weekly).

Exercise	Muscle(s) focused on	Frequency M T W Th F S S	Intensity (Weight lifted)	Reps	Sets
1					
2					
3					
4					
5					
6					
7					
8					

Steps to Ensure Success and Enjoyment

1. **Warm-up.** Doing a 5–15 minute aerobic warm-up that combines walking, light jogging, or cycling, plus slow arm swings combined with a few light calisthenics, is perfect.
2. **Breathe.** Do not hold your breath while lifting weights. Exhale while lifting the weight, and inhale while returning the weight. Additionally, a few controlled deep breaths in through the nose and out through the mouth can help recovery between sets and/or lifts.
3. **Start slow.** Use a weight or an exercise that you feel confident about using. Starting too aggressively may lead to rapid failure or increase your risk of injury.
4. **Play it safe.** Inspect the weight you are about to lift to make sure it's the right load. If you plan to lift with free weights, use a spotter and always be sure the weights are secure.
5. **Cooldown.** Repeat a 5–15 minute aerobic activity with stretching of the muscles used. This period is the most important for maintaining and/or gaining flexibility.
6. **Soreness.** If delayed muscle soreness develops, mild stretching of the sore muscles and repeating the same activities using a lower intensity will relieve much of the discomfort.
7. **Track your progress.** Keep a training log, or establish an assessment battery you can complete every few months. This will help document improvements and plan for the future.

FUNCTIONAL STRENGTH TRAINING

As stated previously, not only are the systematic and progressive increases in overload a necessity for optimal changes in strength, but specificity is important too. Functional strength training attempts to address the specificity to an even greater extent than modification of mode, volume, and frequency. Using stability balls, medicine balls, foam pads, soft discs, and balance boards, it tries to combine neuromuscular control with strength development. These exercises put a premium on balance and require the person to control movement in all three planes. This same idea is the rationale of many people to train with free weights versus machines. Machines stress a muscle or muscle group, but do not require the person to balance the resistance as it is moving. Free weights on the other hand require the person to control the load while moving it through a full range of motion. Functional strength training adds yet an additional dimension forcing the lifter to not only balance the resistance, but also control his/her body while completing the movement. An additional benefit to functional strength training is the enhancement of core strength. Core strength has become a popular term that basically implies one's strength to control the trunk and how much each limb is allowed to move during activity.

For example, functional strength training would give a person strength for daily activities, such as lifting heavy boxes, unloading the car or trunk, pulling open a heavy door, raking leaves, shoveling snow, carrying a child, or more recreational activities like hiking a mountain trail or paddling a canoe.

If you're an athlete, functional strength training can improve performance by forcing your muscles to work as one functional unit. The terms core and functional are often viewed as being similar; however, functional strength training ought to be considered as a broader-based training regimen. We have presented the basics of core training in Chapter 4. Working muscles of the pelvis, trunk, and shoulder stabilizers are the mainstays of core training. Functional strength training expands this domain to include more traditional forms of strength training with an added twist. This twist is most often some element of instability.

Incorporating medicine balls, tubing, stability balls, rollers, and foam pads is commonplace in functional strength-training programs. According to Tom Venuto (2005), a fitness trainer and body builder, there appear to be six commonalities among good functional training programs. They include (a) doing more unsupported exercises with attempts to involve core and stabilizing muscles for extended periods of time; (b) using a stability ball to create unstable situations; (c) performing abdominal exercises that are integrated with other movements, including rotational movements, as well as some that isolate just the abdominals; (d) performing more unilateral work, such as using dumbbells that force the lifter to stabilize his or her body during the movements; (e) avoiding using machines to perform lifts, since the machine takes away the need for the body to stabilize itself and the weight being lifted; and (f) focusing on using large muscle mass, multi-joint exercises, and fewer isolation movements.

The selected video links are examples of how functional strength training differs from traditional strength training. Keep in mind that a full spectrum of exercises can be used by any level of person; however, without a clear foundational strength base, trying to perform some of the more complex functional strength exercises would be unwise.

Video 1. Functional strength-training workout showing various exercises and equipment to create an unstable platform to force stabilizing muscles to be active throughout the movement.
http://www.youtube.com/watch?v=ggdNcjJg5Dc&feature=fvwrel
Video 2. More traditional or simple functional strength-training exercises using a dumbbell and body weight for resistance.
http://www.youtube.com/watch?v=4dtHHIkzrl4

Video 3. A demo video of some fairly sophisticated routines used to enhance balance during movements.
http://www.youtube.com/watch?v=XM3U1dWHAA8&feature=related

SUMMARY

Some people are fortunate enough (or unfortunate, depending on how one looks at it) to have jobs that provide the daily physical demands needed to maintain muscle mass. But reality suggests that the future will offer less and less need for manual labor or even physical activity of any kind. In much of society, the need to even physically move about is being lost. Elevators, escalators, home shopping networks, video games, e-mail, cell phones, and computer-based work stations at home (eliminating the need to commute to a job site) are all examples of how our daily lives are becoming less active.

On the surface this may appear harmless and it most likely would be if we adapted appropriately. Fewer physical demands mean less activity. Less activity means less need for muscle and less need for food. Will we match our dietary intake to our daily physical requirements? That remains to be seen; however, if current generations are any indication of how our society has adapted, the experts would reply with a resounding NO! Quite simply, we are not adjusting to the lack of daily activity and we are getting fatter as a result of it. So, how much strength do you need and how do you get it? It is simple. Be active!

On a daily basis, you need to do some:

1. Aerobic activity that will stimulate the large muscles of the legs. Occasionally, add a little greater stress to those same muscles in order to recruit all the fiber types into the activity. If that requires weight training, so be it.
2. Activity where there is a demand for muscular strength of the upper body. Daily chores or simple calisthenics work equally well.
3. Abdominal crunches and/or "the plank" to maintain a sound level of muscular endurance for the trunk.

The rewards are not only medicinal but aesthetic as well. There is no equal to having adequate strength for activities of daily living. We lose what we fail to use and if we want it later, we have to use it now, every day.

References

American College of Sports Medicine. (2010). The recommended quantity and quality of exercise for developing cardiorespiratory and muscular fitness in healthy adults. *Medicine and Science in Sport and Exercise, 30*, 975–991.

Carpinelli, R. N., Otto, R., & Winett, R. A. (2004, June). A critical analysis of the ACSM position stand on resistance training: Insufficient evidence to support recommended training protocols. *Journal of Exercise Physiology Online, 7*(3), 1–60.

Garnica, R. A. (1986). Muscle power in young women after slow and fast isokinetic training. *Journal of Orthopedics and Sports Physical Therapy, 8*(1), 1–9.

Hall, G. L., Hetzler, R. K., Perrin, D., & Weltman, A. (1992). Relationship of timed sit-up tests to isokinetic abdominal strength. *Research Quarterly for Exercise and Sport, 63*, 80–84.

Knudson, D., & Johnston, D. (1995). Validity and reliability of a trunk bench curl-up test of abdominal endurance. *Journal of Strength and Conditioning Research, 9*, 165–169.

McGill, S. (2002). *Low-back disorders: Evidence-based prevention and rehabilitation.* Leeds, UK: Human Kinetics.

Physical Activity Guidelines for Americans. (2008). Retrieved from http://www.health.gov/PAGuidelines/

Venuto, T. (2005). *Functional strength training vs. bodybuilding: Is bodybuilding the worst thing that ever happened to strength training?* Retrieved from http://www.shawnlebrunfitness.com/build-muscle/bodybuilding.html

Wagner, M., & Oden, W. (2011). *Fundamentals of weight training*. Dubuque, IA: Kendall Hunt.

Wagner, M, & Oden, G. (2013). Strength training for Total Health and Wellness, Dubuque, IA: Kendall Hunt.

Watts, K., Jones, E., Davis, E., & Green, D. (2005). Exercise training in obese children and adolescents. *Sports Medicine, 35*, 375–392.

Wescott, W., & Baechle, T. (1998). *Strength training past 50*. Champaign, IL: Human Kinetics.

Whitehead, J. R., et al. (2010). *Strength training improves flexibility too*. Retrieved from http://www.acsm.org/about-acsm/media-room/news-releases/2011/08/01/study-strength-training-improves-flexibility-too

WORKOUT LOG

DATE: EXERCISE	SET 1 Rep	SET 1 Wt	SET 2 Rep	SET 2 Wt	SET 3 Rep	SET 3 Wt	SET 4 Rep	SET 4 Wt

DATE: EXERCISE	SET 1 Rep	SET 1 Wt	SET 2 Rep	SET 2 Wt	SET 3 Rep	SET 3 Wt	SET 4 Rep	SET 4 Wt

DATE: EXERCISE	SET 1 Rep	SET 1 Wt	SET 2 Rep	SET 2 Wt	SET 3 Rep	SET 3 Wt	SET 4 Rep	SET 4 Wt

CHAPTER 5

PERSONAL GROWTH OPPORTUNITY 1

Muscular Strength/Endurance Lab and Worksheet

Instructions: Complete either Part A, Part B, or both if you wish.

Part A

For assessing strength and endurance, use the procedures found in Chapter 5. Complete each test with a partner. No special equipment is required. Record the number of repetitions in the "Actual Value" column below.

To determine whether you meet the health standard for each test, refer to Table 5.6.

Males—complete all four tests: bench jumps, push-ups, crunches, and modified dips.

Females—complete the three appropriate tests: bench jumps, either modified push-ups or standard push-ups, and crunches. If you are an athlete who requires considerable upper body strength, feel free to try the modified dip test. A realistic minimum number would be 20 repetitions.

Your overall score can be calculated by giving yourself points for all tests as follows:

4 points	Exceed the health standard
3 points	Meet the standard
2 points	Barely under minimum standard
1 point	Not very close to minimum standard

TEST	ACTUAL VALUE	MEET HEALTH STANDARD? (Y/N)	POINTS
Bench Jumps			
Push-ups/Modified Push-ups			+
Crunches			+
Modified Dips (males only)			+
		Overall Score	=

If your overall strength score is ≥8 for females and ≥10 for males, you've met the health standards with reasonable success. Review the areas that perhaps need improvement and think about how you might be able to do that.

Part B

If you have access to free weights and/or machines and you have received some general instruction or experience using such weights, you can complete the combined total body strength and endurance test described in Chapter 5. This could be used in place of the above-described tests or done in addition to the above tests.

Use the percentages shown in Table 5.3 for each specific lift. An example is provided for you in page 89. Use Table 5.5 to determine if you meet and/or exceed the healthy standards for combined strength and endurance. Give yourself points using the same scale as used in Part A.

TEST	NO. OF REPS	MEET HEALTH STANDARD? (Y/N)	POINTS
Leg Extension			
Leg Curl			+
Bench Press			+
Lat Pulls			+
Arm Curls			+
		Overall Score	=

If your strength/endurance score is ≥13 (for both females and males), you have met the health standards with reasonable success. Review the areas that perhaps need improvement and think about how you might be able to do that.

Question

Name six fundamental safety issues for safe weight training.

1. _____

2. _____

3. _____

4. _____

5. _____

6. _____

Nutrition

© Monkey Business Images, 2014. Used under license from Shutterstock, Inc.

Specific Objectives

1. List and explain the Dietary Guidelines for Americans.
2. Design an eating pattern that conforms to ChooseMyPlate.
3. List and explain the roles of the various nutrients needed by the body.
4. Comprehend the various types of dietary fats and their impact on cardiovascular health.
5. Identify the role of vitamins and minerals in the human body.
6. Present specific steps for reducing dietary intake of sodium, sugar, fat, saturated fat, trans-fat, and cholesterol.
7. Describe the important considerations of vegetarianism.
8. Explain the pros and cons of dietary supplements.
9. Plan for healthy eating in fast-food and other restaurants.
10. Incorporate information from food labels into dietary decisions.
11. Conduct a diet analysis and make plans for improvement.

Adapted from *Fitness for Life, Fourth Edition* by Bill Hyman, Gary Oden, David Bacharach, Tim Sebesta. Copyright © 2011 by Kendall Hunt Publishing Company. Reprinted by permission.

Most people know that eating right is a critical factor in how we look and feel and that we may even be able to reduce our risks of certain health problems by following sound dietary principles. We know that proper nutrition is important, yet we remain trapped in old eating patterns that are not conducive to positive health. Many individuals feel as though their current diet is so bad that it would be futile to attempt to attain prudent eating habits. Some realize that minor adjustments could provide benefits, but lack the knowledge of basic nutritional principles. Others know what needs to be done, yet mistakenly believe that it would be very costly and inconvenient for them to pursue a healthy diet, and still others are misled by the abundance of unscientific and misleading nutrition information that is often disseminated.

None of these situations needs to be the case. Healthful and enjoyable eating habits have been attained by millions of Americans and are certainly attainable by anyone, including college students. Most diets need only minor adjustments to provide the benefits of good health, and with some study of the information provided in this chapter, good eating habits can be adopted for lifelong health. Unfortunately, there is a great deal of misinformation and misrepresentation in the area of nutrition, which is very misleading to the average consumer. Nutrition information can be presented in a very simple format, or it can be made to appear quite complicated, and while certain individuals may desire to study the science of nutrition in detail, most people simply want to know the basic guidelines in order to make easy lifestyle application of good nutrition principles. For this reason, several reputable government agencies and professional organizations have published documents that provide excellent information to help the general public sort through the vast array of information to make decisions. Although some of the specific information in those documents has been debated, a proper diet is virtually assured if one follows the general recommendations provided.

The 2015–2020 Dietary Guidelines for Americans from the U.S. Department of Agriculture (USDA) provide several key recommendations for achieving optimal nutrition (U.S. Department of Health and Human Services & USDA, 2010). Since these Guidelines provide an excellent framework for a healthy diet, they will serve as the center of our discussion. The following snapshot is taken from the Guidelines and contains practical suggestions for incorporating them into your daily eating plan.

A SNAPSHOT OF THE 2015-2020 DIETARY GUIDELINES FOR AMERICANS

1. **Follow a healthy eating pattern across the lifespan.** All food and beverage choices matter. Choose a healthy eating pattern at an appropriate calorie level to help achieve and maintain a healthy body weight, support nutrient adequacy, and reduce risk for chronic disease.
2. **Focus on variety, nutrient density, and amount.** To meet nutrient needs within calorie limits, choose a variety of nutrient-dense foods across and within all food groups in recommended amounts.
3. **Limit calories from added sugars and saturated fats and reduce sodium intake.** Consume an eating pattern low in added sugars, saturated fats, and sodium. Cut back on foods and beverages higher in these components to amounts that fit within healthy eating patterns.
4. **Shift to healthier food and beverage choices.** Choose nutrient-dense foods and beverages across and within all food groups in place of less healthy choices. Consider cultural and personal preferences to make these shifts easier to accomplish and maintain.

5. **Support healthy eating patterns for all.** Everyone has a role in helping to create and support healthy eating patterns in multiple settings nationwide, from home to school to work to communities.

What is a Healthy Eating Pattern?

An eating pattern can be defined as the combination of foods and beverages that make up an individual's complete dietary intake over time. An eating pattern is more than the sum of its parts; it represents the totality of what individuals habitually eat and drink, and these dietary components act synergistically in relation to health. A healthy eating pattern should be tailored to the individual's personal, cultural and traditional preferences as well as food budget. An individual's healthy eating pattern will vary according to their calorie level to help achieve and maintain a healthy body weight, support nutrient adequacy, and reduce risk for chronic disease.

Key Recommendations

The Key Recommendations for healthy eating patterns should be applied in their entirety to reflect an overall healthy eating pattern.

- Consume a healthy eating pattern that accounts for all food and beverages within an appropriate calorie level.

  A healthy eating pattern includes:
  - A variety of vegetables from all of the subgroups–dark green, red and orange, legumes (beans and peas), starchy, and other
  - Fruits, especially whole fruits
  - Grains, at least half of which are whole grains
  - Fat-free or low-fat dairy, including milk, yogurt, cheese, and/or fortified soy beverages
  - A variety of protein foods, including seafood, lean meats and poultry, eggs, legumes (beans and peas), and nuts, seeds, and soy products.
  - Oils
- *A healthy eating pattern limits:*
  - Saturated and trans fats, added sugars, and sodium.

Key Recommendations that are quantitative are provided for several components of the diet that should be limited. These components are of particular public health concern, and the specified limits can help individuals achieve healthy eating patterns within calorie limits:

- Consume less than 10 percent of calories per day from added sugars
- Consume less than 10 percent of calories per day from saturated fats
- Consume less than 2,300 milligrams (mg) per day of sodium
- If alcohol is consumed, it should be consumed in moderation–up to one drink per day for women and up to two drinks per day for men–and only by adults of legal drinking age.

In addition to diet, physical activity is important to promote health and reduce the risk of chronic disease. Diet and physical activity are the two parts of the calorie balance equation to help manage body weight. To help individuals maintain and achieve a healthy body weight, the Dietary Guidelines includes a Key Recommendation to:

■ Meet the *Physical Activity Guidelines for Americans*.

Key Elements of Healthy Eating Patterns

A premise of the *Dietary Guidelines* is that nutritional needs should be met primarily from foods. All forms of foods–fresh, canned, dried, and frozen–can be included in healthy eating patterns. Importantly, foods should be in the most nutrient-dense form possible. These foods contain essential vitamins and minerals, dietary fiber, and other naturally occurring substances that may have positive health effects. Nutrient-dense foods include all vegetables, fruits, whole grains, seafood, eggs, beans and peas, nuts and seeds, fat-free and low-fat dairy products and lean meats and poultry, when purchased, prepared, served and consumed with little to no added saturated fats, sugars, refined starches, and sodium.

© Elena Schweitzer, 2014. Used under license from Shutterstock, Inc.

© Hurst Photo, 2014. Used under license from Shutterstock, Inc.

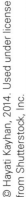

© Hayati Kayhan, 2014. Used under license from Shutterstock, Inc.

THE DASH EATING PLAN

Another eating plan highlighted in the 2015–2020 Dietary Guidelines is known as the DASH diet. DASH stands for Dietary Approaches to Stop Hypertension and is based on the findings of several DASH research studies. Hypertension, or high blood pressure, is known as the silent killer and is discussed thoroughly in Chapter 8. Research studies show that diet affects hypertension and that blood pressure can be lowered by following a particular eating plan. The DASH diet is very consistent with the Dietary Guidelines and ChooseMyPlate, as it limits sodium, saturated fatty acids, and cholesterol and focuses on increasing intake of foods rich in potassium, calcium, magnesium, protein, and fiber. It is rich in fruits, vegetables, fat-free or low-fat milk and milk products, whole grains, fish, poultry, seeds, and nuts. The DASH plan can be viewed in its entirety at the following website:

www.nhlbi.nih.gov/health/public/heart/hbp/dash/new_dash.pdf

CHOOSEMYPLATE

ChooseMyPlate (United States Department of Agriculture (USDA), 2018) replaced the Food Pyramid in 2011 and is another helpful guide to good eating. It is important to note that the Dietary Guidelines for Americans and ChooseMyPlate are consistent with and complement each other. They support the same basic nutrition information. ChooseMyPlate also places emphasis on regular physical activity and offers an individualized approach to building a healthy diet. Each section of the plate represents a different food group. With all nutrients, the amount needed by an individual varies depending on age, gender, and activity level, and more specific and detailed information on how to personalize your plate for optimal results can be found at the USDA website highlighted below:

www.ChooseMyPlate.gov

The first section of the plate represents grains. Foods from this group are excellent sources of complex carbohydrates, fiber, iron, niacin, and vitamin B1, among other nutrients. Everyone needs to consume six ounces of grains daily, with at least half of them being whole grains. One ounce equals one slice of bread, one cup of ready-to-eat cereal, or one-half cup of cooked rice, pasta, or cereal. The second section of the plate is made up of vegetables. Everyone should strive to eat more dark-green, orange, and red vegetables. Two to three cups each day are recommended, and a one-cup serving is considered as one cup of raw or cooked vegetables or two cups of leafy green vegetables. The third section of the plate is the fruits. A variety of fruits (fresh, frozen, canned, or dried—the Academy of Nutrition and Dietetics, formerly the American Dietetic Association [ADA], encourages all of them) should be consumed. The recommended amount is one and one-half to two cups daily, and a cup is considered as one cup of fruit juice, one-half cup of dried fruit, or one cup of cut fruit. Go easy on the fruit juice, since it adds calories to the diet without significantly contributing to a feeling of fullness. Fruits and vegetables are also carbohydrate-rich foods and provide fiber, vitamins C, B6, A, and E, as well as folic acid. The fourth part of the plate is meat and beans, which provide protein, niacin, iron, and vitamin B1, as well as other important nutrients. Low-fat choices of lean meats and poultry should be chosen, with meats being baked, broiled, or grilled. For variety, include fish, beans, peas, nuts, and seeds to provide the valuable nutrients from this group. Five to six ounces a day are recommended, and one ounce is a one-ounce serving of meat, fish, or poultry, one-fourth cup of cooked dry beans, one egg, one tablespoon of peanut butter, or one-half ounce of nuts or seeds. The final part of ChooseMyPlate consists of dairy foods. Dairy foods provide calcium, protein, vitamin B12, and other nutrients. It is recommended that dairy choices be fat free or low fat, and the recommended daily amount is three cups. One cup is a cup of milk or yogurt, one and one-half ounces of natural cheese, or two ounces of processed cheese. It is important to note that while oils are not found on the plate, they are common in our diets, so healthy choices should be made in this area as well. Oils are fats that are liquid at room temperature, like the vegetable oils used in cooking, but are found in other food sources as well. Choose oils that are unsaturated and with little or no trans-fats. Most oils should be chosen from fish, nuts, and vegetable oils, with a limitation of fats like butter, stick margarine, shortening, and lard. While some oil intake is needed for health, oils still contain calories. In fact, oils and solid fats both contain about 120 calories per tablespoon. Therefore, the amount of oil consumed needs to be limited to balance total calorie intake. The amount of oils varies greatly from product to product. The ChooseMyPlate plan emphasizes that one size does not fit all; so a visit to the USDA website can be of great assistance in formulating a prudent eating plan.

USDA

United States Department of Agriculture

10 tips
Nutrition
Education Series

MyPlate
MyWins

Based on the
Dietary
Guidelines
for Americans

Choose MyPlate

Use MyPlate to build your healthy eating style and maintain it for a lifetime. Choose foods and beverages from each MyPlate food group. Make sure your choices are limited in sodium, saturated fat, and added sugars. Start with small changes to make healthier choices you can enjoy.

1 Find your healthy eating style
Creating a healthy style means regularly eating a variety of foods to get the nutrients and calories you need. MyPlate's tips help you create your own healthy eating solutions—"MyWins."

2 Make half your plate fruits and vegetables
Eating colorful fruits and vegetables is important because they provide vitamins and minerals and most are low in calories.

3 Focus on whole fruits
Choose whole fruits—fresh, frozen, dried, or canned in 100% juice. Enjoy fruit with meals, as snacks, or as a dessert.

Fruits

4 Vary your veggies
Try adding fresh, frozen, or canned vegetables to salads, sides, and main dishes. Choose a variety of colorful vegetables prepared in healthful ways: steamed, sauteed, roasted, or raw.

Vegetables

5 Make half your grains whole grains
Look for whole grains listed first or second on the ingredients list—try oatmeal, popcorn, whole-grain bread, and brown rice. Limit grain-based desserts and snacks, such as cakes, cookies, and pastries.

Grains

6 Move to low-fat or fat-free milk or yogurt
Choose low-fat or fat-free milk, yogurt, and soy beverages (soymilk) to cut back on saturated fat. Replace sour cream, cream, and regular cheese with low-fat yogurt, milk, and cheese.

Dairy

7 Vary your protein routine
Mix up your protein foods to include seafood, beans and peas, unsalted nuts and seeds, soy products, eggs, and lean meats and poultry. Try main dishes made with beans or seafood like tuna salad or bean chili.

Protein

8 Drink and eat beverages and food with less sodium, saturated fat, and added sugars
Use the Nutrition Facts label and ingredients list to limit items high in sodium, saturated fat, and added sugars. Choose vegetable oils instead of butter, and oil-based sauces and dips instead of ones with butter, cream, or cheese.

Limit

9 Drink water instead of sugary drinks
Water is calorie-free. Non-diet soda, energy or sports drinks, and other sugar-sweetened drinks contain a lot of calories from added sugars and have few nutrients.

10 Everything you eat and drink matters
The right mix of foods can help you be healthier now and into the future. Turn small changes into your "MyPlate, MyWins."

Center for Nutrition Policy and Promotion
USDA is an equal opportunity provider, employer, and lender.

Go to **ChooseMyPlate.gov**
for more information.

DG TipSheet No. 1
June 2011
Revised October 2016

Figure 6.1 • ChooseMyPlate guidelines.

THE HEALTHY MEDITERRANEAN-STYLE PATTERN

In addition to the eating pattern presented in the Dietary Guidelines, another eating pattern has received considerable attention as a plan that also provides nutrients and results in low rates of diet-related disease and a longer life expectancy. The Healthy Mediterranean-Style Pattern is an adaptation of the Healthy U.S.-Style Pattern, as it modifies amounts recommended from some food groups to more closely reflect eating patterns that have been associated with positive health outcomes in studies of Mediterranean-Style diets (the foods and cooking styles of countries around the Mediterranean Sea).

The Mayo Clinic emphasizes the research on the benefits of this diet, including reducing the risk of heart disease, lowering LDL cholesterol, reducing the incidence of cancer, Parkinson's disease, Alzheimer's disease, and when supplemented with extra-virgin olive oil and mixed nuts, a reduced risk of breast cancer in women. It is also associated with a reduced risk of cardiovascular mortality as well as overall mortality. Thus, this eating style is encouraged by most major scientific organizations, and the Mediterranean style pattern is included in the Dietary Guidelines.

The Mediterranean diet incorporates the basics of healthy eating found in the Dietary Guidelines - with minor variations in proportions of certain foods. It includes plenty of fruits, vegetables, pasta, and rice and very few saturated or trans-fats. It includes beans and lentils, which are loaded with plant protein, fiber, carbohydrate and other nutrients and naturally low in fat. Most grains are whole grains, and breads are not eaten with butter or margarine, but dipped in olive oil or eaten plain. Heart healthy and protein packed fish is a staple in the diet, and nuts play a central role as well - but not in large amounts due to their fat content, although the fat found in most nuts is not saturated fat. The fat in the diet comes primarily from mono- and poly-unsaturated fats. Overall, the dietary emphases of the plan are:

- Eating primarily plant-based foods, such as fruits and vegetables, whole grains, legumes and nuts
- Replacing butter with healthy fats such as olive oil and canola oil
- Using herbs and spices instead of salt to flavor foods
- Limiting red meat to no more than a few times a month
- Eating fish and poultry at least twice a week
- Drinking red wine in moderation (optional)

(American Academy of Nutrition and Dietetics, 2017; Mayo Clinic, 2017)

THE NUTRIENTS

There are six categories of nutrients needed by the human body. The macronutrients are the energy (calorie)-providing nutrients—fats, carbohydrates, and proteins. The micronutrients, namely, vitamins, minerals, and water, do not provide energy (calories). Figure 6.2 illustrates the percentages of the macronutrients recommended for a balanced diet.

Fats

Dietary fat has been vilified, but we all need some fat in our diet. Fats provide an avenue for the transportation and storage of fat-soluble vitamins (A, D, E, and K) and are important in the regulation of certain body functions. They help form cell membranes and hormones. They add flavor to food and provide

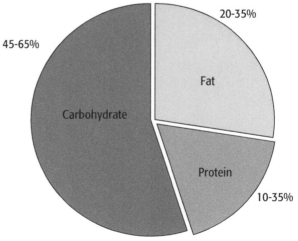

Figure 6.2 • Recommended calories from the macronutrients.

TABLE 6.1 Your Fat Budget

Fat Budget for Men			
Age	Weight	Fat Budget	Based on Average Caloric Need of:
19–24	140–160	90 g	2700
	160–180	105 g	3150
	180–200	115 g	3450
25–50	140–160	85 g	2550
	160–180	95 g	2850
	180–200	105 g	3150
Over 50	140–160	70 g	2100
	160–180	75 g	2250
	180–200	85 g	2550

Fat Budget for Women			
Age	Weight	Fat Budget	Based on Average Caloric Need of:
19–24	110–130	70 g	2100
	130–150	80 g	2400
	150–170	90 g	2700
25–50	110–130	65 g	1950
	130–150	75 g	2250
	150–170	85 g	2550
Over 50	110–130	55 g	1650
	130–150	65 g	1950
	150–170	75 g	2250

This fat budget is calculated for thirty percent of the total calories of average caloric needs. If you wish to consume a higher or lower percentage of calories from fat (recommended from 20 to 35 percent), or if you believe you do not have the same average caloric needs for your sex, age, and weight, you can calculate your own fat budget with the following equation:

FAT BUDGET (in grams) = (CALORIC NEEDS × 0.3) / 9

For example, if you determine that you consume approximately 2,000 calories per day, your fat budget would be calculated as follows:

FB = (2000 × 0.3) / 9

FB = 600 / 9

FB = 67 grams per day

satiety—that satisfied feeling of fullness experienced after a meal. Many foods containing fat are good sources of high-quality protein. Fats also provide energy at a rate of nine calories per gram, making them the most concentrated form of energy for the body. Yet while an excellent source of concentrated energy, this also makes fat the fattening nutrient, and anyone interested in losing weight will certainly need to limit fat intake. The amount of fat actually needed is significantly less than most people's current intake. A good goal for fat intake is between 20 and 35 percent of total calories. Table 6.1 can help you determine your fat budget.

While some dietary fat is needed, the high-fat diet has been identified as a contributor to poor health. A diet high in fat, saturated fat, trans-fat, and cholesterol contributes significantly to one's risk for the number one killer of Americans—heart disease. Table 6.2 compares the fat, saturated fat, cholesterol, and calories from selected foods. Excessive dietary cholesterol causes increases in serum cholesterol (cholesterol in the bloodstream) levels. For this reason, it is important to include fewer high-cholesterol products in our diet. Numerous products are attempting to capitalize on the health-conscious consumer by touting their low-cholesterol or cholesterol-free qualities. It is important to note that although these are certainly good qualities, knowing that a product is low in cholesterol or cholesterol free is not enough. Some foods contain no cholesterol, but are high in saturated fats or trans-fats. As a rule, food products that come from plant sources never contain cholesterol. Cholesterol is present only in foods of animal origin.

Even more important than dietary cholesterol is the role of saturated fat and trans-fat in serum cholesterol levels. Each of these raises the level of low-density lipoprotein (LDL) in the blood. LDL is the type of cholesterol that adheres to the inside walls of the arteries, causing a condition known as atherosclerosis, or the build-up of fatty deposits on artery walls. This interferes with the flow of blood through those arteries. Therefore, LDL is often referred to as bad cholesterol. Foods high in saturated fat and trans-fats are those most likely to be converted into LDL, so it is very important to limit their consumption. Saturated fat should comprise no more than 10 percent of total calories, and trans-fat intake should be kept as low as possible. Saturated fats are usually solid at room temperature and include foods like whole dairy products, fatty meats such as bacon, lunch meats, sausage, and heavily marbled steaks and roasts, fried and breaded foods, many desserts, sauces, gravies and oils, and products that have been hydrogenated. Hydrogenation is used to change the texture and prolong the shelf life of a product, and trans-fats are created through this process. Trans-fats behave like saturated fat and raise LDL levels. Margarine and shortening are often hydrogenated, and numerous processed foods contain oils with some degree of hydrogenation. Fortunately for nutrition-conscious consumers, the amount of trans-fat in foods is provided on food labels, and the U.S. Food and Drug Administration has taken initial steps toward potentially eliminating most trans-fat from the food supply.

TABLE 6.2 Comparison of Calories, Fat, Saturated Fat and Cholesterol Content of Selected Foods

Food	Calories	Fat	Saturated Fat	Cholesterol
Dairy Products/Eggs				
1 cup whole milk	150	8	5	33
1 cup 2% milk	120	5	3	18
1 cup skim milk	86	trace	trace	4
1 cup ice cream	269	14	8	59
1 cup sherbet	204	2	2	8
1 oz cheddar cheese	114	9	6	30
1 oz part skim mozzarella cheese	80	5	3	15
1 medium egg	66	4	1.5	187
1 egg white	16	0	0	0
Meat and Meat Products				
3 oz. water packed tuna	100	1	trace	26
6 large fried shrimp	109	6	1	80
3 oz. baked salmon	184	9	1.6	74
3 oz. ground beef patty	240	17	6.5	75
3 oz. broiled sirloin (fat trimmed)	166	6	2.5	76
3 medium bacon slices	109	9	3	16
3 oz. roasted ham (fat trimmed)	179	8	3	80
fried chicken (1/2 breast)	364	18	5	119
roasted chicken (1/2 breast)	142	3	1	73
Snack Foods and Fats				
1 tbsp butter	100	11.5	7	31
1 tbsp margarine	100	11.5	2	0
1 tbsp corn oil	120	14	2	0
1 tbsp mayonnaise	100	11	2	8
1 oz. avocado	50	5	1	0
4 chocolate chip cookies	185	9	3.5	8
1 slice pecan pie	452	21	4	106

One additional warning about saturated fats is needed here. While most oils from plants are low in saturated fat, there are two notable exceptions. They are palm oil, which is 82 percent saturated, and coconut oil, which is 87 percent saturated. These two oils are harvested from plants that are grown in tropical regions and are therefore referred to as tropical oils. Steps should be taken to minimize or avoid consumption of these oils.

Two other types of dietary fat have interesting effects on serum cholesterol levels. Polyunsaturated and monounsaturated fats (often referred to as PUFAs and MUFAs) are the two unsaturated fats. They are found mainly in many fish, nuts, seeds, and oils from plants. Some examples of foods that contain these fats include salmon, trout, herring, avocados, olives, walnuts, and liquid vegetable oils (such as soybean, corn, safflower, canola, olive, and sunflower oils). These unsaturated fats do not raise LDL cholesterol; in fact some studies suggest they can help lower LDL cholesterol slightly when included as part of a low-saturated and trans-fat diet. They should be substituted for saturated fat whenever possible. One other type of fat that has received considerable attention is the omega-3 fatty acids. Omega-3 (n-3 polyunsaturated) fatty acids are essential fats that your body needs to function properly but does not make. Humans must get these fatty acids through food, which means getting EPA (eicosapentaenoic acid) and DHA (docosahexaenoic acid) from seafood and ALA (alpha-linolenic acid) from sources such as walnuts, flaxseed, and canola and soybean oils. Omega-3 fatty acids, particularly EPA and DHA, have been shown to benefit the heart of healthy people and those at high risk for—or those who already have—cardiovascular disease. The American Heart Association (2018) recommends eating fish (particularly fatty fish) at least two times (two servings) a week. Each serving is 3.5 ounce cooked, or about ¾ cup of flaked fish. Fatty fish like salmon, herring, lake trout, sardines, and albacore tuna are high in omega-3 fatty acids. A similar compound is omega-6 fatty acids. While some controversy exists concerning their role in heart health, the American Heart Association considers them heart healthy and recommends that 5–10 percent of daily calories be omega-6 fats. They are found in nuts, seeds, and vegetable oils.

Although there is certainly a difference in the types of fatty acids and the effect they have on cholesterol levels, it is important to remember that they are all fats and that they all contain nine calories per gram. Total fat consumption should be 20–35 percent of our total caloric intake, and consuming a higher percentage of calories as fat means consuming a lower percentage of calories as carbohydrate or protein—and it is usually carbohydrate consumption that is compromised. And at nine calories per gram, a reduction in dietary fat intake is a major step toward reducing total caloric consumption, which is one-half of the energy balance equation necessary for a healthy weight.

The fatty acid composition of many fats and oils is shown in Figure 6.3 and a chart with suggestions for substitutions for many high-fat food items is shown in Table 6.3. Additional tips for reducing dietary fat include the following:

1. Use fats and oils sparingly in cooking.
2. Use small amounts of salad dressings and spreads, such as butter, margarine, and mayonnaise. One tablespoon of most of these spreads provides 10–11 grams of fat, and 90–100 calories.

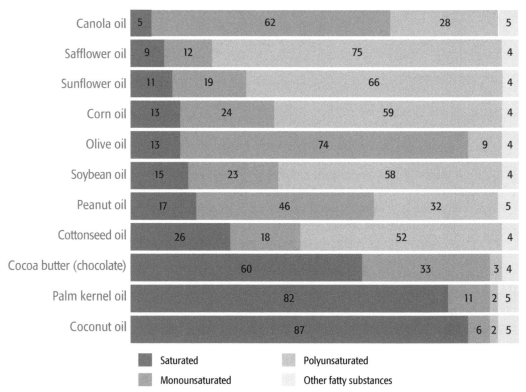

Figure 6.3 • Percentages of saturated, polyunsaturated, and monounsaturated fats in common vegetable oils.
Source: *Health: The Basics* 2nd edition. Donatelle & Davis.

TABLE 6.3 Cutting the Fat

The following substitutions are helpful in reducing dietary fat.

The comparative grams of fat are shown for some items.

Instead of:	Try
Butter or margarine	Butter substitutes
Regular yogurt	Non-fat yogurt
Regular salad dressing	Non-fat salad dressing
Mayonnaise	Mustard or low-fat salad dressing
Tuna in oil	Tuna in water
Fried foods	Baked or broiled foods
Dark meat poultry	Light meat poultry
Prime beef	Choice or select beef
Bacon and sausage	Lean ham
Burger and fries	Soup and salad
Pepperoni pizza	Canadian bacon pizza
Whole-milk dairy products	Skim or low-fat dairy products
Regular cheese	Low-fat cheese, skim milk mozzarella
Pastries (38 g or more)	Hot cereals (2 g)
Muffins (5–12 g)	English muffins (1–2 g)
Croissant (12 g)	Bread (1 g)
Fried chicken (30 g)	Grilled chicken (3 g)
Fried potatoes (12 g)	Baked potato (trace)
In cooking:	**Try**
1 cup of oil	1 cup of applesauce
Whole eggs (6 g)	2 egg whites (trace)
When reaching for a snack:	**Try**
Candy bar	Fresh fruit
Ice cream bars (8–30 g)	Frozen fruit bars (0 fat)
Ice cream (11–18 g)	Sherbet, low-fat yogurt, or ice milk (2–4 g)
Doughnuts (14 g)	Bagels (2 g)
Devil's food cake	Angel food cake
High-fat cookies and crackers	Fat-free cookies and crackers
Fried corn and potato chips	Baked chips or pretzels

3. Choose liquid vegetable oils most often because they are lower in saturated fat.
4. Become a label reader to check how much fat and saturated fat are in a serving.
5. Choose lean meat, fish, poultry, and dried beans and peas as your low-fat protein sources.
6. Trim the fat from meat; remove the skin from poultry. (When cooking, the skin can be left on poultry without adding fat, provided it is removed before the chicken is eaten.)
7. Moderate the use of egg yolks and organ meats, both of which are high in cholesterol. While an egg contains about 185 mg of cholesterol, no fat or cholesterol is found in egg whites. Use them freely.
8. Choose skim milk or low-fat milk and fat-free or low-fat yogurt and cheese most of the time.

Carbohydrates

Carbohydrates are the body's preferred form of energy for sustaining daily activity. Many individuals believe that carbohydrates are the fattening nutrient, but they are not. Carbohydrates supply only four calories per gram, and many high-carbohydrate foods provide substantial amounts of other important nutrients, specifically vitamins and minerals, along with dietary fiber. Most high-carbohydrate foods, which include fruits, vegetables, and whole-grain products, are considered nutrient dense and should make up 45–65 percent of one's daily caloric intake. A nutrient-dense food is one that contains relatively high levels of nutrients packed into a relatively low number of calories. A good example of a specific nutrient-dense food is broccoli. One cup of the cooked vegetable provides only 46 calories and virtually no fat, yet contains 98 mg of vitamin C—the Dietary Reference Intake (DRI; explained below) is only 75–90 mg—almost half of the DRI for vitamin A, 20 percent of the DRI for calcium, 10 percent for iron, as well as additional B vitamins, potassium, magnesium, and other minerals. On the other hand, a non-nutrient-dense food is a typical candy bar, weighing in at 280 calories and 14 grams of fat, five grams of which are saturated. It is almost completely void of any valuable nutrients.

There is an important difference in types of carbohydrates. Carbohydrates fall into one of two categories: simple or complex. Simple carbohydrates consist of sugars, such as fructose, sucrose, dextrose, and others, and provide no significant nutritional value. Simple sugars are either monosaccharides (single sugars, like fructose and glucose) or linked combinations of monosaccharides called disaccharides (double sugars, like sucrose and lactose). Complex carbohydrates are polysaccharides, which are longer chains of saccharides, the most notable of which is starch. Starchy foods like potatoes, grains, and legumes are very important for good nutrition. They are low in fat and are cholesterol free, low in calories, high in fiber, and usually nutrient dense. Complex carbohydrates should make up the majority of the calories in our diet, while simple sugars should be held to a minimum. The body does not need the carbohydrate from added sugars (sugars and syrups added to foods during preparation or processing or added at the table). These added sugars have been shown to increase risks of cardiovascular disease and obesity (and therefore additional disease related to obesity). The American Heart Association (2018) recommends no more than six teaspoons (100 calories) per day of added sugar for women and no more than nine teaspoons (150 calories) per day for men. The average American consumes about 22 teaspoons per day (350 calories). The major source of added sugars in typical U.S. diets is beverages, which include soft drinks, fruit drinks, sweetened coffee and tea, energy drinks, alcoholic beverages, and flavored waters. Beverages account for almost half (47 percent) of all added sugars consumed by the U.S. population. The other major source of added sugars is snacks and sweets, which includes grain-based desserts such as cakes, pies, cookies, brownies, doughnuts, sweet rolls, and pastries; dairy desserts such as ice cream, other frozen desserts, and puddings; candies; sugars; jams; syrups; and sweet toppings. Together, these food categories make up more than 75 percent of intake of all added sugars (U.S. Department of Health and Human Services, 2015).

Mention must be made here of low-carb diets which remain popular. Many weight-loss efforts now approach the process through carbohydrate restriction. In weight-loss efforts, it is critical to remember that the total number of calories consumed is the essential dietary factor relevant to body weight. Diets composed of less than 45 percent of total calories as carbohydrate or more than 35 percent of total calories as protein are generally no more effective than other calorie-controlled diets for long-term weight loss and weight maintenance. Since carbohydrates should make up the majority of daily caloric intake, the emphasis on lowered carbohydrate intake has clearly been misguided. Excessive intake of any nutrient can make weight control very difficult, so carbohydrates, like all sources of calories, must be balanced with physical activity for maintenance of a healthy weight. Also, it is true that all carbohydrates are not the same. As explained above, most of the simple carbohydrates provide little nutritional value, so it is best to minimize them in the diet; but reducing the nutrient-dense, complex carbohydrates would deprive the body of its most valuable source of low-calorie, nutrient-rich foods.

Proteins

Proteins are the major building blocks in the human body and are major components of nearly every human cell. They play an important role in the development of antibodies, enzymes, blood, skin, bone, and muscle. Proteins also supply the body with energy in the absence of available carbohydrates and fats. Like carbohydrates, they provide four calories per gram. Proteins are made up of amino acids. There are 20 amino acids that the human body uses, 9 of which are called indispensable or essential, because the body cannot manufacture them. The other 11 are called dispensable or non-essential, because they can be manufactured in the liver. A high-quality protein, or complete protein, is one that contains all nine indispensable amino acids and comes primarily from animal sources. Plant-source protein usually does not contain all of the indispensable amino acids and is called incomplete protein. Incomplete protein, however, can be combined so that all needed amino acids are provided. This practice is the concept of complimentary proteins and is included in the discussion of vegetarianism later in this chapter. Proteins should make up 10–35 percent of total calories.

Vitamins

Vitamins are organic compounds needed by the body in small amounts. Although they do not provide calories, they do help transform food into energy. They also promote the growth and repair of tissue and assist in the utilization of minerals. Vitamins may be classified as fat-soluble or water-soluble. Fat-soluble vitamins A, D, E, and K are stored in the body's adipose (fat) tissue and can potentially reach toxic levels if very high doses are consumed over a period of time. Water-soluble vitamins B complex and C are excreted by the body, so they should be consumed on a daily basis. A guide to vitamin functions, sources and daily values is found in Table 6.4.

Folic acid (folate) is a B vitamin that is now widely recognized as an important nutrient for the prevention of a specific type of birth defect known as neural tube defects. Neural tube defects are conditions in which the baby's brain or spine does not form properly. The two most common of these defects are spina bifida and anencephaly, and they can result in serious disability or death. Spina bifida is the condition resulting in the incomplete closure of the spinal column. A sac of fluid comes through the babies back and part of the spinal cord in this sac is damaged. Potential problems associated with this birth defect are inability to move lower body parts, loss of bowel and bladder control, and learning disabilities. Anencephaly is the improper formation and absence of part of the brain and skull bones. Babies with this condition usually die before birth in a miscarriage or shortly after birth. About 3,000 pregnancies are affected by a neural tube defect each year in the United States, and the March of Dimes (2016) projects that up to 70 percent of these defects could be prevented through adequate folic acid intake by women starting before they become pregnant.

Clearly, adequate folic acid intake is important. The DRI for folate is 400 micrograms, and it is even higher during pregnancy and lactation. Many breakfast cereals are fortified with 100 percent of the needed daily value of folic acid, and several other foods

TABLE 6.4 Vitamins: Sources, Functions, and Daily Values

Vitamin	What It Does	Where Is It Found	Daily Value*
Biotin	■ Energy storage ■ Protein, carbohydrate, and fat metabolism	■ Avocados ■ Cauliflower ■ Eggs ■ Fruits (e.g., raspberries) ■ Liver ■ Pork ■ Salmon ■ Whole grains	300 mcg
Folate/Folic Acid *Important for pregnant women and women capable of becoming pregnant*	■ Prevention of birth defects ■ Protein metabolism ■ Red blood cell formation	■ Asparagus ■ Avocado ■ Beans and peas ■ Enriched grain products (e.g., bread, cereal, pasta, rice) ■ Green leafy vegetables (e.g., spinach) ■ Orange juice	400 mcg
Niacin	■ Cholesterol production ■ Conversion of food into energy ■ Digestion ■ Nervous system function	■ Beans ■ Beef ■ Enriched grain products (e.g., bread, cereal, pasta, rice) ■ Nuts ■ Pork ■ Poultry ■ Seafood ■ Whole grains	20 mg
Pantothenic Acid	■ Conversion of food into energy ■ Fat metabolism ■ Hormone production ■ Nervous system function ■ Red blood cell formation	■ Avocados ■ Beans and peas ■ Broccoli ■ Eggs ■ Milk ■ Mushrooms ■ Poultry ■ Seafood ■ Sweet potatoes ■ Whole grains ■ Yogurt	10 mg
Riboflavin	■ Conversion of food into energy ■ Growth and development ■ Red blood cell formation	■ Eggs ■ Enriched grain products (e.g., bread, cereal, pasta, rice) ■ Meats ■ Milk ■ Mushrooms ■ Poultry ■ Seafood (e.g., oysters) ■ Spinach	1.7 mg
Thiamin	■ Conversion of food into energy ■ Nervous system function	■ Beans and peas ■ Enriched grain products (e.g., bread, cereal, pasta, rice) ■ Nuts ■ Pork ■ Sunflower seeds ■ Whole grains	1.5 mg

Vitamin	What It Does	Where Is It Found	Daily Value*
Vitamin A	▪ Growth and development ▪ Immune function ▪ Reproduction Red blood cell formation ▪ Skin and bone formation ▪ Vision	▪ Cantaloupe ▪ Carrots ▪ Dairy products ▪ Eggs ▪ Fortified cereals ▪ Green leafy vegetables (e.g., spinach and broccoli) ▪ Pumpkin ▪ Red peppers ▪ Sweet potatoes	5,000 IU
Vitamin B$_6$	▪ Immune function ▪ Nervous system function ▪ Protein, carbohydrate, and fat metabolism ▪ Red blood cell formation	▪ Chickpeas ▪ Fruits (other than citrus) ▪ Potatoes ▪ Salmon ▪ Tuna	2 mg
Vitamin B$_{12}$	▪ Conversion of food into energy ▪ Nervous system function ▪ Red blood cell formation	▪ Dairy products ▪ Eggs ▪ Fortified cereals ▪ Meats ▪ Poultry ▪ Seafood (e.g., clams, trout, salmon, haddock, tuna)	6 mcg
Vitamin C	▪ Antioxidant ▪ Collagen and connective tissue formation ▪ Immune function ▪ Wound healing	▪ Broccoli ▪ Brussels sprouts ▪ Cantaloupe ▪ Citrus fruits and juices (e.g., oranges and grapefruit) ▪ Kiwifruit ▪ Peppers ▪ Strawberries ▪ Tomatoes and tomato juice	60 mg
Vitamin D *Nutrient of concern for most Americans*	▪ Blood pressure regulation ▪ Bone growth ▪ Calcium balance ▪ Hormone production ▪ Immune function ▪ Nervous system function	▪ Eggs ▪ Fish (e.g., herring, mackerel, salmon, trout, and tuna) ▪ Fish liver oil ▪ Fortified cereals ▪ Fortified dairy products ▪ Fortified margarine ▪ Fortified orange juice ▪ Fortified soy beverages (soymilk)	400 IU
Vitamin E	▪ Antioxidant ▪ Formation of blood vessels ▪ Immune function	▪ Fortified cereals and juices ▪ Green vegetables (e.g., spinach and broccoli) ▪ Nuts and seeds ▪ Peanuts and peanut butter ▪ Vegetable oils	30 IU
Vitamin K	▪ Blood clotting ▪ Strong bones	▪ Green vegetables (e.g., broccoli, kale, spinach, turnip greens, collards, Swiss chard, mustard greens)	80 mcg

* The Daily Values are the amounts of nutrients recommended per day for Americans 4 years of age or older. Source: http://www.fda.gov/nutritioneducation

* The Daily Values are the amounts of nutrients recommended per day for Americans 4 years of age or older.

TABLE 6.5 Foods High in
Folic Acid

- Leafy green vegetables, like spinach, broccoli, and Romaine lettuce
- Asparagus
- Beans, peas, and lentils
- Fruits like lemons, bananas, and melons
- Fortified and enriched products, like some breads, juices, and cereals
- Orange juice from concentrate and other citrus fruits
- Many breakfast cereals have 100 percent of the daily value for folic acid in each serving – Many food labels will identify folic acid content.

can provide folic acid as well. Women who are pregnant or may become pregnant may also wish to discuss taking a folic acid supplement with their health care provider. Foods high in folic acid are found in Table 6.5.

Vitamin C is a water-soluble vitamin, which must be consumed regularly for good health. It is needed for normal growth and development and is critical in the formation of collagen, a protein used to make tendons, ligaments, blood vessels, scar tissue, and skin. Vitamin C is important in wound healing and for the maintenance and repair of teeth, bones, and cartilage. It is also considered an antioxidant—compounds that are thought to block some of the damage caused by free radicals. Free radicals are by-products of the process of our body's transforming food into energy and may damage human cells (National Institutes of Health, 2011). The relationship between antioxidants and free radicals is discussed later in this chapter. When one is deficient in vitamin C, several health affects become evident, including inflammation and bleeding of the gums, dry scaly skin, impaired wound healing, nosebleeds, easy bruising, weakened tooth enamel, and decreased resistance to infection. Although it has been touted by many as a way to prevent the common cold, there is currently no conclusive data that show vitamin C to be effective in preventing the common cold. Since vitamin C cannot be manufactured or stored by the body, it must be regularly included in a healthy diet. Fortunately, vitamin C is relatively easy to attain. Fruits and vegetables contain vitamin C, and the readily available sources of citrus fruits and juices are quite popular in the American diet. Rich sources include broccoli, cantaloupe, tomatoes, strawberries, green and red peppers, leafy green vegetables, sweet and white potatoes, watermelon, brussels sprouts, cauliflower, cabbage, papaya, mango, pineapples, and several types of berries. Adults need 75–90 (75 for women; 90 for men; slightly higher for women during pregnancy and lactation) milligrams of vitamin C daily, and because smoking depletes vitamin C, smokers need an additional 35 milligrams each day. Women who are pregnant and lactating may need more vitamin C. However, very high doses (greater than 2,000 milligrams per day) can lead to gastrointestinal distress.

Minerals

Minerals are inorganic compounds that are also needed in small amounts. They serve primarily as structural elements, but also regulate a number of processes in the body such as muscle contraction, blood clotting, and protein synthesis to name a few. Some of the major minerals needed by the body include iron, calcium, phosphorus, potassium, magnesium, sodium, and chloride. A guide to the functions, sources, and daily values is found in Table 6.6.

One mineral that warrants special attention is iron. Iron is a part of many enzymes and is a vital part of blood protein, hemoglobin, and the muscle protein myoglobin, both of which carry oxygen. While men require more of most vitamins and minerals, iron is an exception. Adult women require considerably more daily iron than adult men (18 mg per day for women and 8 mg per day for men) primarily due to losses of iron during menstruation. During pregnancy, iron needs increase even more, and a supplement may be recommended by a health care provider. If adequate amounts of iron are not consumed, the individual is at risk of anemia. Anemia is a low level of blood hemoglobin usually caused by inadequate iron in the diet or by poor iron absorption. The low hemoglobin levels cause less oxygen to be delivered to body cells, resulting in lowered energy levels. The body's ability to absorb and use iron is affected by several factors, one of which is the type of iron consumed. Heme iron is found in animal sources and is efficiently absorbed by the body. Nonheme iron, on the other hand, is found in vegetable sources, and is less available. The iron content of several selected foods is found in Table 6.7.

TABLE 6.6 Selected Minerals: Sources, Functions, and Daily Values

Vitamin	What It Does	Where Is It Found	Daily Value*
Calcium *Nutrient of concern for most Americans*	▪ Blood clotting ▪ Bone and teeth formation ▪ Constriction and relaxation of blood vessels ▪ Hormone secretion ▪ Muscle contraction ▪ Nervous system function	▪ Almond, rice, coconut, and hemp milks ▪ Canned seafood with bones (e.g., salmon and sardines) ▪ Dairy products ▪ Fortified cereals and juices ▪ Fortified soy beverages (soymilk) ▪ Green vegetables (e.g., spinach, kale, broccoli, turnip greens) ▪ Tofu (made with calcium sulfate)	1,000 mg
Chloride	▪ Acid-base balance ▪ Conversion of food into energy ▪ Digestion ▪ Fluid balance ▪ Nervous system function	▪ Celery ▪ Lettuce ▪ Olives ▪ Rye ▪ Salt substitutes ▪ Seaweeds (e.g., dulse and kelp) ▪ Table salt and sea salt ▪ Tomatoes	3,400 mg
Chromium	▪ Insulin function ▪ Protein, carbohydrate, and fat metabolism	▪ Broccoli ▪ Fruits (e.g., apple and banana) ▪ Grape and orange juice ▪ Meats ▪ Spices (e.g., garlic and basil) ▪ Turkey ▪ Whole grains	120 mcg
Copper	▪ Antioxidant ▪ Bone formation ▪ Collagen and connective tissue formation ▪ Energy production ▪ Iron metabolism ▪ Nervous system function	▪ Chocolate and cocoa ▪ Crustaceans and shellfish ▪ Lentils ▪ Nuts and seeds ▪ Organ meats (e.g., liver) ▪ Whole grains	2 mg
Iodine	▪ Growth and development ▪ Metabolism ▪ Reproduction ▪ Thyroid hormone production	▪ Breads and cereals ▪ Dairy products ▪ Iodized salt ▪ Potatoes ▪ Seafood ▪ Seaweed ▪ Turkey	150 mcg
Iron *Nutrient of concern for young children, pregnant women, and women capable of becoming pregnant*	▪ Energy production ▪ Growth and development ▪ Immune function ▪ Red blood cell formation ▪ Reproduction ▪ Wound healing	▪ Beans and peas ▪ Dark green vegetables ▪ Meats ▪ Poultry ▪ Prunes and prune juice ▪ Raisins ▪ Seafood ▪ Whole grain, enriched, and fortified cereals and breads	18 mg

* The Daily Values are the amounts of nutrients recommended per day for Americans 4 years of age or older.

(Continued)

TABLE 6.6 (Continued)

Vitamin	What It Does	Where Is It Found	Daily Value*
Magnesium	▪ Blood pressure regulation ▪ Blood sugar regulation ▪ Bone formation ▪ Energy production ▪ Hormone secretion ▪ Immune function ▪ Muscle contraction ▪ Nervous system function ▪ Normal heart rhythm ▪ Protein formation	▪ Avocados ▪ Bananas ▪ Beans and peas ▪ Dairy products ▪ Green leafy vegetables (e.g., spinach) ▪ Nuts and pumpkin seeds ▪ Potatoes ▪ Raisins ▪ Wheat bran ▪ Whole grains	400 mg
Manganese	▪ Carbohydrate, protein, and cholesterol metabolism ▪ Cartilage and bone formation ▪ Wound healing	▪ Beans ▪ Nuts ▪ Pineapple ▪ Spinach ▪ Sweet potato ▪ Whole grains	2 mg
Molybdenum	▪ Enzyme production	▪ Beans and peas ▪ Nuts ▪ Whole grains	75 mcg
Phosphorus	▪ Acid-base balance ▪ Bone formation ▪ Energy production and storage ▪ Hormone activation	▪ Beans and peas ▪ Dairy products ▪ Meats ▪ Nuts and seeds ▪ Poultry ▪ Seafood ▪ Whole grain, enriched, and fortified cereals and breads	1,000 mg
Potassium *Nutrient of concern for most Americans*	▪ Blood pressure regulation ▪ Carbohydrate metabolism ▪ Fluid balance ▪ Growth and development ▪ Heart function ▪ Muscle contraction ▪ Nervous system function ▪ Protein formation	▪ Bananas ▪ Beet greens ▪ Juices (e.g., carrot, pomegranate, prune, orange, and tomato) ▪ Milk ▪ Oranges and orange juice ▪ Potatoes and sweet potatoes ▪ Prunes and prune juice ▪ Spinach ▪ Tomatoes and tomato products ▪ White beans ▪ Yogurt	3,500 mg
Selenium	▪ Antioxidant ▪ Immune function ▪ Reproduction Thyroid function	▪ Eggs ▪ Enriched pasta and rice ▪ Meats ▪ Nuts (e.g., Brazil nuts) and seeds ▪ Poultry ▪ Seafood ▪ Whole grains	70 mcg

* The Daily Values are the amounts of nutrients recommended per day for Americans 4 years of age or older.

Vitamin	What It Does	Where Is It Found	Daily Value*
Sodium *Nutrient to get less of*	■ Acid-base balance ■ Blood pressure regulation ■ Fluid balance ■ Muscle contraction ■ Nervous system function	Breads and rolls ■ Cheese (natural and processed) ■ Cold cuts and cured meats (e.g., deli or packaged ham or turkey) ■ Mixed meat dishes (e.g., beef stew, chili, and meat loaf) ■ Mixed pasta dishes (e.g., lasagna, pasta salad, and spaghetti with meat sauce) ■ Pizza ■ Poultry (fresh and processed) ■ Sandwiches (e.g., hamburgers, hot dogs, and submarine sandwiches) ■ Savory snacks (e.g., chips, crackers, popcorn, and pretzels) ■ Soups ■ Table salt	2,400 mg
Zinc	■ Growth and development ■ Immune function ■ Nervous system function ■ Protein formation ■ Reproduction ■ Taste and smell ■ Wound healing	■ Beans and peas ■ Beef ■ Dairy products ■ Fortified cereals ■ Nuts ■ Poultry ■ Seafood (e.g., clams, crabs, lobsters, oysters) ■ Whole grains	15 mg

* The Daily Values are the amounts of nutrients recommended per day for Americans 4 years of age or older.

TABLE 6.7   Selected Sources of Dietary Iron

1 cup cooked spinach	6.4 mg	1 baked potato	2.8 mg
1 cup cooked lima beans	5.9 mg	3.5 oz boiled shrimp	2.2 mg
3 oz fried liver	5.3 mg	3 oz ground beef patty	2.1 mg
1 cup cooked navy beans	5.1 mg	1 cup spaghetti	2.0 mg
4 oz hamburger patty	4.8 mg	1 cup cooked oatmeal	1.6 mg
1 cup canned kidney beans	4.6 mg	1/2 roasted chicken breast	.89 mg
1 cup cooked split peas	3.4 mg		
1 cup cooked black-eyed peas	3.3 mg	Many breakfast cereals are enriched with iron—check the label.	
1 cup cooked white rice	2.9 mg		

Another important mineral that deserves special attentions is calcium. Inadequate intake and poor absorption of calcium contribute to osteoporosis, or the loss of bone density. This condition, which is most prevalent in postmenopausal women, can result in bone fractures. Adequate calcium consumption, mainly from low-fat dairy products, is important beginning at an early age and continuing throughout the lifespan for the prevention of osteoporosis. Osteoporosis, including additional risk factors and guidelines for prevention, is discussed thoroughly in Chapter 8.

Getting Adequate Vitamins and Minerals—The DRIs

The Food and Nutrition Board of the National Academy of Sciences has, for several years, analyzed scientific data to determine just how much of the various vitamins and minerals are needed for good health. Previously, their recommendations were published in the form of the RDAs—Recommended Dietary Allowances—and provided the levels of vitamins and minerals needed to prevent deficiency. Their recommendations are now known as the Dietary Reference Intakes (DRIs) and recommend levels that are thought to decrease the risk of chronic, diet-related diseases (Institute of Medicine of the National Academies, 2014). While they are only estimates and are developed for healthy people, they provide an excellent guide for attainment of adequate intakes of necessary vitamins and minerals. The DRIs for several key nutrients are provided in Table 6.8.

Water

Sometimes considered the forgotten nutrient, water is essential for health. Once water enters the body, it mixes with other compounds, primarily minerals, to produce fluids critical to all life processes. These body fluids transport important nutrients and other substances to the cells, carry waste away from cells, and allow chemical reactions to take place in the body. They lubricate joints, absorb shock, and cushion the amniotic sac during pregnancy. Water also serves as a solvent for minerals, vitamins, amino acids, glucose, and other substances, regulates body temperature, and maintains blood volume. The average person consumes and excretes (through the kidneys, lungs, and skin) about two and a half liters of water each day. Heavy exercise or other activities leading to fluid loss call for additional water consumption. To assure proper balance and hydration it must be replaced. Many foods, specifically fruits and vegetables, have high water content and can help replace water loss. While information on the necessary amount of water consumption varies greatly (and is affected by overall health, activity level, environment, and whether you are pregnant or breastfeeding), it is recommended that about six to eight glasses (eight ounce) of water be consumed each day.

Fiber

Although not actually classified as a nutrient, fiber is nonetheless an important dietary element. Fiber is the indigestible part of plant foods and is sometimes referred to as roughage or bulk. Fiber attracts water and pushes other foods through the digestive track. There are two types of fiber: soluble and insoluble. Soluble fiber, so named because it dissolves or forms a gel in water, is thought to be helpful in lowering blood cholesterol levels. Soluble fiber is also valuable to the diabetic in that it can aid in the stabilization of blood glucose levels. Good sources include citrus fruits, oats, barley, kidney beans, and apples. Insoluble fiber, named because it does not dissolve in water, is found in numerous fruits, grains, and vegetables. It adds bulk to the intestinal contents and helps waste products move quickly through the digestive track. This is thought to reduce the risk of cancers of the digestive track as well as help prevent constipation, hemorrhoids, and diverticulosis. Diverticulosis is a condition in which a small pouch develops in the colon that bulges outward through a weak spot. About 10 percent of Americans above the age of 40 have diverticulosis. When the pouch becomes inflamed, the condition is called diverticulitis, which can lead to bleeding, infections, tears, or blockages and can result in serious illness if not properly treated. The 2015–2020 Dietary Guidelines recommend 25 grams of fiber a day for women and 38 grams a day for men. Fiber is a very underconsumed food component, as most Americans consume less than 15 grams a day. While including dietary fiber is important, care must be taken not to overdo it. Too much fiber can cause other valuable nutrients to be lost and can cause gastrointestinal

TABLE 6.8 Dietary Reference Intakes (DRIs): Recommended Dietary Allowances and Adequate Intakes, Vitamins

Food and Nutrition Board, Institute of Medicine, National Academies

Life Stage Group	Vitamin A (µg/d)[a]	Vitamin C (mg/d)	Vitamin D (mg/d)[b,c]	Vitamin E (mg/d)[d]	Vitamin K (µg/d)	Thiamin (mg/d)	Riboflavin (mg/d)	Niacin (mg/d)[e]	Vitamin B6 (mg/d)	Folate (µg/d)[f]	Vitamin B12 (µg/d)	Pantothenic Acid (mg/d)	Biotin (µg/d)	Choline (mg/d)[g]
Infants														
0 to 6 mo	400*	40*	10	4*	2.0*	0.2*	0.3*	2*	0.1*	65*	0.4*	1.7*	5*	125*
6 to 12 mo	500*	50*	10	5*	2.5*	0.3*	0.4*	4*	0.3*	80*	0.5*	1.8*	6*	150*
Children														
1–3 y	**300**	**15**	**15**	**6**	30*	**0.5**	**0.5**	**6**	**0.5**	**150**	**0.9**	2*	8*	200*
4–8 y	**400**	**25**	**15**	**7**	55*	**0.6**	**0.6**	**8**	**0.6**	**200**	**1.2**	3*	12*	250*
Males														
9–13 y	**600**	**45**	**15**	**11**	60*	**0.9**	**0.9**	**12**	**1.0**	**300**	**1.8**	4*	20*	375*
14–18 y	**900**	**75**	**15**	**15**	75*	**1.2**	**1.3**	**16**	**1.3**	**400**	**2.4**	5*	25*	550*
19–30 y	**900**	**90**	**15**	**15**	120*	**1.2**	**1.3**	**16**	**1.3**	**400**	**2.4**	5*	30*	550*
31–50 y	**900**	**90**	**15**	**15**	120*	**1.2**	**1.3**	**16**	**1.3**	**400**	**2.4**	5*	30*	550*
51–70 y	**900**	**90**	**15**	**15**	120*	**1.2**	**1.3**	**16**	**1.7**	**400**	**2.4**[h]	5*	30*	550*
>70 y	**900**	**90**	**20**	**15**	120*	**1.2**	**1.3**	**16**	**1.7**	**400**	**2.4**[h]	5*	30*	550*
Females														
9–13 y	**600**	**45**	**15**	**11**	60*	**0.9**	**0.9**	**12**	**1.0**	**300**	**1.8**	4*	20*	375*
14–18 y	**700**	**65**	**15**	**15**	75*	**1.0**	**1.0**	**14**	**1.2**	**400**[i]	**2.4**	5*	25*	400*
19–30 y	**700**	**75**	**15**	**15**	90*	**1.1**	**1.1**	**14**	**1.3**	**400**[i]	**2.4**	5*	30*	425*
31–50 y	**700**	**75**	**15**	**15**	90*	**1.1**	**1.1**	**14**	**1.3**	**400**[i]	**2.4**	5*	30*	425*
51–70 y	**700**	**75**	**15**	**15**	90*	**1.1**	**1.1**	**14**	**1.5**	**400**	**2.4**[h]	5*	30*	425*
>70 y	**700**	**75**	**20**	**15**	90*	**1.1**	**1.1**	**14**	**1.5**	**400**	**2.4**[h]	5*	30*	425*
Pregnancy														
14–18 y	**750**	**80**	**15**	**15**	75*	**1.4**	**1.4**	**18**	**1.9**	**600**[j]	**2.6**	6*	30*	450*
19–30 y	**770**	**85**	**15**	**15**	90*	**1.4**	**1.4**	**18**	**1.9**	**600**[j]	**2.6**	6*	30*	450*
31–50 y	**770**	**85**	**15**	**15**	90*	**1.4**	**1.4**	**18**	**1.9**	**600**[j]	**2.6**	6*	30*	450*
Lactation														
14–18 y	**1,200**	**115**	**15**	**19**	75*	**1.4**	**1.6**	**17**	**2.0**	**500**	**2.8**	7*	35*	550*
19–30 y	**1,300**	**120**	**15**	**19**	90*	**1.4**	**1.6**	**17**	**2.0**	**500**	**2.8**	7*	35*	550*
31–50 y	**1,300**	**120**	**15**	**19**	90*	**1.4**	**1.6**	**17**	**2.0**	**500**	**2.8**	7*	35*	550*

Note: This table (taken from the DRI reports, see www.nap.edu) presents Recommended Dietary Allowances (RDAs) in **bold type** and Adequate Intakes (AIs) in ordinary type followed by an asterisk (*). An RDA is the average daily dietary intake level; sufficient to meet the nutrient requirements of nearly all (97–98 percent) healthy individuals in a group. It is calculated from an Estimated Average Requirement (EAR). If sufficient scientific evidence is not available to establish an EAR, and thus calculate an RDA, an AI is usually developed. For healthy breastfed infants, an AI is the mean intake. The AI for other life stage and gender groups is believed to cover the needs of all healthy individuals in the groups, but lack of data or uncertainty in the data prevent being able to specify with confidence the percentage of individuals covered by this intake.

a As retinol activity equivalents (RAEs): 1 RAE = 1 μg retinol, 12 μg β-carotene, 24 μg α-carotene, or 24 μg β-cryptoxanthin. The RAE for dietary provitamin A carotenoids is two fold greater than retinol equivalents (RE), whereas the RAE for preformed vitamin A is the same as RE.

b As cholecalciferol: 1 μg cholecalciferol = 40 IU vitamin D.

c Under the assumption of minimal sunlight.

d As α-tocopherol includes *RRR*-α-tocopherol, the only form of α-tocopherol that occurs naturally in foods, and the *2R*-stereoisomeric forms of α-tocopherol (*SRR*-, *RSR*-, *RRS*-, and *RSS*-α-tocopherol) that occur in fortified foods and supplements. It does not include the *2S*-stereoisomeric forms of α-tocopherol (*SRR*-, *SSR*-, *SRS*-, and *SSS*-α-tocopherol), also found in fortified foods and supplements.

e As niacin equivalents (NE). 1 mg of niacin = 60 mg of tryptophan; 0–6 months = preformed niacin (not NE).

f As dietary folate equivalents (DFE). 1 DEF = 1 μg food folate = 0.6 μg of folic acid from fortified food or as a supplement consumed with food = 0.5 μg of a supplement taken on an empty stomach.

g Although AIs have been set for choline, there are few data to assess whether a dietary supply of choline is needed at all stages of the life cycle, and it may be that the choline requirement can be met by endogenous synthesis at some of these stages.

h Because 10 to 30 percent of older people may malabsorb food-bound B12, it is advisable for those older than 50 years to meet their RDA mainly by consuming foods fortified with B12 or a supplement containing B12.

i In view of evidence linking folate intake with neural tube defects in the fetus, it is recommended that all women capable of becoming pregnant consume 400 μg from supplements or fortified foods in addition to intake of food folate from a varied diet.

j It is assumed that women will continue consuming 400 μg from supplements or fortified food until their pregnancy is confirmed and they enter prenatal care, which ordinarily occurs after the end of the periconceptional period—the critical time for formation of the neural tube.

Sources: Dietary Reference Intakes for Calcium, Phosphorous, Magnesium, Vitamin D, and Fluoride (1997); *Dietary Reference Intakes for Thiamin, Riboflavin, Niacin, Vitamin B6, Folate, Vitamin B12, Pantothenic Acit, Biotin, and Choline* (1998); *Dietary Reference Intakes for Vitamin C, Vitamin E, Selenium, and Carotenoids* (2000); *Dietary Reference Intakes for Vitamin A, Vitamine K, Arsenic, Boron, Chromium, Copper, Iodine, Iron, Manganese, Molybdenum, Nickel, Silicon, Vanadium, and Zinc* (2001); *Dietary Reference Intakes for Water, Potassium, Sodium, Chloride, and Sulfate* (2005); and *Dietary Reference Intakes for Calcium and Vitamin D* (2011). These reports may be accessed via www.nap.edu.

Dietary Reference Intakes (DRIs): Recommended Dietary Allowances and Adequate Intakes, Elements
Food and Nutrition Board, Institute of Medicine, National Academies

Life Stage Group	Calcium (mg/d)	Chromium (µg/d)	Copper (µg/d)	Fluoride (mg/d)	Iodine (µg/d)	Iron (mg/d)	Magnesium (mg/d)	Manganese (mg/d)	Molybdenum (µg/d)	Phosphorus (mg/d)	Selenium (µg/d)	Zinc (mg/d)	Potassium (g/d)	Sodium (g/d)	Chloride (g/d)
Infants															
0 to 6 mo	200*	0.2*	200*	0.01*	110*	0.27*	30*	0.003*	2*	100*	15*	2*	0.4*	0.12*	0.18*
6 to 12 mo	260*	5.5*	220*	0.5*	130*	11	75*	0.6*	3*	275*	20*	3	0.7*	0.37*	0.57*
Children															
1–3 y	700	11*	340	0.7*	90	7	80	1.2*	17	460	20	3	3.0*	1.0*	1.5*
4–3 y	1,000	15*	440	1*	90	10	130	1.5*	22	500	30	5	3.8*	1.2*	1.9*
Males															
9–13 y	1,300	25*	700	2*	120	8	240	1.9*	34	1,250	40	8	4.5*	1.5*	2.3*
14–18 y	1,300	35*	890	3*	150	11	410	2.2*	43	1,250	55	11	4.7*	1.5*	2.3*
19–30 y	1,000	35*	900	4*	150	8	400	2.3*	45	700	55	11	4.7*	1.5*	2.3*
31–50 y	1,000	35*	900	4*	150	8	420	2.3*	45	700	55	11	4.7*	1.5*	2.3*
51–70 y	1,000	30*	900	4*	150	8	420	2.3*	45	700	55	11	4.7*	1.3*	2.0*
>70 y	1,200	30*	900	4*	150	8	420	2.3*	45	700	55	11	4.7*	1.2*	1.8*
Females															
9–13 y	1,300	21*	700	2*	120	8	240	1.6*	34	1,250	40	8	4.5*	1.5*	2.3*
14–18 y	1,300	24*	890	3*	150	15	360	1.6*	43	1,250	55	9	4.7*	1.5*	2.3*
19–30 y	1,000	25*	900	3*	150	18	310	1.8*	45	700	55	8	4.7*	1.5*	2.3*
31–50 y	1,000	25*	900	3*	150	18	320	1.8*	45	700	55	8	4.7*	1.5*	2.3*
51–70 y	1,200	20*	900	3*	150	8	320	1.8*	45	700	55	8	4.7*	1.3*	2.0*
>70 y	1,200	20*	900	3*	150	8	320	1.8*	45	700	55	8	4.7*	1.2*	1.8*
Pregnancy															
14–18 y	1,300	29*	1,000	3*	220	27	400	2.0*	50	1,250	60	12	4.7*	1.5*	2.3*
19–30 y	1,000	30*	1,000	3*	220	27	350	2.0*	50	700	60	11	4.7*	1.5*	2.3*
31–50 y	1,000	30*	1,000	3*	220	27	360	2.0*	50	700	60	11	4.7*	1.5*	2.3*
Lactation															
14–18 y	1,300	44*	1,300	3*	290	10	360	2.6*	50	1,250	70	13	5.1*	1.5*	2.3*
19–30 y	1,000	45*	1,300	3*	290	9	310	2.6*	50	700	70	12	5.1*	1.5*	2.3*
31–50 y	1,000	45*	1,300	3*	290	9	320	2.6*	50	760	70	12	5.1*	1.5*	2.3*

Note: This table (taken from the DRI reports, see www.nap.edu) presents Recommended Dietary Allowances (RDAs) in bold type and Adequate Intakes (AIs) in ordinary type followed by an asterisk (*). An RDA is the average daily dietary intake level; sufficient to meet the nutrient requirements of nearly all (97–98 percent) healthy individuals in a group. It is calculated from an Estimated Average Requirement (EAR). If sufficient scientific evidence is not available to establish an EAR, and thus calculate an RDA, an AI is usually developed. For healthy breastfed infants, an AI is the mean intake. The AI for other life stage and gender groups is believed to cover the needs of all healthy individuals in the groups, but lack of data or uncertainty in the data prevent being able to specify with confidence the percentage of individuals covered by this intake.

Sources: Dietary Reference Intakes for Calcium, Phosphorous, Magnesium, Vitamin D, and Fluoride (1997). Dietary Reference Intakes for Thiamin, Riboflavin, Niacin, Vitamin B6, Folate, Vitamin B12, Pantothenic Acid, Biotin, and Choline (1998); Dietary Reference Intakes for Vitamin C, Vitamin E, Selenium, and Carotenoids (2000); and Dietary Reference Intakes for Vitamin A, Vitamin K, Arsenic, Boren, Chromium, Copper, Iodine, Iron, Manganese, Molybdenum, Nickel, Silicon, Vanadium, and Zinc (2001): Dietary Reference Intakes for Water, Potassium, Sodium, Chloride, and Sulfate (2005); and Dietary Reference Intakes for Calcium and Vitamin D (2011). These reports may be accessed via www.nap.edu.

Reprinted with permission from *Dietary Reference Intakes for Calcium and Vitamin D, 2011 by Joyce L. Vedral, Institute of Medicine Staff.* Copyright © 2011 by the National Academy of Sciences, Courtesy of the National Academies Press, Washington, D.C.

upset, including constipation if water consumption is not increased. The fiber content of selected foods is shown in Table 6.9.

Antioxidants

One set of valuable nutrients are now widely recognized as having several beneficial qualities and are known as the antioxidants. These antioxidants include vitamins C and E, beta carotene, selenium, and carotenoids (found in green, yellow, and orange vegetables) and appear to promote health by repairing damage done by free radicals. Free radicals are by-products of cell oxidation, and their production is increased by cigarette smoke, excessive sun exposure, stress, certain drugs, and environmental factors. They damage cells and may cause genes to mutate and are linked to increased risk of arthritis, cancer, cardiovascular disease, and other disorders. Dietary antioxidants may reduce or prevent the formation of free radicals and may help remove them from the body. Antioxidants are supplied by a diet rich in fruits and vegetables.

VEGETARIANISM

An increasingly popular nutritional choice is vegetarianism. The Academy of Nutrition and Dietetics takes the position that "appropriately planned vegetarian diets, including total vegetarian or vegan diets, are healthful, nutritionally adequate, and may provide health benefits in the prevention and treatment of certain diseases. Well-planned vegetarian diets are appropriate for individuals during all stages of the lifecycle, including pregnancy, lactation, infancy, childhood, and adolescence, and for athletes." Individuals may choose to practice vegetarianism for a variety of reasons, including religious beliefs, personal ethical beliefs, and health concerns. Sound scientific studies show a positive relationship between vegetarianism and the reduced risk for diseases, including obesity, coronary artery disease, hypertension, diabetes mellitus, and some types of cancer (ADA, 2009). However, vegetarianism should not be labeled a good or bad eating style, as the overall diet must be considered. The diet must be "appropriately planned". Carelessness or lack of knowledge in the area of vegetarianism can lead to nutritional deficiencies.

One of the major concerns vegetarians must address is the inclusion of complementary proteins into their diet. Complete proteins (those containing all of the essential amino acids) are found primarily in animal products. However, certain incomplete proteins that contain some of the amino acids can be combined to create complete protein. Legumes, or beans and peas, are good to combine with grains as well as nuts and seeds to make complete protein. Examples of these combinations are beans with rice or peanut butter with whole-wheat bread. Vegetarians who consume a wide variety of plant foods and are careful about their combinations can fulfill their protein needs on this diet. Other nutrients, specifically vitamins D and B12, may also be difficult to attain through the vegetarian diet. Vegetarians must be diligent and knowledgeable to make this eating style work. It is recommended that anyone considering the practice of becoming a vegetarian consult with a registered dietitian (RD) before adopting this eating plan in order to discuss potential deficiencies and how to prevent them. A nutritional supplement may be recommended.

TABLE 6.9 Good Sources of Dietary Fiber

Fruits	Grams
1 medium apple	4–5
1 banana	3
1 cup blueberries	5
10 dates	7
1 orange	3
1 pear	5
1 cup strawberries	3
1 watermelon slice	2–3

Vegetables	Grams
1 artichoke	4
1 raw carrot	2
1/2 cup cream style corn	6
1 cup chopped lettuce	1
1/2 cup green peas	6
1 cup cooked spinach	6
1 cup cooked squash	5–6
1 tomato	2

Legumes	Grams
1 cup cooked black beans	15
1 cup cooked green beans	3
1 cup pork and beans	18
1 cup cooked black-eyed peas	11
1 cup kidney beans	20
1 cup cooked navy beans	16
1 cup cooked pinto beans	19

Grains	Grams
1 bagel	1
1 whole grain slice of bread	1–3
4 graham crackers	3
1 bran muffin	2
hot dog/hamburger bun	1
1 cup cooked oatmeal	7–9
1/2 cup Grape-Nuts cereal	3.5
1 cup Nature Valley granola	7.5
3/4 cup Shredded Wheat cereal	4
1 cup cooked macaroni	1
1 cup cooked rice	2.5–4
1 cup cooked spaghetti	1–2

Other	Grams
1 cup almonds	15
1 cup cashews	8
1 cup shredded coconut	11
1 tbsp peanut butter	1
1/4 cup sunflower seeds	2

NUTRITIONAL SUPPLEMENTS

Over half of Americans take vitamin supplements (Kantor et al, 2016). This indicates that many individuals are concerned that they are not meeting their bodies' nutritional needs through dietary measures. While there are varied opinions concerning the necessity of supplements, most nutrition scientists agree that the needed levels of nutrients are easily attainable through a balanced diet. Some individuals believe that if some nutrients are good, then more must be better, but there is no evidence that this is the case. In fact, individuals who insist on supplementing their nutrient intake should exercise caution, since there is a possibility of excessive intake of certain nutrients, especially the fat-soluble vitamins A, D, E, and K. While the water-soluble vitamins B and C are not stored in fat and any excesses are readily excreted, fat-soluble vitamins are stored in the fatty tissue of the body. Continued high intake of fat-soluble vitamins can lead to a dangerous accumulation of these substances, causing a condition known as vitamin toxicity or hyper-vitaminosis. Kidney and liver damage, as well as other health problems, can result from the consumption of these megadoses of vitamins and some minerals. High levels of some nutrients may also interfere with the absorption of other crucial nutrients. Therefore, any supplement that provides greater than 100 percent of the DRI for any vitamin or mineral is discouraged.

Furthermore, supplements may fall short in offering another valuable component to the diet. It is known that many foods contain compounds which provide specific health benefits. Substances known as phytochemicals, found in plants, especially fruits and vegetables, may help prevent cancer, diabetes, hypertension, and cardiovascular disease. These potentially valuable substances are not provided through typical supplementation, but are supplied by consuming a variety of foods from plants. Phytochemicals include compounds like allyl sulfides (garlic and onions), lycopene (tomatoes and peppers), carotenoids (carrots, cilantro, celery), flavonoids and gingerols (herbs and spices), silymarin (artichokes), and phenols and ellagic acid (grapes, berries, melons), just to name a few.

The "pill mentality" is another risk of supplementation. This refers to the mind-set that efforts to consume a good diet are unnecessary because nutritional needs can be met by taking a supplement. Clearly, a pill is no substitute for a balanced diet, and consuming a supplement does not correct the problems found in a high-fat, high-calorie diet.

While supplements are quite popular and are available over the counter, the decision to take them is one that should not be made lightly. A vitamin/mineral supplement may help when:

- You are eating less than 1,600 calories per day, or you are on a low-calorie weight-loss diet
- You are elderly and not eating as much as you should
- You are a strict vegetarian or vegan
- You are pregnant or a woman of child-bearing age
- You have a medical condition that limits your food choices.

A registered dietitian can help you evaluate your eating pattern and determine whether a vitamin/mineral supplement is right for you (ADA, 2011).

ALCOHOL CONSUMPTION

Alcohol is a source of calories, providing seven calories per gram, but no nutritional value. It contains empty calories and is an excellent place to cut calories in a weight-loss attempt, since calories can be eliminated without sacrificing nutrient intake. In addition, those who drink beyond moderation are at risk of alcohol-related problems, including malnutrition and undernutrition, since the drinker may rely on alcohol to provide calories and may neglect the consumption of nutrient-dense foods. While the direct link is unknown, evidence suggests that light drinking may bestow some health benefits, specifically heart disease risk reduction. Antioxidants and other compounds known as flavanoids (and a specific component called resveratrol) found in alcohol and red wine may have positive influences on cholesterol levels and clot formation. However, it is not recommended that one begin drinking in order to attain those benefits, and for responsible adults who do choose to consume alcohol, any alcohol consumption beyond moderation (no more than one drink per day for women and two drinks per day for men) should be avoided.

FAST FOODS AND EATING OUT

Whether eating out or buying carryout, Americans are consuming more and more of their calories from full-service and fast-food restaurant fare. In 2014, U.S. households, for the first time, spent over fifty percent of their total food dollars on food away from home. Almost three of four Americans eat out once a week, and 35 percent eat out two to three days a week or more (USDA, 2016). During 2007–2010, American adults consumed, on average, 11.3 percent of their total daily calories from fast food. For ages 20–39, that percentage is more than 15 (CDC, 2013). Fast-food establishments are the most frequent source of outside food. When meals are selected based primarily on speed and convenience, nutrition is likely to suffer. Most fast-food menu items are notoriously high in fat, saturated fat, calories, and sodium, and low in fiber and other valuable nutrients. However, eating fast food and maintaining a balanced diet need not be mutually exclusive. Most fast-food chains incorporate a few menu items for health-conscious customers. As indicated in Table 6.10, fast-food selections vary greatly in fat and calorie content. Most fast-food restaurants will provide information on the nutritional value of menu items on request, and most provide nutritional data on their websites. Try these suggestions from ChooseMyPlate (2016) for maintaining nutritional balance while eating away from home:

- As a beverage choice, ask for water or order fat-free or low-fat milk, unsweetened tea, or other drinks without added sugars.
- Ask for whole-wheat bread for sandwiches.
- In a restaurant, start your meal with a salad packed with veggies, to help control hunger and feel satisfied sooner.
- Ask for salad dressing to be served on the side. Then use only as much as you want.
- Choose main dishes that include vegetables, such as stir fries, kebobs, or pasta with a tomato sauce.
- Order steamed, grilled, or broiled dishes instead of those that are fried or sautéed.
- Choose a "small" or "medium" portion. This includes main dishes, side dishes, and beverages.
- Order an item from the menu instead heading for the "all-you-can-eat" buffet.
- If main portions at a restaurant are larger than you want, try one of these strategies to keep from overeating:
  - Order an appetizer-sized portion or a side dish instead of an entrée.
  - Share a main dish with a friend.
  - If you can chill the extra food right away, take leftovers home in a "doggy bag."
  - When your food is delivered, set aside or pack half of it to go immediately.
  - Resign from the "clean your plate club"—when you've eaten enough, leave the rest.
- To keep your meal moderate in calories, fat, and sugars:

TABLE 6.10 Making Healthier Fast-Food Selections (Compare the Fat and Calories)

Compare the Fat and Calories	Fat (grams)	Saturated Fat (grams)	Calories
Jack in the Box Ultimate Cheeseburger	49	21	820
Jack in the Box Chicken Fajita Pita	11	5	320
McAlister's McClub Sandwich	39	8	810
McAlister's Grilled Chicken Salad	24	11	490
Burger King Double Whopper with Cheese	64	24	980
Burger King Grilled Chicken Sandwich	19	4	470
Burger King Veggie Burger	15	2.5	390
McDonald's Big Breakfast/Hotcakes	65	25	1350
McDonald's Egg McMuffin	12	6	300
McDonald's 20 Piece Chicken Nugget	53	9	890
McDonald's Southwest Grilled Chicken Salad	11	4.5	350
Papa John's The Meats (1 large slice)	17	7	380
Papa John's Hawaiian Chicken (1 large slice)	6	2	260
Subway 6" Chicken & Bacon Ranch Melt	30	10	590
Subway 6" Black Forest Ham	4.5	1	290
Buffalo Wild Wings Boneless Wings (small) - Sweet BBQ Sauce	82	26	1370
Chicken Street Tacos	36	7	560

- Ask for salad dressing to be served "on the side" so you can add only as much as you want.
- Order foods that do not have creamy sauces or gravies.
- Add little or no butter to your food.
- Choose fruits for dessert most often.
- On long commutes or shopping trips, pack some fresh fruit, cut-up vegetables, low-fat string cheese sticks, or a handful of unsalted nuts to help you avoid stopping for sweet or fatty snacks.

When eating out at traditional-style restaurants, consider these tips:

- Ask your server about low-fat entrées and low-calorie options on their menu. Inquire about the method of preparation—just because it sounds healthy does not make it healthy.
- If there are terms on the menu that you don't recognize, ask what they mean. Hints to high-fat selections include parmigiana, hollandaise, carbonara, bernaise, batter-dipped, au gratin, Alfredo, and tempura.
- Ask your server if certain items can be served in a healthier manner. Can skim products be substituted for whole dairy products? Can products with lots of butter be served with lower fat dips or sauces? Ask for sauces, dressing, and gravies on the side.
- Order a sure-fire nutrient-dense side dish with your entrée, such as steamed rice or lightly stir-fried vegetables.
- Ask if "heart-healthy" indicators are available to help you make healthier choices.
- Share an entrée with a friend. With today's portion sizes, you can still fill up and save money too.
- Don't feel compelled to clean your plate. If you do order too much, take a container to-go.
- Eat slowly. Fast eaters tend to eat more.

READING FOOD LABELS

One of the most valuable sources of nutrition information can be found on the food label, and fortunately for consumers, understanding that information is easier than ever. As shown in Box 6.1, these food labels are presented in an easy-to-read and straightforward format. Some of the most valuable information includes the number of calories per serving and the number of calories that come from fat. This can be of assistance in following the dietary guidelines and in keeping fat consumption at 20–35 percent of calories consumed. The indication of the amount of saturated fat, trans-fats, and cholesterol can be quite helpful, and the amount of vitamins and minerals provided per serving can assist in the selection of more nutrient-dense foods. The amount of fiber provided can also be valuable in the effort to consume the recommended 25–38 grams per day.

HEALTHY SNACKING

Most people eat between meals, and most traditional snack foods are high calorie, non–nutrient dense, and draw a high percentage of their calories from fat. A typical candy bar, used in an earlier example, contains about 250–300 calories, with approximately 40–50 percent of those calories coming from fat. However, snacks can actually help you work toward good nutrition. By choosing nutrient-rich foods from the ChooseMyPlate food groups, snacks can boost your energy between meals and supply essential vitamins and minerals. Through careful selection and rare indulgence into the traditional high-fat snack treats, snacking can be healthy. Some suggestions for healthy snacking include:

- **Consider snacks as miniature meals.** Consume meal-like snacks such as fruit, raw vegetables, bagels or yogurt, instead of traditional snack foods.
- **Designate a snack spot in the pantry and the refrigerator**. Intentional stock with nutrient-dense foods.
- **Compensate for traditional snack foods**. When high-fat, high-calorie snacks are chosen, work in some additional exercise and keep the fat content of that day's meals to a minimum.
- **Avoid overeating in a hurry**. It is easy to reach for a snack and consume several portions or servings without giving it any thought. Think about what and how much you are eating, and consume the snack slowly.
- **Have an occasional treat**. Don't feel like you must give up your favorite snack foods forever. Eating a traditional snack food is acceptable if it is occasional and moderate.

NUTRITION FOR THE HIGHLY ACTIVE PERSON

Many people mistakenly believe that if they are highly active, their nutritional needs cannot be met through diet alone. Sports supplements have become a multibillion-dollar industry on the basis of this misconception. In fact, active individuals can easily meet all of their body's needs by consuming a healthy diet. As energy expenditure increases, energy needs also increase, so the athletic individual commonly consumes a greater number of calories for fuel than the less-active person. The percentage of nutrients in the total diet, however, should remain the same, with carbohydrates comprising about 45–65 percent of total calories. Fat should still be kept to about 20–35 percent of the total calories, with protein remaining at 10–35 percent of calories. Many individuals in training are concerned that they are not getting enough protein from their diet. However, while protein requirements are higher for athletes, they are not high enough to require protein supplements, since the increase in total caloric consumption more than compensates for any additional needs. The recommended daily protein intake is 0.8 gram per kilogram of body weight. This recommendation includes a margin of safety high enough to cover almost all

BOX 6.1

Six Steps to Label Reading

The Nutrition Facts label is for a particular brand of macaroni and cheese. It would normally appear on the back of the package. The numbers and percentages on it are significant. They tell you whether this brand of macaroni and cheese is a good food choice for you as part of your overall diet on any given day.

1. Serving Size 1 cup (228g)
Line 1 tells you the size of one serving. Compare it immediately to line 2, which tells you how many servings of that size are in the package or container.

The other numbers on the label – lines 4 through 18 – refer to one serving only. If you actually eat 2 or 3 servings at one time, you should multiply each of those numbers by 2 or 3.

In our example, one serving of macaroni and cheese equals one cup. There are, however, two servings in this package. If you eat the contents of the whole package at one meal, you should multiply each of the numbers between lines 4 and 18 by 2 to get an accurate picture of what you are consuming.

4. Calories 250   Calories from Fat 110
19. Calories   2,000   2,500
Line 4 tells you how many calories are in one serving of the labeled food. The point of comparison, 2,000 calories per day, is found in line 19.

Line 4 of the macaroni and cheese label indicates 250 calories in one serving. That is a little more than 1/10 of a total daily intake of 2,000 calories. One serving leaves room on the plate for some other items. Two servings plus other items may push the meal beyond an appropriate number of calories for one of your day's three meals plus snacks.

Note: The 2,000-calorie diet relates to an average-size, *active* person. At line 19, the label also offers information on a 2,500 calorie per day diet for a larger, active person. In fact, your calorie intake may be higher or lower than either of these scales. If so, you may want to make mental adjustments when considering the numbers on each line.

> **The limits and goals cited in this brochure relate to a diet of 2,000 calories per day. The limits and goals may be higher for a 2,500 diet.**

Calories 250   Calories from Fat 110
Line 4 lists calories that come from fat rather than from carbohydrate or protein. This number can be compared with the total number of calories in one serving, which is listed on the same line.

For example, line 4 of our macaroni and cheese label indicates that one serving contains 110 calories from fat and a total of 250 calories. That means that almost half (44 percent) of the calories in this item are from fat.

Nutritionists recommend that less than 30 percent of daily intake of calories come from fat. That does not mean that every item eaten during the day should have less than 30 percent of calories from fat. But if you choose to eat even one serving of this brand of macaroni and cheese, it would be a good idea to choose items lower in fat to accompany it and for other meals.

6. Total Fat 12g   18%
20. Total Fat   Less than   65g
Line 6 refers to the sum of different fats included in one serving of the labeled item. Total fat can be compared first with the recommended limit for a day's consumption of fat in line 20.

For example, line 20 of the macaroni and cheese label tells us that the recommended limit for total fat consumption is less than 65 grams. Line 6 indicates that there are 12 grams of fat in one serving. So the total fat in this possible food choice is just under 1/5 of the daily total. In fact, the label tells us the actual percentage is 18 percent.

When examining percentages on the Nutrition Facts label, 20 percent is considered high and 5 percent, low. There may be a packaged macaroni and cheese or another packaged food choice that has a lower percentage of fat. You can compare that 18 percent with the corresponding figure for total fat for the same serving size on other labels.

7. Saturated Fat 3g   15%
21. Sat Fat   Less than   20g
Saturated fat helps raise your cholesterol level. Line 7 tells you how much of this fat is in one serving of a labeled item. Compare that figure with the limit listed in line 21.

For example, line 21 on the macaroni and cheese label indicates less than 20 grams is the recommended daily limit for saturated fat. One serving contains 3 grams, which isn't terrible but is not good either. Remember, 20 percent is considered high and 5 percent, low. The label gives you the exact percentage, which is 15 percent.

Always look for the product with the lowest level of saturated fat. You can compare the 3 grams or 15 percent with the corresponding figures for saturated fat on other labels.

Note: Trans-fat also helps to raise cholesterol levels. So the harmful effect of

The AICR Guide to the Nutrition Facts Label

Nutrition Facts		
Serving Size 1 cup (228g)		
Servings Per Container 2		
Amount Per Serving		
Calories 250	Calories from Fat 110	
		% Daily Value*
Total Fat 12g		**18%**
Saturated Fat 3g		15%
Trans Fat 1.5g		
Cholesterol 30mg		**10%**
Sodium 470mg		**20%**
Total Carbohydrate 31g		**10%**
Dietary Fiber 0g		0%
Sugars 5g		
Protein 5g		
Vitamin A		**4%**
Vitamin C		**2%**
Calcium		**20%**
Iron		**4%**

* Percent Daily Values are based on a 2,000 calorie diet. Your Daily Values may be higher or lower depending on your calorie needs:

	Calories	2,000	2,500
Total Fat	Less than	65g	80g
Sat Fat	Less than	20g	25g
Cholesterol	Less than	300mg	300mg
Sodium	Less than	2,400mg	2,400mg
Total Carbohydrate		300g	375g
Dietary Fiber		25g	30g

saturated fat is compounded by the presence of trans-fat in the same product.

8. *Trans* Fat   1.5g
Beginning in 2006, food manufacturers are required to offer information on trans-fat on the Nutrition Facts label. The only fact required is the number of grams present in a single serving.

No limit has been set for trans-fat, so there is no point of comparison on the label. However, trans-fat acts like saturated fat. It raises your bad cholesterol level. You can therefore add the number of grams of trans-fat to the number of grams of saturated fat. Then compare the total to the limit for saturated fat in line 21.

For example, add the 1.5 grams transfat on our macaroni and cheese label to the 3 grams of saturated fat. The total is 4.5 grams or roughly 1/5 or 20 percent of the recommended limit of less than 20 grams of saturated fat.

The presence of 1.5 grams of trans-fat in this food item raises the level of undesirable fat to a high level.

9. Cholesterol 30mg   10%
22. Cholesterol   Less than   300mg
Line 9 tells you how much cholesterol there is in a labeled item. Compare this number to the recommended limit for cholesterol in line 22.

In our example, the label indicates 30 milligrams of cholesterol in this macaroni and cheese. The recommended limit

Reprinted from the American Institute for Cancer Research, www.aicr.org.

for cholesterol is less than 300 milligrams. That means this product has 1/10 of the daily limit. In fact, the label gives you the 10 percent figure.

Now compare that 30 milligrams with the amount of cholesterol in the same serving size of similar products. Try to find one that has less cholesterol per serving.

Nutritionists advise us to choose foods that keep consumption of saturated fat, trans-fat, and cholesterol as low as possible.

10. Sodium 470mg   **20%**
23. Sodium   **Less than**   **2,400mg**

Line 10 indicates how much sodium there is in a single serving of a labeled product. Compare that number with the recommended limit in line 23.

The macaroni and cheese label indicates the presence of 470 milligrams in one serving. The limit listed in line 23 is less than 2,400 milligrams per day. So one serving contains roughly 1/5 or 20 percent of the daily limit. Remember, 5 percent is considered low and 20 percent is considered high.

Now make the second comparison. Look at the label on a similar product to find out if the amount of sodium for the same serving size is lower.

Note: The Institute of Medicine recently lowered the recommended limit on sodium to 2,300 milligrams. Some people may be advised to consume substantially less (as low as 1,500 mg) for blood pressure control.

11. Total Carbohydrate 31g   **10%**
24. Total Carbohydrate   **300g**

Line 11 includes all added and natural carbohydrates in a single serving of the labeled item. This figure can be compared with the recommended daily total for carbohydrate in line 24.

The figure in line 24 is 300 grams. Note that the phrase "less than" does not appear. This is a recommended total to achieve. Carbohydrates will make up the bulk of your diet if you eat mostly vegetables, fruit, whole grains, and beans. They should make up 45–65 percent of your 2,000 calories, leaving less room for fat.

Compare the amount of carbohydrate in the macaroni and cheese label (31 grams) with the total recommended in line 24 (300 grams). That's 1/10 or 10 percent. Since you are trying to achieve the limit, that 10 percent is only a middling score.

Note: Diabetic patients should consult with a registered dietitian or their physician to determine an appropriate carbohydrate intake.

12. Dietary Fiber 0g   **0%**
25. Dietary Fiber   **25g**

Line 12 tells you the amount of dietary fiber in one serving of the labeled item. Compare that figure with the recommended

amount listed in line 25. Note that the phrase "less than" does not precede this recommendation. That means that 25 grams is a goal to achieve.

Line 12 on the macaroni and cheese label indicates there is 0 fiber in one serving. This food choice won't help you reach that 25 grams a day for good health.

You could add a variety of fiber-rich vegetables and whole grains to your plate. Or compare that 0 grams to the figure for dietary fiber on other food labels to find another choice with more fiber for your meal.

13. Sugars 5g

There is no recommended limit (or goal) for sugar consumption offered on the Nutrition Facts label. To get an idea of how much sugar a serving of this product contains, you have to look beyond the information offered on the label.

For example, in line 13 our macaroni and cheese label indicates 5 grams of sugar in a single serving. There are 4 grams of sugar in a teaspoon. So this item is fairly low in sugar—barely more than a single teaspoon. Furthermore, much of it is probably naturally occurring sugar.

On the other hand, many soft drinks contain as many as 32 grams of sugar, which equals 8 teaspoons of sugar added to the product.

Another way of assessing the sugar level in a serving of the same product is to examine the list of ingredients, which is usually found beneath the Nutrition Fact label. If terms like sugar, honey, corn syrup, fructose, maltose, or dextrose are listed, sugar has been *added* to the product. If any or several of those terms appear near the top of the list, a lot of sugar has been added.

Added sugar adds calories without any nutritional value. Nutritionists advise us to keep our consumption of *added sugar* as low as possible.

14. Protein 5g

Line 14 lists the amount of protein in a labeled item. As with sugar, the label offers no figure with which to compare this number. Protein is high in meats, dairy and available in many vegetables. Most Americans get more than enough.

In the macaroni and cheese label, line 14 shows 5 grams of protein. That's not a lot. But most people eating a typical American diet would make up the difference during the course of three meals.

Note: People who have recently chosen a vegetarian diet may need to refer to this line. They should try to consume 50 grams of protein per day. One serving of this packaged macaroni and cheese would provide only 5 grams of 1/10 of the recommended total.

15. Vitamin A	**4%**
16. Vitamin C	**2%**
17. Calcium	**20%**
18. Iron	**4%**

Lines 15 through 18 list some of the vitamins and minerals that may be present in a labeled food. Manufacturers are required to list vitamins A and C and the minerals calcium and iron. Others may be listed if a food is fortified with them, a claim is made about them, or the manufacturer chooses to do so.

In this part of the label, the information that allows a significant comparison is lacking, but the comparison has been made for you. For example, in line 15 of our macaroni and cheese label, the amount of vitamin A is described as 4 percent. That means one serving contains 4 percent of the amount recommended for daily intake by the Food and Nutrition Board.

Lines 15 through 18 tell us that one serving of this macaroni and cheese is not a good source of vitamin A, vitamin C, or iron. But it does provide 1/5 of the amount of calcium recommended for dairy intake.

Note: It's always more complicated than you think. The percentages in lines 15–18 do allow you to compare the level of vitamins or minerals in different products. But they do not represent an accurate percentage of the recommended amount for daily consumption. They don't reflect nutrition recommendations developed since 1968—recommendations that are based on more recent research.

Conclusion

By comparing numbers on the Nutrition Facts label, you should be able to decide if the labeled food item is a good choice for you.

In our example, the label discloses that this macaroni and cheese has a high percentage of calories from fat and is high in the combination of saturated fat and trans-fat that can raise your bad cholesterol level. It is also high in sodium.

On the other hand, it is low in important vitamins and contains no fiber at all.

In other words, it is high where it should be low and low where it should be high. Its only virtue is the presence of 20 percent of the calcium recommended for daily intake.

Does this assessment mean that you should never eat this brand of macaroni and cheese? Your first option is to choose another product. But if you do choose this item, AICR recommends limiting yourself to single serving and balancing it with vegetables, fruits or beans, as well as choosing lower fat dishes during the rest of the day for lower cancer risk.

individuals. Athletes, however, need 1.2–1.7 grams of protein per kilogram of body weight per day (Academy of Nutrition and Dietetics, 2012; Stoler, 2013). Even these levels are easily met through the increase in caloric consumption needed to meet a highly active person's energy needs (Neiman, 2011). Consuming protein above these levels will not build muscle faster—in fact, it may contribute to body fat. Personal Growth Opportunity 6.1 is provided to help you determine your daily protein needs. A review of the protein content of selected foods in Table 6.11 demonstrates the ease with which these levels can be attained.

The active individual does have additional fluid needs. However, the belief that these needs cannot be met with water, and that a special fluid replacement drink is needed, is erroneous. Proper hydration is important, but an increase in water consumption can assure adequate hydration.

YOUR PLAN OF ACTION

Now that you are more aware of the necessary steps for good nutrition, how will you incorporate them into your personal dietary practices? You might find the following suggestions valuable in your quest:

1. **Compare your diet to ChooseMyPlate**—By recording everything you eat over a two-day period, you can identify strengths and weaknesses in your diet and create targets for change. Calculate the number of servings you consume from each food

TABLE 6.11   Protein Content of Selected Foods

Food	Size		Protein
Whole Milk	1 cup	=	8 g
Skim Milk	1 cup	=	10 g
1 Egg		=	6 g
Cheese	1 ounce	=	6–10 g
Ice Cream	1 cup	=	5 g
Yogurt	8 oz	=	12 g
Fish	3 oz	=	17–24 g (Tuna = 24 g)
Beef	3 oz	=	20–24 g
Pork	3 oz	=	20 g
Poultry	3 oz	=	20–25 g
Rice (cooked)	1 cup	=	4 g
Macaroni & Cheese	1 cup	=	17 g
Spaghetti/Meatballs	1 cup	=	19 g
Nuts	1 cup	=	20–35 g
Dry Beans/Peas (cooked)	1 cup	=	15–20 g
Peanut Butter	1 tbsp	=	4 g
Double Whopper w/cheese		=	51 g (61 g fat)
One slice of Pizza		=	15–20 g
Big Mac		=	25 g
Wendy Big Classic w/cheese		=	30 g
Ultimate Cheeseburger		=	47 g (69 g fat)
Fajita Pita		=	24 g (8 g fat)

group, and compare this information to the recommendations in ChooseMyPlate. You can also conduct a more detailed diet analysis at the ChooseMyPlate.gov website. If you find that your servings are too low in some groups or too high in others, commit to make those changes today.

2. **Set some goals**—Do not try to perform a total overhaul of your diet right away. From the assessment of your diet, identify two changes that could lead to more nutrient-dense food consumption. Then set goals to consume more, or less, of those food items that you identified for change. By maintaining awareness of these two changes, you are more likely to make wiser choices.

3. **Be aware of settings that create challenge**—If you typically go for a box of cookies as soon as you get home from class or work, or like to stop at a particular vending machine frequently, these are habits that could be targeted for change. Make it a point to avoid the vending machine by walking a different route so that you do not have to pass by it. Stop by the supermarket to purchase some fresh fruit on the way home so the cookies are not so tempting.

4. **Become a label reader**—Become familiar with what your favorite foods have to offer, or do not offer. Determine if certain foods make notably higher contributions to your fat intake than others, then take steps to reduce those foods in your diet. Conversely, you can identify nutrient-dense foods through label reading and try to consume those foods more often.

5. **When eating out, share an entrée**—Since ordering out usually makes it a bit more difficult to eat within the goals and guidelines, and since portion sizes at many restaurants have gotten bigger, sharing an entrée and ordering an extra dinner salad may help you stick with your plans for dietary changes. You may be surprised how much money it can save you too.

6. **Be a smart shopper**—Many food choices would be much easier if more preparation was made while shopping for foods in the supermarket. By going shopping with a specific goal of purchasing nutritious foods, you will find that you are setting yourself up for success when you get home. Purchasing fresh fruits, vegetables, and other nutrient-dense items instead of cookies, snacks, and ice creams will provide more healthful selections when mealtime rolls around. When selecting snack foods, be sure to select healthy snacks. And the old suggestion you have probably heard can actually be very helpful: "Do not go shopping while you are hungry." You may come home with a basket full of foods that do not fit with your healthy diet.

References

American Academy of Nutrition and Dietetics (2017). Make it Mediterranean. Retrieved from: https://www.eatright.org/food/planning-and-prep/cooking-tips-and-trends/make-it-mediterranean

American Dietetic Association. (n.d.-a). *Dietary supplements*. Retrieved from http://www.eatright.org/Public/content.aspx?id=7918&terms=vitamin+supplement

American Dietetic Association. (n.d.-b). *To supplement or not to supplement*. Retrieved from http://www.eatright.org/Public/content.aspx?id=4294967946&terms=vitamin+supplement

American Heart Association (2018). *Added sugars*. Retrieved from: http://www.heart.org/HEARTORG/HealthyLiving/HealthyEating/HealthyDietGoals/Fish-and-Omega-3-Fatty-Acids_UCM_303248_Article.jsp#.WsI2AOSWyUk

American Heart Association (2015). Added sugars add to you risk of dying from heart disease. Retrieved from: http://www.heart.org/HEARTORG/HealthyLiving/HealthyEating/Nutrition/Added-Sugars-Add-to-Your-Risk-of-Dying-from-Heart-Disease_UCM_460319_Article.jsp#.Wo20fuSWyUk

American Heart Association (2018). Fish and Omega 3 Fatty Acids. Retrieved from: http://www.heart.org/HEARTORG/HealthyLiving/HealthyEating/HealthyDietGoals/Fish-and-Omega-3-Fatty-Acids_UCM_303248_Article.jsp#.WsI2AOSWyUk

Coulston, A. M., & Boushey, C. J. (2008). *Nutrition in the prevention and treatment of disease* (2nd ed.). New York, NY: Elsevier.

Craig, W. J., & Mangels, A. R. (2009). The ADA position paper on vegetarian diets. *Journal of the American Dietetic Association, 109*(7), 1266–1282.

Institute of Medicine of the National Academies. (2014). *Dietary Reference Intakes (DRIs): Recommended dietary allowances and adequate intakes.* Retrieved from http://www.iom.edu/Activities/Nutrition/SummaryDRIs/~/media/Files/Activity%20Files/Nutrition/DRIs/RDA%20and%20AIs_Vitamin%20and%20Elements.pdf

Johnson RK, Appel LJ, Brands M, et al. Dietary sugars intake and cardiovascular health: a scientific statement from the American Heart Association. Circulation. 2009;120:1011–20.

Kantor, E.D., Rehm, C.D., Mengmeng, D., White, E., and Giovannucci, L. (2016). Trends in dietary supplement use among US adults from 1999–2012. Journal of the American Medical Association. (14) 316. Doi: 10.1001/jama.2016.14403

March of Dimes. (2013). *Birth defects: Spina bifida.* Retrieved from http://www.marchofdimes.com/baby/birthdefects_spinabifida.html

March of Dimes (2016). Neural Tube Defects. Retrieved from: https://www.marchofdimes.org/baby/neural-tube-defects.aspx

National Institutes of Health. (2006). *Your guide to lowering your blood pressure with DASH.* Retrieved from http://www.nhlbi.nih.gov/health/public/heart/hbp/dash/new_dash.pdf

National Institute of Health. (2013). *Diverticulosis and diverticulitis.* Retrieved from www.digestive.niddk.nih.gov/ddiseases/pubs/diverticulosis

National Institutes of Health. (2014a). *Antioxidants.* Retrieved from http://www.nlm.nih.gov/medlineplus/antioxidants.html

National Institutes of Health. (2014b). *Iron in diet.* Retrieved from http://www.nlm.nih.gov/medlineplus/ency/article/002422.htm

National Institutes of Health. (2014c). *Vitamin C.* Retrieved from http://www.nlm.nih.gov/medlineplus/ency/article/002404.htm

Rosenbloom, C. A. (Ed.). (2012). *Sports nutrition: A practice manual for professionals.* Chicago, IL: Academy of Nutrition and Dietetics.

Stoler, F. D. (2013). *Sports nutrition unplugged.* American Academy of Sports Medicine. Retrieved from http://www.acsm.org/access-public-information/acsm%27s-sports-performance-center/sports-nutrition-un-plugged

Thompson, J. and Manore, M. (2018). *Nutrition: An applied approach, 5th edition.* San Francisco: Benjamin Cummings.

U.S. Department of Agriculture. *ChooseMyPlate* (2018). Retrieved from: https://www.choosemyplate.gov/

U.S. Department of Agriculture. (2013). *Tips for eating healthy when eating out.* Retrieved from http://www.choosemyplate.gov/healthy-eating-tips/tips-for-eating-out.html

U.S. Department of Agriculture. (2014). ChooseMyPlate. Retrieved from www.ChooseMyPlate.gov

U.S. Department of Agriculture. (n.d.). *Let's eat out: Americans weight taste, convenience, and nutrition.* Retrieved from http://www.ers.usda.gov/publications/eib19/eib19.pdf

United Stated Department of Agriculture (2016). Food Expenditures. Retrieved from: https://www.ers.usda.gov/data-products/food-expenditures/food-expenditures/#Food Expenditures

U.S. Department of Health and Human Services and U.S. Department of Agriculture. *2015–2020 Dietary Guidelines for Americans.* 8th Edition. December 2015. Available at https://health.gov/dietaryguidelines/2015/guidelines/.

U.S. Department of Health and Human Services & U.S. Department of Agriculture. (2010, December). *Dietary Guidelines for Americans, 2010* (7th ed.). Washington, DC: U.S. Government Printing Office.

CHAPTER 6

PERSONAL GROWTH OPPORTUNITY 1

Protein Worksheet: Calculating Your Daily Protein Needs

The Recommended Dietary Allowance for protein is 0.8 grams of protein per kilogram of body weight per day. You can calculate your specific protein needs by using the worksheet:

1. Convert your body weight in pounds to kilograms. Since one kilogram equals 2.2 pounds, the equation is:

   Body weight in pounds ÷ 2.2 = body weight in kilograms.

   If John weighs 175 pounds, his weight in kilograms would be:

   175 ÷ 2.2 = 79.5 (or 80) kilograms.

   Body weight in pounds _____ ÷ 2.2 = _____ body weight in kilograms

2. Multiply your weight in kilograms by 0.8. John's protein needs would be:

   80 × 0.8 = 64 grams of protein per day.

   Body weight in kilograms _____ × 0.8 = _____ grams of protein needed each day.

   Sixty-four grams of protein supply 256 calories. If John is consuming approximately 15 percent (10–35 percent is the recommendation) of his calories from protein, he is consuming plenty of protein—nearly 80 grams—in only 2,100 calories per day.

3. If John is a highly active individual who believes he requires more than the recommended 0.8 grams per kilogram per day, he may choose to base his protein needs on 1.2 grams (or up to 1.7 grams) per kilogram per day:

   80 × 1.2 = 96 grams of protein per day.

   Body weight in kilograms _____ × 1.2 = _____ grams of protein possibly needed for a strength or endurance athlete in heavy training.

   These 96 grams of protein now provide 384 calories. If protein now comprises about 15 percent of his total calories, this would result in a daily caloric consumption of about 2,560 calories per day. If he is indeed a strength or endurance athlete in heavy training, his additional energy expenditure will likely require more than 2,560 calories, so again, protein needs are easily met through a balanced diet.

Weight Control

© tmbphotis, 2014. Used under license from Shutterstock, Inc.

Specific Objectives

1. Describe the incidence of obesity in America.
2. Describe the difference between overfat and obese.
3. List the major health effects of obesity.
4. Understand the possible cause of obesity.
5. Explain how current theories of obesity relate to weight-loss and weight-control efforts.
6. Understand the difference between upper- and lower-body obesity.
7. Explain the role of heredity in body weight.
8. Explain the role of aerobic and anaerobic exercise in weight control.
9. Explain the role of diet in weight control.
10. Describe the changes occurring in resting metabolism as a result of diet and exercise.
11. Identify the false claims and dangers of over-the-counter diet aids.
12. Describe the proper choices for a weight-loss plan.

Adapted from *Fitness for Life, Fourth Edition* by Bill Hyman, Gary Oden, David Bacharach, Tim Sebesta. Copyright © 2011 by Kendall Hunt Publishing Company. Reprinted by permission.

OVERVIEW

Americans are among the heaviest people in the world, and despite wishes to the contrary, we just keep getting heavier. The average male adult now weights 195.7 lb and the average female adult 166.3 lb. The number of overweight children, adolescents, and adults has risen over the past four decades, with current reports indicating that nearly two-thirds of U.S. adults are overweight. In addition, nearly one-third of U.S. adults are obese. The prevalence has steadily increased over the years among both genders, all ages, and all racial/ethnic groups. The prevalence of obesity has more than doubled increasing from 13 percent in 1960 to more than 37 percent by the 2014 (Table 7.1). In 2016, obesity prevalence by state ranged from 20.5 percent in Colorado to 34.7 percent in Louisiana. Eleven states had an obesity rate between 20 and 25 percent whereas 13 states had an obesity rate equal to or greater than 30 percent. The number of overweight children and adolescents has also risen over the past four decades with the latest estimates showing 17 percent of children (ages 6–11) and 17.5 percent of adolescents (ages 12–19) being overweight (National Center for Health Statistics, 2017).

Obesity is common, serious and costly. Medical conditions associated with being overweight or obese include heart disease, stroke, type 2 diabetes, and certain types of cancer. The estimated medical cost of obesity in the U.S. exceeds $190 billion yearly (www.heathlycommunitiesheathlyfuture.org). There is no simple cause for overweight and obesity; factors vary by individual. In some cases, there may be genetic predisposition to being overweight; however, the vast majority of people simply are brought up making unhealthy food choices, eating foods high in saturated fat and laden with sugar, which add significant calories to their diet. This can either be by choice or because they do not have the financial ability to purchase healthier, less caloric options. Other significant factors causing weight gain are regularly eating over-sized portions, which increases calorie intake, and not getting enough exercise. People who are physically active are less likely to be overweight or obese.

STRIVING FOR THE LEAN IDEAL

A longing to be thin has overcome millions of Americans. Whether it be for health benefits or cosmetic purposes, a large number of people have a habit of looking at the image in the mirror or at the number on the scale and deciding whether that body size and shape is acceptable. Many are not pleased, and for some the quest for the perfect physique has become an obsession. This often leads to frustration since the image of the perfect body that has been set before us is simply unattainable for many people. Some not only experience frustration, but also enter into eating behaviors that can be dangerous. This chapter explores the obsession with thinness, looking at the health benefits of achieving and maintaining a desirable body weight, as well as the pros and cons of getting trapped in the strife for the ideal. In addition, this chapter discusses proper weight-control techniques.

TABLE 7.1 Estimated (Age-Adjusted) Percentage of US Adults with Overweight and Obesity by Sex, 2013-2014

	All (Men and Women)	Men	Women
Overweight or Obesity	70.2	73.7	66.9
Overweight	32.5	38.7	26.5
Obesity (including extreme obesity)	37.7	35	40.4
Extreme obesity	7.7	5.5	9.9

National center for Health statistics

BOX 7.1

Fast Food Contributes to Obesity

Regularly eating away from home, particularly at fast food restaurants has a strong correlation to excess weight. Fast food restaurants carry items that significantly increase your total daily calorie intake, putting your calorie balance out of whack. It's not uncommon for a meal at a fast food restaurant to contain an entire day's worth of calories. When researchers examined the influence of fast food consumption on body weight, they found that the more frequently people ate fast food, the more they weigh. In a study published in the journal Preventing Chronic Diseases in 2011, scientists found that eating fast food three times per week increased the risk of obesity by 33 percent.

If you have a habit of eating fast food, it's best to cut back on your intake. When you do eat out at a fast food restaurant, select the smallest size available and choose a healthy side dish such as vegetables. These changes help reduce the overall calorie intake of the meal.

How did we ever reach the point that we feel that our bodies have to look like movie stars and fashion models to be acceptable? Perhaps it comes from looking at too many movie stars and fashion models. The media has undoubtedly been a very powerful influence when it comes to body image. Throughout time, a current trend or style has been promoted as the perfect body. Even though the desired look has changed, there has always been a social expectation that some body parts should be more developed than others. At one time, size was in, and the bigger the better. Classic artwork depicts full-bodied women as the ideal, and as recently as the 1950s, the Marilyn Monroe look of voluptuous curves was considered everybody's dream figure. In the 1960s, thinness began to become the latest fashion. Since that time, television, movies, and print ads have consistently presented the message that if you do not have a fashion model's body, you lack in attractiveness. And most people do not have a fashion model's body.

This social phenomenon of a desire to be thin has driven millions of Americans to the task of losing weight. Oftentimes, the message of the importance of maintaining a healthy weight has been lost in the cosmetic desire to be attractive. Individuals frequently turn to fraudulent, ineffective, and sometimes dangerous methods of weight loss only to find themselves frustrated, lighter in the pocketbook, and possibly compromising their health. Too often, the media and social expectations, not the pursuit of health, drive one's actions. Dieting has become big business in the United States. About 50 million adults go on a diet each year, and those people will spend over $60 billion on diet products and programs (www.money.usnews.com). The majority of that money is being wasted. Diet books, special nutrition plans, exercise gimmicks, fat farms, diet drugs, and weight-loss centers abound, each marketing itself to potential clients as the best way to lose weight. These approaches often take advantage of ignorance and the desire for the quick and easy fix. The truth is that most of them are unsuccessful avenues toward weight loss. In fact, less than 20 percent of those engaged in an effort to lose weight actually lose the weight and keep the weight off (Wing & Phelan, 2006).

WHAT IS OVERWEIGHT, OVERFAT, AND OBESITY?

Overweight refers to an excessive amount of body weight. An excessive amount of body weight is not always a negative. It can be common for athletes to have excessive weight yet not be over fat or obese. It is the large amount of lean body mass of the athlete that will show the athlete to be overweight. Overfat refers to an excessive amount of body fat above what would be considered ideal, whereas obesity refers to having more than 10 percent body fat above what would be considered ideal. Ideal percent body fat or body composition differs for men and women. As a rule, women have more body fat than do men. Most health professionals agree that ideal body fat for men is 15 percent and for women 22 percent. Therefore, for men obesity would be defined as a body fat percentage of 25 or above. For women, percent body fat to be considered obese would be 32 or above. Body mass index (BMI; defined in Chapter 3) is also used to define overweight and obesity. A BMI between 25 and 30 is considered overweight and a BMI above 30 is considered obese. As mentioned in Chapter 3, BMI does not consider the amount of lean mass a person may have, therefore BMI is not a great indicator of overweight and obesity.

BODY FAT DISTRIBUTION

Health care professionals are not only concerned with how much fat a person has, but also where the fat is located on the body. Recent information is showing that it makes a difference where the excess fat is deposited, with respect to medical complications. Health risks are greater for people who have

TABLE 7.2 Leading Causes of Obesity in America

1. Over-sized portions

2. Unhealthy food choices

3. Not getting enough exercise

Source: https://www.livestrong.com/article/262489-the-leading-causes-of-obesity-in-america/

most of their body fat in the upper body, especially the truck and abdominal areas. This is called android obesity. Gynoid obesity, which is characterized by deposition of body fat in the hips and thighs, shows less vulnerability to health risks.

HEALTH EFFECTS OF OBESITY

The National Institutes of Health recognizes obesity as a condition that poses significant health risks (Table 7.3). One-third of premature deaths in the United States are attributable to poor diet and inactivity, making this combination second only to tobacco use in behavioral causes of death (Centers for Disease Control and Prevention [CDC], 2018). Obesity has been linked to numerous disorders and causes of death, including high blood pressure, elevated cholesterol levels, kidney and liver disorders, diabetes, heart disease, gallbladder disease, osteoarthritis, some types of cancer, and breathing problems. Obesity is also a factor in early death, with most of the increase in mortality resulting from coronary heart disease. It is estimated that if all Americans would achieve a normal body weight, life expectancy in the United States would increase by three years, there would be 35 percent less congestive heart failure and stroke, and 25 percent less heart disease (CDC, 2018). Some of the major health problems associated with obesity are discussed below.

Psychological Burden

Society creates tremendous pressures on people, particularly on females, to be thin. Obese people often suffer from feelings of guilt, depression, anxiety, and low self-esteem. This can be the greatest harm caused by obesity, especially among adolescents. Obese people are often subjected to prejudice and discrimination.

Hypertension

A person's risk of developing high blood pressure is doubled if he/she is obese. This is true both in adults and children. Known as the "silent killer" because of the absence of outward warning signs, high blood pressure affects approximately 26 percent of obese men and women in America.

Hypertension is discussed in more detail in Chapter 8.

Blood Lipid Levels

Overweight individuals are more prone to suffer from hypercholesterolemia, or elevated levels of serum cholesterol and increased triglyceride. Also, the risk ratio, or ratio of total cholesterol to high-density cholesterol, is higher in the obese, and this is a major indicator of risk for heart disease. On the brighter side, weight loss is an excellent way to lower the heart disease risk, which is posed by elevated cholesterol and triglyceride. For every pound lost, there is approximately a 1-mg reduction in total cholesterol (Nieman, 2011).

Diabetes

The obese have a rate of diabetes that is three times the rate of the nonobese (Nieman, 2011). Nearly 80 percent of patients with

TABLE 7.3 Health Consequences of Obesity

Increase in Risk	
Male	**Female**
Cancer	Cancer
Colon/rectum	breast
Prostate	cervix
	endometrium
	gallbladder
Low back pain	Low back pain
	Impaired fertility
	Fetal defects

Moderate Increase in Risk
Male and Female
Heart disease
Stroke
Osteoarthritis
Gout

Great Increase in Risk
Male and Female
Diabetes
Hypertension
Sleep apnea
Gallbladder disease

non-insulin-dependent diabetes are obese (National Institute of Diabetes and Kidney Disorders).

Cancers

Certain types of cancer are found in greater numbers in the obese. The American Cancer Society reports that overweight individuals increase their risk of certain types of cancer. Men who are obese are more likely than their nonobese counterparts to develop cancer of the colon, rectum, or prostate. Women who are obese are more likely than their nonobese counterparts to develop cancer of the gallbladder, uterus, cervix, or ovaries. Esophageal cancer has also been associated with obesity (American Cancer Society, 2005).

Osteoarthritis

Osteoarthritis is one of the most prevalent diseases in the United States. Obesity increases the risk for osteoarthritis. Obese people have double the risk of osteoarthritis as nonobese people. Obesity produces change in cartilage cells, which promotes osteoarthritis (Jarvholm, Lewold, Malchau, & Vingard, 2005).

POPULAR THEORIES OF OBESITY

Obesity results from longstanding positive energy balance; in simple terms, people consume more energy than they expend. Explaining why so many Americans fall into this category has been a source of confusion to researchers and the public alike. Theories of obesity fall into three categories: genetic and parental influences, high energy intake, and low energy expenditure (Nieman, 2011).

A person's body weight is determined by the interaction of several complex factors. These include social, emotional, environmental, behavioral, and biological determinants. Although there is still much to be learned about the conditions of overweight and obesity, research has revealed some important information. Evidence points to genetic and parental influence as important factors in explaining why some people find it difficult to avoid obesity. Reports show that 80% of children of two obese parents eventually become obese, with 40% of children with one parent becoming obese, and only 14% of children becoming obese if neither parent is obese (Speakman, 2004). Other researches support the importance of parental obesity in predicting obesity in children. These results, however, do not supply any indication as to the relative importance of genetics versus family lifestyle as related to the development of obesity.

Some evidence points to a genetic link to body fatness. Overweight biological parents appear to be a factor in an individual's experience with his/her own overweightness. In addition, it also appears that the distribution of fat in our parents is likely to determine how and where we store fat. Studies of identical twins who were separated at birth lend evidence to the theory of genetic predisposition. The sets of twins who came from obese biological parents were both likely to be obese later in life, regardless of whether they grew up in a family with fat or thin members. Also, separated twins who eat very different diets as they grow up tend to weigh about the same. These studies have led many to conclude that the role of heredity in obesity is significant. Therefore, the tendency to blame obesity on parental overfeeding during childhood or the suggestion that most people are overweight because they do not have enough self-control is most likely inaccurate (Sorensen et al., 1992).

However, not all research points to such a strong relationship between genetics and body weight. Some large-scale studies conclude that about 25 percent of the variation

---

BOX 7.2

Other Diseases and Health Problems Linked to Obesity

- ❑ Gallbladder disease and gallstones.
- ❑ Fatty liver disease (also called nonalcoholic steatohepatitis or NASH).
- ❑ Gastroesophageal reflux. This problem occurs when the lower esophageal sphincter does not close properly and stomach contents leak back or reflux into the esophagus.
- ❑ Gout, another disease affecting the joints.
- ❑ Pulmonary problems, including sleep apnea.

between people's fat mass is due to biological inheritance, with lifestyle, cultural, and environmental factors being responsible for the other 75 percent of the variance.

While individuals should be aware of the importance of genetic predisposition toward body fatness, we must be careful how we utilize that information. Some may be inclined to use it as an excuse. "I come from a fat family, therefore, I can't do anything about my weight" is sometimes offered as the reason for a person having this health-compromising condition, whereas in reality, he/she has done very little to address this problem which is oftentimes preventable. There are numerous individuals who maintain a healthy weight in spite of having a "family history" of obesity. Individuals who feel as though they do have a genetic predisposition toward overweight and obesity should view their situation as an increased challenge, which can effectively be addressed with a thorough understanding of the weight-loss process.

Diet

The concept of weight control through diet is a very simple one. However, this simple concept is extremely difficult for most Americans to follow. Simply stated, in order for a person to maintain his/her current weight, he/she must maintain a neutral energy balance. This means that the number of calories consumed and the number of calories expended are equal; they neutralize each other. If a person consumes more calories than he/she uses, a positive energy balance exists and weight gain occurs. For example, if Johnny eats a 300-calorie ice cream cone each day and these calories are above and beyond his daily expenditure of calories, then Johnny will gain one pound of fat approximately every 12 days (3,500 calories = 1 pound). In order for a person to lose weight, a negative energy balance must exist. A negative energy balance exists when a person expends more calories than he/she consumes. If Johnny expends 300 calories each day through some type of activity, and these calories are above and beyond his daily expenditure of calories, then Johnny will lose one pound of weight approximately every 12 days. Notice that the term fat was used when referring to weight gain but the term weight was used when referring to weight loss. This is because fat is the body's storage form of energy. Every calorie that a person consumes above what is used is stored as fat. This is the case regardless of the type of food eaten. The overconsumption of calories from carbohydrates, fat, or protein is all stored as excess body fat. On the other hand, when a person loses weight, he/she may or may not lose fat.

Even though our goal in weight loss is to shed fat, we sometimes lose as much lean weight as we do fat weight. Without an appropriate exercise program, weight loss will consist of a combination of fat and lean body mass. (This topic will be covered in more detail later in this chapter.)

As we can see, in order for weight loss to occur, a negative energy balance must exist, and in order for this weight loss not to include lean tissue, an exercise program must be implemented. The question that should be addressed at this time is "What is the best way to create a negative energy balance."

A negative energy balance can be created in two ways: through diet or exercise. Which would be most advantageous for weight loss? Without a doubt, a reduction in the number of calories consumed leads to weight loss more quickly than any form of reasonable exercise. If a person decides to cut back on the number of calories consumed, weight loss will be proportional to the caloric deficit created. As mentioned earlier, 3,500 calories constitutes one pound, therefore, anytime a person has a caloric deficit of 3,500 calories, one pound is lost. For someone in need of large weight loss, diet would be the fastest means to accomplish that goal. For example, if a person has a typical calorie intake of 3,000 calories daily and decides to cut back to 2,000 calories a day, then one pound could be lost every 3.5 days. For someone in need of losing 20, 30, 40, or even more weight this would seem to be the best way to achieve desired results. In a six-week period, the total weight loss would seem to be 12 pounds; in three months the loss would equal 26 pounds. Many people will look at this and say, "WOW! I didn't know weight loss could be so simple or easy." In addition, people will think "WOW! If cutting back from 3,000 to 2,000 calories can result in this much loss, just think what I can lose if I only eat 1,000 calories a day, or even better, what about 500 calories?" Hopefully these people will continue to read and come to another conclusion. The above example does have flaws. In theory, going from 3,000 to 2,000 calories a day could result in the stated weight loss, but in reality this does not happen. Resting metabolism plays a significant role in body-weight regulation, with a high metabolic rate causing weight loss to occur quickly and a slow metabolism causing weight loss to be slow. The resting metabolism for a 121-pound female amounts to approximately 1,190 calories per day or about 60 to 75 percent of total energy expenditure. As most individuals who have dieted know, the rate of weight loss slows during the course of dieting. This is brought about by a decreasing metabolism which occurs as a result of a reduction in calories consumed. Weight loss is most rapid during the initial days of a diet with weight loss becoming more and more difficult as the duration of the diet increases. Metabolic adjustment begins within a couple of days of caloric deficiency and will adjust to the new lower level in three to four weeks. In order for weight loss to continue, the individual will need to continue to reduce the number of calories consumed which can lead to many nutritional deficits.

In addition to the problem of reducing the caloric intake to dangerously low levels, a second major problem is created when weight is lost by diet alone. Most individuals who choose to lose weight by low-calorie diets gain the weight back in a very short time after they stop the diet. The reason for this is simple. People who are overweight, for the most part, like to eat. Their lifestyle is one that enjoys the pleasure obtained from food. If these people diet and lose weight and then go back to their previous lifestyle and eating habits, then weight gain is very rapid.

Since the resting metabolic rate (RMR) decreased while dieting, the amount of food they can now eat and still maintain current weight is much less. It is true that resting metabolism increases with the increase in food intake after an individual stops dieting; however, the time for the resting metabolism to increase is much longer than it was for the RMR to decrease during weight loss. Most people will experience a gain in weight which exceeds the loss they accomplished through their diet.

A third problem associated with the reduction in calories consumed is the dedication and discipline it takes to eat less. In America, we associate food with pleasure and good times. We celebrate joyous occasions with food and drink. If we reduce our food consumption, even to a small degree, we take some of the joy out of life. (Hopefully, through the weight loss, we replace this joy loss and add more.) Even though the weight loss equation is a very simple one, it is difficult to follow.

The following equations can be used for estimating RMR. For female, RMR (calories/day) $= (10 \times w) + (6.25 \times h) - (5 \times a) - 161$, and for males, RMR (calories/day) $= (10 \times w) + (6.25 \times h) - (5 \times a) + 5$.

w = weight in kg (weight in pounds divided by 2.2)

h = height in cm (inches $\times$ 2.54)

a = age

© Jacek Chabraszewski, 2014. Used under license from Shutterstock, Inc.

Exercise

Exercise is the second important component of weight control. Exercise offers a number of significant advantages to people attempting to achieve long-term weight loss. First and foremost, exercise increases energy expenditure, helping to create a negative energy balance necessary for weight loss. Unfortunately, the amount of energy expended during most exercise programs (walking, jogging, swimming, cycling, etc.) with the typical frequency and duration (three to five days per week, 20–30 minutes per session) is a modest 600–1,200 calories per week. Thus, exercise can be said to have very little effect on short-term weight control.

The importance of exercise in weight control is more clearly established in regard to long-term weight loss and weight-loss maintenance. In looking at the cumulative effect of increased energy expenditure for a year, the results are impressive (600–1,200 calories per week for 52 weeks = 9–18 pounds per year). The wonderful fact of this weight loss is that it can be permanent. Many times individuals look for the "quick fix," in other words, they want instant results!

People want to lose large amounts of weight and lose it fast. Exercise may not be the "quick fix" they want, but it is the best fix for a person. When we look at the facts concerning long-term weight loss, one conclusion is clear: exercise is a requirement for most individuals! Evidence that demonstrates the importance of exercise on weight control includes data that show that both obese children and adults exercise less than normal-weight people. Studies show that overweight children tend to be less active than lean children participating in sports. For example, while playing tennis, obese girls have been found to be inactive 77 percent of the time compared with 56 percent of the time for normal-weight girls. In general, lean children spend up to 40 percent more time in physical activity than obese children (Nieman, 2011). Obese men informally walk an average of three and seven-tenths miles per day compared with

---

BOX 7.3

Components of a Weight Loss Program

1. **It Starts With Food** – Good nutrition is the foundation of any weight loss program. The first step in good nutrition is choosing whole foods and avoiding processed foods. Processed foods are often high in sugar, fat, salt and calories but low in nutrients. Whole foods like fresh vegetables, fruits, eggs and lean meats are nutrient dense, which means they fill you up and meet your body's requirements for good health. To lose weight, you will need to consume fewer calories than you expend, so it is important to be aware of calories and portion sizes.
2. **Next Comes Activity** – Once you've made improvements to your diet, it's time to increase your daily activity. Choose an activity that you enjoy and can do regularly. It should be something that can fit easily into your daily routine. Walking is a good place to start for many people. A 30-minute walk burns around 100 calories, on average. If walking isn't the right activity for you, find one that is – biking, swimming, rowing or whatever you enjoy and can accomplish most days.
3. **Now Change Your Thoughts** – If you are overweight, chances are this is not your first attempt at losing weight. Maybe you've lost a significant amount of weight in the past only to regain it. That's not uncommon among people who struggle with excess weight. According to the American Psychological Association, understanding and modifying the behaviors and emotions related to weight management are essential to successful weight loss. It's important to leave the past where it belongs – in the past. Believe in your success and surround yourself with people who boost your self-esteem and support your weight loss efforts.
4. **Take the Long View** – The Weight-control Information Network, or WIN, a service of the National Institute of Diabetes and Digestive and Kidney Diseases, recommends a gradual approach to weight loss. Aim for 1/2 to 2 pounds per week. Rather than going on a very restrictive diet, strive for lasting lifestyle changes that support modest, steady weight loss. And don't expect perfection. When you falter, just get back on track at your next opportunity. Focus on making long-term, lasting changes and you will reach a healthy weight.

six miles per day for men of normal weight; while obese females walk two miles per day compared with four and ninth-tenths miles per day for normal-weight women. Obese individuals spend less time on their feet and stay in bed longer than normal-weight people. If the obese individual is given a choice between walking up the stairs or riding the escalator, he/she is more likely to choose the escalator. Even with small children, ages four to eight, data show increased body fat levels if daytime activity is less than normal. Even though weight loss may not be rapid, the goal of weight loss should be to lose it for a lifetime. Consistent participation in aerobic activity burns substantial amounts of calories. Anaerobic exercise such as weight training does not burn as many calories during a workout, but this type exercise does enhance resting metabolism by increasing the muscle mass. This change results in an increased daily-calorie expenditure for an individual. Enhancing muscle mass can be viewed as an investment in future weight control. This is one reason why both aerobic and anaerobic exercise are suggested for weight loss and weight maintenance. The energy expenditure of weight-bearing exercise (walking, jogging, games, etc.) is dependent on the body weight of the individual. If two people, one weighing 110 pounds and the other weighing 220 pounds, jog one mile together, the 220 pound person expends more calories because it requires more energy to move a heavier weight from one location to another. Table 7.4 provides an estimate of caloric expenditure for selected activities. Appendix D provides you with a caloric expenditure scale that will help you identify the ideal number of calories to be burned each week to provide optimal health.

EXERCISE AND RESTING METABOLISM

Another benefit of exercise in regard to weight control is the effect that exercise has on resting metabolism. For many years, people in the fitness and wellness professions preached that exercise has a significant positive effect on RMR and referred to that effect as the "after burn" of exercise. One can still watch an informative commercial on television and see some "fitness expert" discussing the wonderful "after burn" of exercise. The truth of the matter is this "after burn" of exercise is not very significant. Research indicates that additional calories are expended after the exercise bout is concluded, but the number of calories is small. For example, jogging (12 minutes per mile), walking, or cycling at a moderate intensity (50–60 percent of maximum heart rate) causes the metabolic rate to stay elevated for 20 to 30 minutes after the exercise, burning an additional ten to 12 calories (Neiman, 2011). When exercise intensity is increased to 75 percent, RMR is increased for about 30 to 45 minutes, with a caloric expenditure of an extra 15 to 30 calories. For an obese person who takes a one- or two-mile walk per day, the extra calories expended hardly seem enough to be meaningful. On the other hand, the effect exercise has on chronic metabolic rate may be a bit more attractive. Since the overwhelming majority of calories a person expends per day is a result of that person's RMR, any increase is a bonus. Research has indicated that RMR increases chronically through an exercise program (Nieman, 2011).

The amount of increase is dependent on the type, intensity, and duration of the exercise program. A relationship does exist between type, intensity, duration, and amount of increase in RMR. The more intense and longer a person exercises, the greater the increase. For the obese person who performs very low-intensity exercise, the increase may be minor; however, for the obese person who performs higher-intensity exercise, the increase can be very significant. Many people reading this text will say "Oh No! High-intensity exercise! This doesn't sound like much fun!" Over

TABLE 7.4 Calories Expended per Hour in Various Physical Activities (Performed at Recreational Level)*

| Activity | Calories Used per Hour | | | | |
	100 lb (145.5 kg)	120 lb (54.6 kg)	150 lb (68 kg)	180 lb (82 kg)	200 lb (91 kg)
Archery	180	204	240	276	300
Backpacking (40-lb pack)	307	348	410	472	513
Badminton	255	289	340	391	425
Baseball	210	238	280	322	350
Basketball (half court)	225	255	300	345	375
Bicyding (normal speed)	157	178	210	242	263
Bowling	155	176	208	240	261
Canoeing (4 mph)	276	344	414	504	558
Circuit Training	247	280	330	380	413
Dance, Ballet (choreographed)	240	300	360	432	480
Dance, Exercise	315	357	420	483	525
Dance, Modern (choreographed)	240	300	360	432	480
Dance, Social	174	222	264	318	348
Fencing	225	255	300	345	375
Fitness Calisthenics	232	263	310	357	388
Football	225	255	300	345	375
Golf (walking)	187	212	250	288	313
Gymnastics	232	263	310	357	388
Handball	450	510	600	690	750
Hiking	225	255	300	345	375
Horseback Riding	180	204	240	276	300
Interval Training	487	552	650	748	833
Jogging (5½ mph)	487	552	650	748	833
Judo/Karate	232	263	310	357	388
Mountain Climbing	450	510	600	690	750
Pool; Billiards	97	110	130	150	163
Racquetball; Paddleball	450	510	600	690	750
Rope Jumping (continuous)	525	595	700	805	875
Rowing Crew	615	697	820	943	1,025
Running (10 mph)	625	765	900	1,035	1,125
Sailing (pleasure)	135	153	180	207	225
Skating, Ice	262	297	350	403	438
Skating, Roller	262	297	350	403	438
Sking, Cross-Country	525	595	700	805	875
Sking, Downhill	450	510	600	690	750
Soccer	405	459	540	621	775
Softball (fast)	210	238	280	322	350
Softball (slow)	217	246	290	334	363
Surfing	416	467	550	633	684
Swimming (slow laps)	240	272	320	368	400
Swimming (fast laps)	420	530	630	768	846
Table Tennis	180	204	240	276	300
Tennis	315	357	420	483	525
Volleyball	262	297	350	403	483
Walking	204	258	318	372	426
Waterskiing	306	390	468	564	636
Weight Training	352	399	470	541	558

*Note: Locate your weight to determine the calories expended per hour in each of the activities shown in the table based on recreational involvement. More vigorous activity, as occurs in competitive athletics, may result in greater caloric expenditures.

Reprinted, with permission, from C.B. Corbin and R. Lindsey, 2007, *Fitness for Life, 5th ed.* (Champaign, IL: Human Kinetics), 231.

the past few years, the fitness world has been educating people on the proper exercise programs, with the trend being that low-intensity exercise is as good as higher intensities. The truth is, the higher the intensity, the greater the benefit, as long as it is aerobic. It is important that everyone realize that this does not mean that obese individuals should only perform high-intensity exercise. First, you need to know what constitutes high-intensity exercise. Aerobic exercise that requires a heart rate above 60 percent of a person's maximum heart rate reserve (refer back to Karovens formula in chapter 2) is classified as high intensity. This intensity is not severe to the point of great discomfort. Most people, whether lean or fat, can exercise at 60 percent of maximum heart rate reserve by performing a walking program. High intensity exercise feels challenging, however, it is not to the point that a person cannot continue for an extended period of time. If you are short of breath, are in pain or can't work out as long as you had planned, your exercise intensity is probably higher than your fitness level allows. While on the subject of low-intensity exercise, one other point should be made. You have probably heard that low-intensity exercise burns more fat. Although this is a true statement, it is also a very misleading statement.

When the body burns a calorie, the source of the calorie does not matter. This means that regardless of fat, protein, or carbohydrate, a calorie is a calorie in terms of weight loss. It does not matter if the calorie is a fat, protein, or carbohydrate! In fact, the major source of energy while the body is at total rest is fat. Therefore, if we buy into the low-intensity fat-burning philosophy, we should become couch potatoes in order to burn the most fat.

So, this would not be wise from a weight-control standpoint. From an RMR standpoint, it is clear that the higher the intensity, the greater the benefit. However, any exercise expends calories and will enhance a person's ability to lose weight.

Anaerobic exercise is also very important when programming exercise for weight control. As a person begins to diet and reduces the number of calories consumed, the natural reaction in the body is for RMR to decrease. The body always adjusts to the number of calories eaten, whether it is an increase or a decrease in calories. This is demonstrated by the early weight loss or weight gain individuals experience when they eat either a very low- or very high-calorie diet. This weight loss or gain is large, but as the duration of the diet continues, the amount of weight lost or gained decreases, even though the individual(s) have been very faithful to their diet. Frustration is a common occurrence with people who achieve early weight loss success but experience the difficulty in losing weight after metabolism drops.

RMR will remain higher if exercise is included in the weight-loss program. People who exercise aerobically and diet have more success maintaining RMR than individuals who do not exercise. Most research indicates that aerobic exercise slows the decreased RMR brought about by dieting. Slowing the decrease in RMR does not mean that aerobic exercise completely stops the decline. As much as the proponents of fitness like for everyone to believe that aerobic exercise stops RMR from decreasing, the fact is only a slowing takes place. Another benefit provided by aerobic exercise in weight control is its effect on the maintenance of lean body mass. As was mentioned earlier, a person should be concerned about his/her percentage of body fat, not scale weight. This is hard for most people. Anytime we go to the doctor, we get weighed. Most people have scales in the bathroom and it is easy to step on and look at the weight. Very few people have the opportunity to have a body fat measurement performed. However, it is the percentage of fat that is important, not weight. Weight loss through diet alone causes a much greater loss in weight than in body fat. A person using only a reduction in calorie intake, without exercise, experiences a loss not only in fat, but also in lean tissue. This is not good! Exercise is necessary to prevent the loss in lean tissue.

Data have shown that weight loss through diet alone can be as much as 50 percent fat and 50 percent lean tissue. Aerobic exercise can be useful in reducing the amount of lean tissue loss, but it cannot eliminate it. Anaerobic exercise in the form of weight training is the only way to completely stop lean body tissue loss. Most individuals think aerobic activity is most beneficial in weight control. This concept is true since more calories are burned from aerobic activity; however, preservation of lean tissue is accomplished best through weight training. For optimal body fat loss, a lower calorie diet in combination with aerobic and anaerobic exercise is needed. Weight training while dieting gives a person the dual benefit of maintaining or even increasing lean body weight and also maintaining RMR. As a result of weight training, the amount of weight loss a person achieves could decrease. For some individuals this can be discouraging. However, as mentioned, the amount of weight lost is not the significant factor, but the amount of fat lost is. When one weight-trains, lean body mass increases and fat body mass decreases. This increase in lean mass causes scale weight to stay the same or decrease at a much slower rate, but percent body fat has a significant decrease.

Again, it is body fat that needs to be lost, not necessarily the weight. Increasing the lean body weight increases the RMR by giving the person more active tissue. Lean tissue is more metabolically active than fat tissue; therefore, the more lean tissue a person possesses, the higher the RMR. It would be nice if everyone who is trying to control his/her weight had the capability of body fat testing; then he/she would not have to rely on the bathroom scale to judge his/her success, but this is just not the case. A better judge of weight than the bathroom scale method may be as simple as the fit of one's clothes. If clothing which has been too small in the past begins to fit, or clothing which is currently being worn is becoming too large, then the weight-control program is working.

EXERCISE AND APPETITE

The relationship of exercise and appetite is another interesting subject in regard to weight control. Studies examining the effect of exercise on appetite have shown mixed results. These data reveal that exercise may increase, decrease, or have no effect on food intake. Until recent years, the scientific community adopted the position that one hour of low- to moderate-intensity exercise reduces appetite. The theory was that food intake decreases during the early days of exercise and persists until the level of exercise is increased to above-moderate levels. At this point, the appetite increases to be in balance with energy expenditure. Other researchers tried to duplicate the results of the earlier studies without success. Studies have shown that there is a large amount of individual variability in what and how much people eat when they exercise. For some people, exercise helps to control appetite while for others, it seems to do the opposite (Hopkins, M., King, N.A., and Blundell, 2010).

SUCCESSFUL WEIGHT CONTROL

Obesity, even though a chronic illness, for the most part has been treated as an acute illness. Most treatment plans for obesity advertise rapid weight loss and make little attempt to involve behavior modification that is necessary for long-term success. Remember, weight control is a lifelong effort, and having realistic expectations about weight loss is an important consideration. Since the ultimate goal of a weight-loss program is to lose weight and keep it off, a nutritionally sound, low-calorie diet that is applicable to the individual's lifestyle is most appropriate. A weight-loss program that includes diet, exercise, and behavior modification is more likely to lead to

BOX 7.4

How to Lose Weight: The NHLBI Obesity Education Initiative

In 1998, the first federal guidelines for the treatment of overweight and obesity in adults were released by the National Heart, Lung, and Blood Institute (NHLBI) as a part of its nationwide Obesity Education Initiative. With nearly 100 million overweight Americans, the NHLBI has made education about overweight and obesity a major priority. Key diet recommendations from this initiative include the following:

❏ The initial goal of a weight-loss regimen should be to reduce body weight by about 10 percent. With success, further weight loss can be attempted, if needed.
❏ Weight loss should be about 1–2 pounds per week for a period of 6 months, with additional plans based on the amount of weight loss. Seek to create a deficit of 500–1,000 calories per day through a combination of decreased caloric intake and increased physical activity.
❏ Reducing dietary fat intake is a practical way to reduce calories. But reducing dietary fat alone without reducing calories is not sufficient for weight loss.

Each pound of body fat represents about 3,500 calories. To follow the NHLBI for weight loss, one must expend 500–1,000 calories more than the amount taken in through the diet. This can be accomplished by increasing energy expenditure 200–400 calories a day through physical activity, and reducing dietary fat intake by 300–600 calories. Each tablespoon of fat represents about 100 calories, so an emphasis on low-fat dairy products and lean meats, and a low intake of visible fats (oils, butter, margarine, salad dressings, sour cream, etc.) is the easiest way to reduce caloric intake without reducing the volume of food eaten.

The NHLBI recommends this diet for weight loss:

❏ Eat 500–1,000 calories a day below usual intake.
❏ Keep total dietary fat intake below 30 percent of calories and carbohydrates at 55 percent or more of total calories.
❏ Emphasize a heart-healthy diet by keeping saturated fats below 10 percent of total calories, cholesterol under 300 mg/day, and sodium less than 2,400 mg/day.
❏ Choose foods high in dietary fiber (20–30 grams/day).

This diet starts in the grocery store. Another challenge is eating healthfully when dining out. Learn to ask for salad dressing on the side and to leave all butter, gravy, or sauces off the dish. Select foods that are steamed, garden fresh, broiled, baked, roasted, poached, or lightly sauteed or stir-fried.

Source: National Institute of Health.

long-term weight control. A successful, long-term weight-control program involves three elements:

1. **Diet.** The number of calories consumed should be reduced.
   ▪ Learn to choose sensible portions of nutritious meals that are lower in fat.
   ▪ Learn to recognize and control environmental cues (like inviting smells or a package of cookies on the counter) that make you want to eat when you are not hungry.
2. **Exercise.** Energy expenditure should be increased at least 200 to 400 calories per day. Any form of physical activity is acceptable.
3. **Behavior Modification.** Several techniques should be used, including:
   ▪ Self-monitoring: Keep a diet diary, with emphasis on recording food amounts and circumstances surrounding the consumption of the food.
   ▪ Control of the events that precede eating: Identification of the circumstances that elicit eating and overeating.
   ▪ Development of techniques to control eating: Typical behavioral-modification techniques are used.
   ▪ Reinforcement through use of rewards: Providing a system of formal rewards enhances progress.

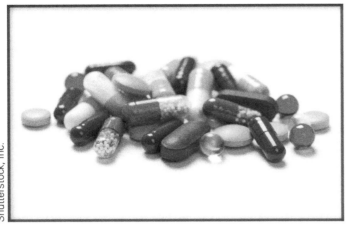

Although obese individuals benefit from these guidelines, there are some individuals who seek additional forms of therapy in search for success. Many people choose very low-calorie diets in order to achieve rapid weight loss. These diets should only be used by severely obese people under medical supervision. Very low-calorie diets contain less than 800 calories and do not contain the necessary amounts of nutrients to maintain a healthy life.

In today's world, diet aids (drinks, powders, diet bars, etc.) are widely available over the counter, and many people are tempted to rely on them for quick and easy weight loss.

However, the promises made by these products are mostly false and the overdependence on these diet aids can be dangerous. The diet aids provide far less than the needed nutritional and calorie requirements and are not complementary to a healthy lifestyle. Although these products can help control hunger and weight in the short-term, they encourage dependence on commercial products rather than the development of healthy eating and exercise habits. The next time you see a commercial for Slim-Fast™, Dynatrim™, or Thin-Trim™, ask yourself: "Should I make this a permanent part of my life?"

Diet pills are another common diet aid. There are many brands of diet pills that can be purchased over the counter, most of which contain ineffective ingredients. Phenyl-propanolamine hydrochloride (PPA), which the Food and Drug Administration has deemed safe and effective as a mild appetite-suppressant, is the most common ingredient of diet pills. However, research on the effectiveness of PPA is equivocal at best. Research indicates the PPA can cause dizziness, high blood pressure, headaches, sleeplessness, and a rapid heart rate. The FDA approves the use of PPA for no longer than 12 weeks.

BOX 7.5

Habits of Those Achieving Success in Weight Loss and Management

Researchers at the University of Pittsburgh and University of Colorado have formed a national registry of people who have lost more than 30 pounds and kept it off for more than a year. Several hundred people are now in this registry, and interesting findings have emerged:

❑ 94 percent of successful losers increased their physical activity level to accomplish their weight loss, with walking the most common activity reported.
❑ 92 percent report that they are continuing to exercise to maintain weight loss. Those most successful in fighting back weight regain typically exercise for at least 1 hour a day, burning at least 400 calories each day.
❑ 98 percent decreased their food intake in some way.
❑ 57 percent received professional help from doctors, registered dietitians, weight watchers, and others.

Nationwide, about 20 percent of overweight and obese individuals are able to lose 10 percent of initial body weight and keep it off for at least 1 year. Weight-loss maintenance gets easier over time. Once weight loss has been maintained for 2–5 years, the chances of longer success greatly increase.

Source: Republished with permission of Annual Reviews, from *Annual Review of Nutrition, Vol. 21,* pp 323–341. Copyright © 2001 by Annual Reviews. Permission conveyed through Copyright Clearance Center, Inc.

Health Benefits of a 10% Weight Loss

Blood Pressure
Decline of about 10 mm Hg in systolic and diastolic blood pressure in patients with hypertension (equivalent to that with most BP medications)

Diabetes
Decline of up to 50% in fasting glucose for newly diagnosed patients

Prediabetes
>30% decline in fasting or 2-hour post-glucose insulin level >30% increase in insulin sensitivity 40% to 60% decline in the incidence of diabetes

Lipids
10% decline in total cholesterol
15% decline in LDL cholesterol
30% decline in triglycerides
8% increase in HDL cholesterol

Mortality
>20% decline in all-cause mortality
>30% decline in deaths related to diabetes
>40% decline in deaths related to obesity
Data from Haslam et al. (2006).

A Systematic Approach to Management Based on BMI and Other Risk Factors

BMI	Suggested Weight Loss	Deciding Factors for Treatment Level
<18.5	• None • Consider weight gain	• Keep at same or move to less intensive strategy: • No cardiovascular risk factors • Lower body obesity/overweight • No previous weight-loss attempts • <25 lb to lose or goal of less than 5% to 10% weight loss
18.5–26.9	• Exercise • Diet modification • Counseling	
27–29.9	• Weight loss program • Behavioral health services • Self-help materials or program	
30–34.9	• Weight loss program • Pharmacotherapy • Meal-replacement	• Consider move to more intensive strategy • Any cardiovascular risk factors present • Metabolic syndrome present • Abdominal obesity/overweight • Previous weight-loss attempt failure at current level • >25 lb to lose or goal of more than 10% weight loss
35–39.9	• Very low energy diet • Residential programs • Pharmacotherapy	
≥40	• Very low energy diet • Suggest surgery	

From *Exercise Testing and Prescription: A Health Related Approach, 7/e* by David Nieman. Copyright © 2011 by The McGraw-Hill Education. Reprinted by permission.

DANGEROUS DIETING

As mentioned earlier in this chapter, our society has created tremendous pressure for individuals to be thin. The "thin is in" look has become synonymous with attractiveness and social status and is probably more evident in females than in males. While we have stated that about two-thirds of Americans are overweight, many more are dissatisfied with their body image. Research has exemplified this as more than eighty percent of women between the ages of 12 and 23 were dissatisfied with their weight (Ross, 2012). Additionally, a telephone survey a several years ago indicated that most participants would change their body if given the opportunity, while only 13 percent preferred to stay the same (Princeton Survey Research Associates, 1990). A more recent survey conducted by Cornell University and reported by Shape (Shape, August 2015), revealed that 90 percent of females are unhappy with their weight.

Those who have a dissatisfaction with body image sometimes feel pressured into trying to conform to the "ideal" body size and shape. Weight reduction, by whatever means they feel might work, captivates their thoughts and energies as they nurture the attitude that losing weight is a good thing, and the more they lose, the more attractive, accepted, and successful they are. The relentless pursuit of thinness can result in serious and sometimes life-threatening eating disorders.

About one percent of adolescent females suffer from an eating disorder known as anorexia nervosa (National Association of Anorexia Nervosa and Associated Disorders, 2017). This dangerous condition is marked by suppression of appetite and intentional caloric deprivation, which results in a wasting away of body mass or self-starvation. There also exists an intense fear of becoming overweight, and weight loss does not weaken that fear. Due to a psychological distortion of body image, the anorexic sees him/herself as fat, even if extremely underweight.

Weight loss is pursued through extremes in the limitation of caloric intake, often including fasting. Strenuous exercise, the use of laxatives and diuretics, and sometimes self-induced vomiting are also tools of the anorexic. The onset of puberty often marks the beginning of this disorder, and it is most evident by a wasted-away, or emaciated, look.

A related disorder is bulimia nervosa. According to the National Association of Anorexia Nervosa and Associated Disorders, 5.1 percent of college-age-women suffer from bulimia. About 50 percent of people who have been anorexic develop bulimia or bulimic patterns (National Association of Anorexia Nervosa and Associated Disorders, 2017). This disorder, known as the binge-purge syndrome, is marked by high amounts of food/caloric consumption followed by self-induced vomiting and the use of laxatives and diuretics. Compulsive exercise also may be a characteristic of bulimia as the person attempts to burn away as many of the recently consumed calories as possible. Although related and often coexistent, bulimia differs significantly from anorexia in that the individual may maintain a normal body weight due to the binges he/she experiences. This allows the bulimic to hide his/her problem, thereby making it difficult for friends and family members to identify the bulimic.

Anorexia and bulimia nervosa are sometimes combined with episodes of crash dieting. Eventually, half of those with anorexia develop bulimia.

While manifesting themselves in dangerous dietary behaviors, eating disorders must be recognized as more than just nutritional problems. They are mental disorders and must be treated as such. While the causes and contributing factors are complex, researchers have been able to provide some insight into the roots of these dangerous behaviors.

Muscle dysmorphic is another dangerous disorder in which a person becomes obsessed with the idea that they are not muscular enough. Those who suffer from muscle dysmorphic tend to hold the delusions that they are skinny or too small but are above average in musculature. Sometimes this is referred to as reverse anorexia nervosa.

Causes and Contributors

A low self-esteem is often at the root of these behaviors. While the victims may appear to be very successful to others, they have become susceptible to expectations of perfection. They typically meet with success in academics, athletics, and social scenarios, but success is not enough. The strife for absolute perfection leaves them feeling less than adequate, and they are driven to take total control in some areas of their lives. They often share a fear of becoming fat and choose eating habits in response to this fear. These people are determined to exhibit a control over this area of their lives. Females comprise about 90 percent of people with eating disorders.

Perhaps the pressure toward perfection comes from some outside sources. Victims of eating disorders often come from families who place unrealistically high expectations on the child members. Overemphasis on physical attractiveness and promotion of the physical ideal by the parents and other family members may be a significant contributor to the development of an eating disorder. In addition, environments that place overemphasis on physical appearance for some type of athletic or social performance may create the mind-set that control of body weight is the most important factor in the person's success. Anorexia athletica is a condition found among individuals who engage in eating disorders to control their weight in order to enhance athletic performance. Gymnasts, distance runners, dancers, and others involved in performance- or appearance-related activities, in which lower weights are seen as an advantage, are more susceptible to these problems.

Eating habits may also be seen as an avenue to dealing with stress and anxiety. Mentally healthy individuals develop various resources for dealing with stressors, but the less resourceful person may turn to unhealthy coping activities.

Control over one's body may temporarily provide the buffer needed to deal with these stressors, but then they become dangerous.

Finally, eating disorders do appear to run in families, but as with obesity and many other health problems, it is unclear to what degree heredity plays a role. Genetic factors may predispose a person to an eating disorder, but psychological, behavioral, and environmental factors are also strong.

BOX 7.6

Binge-Eating Disorder

Diagnostic Criteria
  A. Recurrent episodes of binge eating. An episode of binge eating is characterized by both of the following:
    1. Eating, in a discrete period of time (e.g., within any 2-hour period), an amount of food that is definitely larger than what most people would eat in a similar period of time under similar circumstances.
    2. A sense of lack of control over eating during the episode (e.g., a feeling that one cannot stop eating or control what or how much one is eating).
  B. The binge-eating episodes are associated with three (or more) of the following:
    1. Eating much more rapidly than normal.
    2. Eating until feeling uncomfortably full.
    3. Eating large amounts of food when not feeling physically hungry.
    4. Eating alone because of feeling embarrassed by how much one is eating.
    5. Feeling disgusted with oneself, depressed, or very guilty afterward.
  C. Marked distress regarding binge eating is present.
  D. The binge eating occurs, on average, at least once a week for 3 months.
  E. The binge eating is not associated with the recurrent use of inappropriate compensatory behavior as in bulimia nervosa and does not occur exclusively during the course of bulimia nervosa or anorexia nervosa.

From *Diagnostic and Statistical Manual of Mental Disorders* (5th ed.) by American Psychiatric Association, 2013.

HEALTH THREATS FROM EATING DISORDERS

Both anorexia and bulimia pose the risk of serious medical complications. Anorexia can deprive the body of nourishment to the point that the heart and brain suffer damage. As the body slows down to conserve energy due to the absence of caloric intake, several health problems arise. Amenorrhea, or suppression of the menstrual cycle, occurs, and vital functions such as respiration, heart rate, and blood pressure drop. The skin and hair become unhealthy, with nails and hair becoming brittle and dry. The risk of dehydration is also increased. Other risks include anemia, calcium loss and brittle bones, swollen joints, and light-headedness. Eventually, heart failure can occur.

The specific risks associated with bulimia are related to the acts of binging and purging. Esophageal inflammation and severe tooth decay are common due to the presence of stomach acids from vomiting. More serious complications of stomach rupture and heart failure due to mineral loss may occur.

Treatment

Treatment for an eating disorder is quite complex. The problem requires more serious intervention than simply instilling healthier eating habits or restoring a person's body mass. Certainly, medical care must be available to combat the serious physical problems brought on by this disease, but psychological assistance is crucial in addressing the underlying mental or emotional disorder that lies at the root of the problem. Treatment will focus on efforts to improve a patient's self-esteem and that person's overcoming of his/her distorted body image. Struggles with depression, anxiety, and inability to deal with outside pressures must be addressed. A psychiatrist is often called upon for intervention, and various types of individual, group, and family therapy have been used to treat eating disorders. Medically, hospitalization may be necessary if the patient has developed certain medical complications, such as metabolic disturbances, serious depression, and suicidal tendencies, or if he/she has reached a level of being severely underweight. Certain medications have also been found effective in helping the patient deal with his/her depression and other emotional trauma. Finally, nutritional counseling can assist in the patient's development of adequate knowledge and attitudes toward new and healthier eating habits.

Helping the Person

If you suspect that someone you know is suffering from an eating disorder, your assistance could be crucial to the person's ability to overcome the problem. Anorexia Nervosa and Related Eating Disorders, Inc. provides the following suggestions for helping:

1. Be supportive. Provide information about eating disorders.
2. Be a good listener. A good repertoire of supportive comments can be valuable in helping the person find a safe zone to express his/her fears and anxieties. Comments like "I enjoy spending time with you," "That's interesting, I never thought of it like that before," or simply "Tell me more," can make the person feel more comfortable talking to you about his/her problem.
3. Encourage professional help. Counseling, medical treatment, and perhaps even hospitalization may be needed for recovery.
4. Be prepared for denial, resistance, and even hostility.
5. Do what you can to convince the person that recovery has more advantages than the disorder.
6. Realize that the person's recovery is his/her responsibility, not yours. If you sincerely try to help, you are doing the best you can.

Several other organizations provide up-to-date resources on eating disorders. A list of those organizations is provided below:

National Association of Anorexia Nervosa and Associated Disorders (ANAD)
P.O. Box 7
Highland Park, IL 60035
(708) 831-3438

Anorexia Nervosa and Related Eating Disorders, Inc. (ANRED)
P.O. Box 5102
Eugene, OR 97405
(503) 344-1144

American Anorexia/Bulimia Association, Inc. (AABA)
425 East 61st Street, 6th Floor
New York, NY 10021
(212) 891-8686

References

American Cancer Society. (2005). *Cancer facts and figures—2005*. Atlanta, GA: Author.

Anorexia Nervosa and Related Eating Disorders. (1999). *How many people have eating and exercise disorders?*

Centers for Disease Control and Prevention. (2018). *Adult Obesity Facts*. Retrieved from www .cdc.gov/obesity/data/adult.html

Hopkins, M., King, N.A., and Blundell, J.E., (2010). Acute and long-term effects of exercise on appetite control: Is there any benefit for weight control? *Curr Nutr Metab Care*. 13 (6): 635–40, Nov, 2010.

Jarvholm, B., Lewold, S., Malchau, H., & Vingard, E. (2005). Age, body weight, smoking habits, and the risk of osteoarthritis in the hip and knee in men. *European Journal of Epidemiology*, *20*, 537–542.

McGinnis, J. M., & Foege, W. H. (1993). Actual causes of death in the United States. *Journal of the American Medical Association, 270*, 2207–2212.

Nation Association of Anorexia Nervosa and Associated Disorders. (2017). www.anad.org/ get-information-about-eating-disorder/eating-disorders-statistics

National Center for Health Statistics. (2016). Retrieved from: www.cdc.gov/nihs/gov

National Center for Health Statistics. (2012). *Overweight and obesity*. Retrieved from www.cdc .gov/obesity

The National Institutes of Diabetes and Digestive and Kidney Disorders. (1995). *Diabetes in America* (2nd ed., NIH publication #95-1468). Bethesda, MD: Author.

National Institute of Diabetes and Digestive and Kidney Disease. (2018). Retrieved from: www .niddk.nih.gov

Nieman, D. C. (2011). *Exercise testing and prescription: A health-related approach* (7th ed.). New York, NY: McGraw-Hill.

Princeton Survey Research Associates. (1990). *1990 survey would you change your body if possible*. Princeton Research Associates, Princeton, NJ.

Ross, 2012. *Why do Women Hate their Bodies*. psychcentral.com

Speakman, J. R. (2004). Obesity: The integrated roles of environment and genetics. *Journal of Nutrition, 11*, 2090–2105.

U.S. Department of Health and Human Services. (2010). *Healthy People 2010: A Summary Report*. Boston, MA: Jones and Bartlett.

U.S. Department of Health and Human Services. (2000, January). *Healthy People 2010* (Conference ed. in 2 vols.). Washington, DC: Author.

Wing, R., & Phelan, S. (2006). Successful weight loss maintenance. *American Journal of Clinical Nutrition, 82*, 222–225.

Cardiovascular Disease

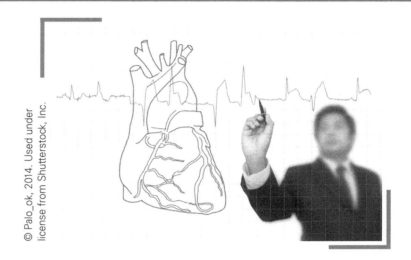

© Palo_ok, 2014. Used under license from Shutterstock, Inc.

Specific Objectives

1. Identify the major forms of cardiovascular disease.
2. Identify the major and minor risk factors associated with cardiovascular disease.
3. Identify the warning signs of heart attack and stroke.
4. Discuss the lifestyle behaviors that contribute to the development of cardiovascular disease.
5. Explain the difference between high-density lipoprotein cholesterol and low-density lipoprotein cholesterol.
6. Identify acceptable levels for blood pressure, blood lipids, glucose, and body fat.
7. Be able to assess a person's risk for cardiovascular disease.
8. Discuss the effects of exercise on reducing cardiovascular disease risk.
9. Understand metabolic syndrome.
10. Discuss what steps an individual can take to keep his/her cardiovascular system healthy and avoid cardiovascular disease.

Adapted from *Fitness for Life, Fourth Edition* by Bill Hyman, Gary Oden, David Bacharach, Tim Sebesta. Copyright © 2011 by Kendall Hunt Publishing Company. Reprinted by permission.

OVERVIEW

The lifestyle in the United States offers so many opportunities. We have the highest standard of living in the world. Transportation is for the most part both convenient and easy; entertainment is readily available; we can drive and even park our cars almost in the location to which we are going; even our food is quick and easy. However, along with the ease of living that we enjoy, there is a price to be paid. The convenience of transportation and the fast foods that we consume at an enormous rate have led to a sedentary lifestyle and high-fat high-calorie diet. This in turn has led to our country having a very high rate of cardiovascular disease (CVD).

CVD is the leading cause of death in the United States, accounting for 1 in 3 deaths in 2017. CVD is disease of any aspect of the cardiovascular system, which includes the heart, blood, and blood vessels. Major forms of CVD include high blood pressure, congenital heart disease, coronary heart disease (CHD), peripheral vascular disease, stroke, rheumatic heart disease, and atherosclerosis. The most predominant form of CVD is CHD. This disease causes a narrowing of the coronary arteries, which supply the heart with nutrients through its blood flow. CHD is the single largest killer of American males and females. About every 38 seconds, an American will die from a coronary event, with 2,300 dying each day. About 41 percent of the people who experience a heart attack in a given year will die from it (American Heart Association, 2018).

The heart, like all other muscles and organs in the body, needs its own blood supply. The myocardium (muscle layer of the heart) is not nourished by the blood being pumped to other parts of the body. The heart's blood is supplied through the coronary artery system (see Figure 8.1). When a portion of the heart does not get adequate blood, it begins to die. When CHD causes the arteries to be closed by about two-thirds, chest pain called angina pectoris can occur during times of excitement or physical exertion. A heart attack, or myocardial infarction, occurs when the blood supply to part of the heart is blocked. This is typically brought about by a blood clot forming in a narrowed coronary pressure, fullness, squeezing, or pain in the center of the chest lasting

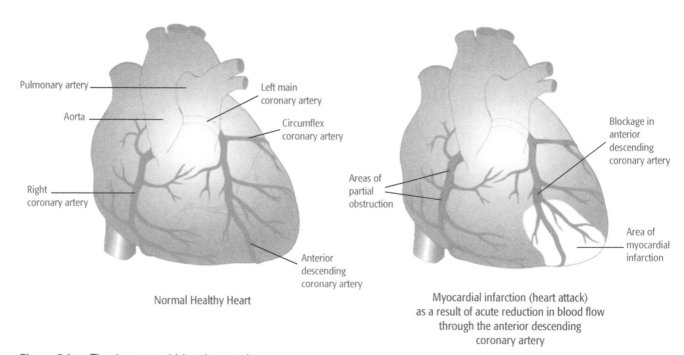

Normal Healthy Heart

Myocardial infarction (heart attack) as a result of acute reduction in blood flow through the anterior descending coronary artery

Figure 8.1 • The heart and blood vessels.

two minutes or more; pain that spreads to the shoulders, neck, or arms; or severe pain, dizziness, fainting, sweating, nausea, or shortness of breath. Sharp, stabbing twinges of pain are usually not signals of a heart attack (see Table 8.1).

Stroke is another predominant form of CVD. Stroke affects the blood vessels that supply oxygen and nutrients to the brain. Atherosclerosis (narrowing of arteries due to buildup of deposits in arterial wall) can cause a blood clot to form inside the cerebral artery and block the blood flow to the brain. The risk factors for stroke are listed in Table 8.3. The prevalence for stroke is less than for heart attack, and stroke numbers have declined significantly over the past 10 years. Current statistics show the prevalence of stroke to be 795,000 incident per year in the United States (AHA, 2018; see Table 8.2). The most important risk factor for stroke is hypertension. As blood pressure increases, the risk for stroke increases accordingly. Some of the warning signals of stroke are dizziness, temporary weakness or numbness on one side of the face, arm or leg, and temporary loss of speech or vision (American Heart Association, 2018).

Hypertension is considered a major risk factor for CHD and stroke; however, hypertension can also be considered a disease in itself. Blood pressure is defined as the force of the blood against the walls of the arteries and veins. This force is created by the heart as it pumps blood to every part of the body. Hypertension or high blood pressure is a condition in which the blood pressure is chronically elevated above the normal or optimal levels (American Heart Association, 2018).

Hypertension is diagnosed if a person has repeated measurements above the optimal levels. For example, if someone has two blood pressure measurements taken on separate occasions and the diastolic pressure is above 90 mm Hg each time, hypertension would

---

TABLE 8.1   What to Do in Case of a Heart Attack

When it comes to a heart attack, delay spells danger. Minutes make a difference, so it's important to know what to do.

Know the Signals of a Heart Attack

- Uncomfortable pressure, fullness, squeezing, or pain in the center of the chest lasting two minutes or more.
- Pain may spread to shoulders, neck, or arms.
- Severe pain, dizziness, fainting, sweating, nausea, or shortness of breath may also occur. Sharp, stabbing twinges of pain are usually not signals of a heart attack.

Know What Emergency Action to Take

- If you are having typical chest discomfort that lasts for two minutes or more, call the local emergency rescue service immediately.
- If you can get to a hospital faster by car, have someone drive you. Find out which hospitals have 24-hour, emergency cardiac care and discuss with your doctor possible choices. Plan in advance the route that's fastest from where you live and work.
- Keep a list of emergency rescue service numbers by your telephone and in a prominent place in your pocket, wallet, or purse.

Know How to Help

- If you are with someone who is having the signals of a heart attack, take action even if the person denies there is something wrong.
- Call the emergency rescue service, or
- Get to the nearest hospital emergency room that has 24-hour emergency cardiac care, and
- Give mouth-to-mouth breathing and chest compressions (CPR) if it is necessary and if you are properly trained.

American Heart Association, 2000.

TABLE 8.2   Risk Factors for Heart Disease, according to the American Heart Association

Risk Factors
Major risk factors that can be changed
1. Cigarette/tobacco smoke
2. High blood pressure
3. High blood cholesterol
4. Physical inactivity
5. Obesity and overweight
6. Diabetes
Major risk factors that cannot be changed
1. Heredity
2. Being male
3. Increasing age
4. Race
Contributing factors
1. Individual response to stress
2. Excessive alcohol
3. Some illegal drugs

Source: American Heart Association. *Heart Disease and Stroke Statistics—2018.*

TABLE 8.3   Risk Factors for Stroke

Risk Factors That Can Be Treated	Risk Factors That Cannot Be Treated
1. High blood pressure	**1.** Age
2. Personal history of heart disease	**2.** Male
3. Cigarette smoking	**3.** Race—African-American
4. High red blood cell count	**4.** Personal history of diabetes mellitus; prior stroke
5. Transient ischemic attacks (TIA)	**5.** Heredity–family history
6. Physical inactivity	**6.** Geographic location–Southeastern U.S.
7. Excessive alcohol intake; intravenous drug abuse	**7.** Season–during periods of extreme temperatures
8. Obesity	**8.** Socioeconomic—more likely among the poor
9. Elevated blood cholesterol	**9.** Asymptomatic carotid bruit–atherosclerosis in carotid artery that causes a sound heard with a stethoscope

Source: American Heart Association.

be determined. Many factors contribute to increased blood pressure. These factors include heredity, obesity, sodium sensitivity, alcohol consumption, age, race, caffeine, and a sedentary lifestyle. Hypertension increases the workload of the heart and arteries and contributes to heart failure and atherosclerosis. Like all muscles in the body, the heart, when required to work harder than normal for a long period of time, tends to enlarge. An enlarged heart has a difficult time keeping up with the demands of the body. Statistics demonstrate that about 50 million Americans have high blood pressure (Table 8.4). Hypertension is most prevalent among the elderly, African Americans, and the obese.

TABLE 8.4 Heart Disease and Stroke Statistics 2018 At-a-Glance

Here are a few key statistics about heart disease, stroke, other cardiovascular diseases and their risk factors, in addition to commonly cited statistics about the American Heart Association's research program. The source for the health statistics is the Association's 2018 Heart Disease and Stroke Statistics Update, which is compiled annually by the American Heart Association, the Centers for Disease Control and Prevention, the National Institutes of Health and other government sources. The years cited are the most recent available for each statistical category. The source for the research information is the Association's Science Operations Department.

Heart Disease, Stroke and other Cardiovascular Diseases

- Cardiovascular disease, listed as the underlying cause of death, accounts for nearly 836,546 deaths in the US. That's about 1 of every 3 deaths in the US.
- About 2,300 Americans die of cardiovascular disease each day, an average of 1 death every 38 seconds.E
- Cardiovascular diseases claim more lives each year than all forms of cancer and Chronic Lower Respiratory Disease combined.
- About 92.1 million American adults are living with some form of cardiovascular disease or the after-effects of stroke. Direct and indirect costs of total cardiovascular diseases and stroke are estimated to total more than $329.7 billion; that includes both health expenditures and lost productivity.
- Nearly half of all NH black adults have some form of cardiovascular disease, 47.7 percent of females and 46.0 percent of males.
- Coronary Heart Disease is the leading cause (43.8 percent) of deaths attributable to cardiovascular disease in the US, followed by Stroke (16.8 percent), Heart Failure (9.0 percent), High Blood Pressure (9.4 percent), diseases of the arteries (3.1 percent), and other cardiovascular diseases (17.9 percent).
- Heart disease accounts for 1 in 7 deaths in the US.
- Cardiovascular disease is the leading global cause of death, accounting for more than 17.9 million deaths per year in 2015, a number that is expected to grow to more than 23.6 million by 2030.
- CVD and stroke accounted for 14% of total health expenditures in 2013-2014. This is more than any major diagnostic group.
- Total direct medical costs of CVD are projected to increase to $749 billion in 2035.

Source: Heart disease and stroke statistics 2018 update: a report from the American Heart Association [published online ahead of print January 31, 2018]. Circulation. DOI: 10.1161/CIR.0000000000000558.

GENDER AND RACE DIFFERENCES IN CARDIOVASCULAR DISEASE STATISTICS

Cardiovascular disease is the leading cause of death for women in the United States. 1 in 3 women's death each year is related to CVD. Many people are surprised by the fact that most CVD deaths each year are women. The death rate for those who have initial heart attack is also much higher for women than for men (26 percent of women die within one year after a heart attack compared with 19 percent of men).

African Americans have the highest risk of developing CVD, with almost 45 percent of men and 47 percent of women experiencing CVD. The Hispanic population has about a 30-percent occurrence rate for CVD, with occurrence being evenly distributed between women and men. However, with the Hispanic population, CVD occurs much earlier in life. It is hard to pull comprehensive facts about Asian Americans, however, CVD is the leading cause of death for this population, accounting for more deaths than all forms of cancer combined. Native Americans have the highest risk for CVD due to the large percentage of this population having diabetes, which is a major risk factor for heart disease and stroke (Center for Disease Control and Prevention, 2017). Finally,

TABLE 8.5 Heart Disease Deaths Vary by Race and Ethnicity

Heart disease is the leading cause of death for people of most ethnicities in the United States, including African Americans, Hispanics, and whites. For American Indians or Alaska Natives and Asians or Pacific Islanders, heart disease is second only to cancer. Below are the percentages of all deaths caused by heart disease in 2013, listed by ethnicity.

Race of Ethnic Group	% of Deaths
American Indians or Alaska Natives	18.4
Asians or Pacific Islanders	22.2
Non-Hispanic Blacks	23.8
Non-Hispanic Whites	23.8
All	23.5

Source: https://www.cdc.gov/heartdisease/facts.htm

there is a 37-percent rate of CVD in white males and a 34-percent rate in white females (Center for Disease Control and Prevention, 2018).

YOUR RISK FOR CARDIOVASCULAR DISEASE

Although CVD is the number one killer in the United States, the fact is that to a large degree we control our own destiny. Preventive medicine is the key to reducing the development of any form of CVD. It is evident that our lifestyle habits largely determine our susceptibility. Most physicians agree that if we ate better, exercised more, smoked less, and maintained proper body composition, it would do more to improve our health than anything they could do for us.

For almost 50 years, research has been conducted in an effort to determine the basic cause of CVD. Large populations have been studied over long periods with their living habits and medical records assessed in relation to the incidence of CVD. These studies have helped identify how CVD develops and what factors predispose one to CVD (Paffenbarger & Hyde, 1984). Risk factors that lead to CVD development can be classified into major and minor categories, with the major factors having much more influence on disease risk. In addition, three of the minor factors are associated with lifestyle behaviors. Although heredity plays a role in CVD, the most important determinant is personal lifestyle. A true statement could probably be made by stating that CVD is not genetically inherited, but we do tend to inherit the lifestyle of our parents. To a large degree, even though we hate to hear it, we do turn into our parents. This simply means that people typically live the type of lifestyle in which they were raised. If, as a child, you ate high-fat foods and were not encouraged to be active, then more than likely those are your habits as an adult. A CVD risk assessment can be used to evaluate the impact of an individual's lifestyle and heredity on the development of CVD (see Personal Growth Opportunity 8.1). Using this assessment can help identify individuals who may be at high risk for disease. In addition, the assessment can educate people regarding the leading risk factors for development of CVD. For example, a person who completes the assessment knows that the ideal blood pressure is 120/80 or lower, that total cholesterol should be below 200 mg/dl, and that smoking or being exposed to environmental smoke significantly increases risk (see Personal Growth Opportunity 8.1 to complete self-assessment CVD risk).

With the exception of gender, age, race, and heredity, the risk factors for CVD are preventable and reversible. A discussion of the risk factors is presented next, along with some recommendations for risk reduction.

PRIMARY OR MAJOR RISK FACTORS

Smoking

Smoking is the number one cause of CVD. Individuals who smoke have a 2.5 times greater than average risk of developing CVD. With 40 percent of all deaths being CVD related and the average risk being high, we would not like our chances if we were smokers. Cancer is the disease that typically is associated with smoking; however, smokers are much more likely to die of heart disease than cancer.

A strong relationship exists between the development of CVD and smoking. This means that the more you smoke, the greater your risk. A one-pack-per-day smoker is at twice the risk as a nonsmoker while a two-pack-per-day smoker is at three times the risk (Neaton & Wentworth, 1992).

It is easy to understand why smoking has such an impact on the development of CVD. As smoke enters the alveoli of the lungs, carbon monoxide competes with oxygen to be carried into the blood. The hemoglobin portion of the red blood cells is the oxygen-carrying component of the blood. As you know, without adequate oxygen the body cannot function; therefore, people must depend on their hemoglobin to transport the needed oxygen. Even though hemoglobin has an affinity for oxygen, it also has an affinity for carbon monoxide. In fact, the affinity for carbon monoxide is stronger than that for oxygen; therefore, oxygen is somewhat ignored. This reduces the amount of oxygen in the blood and forces the heart to pump much more blood in order for adequate oxygen to be delivered.

High Blood Pressure

Although hypertension is considered a type of CVD, high blood pressure is also a major risk factor for developing CHD and stroke. Normal blood pressure is a systolic pressure below 120 mmHg and a diastolic pressure below 80mmHg. As noted in Table 8.6, their are three levels of high blood pressure, with a systolic pressure of 120mm Hg or a diastolic pressure above 80mm Hg constitutes elevated blood pressure. For individuals with elevated blood pressure it is recommended that lifestyle changes be made and blood pressure reassessed in 3-6 months. Stage 1 high blood pressure is a systolic pressure between 130-139mm Hg or a diastolic pressure between 80-89mm Hg. As with elevated blood pressure, lifestyle changes are recommended and a reassessment of blood pressure every 3-6 months. However, if lifestyle changes are not successful in reducing stage 1 blood pressure, your doctor may suggest medication. Stage 2 high blood pressure is a systolic pressure above 140mm Hg or a diastolic pressure above 90mm Hg. A person with stage 2 high blood pressure should incorporate lifestyle changes and medication is likely to be part of the treatment plan. People with stage 2 high blood pressure should reassess every month. As with smoking, CHD has a strong relationship with hypertension. That is to say, the higher the blood pressure, the greater the risk for CHD.

Control of hypertension depends to a large extent on the cause. Some of the causes of hypertension include stress, obesity, and lack of exercise. Control methods may include a weight-loss program, learning how to control stress, and starting an exercise program.

© Simone van den Berg, 2014. Used under license from Shutterstock, Inc.

TABLE 8.6   Know Your Blood Pressure and What to Do about It

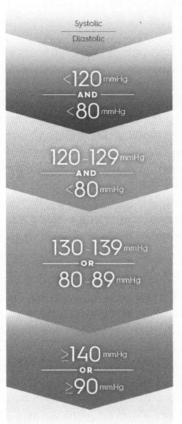

KNOW YOUR BLOOD PRESSURE
—AND WHAT TO DO ABOUT IT

By AMERICAN HEART ASSOCIATION NEWS

Systolic
Diastolic

<120 mmHg
AND
<80 mmHg

120-129 mmHg
AND
<80 mmHg

130-139 mmHg
OR
80-89 mmHg

≥140 mmHg
OR
≥90 mmHg

The newest guidelines for hypertension:

NORMAL BLOOD PRESSURE
*Recommendations: Healthy lifestyle choices and yearly checks.

ELEVATED BLOOD PRESSURE
*Recommendations: Healthy lifestyle changes, reassessed in 3-6 months.

HIGH BLOOD PRESSURE / STAGE 1
*Recommendations: 10-year heart disease and stroke risk assessment. If less than 10% risk, lifestyle changes, reassessed in 3-6 months. If higher, lifestyle changes and medication with monthly follow-ups until BP controlled.

HIGH BLOOD PRESSURE / STAGE 2
*Recommendations: Lifestyle changes and 2 different classes of medicine, with monthly follow-ups until BP is controlled.

*Individual recommendations need to come from your doctor.
Source: American Heart Association's journal Hypertension
Published Nov. 13, 2017

As you may have heard on many occasions, high blood pressure is the silent killer. This statement is made to enforce the fact that individuals do not have any way of knowing their blood pressure unless they have it checked. It should be common practice for a person to monitor his/her blood pressure on a regular basis. If an individual has a family history of high blood pressure or any form of CVD, it is recommended that blood pressure be checked every six months.

For an individual with no family history of this type, one time per year may be adequate.

Hypercholesterolemia

Hypercholesterolemia is a technical name for having too much fat in the blood. Blood fats are responsible for the buildup of plaque on the walls of arteries. The higher an individual's blood lipids or fats, the greater his/her risk is for CVD.

Table 8.8 includes the normal and abnormal values for blood lipids. A person with abnormal blood lipids has double the risk of CVD as a person with normal blood lipids levels. As with smoking and blood pressure, a dose relationship exist. This means that

TABLE 8.7   Lifestyle Modifications to Manage Hypertension*†

Modification	Recommendation	Approximate SBP Reduction (range)
Weight reduction	Maintain normal body weight (body mass index 18.5–24.9 kg/m^2).	5–20 mm Hg/10 kg weight loss
Adopt DASH eating plan	Consume a diet rich in fruits, vegetables, and low-fat dairy products with a reduced content of saturated and total fat.	8–14 mm Hg
Dietary sodium reduction	Reduce dietary sodium intake to no more than 100 mmol/day (2.4 g sodium or 6 g sodium chloride).	2–8 mm Hg
Physical activity	Engage in regular aerobic physical activity such as brisk walking (at least 30 min per day, most days of the week).	4–9 mm Hg
Moderation of alcohol consumption	Limit consumption to no more than 2 drinks (1 oz or 30 mL ethanol; e.g., 24 oz beer, 10 oz wine, or 3 oz 80-proof whiskey) per day in most men and to no more than 1 drink per day in women and lighter weight persons.	2–4 mm Hg

DASH-Dietary Approaches to Stop Hypertension.
*For overall cardiovascular risk reduction, stop smoking.
†The effects of implementing these modifications are dose and time dependent, and could be greater for some individuals.
Source: National High Blood Pressure Education Program. *The Seventh Report of the Joint National Committee on Detection, Evaluation, and Treatment of High Blood Pressure.* National Heart, Lung, and Blood Institute, National Institutes of Health, NIH Pub. No. 03-5233. Bethesda, MD: National Institutes of Health, 2003.

the more abnormal a person's blood lipid levels are, the greater the risk for CVD. Over the past 20 or so years, cholesterol education has improved greatly in the United States. Many people are now aware of cholesterol and its danger. However, most people are not well informed about the different types of cholesterol. Cholesterol can be broken down to subfractions that include low-density lipoproteins (LDL-C), very low-density lipoproteins (VLDL-C), and high-density lipoproteins (HDL-C). These subfractions are very important when determining an individual's risk for CVD. In simple terms, LDL-C has a low density of protein and a high density of fat, while the opposite is true for HDL-C (high protein content, low fat). While LDL-C is harmful because of its ability to cause fatty buildup in blood vessels, HDL-C works as a scavenger, removing fatty buildup in the vessels. The higher the level of HDL-C an individual has, the lower his/her risk is for developing CVD. Evidence exists that suggests that for each 1 mg/dl increase in HDL-C, there is a two-percent reduction for men and a three-percent reduction for women for the development of CVD. Research data also indicate that a one-percent decrease in total cholesterol is associated with a two-percent reduction in CVD (Robergs & Keteyian, 2010).

The following table provides some general guidelines. You should always discuss your own results with your physician.

The National Cholesterol Education Program (NCEP) guidelines given in Table 8.8 show that an LDL-C value below 130 mg/dL is desirable, between 130 and 159 mg/dL is borderline, and 160 mg/dL and above is high risk for CVD. It is obvious that the lower one's LDL-C level, the better. In addition, as indicated in Table 8.8, a HDL-C value below 40 is low and with increased risk for CVD.

It is suggested by many authorities that the ratio between total cholesterol and HDL-C is the strongest indicator of potential CVD risk. A TC/HDL-C ratio of 3.5 or lower

TABLE 8.8   to Healthy Blood Cholesterol and Triglyceride Levels*

Demographic	Total Cholesterol	Non-HDL	LDL	HDL	Triglycerides
Age 19 or younger	Less than 170 mg/dL	Less than 120 mg/dL	Less than 100 mg/dL	More than 45 mg/dL	Less than 150 mg/dL
Men age 20 or older	125 to 200 mg/dL	Less than 130 mg/dL	Less than 100 mg/dL	40 mg/dL or higher	Less than 150 mg/dL
Women age 20 or older	125 to 200 mg/dL	Less than 130 mg/dL	Less than 100 mg/dL	50 mg/dL or higher	Less than 150 mg/dL

Healthy blood cholesterol levels differ by age and sex. If you are age 19 or younger, your total cholesterol levels should be less than 170 milligrams per deciliter (mg/dL) of blood, your non-HDL cholesterol level should be less than 120 mg/dL, your LDL cholesterol level should be less than 100 mg/dL, and your HDL cholesterol level should be more than 45 mg/dL. If you are age 20 or older, your total cholesterol should be between 125 and 200 mg/dL, your non-HDL cholesterol level should be less than 130 mg/dL, your LDL cholesterol level should be less than 100 mg/dL, and your HDL cholesterol level should be 40 mg/dL or higher if you are a man or 50 mg/dl or higher if you are a woman.

When you receive this screening will depend on your age, risk factors, and family history of high blood cholesterol and cardiovascular diseases such as atherosclerosis, heart attack, or stroke.

- **Age 19 or younger.** Screening begins at ages 9 to 11 and should be repeated every 5 years. Screening may be performed as early as age 2 if there is a family history of high blood cholesterol, heart attack, or stroke.
- **Age 20 or older.** Younger adults should be screened every 5 years. Men ages 45 to 65 and women ages 55 to 65 should be screened every 1 to 2 years.

If your blood cholesterol levels are not within the healthy range for your age and sex, your doctor may also recommend heart-healthy lifestyle changes to help you lower or control your high blood cholesterol and order a repeat lipid profile test.

Did you know that cholesterol is an important part of many organs in our body and that high levels of bad types of cholesterol can increase your risk of cardiovascular disease?

*Numerical values are given in milligrams per deciliter. Obtain complete lipoprotein profile after 9- to 12-hour fast.

---

is excellent for men, and 3.0 or lower is excellent for women. For example, a total cholesterol value of 180 and an HDL-C value of 50 would translate into a ratio of 3.6 (180 divided by 50).

Triglycerides are also a blood lipid that, if elevated, can lead to CVD. Most people have been educated concerning blood cholesterol, but not much education has been directed toward triglycerides. Readings of 150 mg/dl or below is considered to be acceptable triglyceride levels with levels above 200 considered high risk. There is a direct relationship between body composition and triglycerides; therefore, the best control for triglycerides may be to control body composition.

Blood lipids can be altered by changes made in an individual's lifestyle. Starting an aerobic exercise program is an excellent way to increase HDL-C and lower LDL-C and triglycerides. Many researchers have demonstrated the beneficial effects of aerobic exercise on blood lipids (Hartung, 1995; Pronk, 1993). Studies suggest that an aerobic exercise program that expends 1,000 calories/week (e.g., ten miles of walking/jogging) at moderate intensity is required to produce lipoprotein changes. Greater changes occur with a greater caloric expenditure.

Exercise intensity is also an important factor in regard to lipid changes. For the past few years, exercise specialists have suggested that low-intensity exercise is as good as or

BOX 8.1

Tips to Control Your Cholesterol

High cholesterol and triglyceride levels can lead to heart disease. Talk to your doctor about your risk for heart disease. Have your cholesterol checked and follow these simple changes to keep your cholesterol at normal levels.

1 Be A Smart Shopper
Choose foods lower in saturated fat, trans fat, and cholesterol. Here are some shopping ideas:

Choose:	Instead of:
Chicken breast or drumstick (skin removed before cooking)	Chicken wing or thigh (skin on while cooking)
Pork—ears, neck bone, feet, ham hocks, round, sirloin, loin	Pork—hog maws, lunch meat, vienna sausage, bacon, ribs
Egg whites	Egg yolks
Skim or 1% milk	Whole milk
Vegetable oil (such as canola, safflower, or sesame)	Lard, butter, shortening

2 Modify How You Cook
Trim the fat from meat, and remove the skin and fat from chicken and turkey before cooking.
Cook ground meat, drain the fat, and rinse with hot tap water. This removes half the fat.
Cool soups, and remove the layer of fat that rises to the top.
Bake, steam, broil, or grill food instead of frying.
Use oils low in saturated fat, such as canola, safflower, and sesame oil.

3 Make Healthy Choices
Choose fresh vegetables and fruits instead of high-fat foods like chips or fries.
Use fat-free or low-fat salad dressing, mayonnaise, or sour cream.
Use small amounts of tub margarine instead of butter.

Source: National Heart, Lung, and Blood Institute. NIH.gov

even better than moderate- and high-intensity exercise. The "no pain, no gain" slogan was said to be outdated and incorrect. This does hold true in regard to total cholesterol, LDL-C, and triglycerides. However, moderate- and high-intensity exercise is necessary for an increase in HDL-C to occur. For low-intensity exercise to be effective in lowering TC, LDL-C, and triglycerides, weight loss must occur. This weight loss must be in the form of body fat, since the greater the amount of fat loss, the greater the decrease in these blood lipids. The independent effect of aerobic exercise on TC, LDL-C, and triglycerides is limited to improving the magnitude of change in triglycerides. TC and LDL-C changes do not seem to change without body fat reduction.

HDL-C increases are directly related to the amount and intensity of the aerobic exercise performance. Exercise that is below 60 percent of maximum heart rate does not seem to have a significant impact on HDL-C. One study performed by Crouse et al. (1995) demonstrated that an increase in exercise intensity produced gains in HDL-C. Subjects performing at 70 percent of maximum heart rate had greater increases in HDL-C than did subjects performing at 60 percent. Likewise, subjects exercising at 80 percent of maximum showed more improvement than did subjects exercising at 70 percent (Table 8.9).

TABLE 8.9 Conditions That Enhance the Effects of Exercise on Blood Lipids

- Patients are currently sedentary
- Lipoprotein levels are abnormal (especially elevated triglycerides or depressed HDL cholesterol)
- Exercise training is long-term (>6 months)
- Body composition changes occur (↑ lean body mass, ↓ body fat)
- Diet is modified (e.g., ↓ saturated fat, ↑ omega-3 or omega-6 fatty acids)

Dietary adjustments are another way to alter blood lipids. Total cholesterol, LDL-C, triglycerides, and even HDL-C can be improved through the proper nutritional practices. The average American consumes between 400 and 600 mg of cholesterol daily; however, the body produces much more than that. The fact that a food product is cholesterol free does not necessarily mean that cholesterol cannot be manufactured from that product. Saturated fats are the biggest concern in the diet. These fats raise cholesterol levels more than anything else in the diet. Any food product that is high in saturated fat, even though it has little or no cholesterol, raises the body's total cholesterol level (Stone et al., 2013).

Saturated fats are found mostly in animal sources (see Table 8.10). Fish and poultry have fewer saturated fats, and therefore they may be a better dietary choice. The American Heart Association has published dietary recommendations for the treatment of hypercholesterolemia (Table 8.11). These recommendations include a fat intake below 30 percent of total calorie consumption with not more than one-third of these calories coming from saturated fat. Since saturated fat has the greatest influence on the production of cholesterol, limiting its intake is the most important dietary control. Monounsaturated fats, such as canola or olive oil, should make up one-third or more of fat calories, since these oils may raise HDL-C levels. Polyunsaturated fats, which may help lower total

TABLE 8.10 Saturated Fat Sources

Food	Amount	Percent Calories from Total Fat	Percent Calories from Saturated Fat	Cholesterol (milligrams)
Fruits		Low	Low	0
Vegetables		Low	Low	0
Grains		Low	Low	0
Nuts		High	Moderate	0
Avocado		88	17	0
Coconut, dried		88	76	0
Milk, nonfat	1 cup	–	–	5
Milk, low-fat	1 cup	30	17	22
Cottage cheese, 4% fat	1/2 cup	35	20	24
Cheese–pasteurized type	1 oz	73	40	25
Cream (half & half)	1/4 cup	79	58	26
Ice cream, regular	1/2 cup	49	27	27
Cheese, cheddar	1 oz	72	40	28
Milk, whole	1 cup	48	27	34
Butter	1 tbs	100	55	35
Margarine	1 tbs	100	18	0
Tuna, canned	3 oz	38	10	55
Chicken, cooked	3 oz	19	6	74
Pork, cooked	3 oz	73	26	76
Beef, cooked	3 oz	77	37	80
Lamb, cooked	3 oz	61	34	83
Egg yolk	1	71	43	220
Liver, fried	2 oz	43	13	250

Source: Whitney, *Understanding Nutrition.* Wadsworth Publishing, 1999.

TABLE 8.11 National Cholesterol Education Program/American Heart Association Guidelines for Dietary Prevention and Treatment of High Serum Cholesterol Levels and Coronary Heart Disease

- Total fat intake should be less than 30 percent of calories.
- Saturated fat intake should be less than 10 percent of calories (Step 2 = <7%).
- Polyunsaturated fat intake should not exceed 10 percent of calories; monounsaturated fat should not exceed 15 percent.
- Cholesterol intake should not exceed 300 mg/day (Step 2 = <200 mg/day).
- Carbohydrate intake should constitute 55 percent or more of calories, with emphasis on complex carbohydrates and high fiber foods.
- Protein intake should provide about 15 percent of the calories.
- Sodium intake should not exceed 2,400 mg/day.
- Alcoholic consumption should be moderate (<2 drinks per day for men, <1 drink per day for women).
- Total calories should be sufficient to maintain the individual's recommended body weight.
- A wide variety of foods should be consumed.

Source: National Cholesterol Education Program and the American Heart Association.

cholesterol without reducing HDL-C, should account for up to one-third of the total fat calories consumed.

In addition to lowering fat consumption, the NCEP recommends limiting dietary cholesterol to under 300 mg/day, which is about the amount of cholesterol found in one large egg.

Cholesterol testing is the first step in gaining control of this risk factor. The NCEP recommends that all adults be tested at least once every five years, beginning at age 20. If an individual has a family history of heart disease, the recommendation is for the testing to occur at least every three years.

Physical Inactivity

In 1993, the American Heart Association identified a sedentary lifestyle as a major risk factor for CVD. Lack of physical activity is on a par with smoking, high blood pressure, and high cholesterol and triglyceride levels as a major factor in determining CVD risk. When compared with the other major risk factors, lack of physical activity affects more of the population than the others combined. Roughly 60 percent of the U.S. population is at risk because of physical inactivity (Table 8.2). This makes lack of exercise the most changeable of all the risk factors. As little as 90 minutes per week of mild exercise is reported to significantly reduce CVD risk. Exercise may include any activity that expends calories. Examples could include hiking, cycling, gardening, swimming, or golf.

Most experts maintain that as long as total energy output is increased, expended through light or moderate exercise, risks of CVD are decreased. A lower risk for CVD was observed in men and women who habitually carried out light exercise (leisure-time walking, cycling, and gardening; Blair et al., 1995). Also, Lee, Hsieh, and Paffenbarger (1995) reported that total energy expenditure and energy expenditure in vigorous activities (greater than 60 percent of maximum) related inversely to CVD mortality. With this information in mind, the guidelines for improving cardiovascular endurance that were presented in Chapter 2 are appropriate to follow in order to reduce CVD risk.

Obesity

As defined in Chapter 3, obesity is considered to be 10 percent above the ideal fat percentage. In addition, some agencies use a body mass index (refer to Chapter 3, for definition) above 30 for defining obesity. Excess body fat places a strain on the cardiovascular system, creating a much less efficient engine. Although obesity is recognized as an independent risk factor for CVD, the risk attributed to obesity may actually be caused by other risk factors that are usually associated with excessive body fat. Risk factors such as high blood lipids, high blood pressure, and diabetes improve with a decrease in body fat.

An increase in daily physical activity, which includes participation in both aerobic and strength-training programs, and a moderate reduction in caloric intake can lead to a significant reduction in percent body fat. The importance of strength training cannot be overlooked in regard to changing one's body composition. If a person does not include strength training while trying to change body composition, the person will lose both weight and lean tissue. The loss of lean tissue would decrease resting metabolism and make it more difficult for a person to maintain a healthy body composition. See Chapter 7 for more recommendations on weight control.

Diabetes

Diabetes mellitus (commonly called diabetes) is a condition in which the blood glucose (sugar) is inhibited from entering the cell. This condition is created because the pancreas either stops producing insulin, does not produce enough insulin to meet the body's needs, or the body cannot use insulin. As a result, blood glucose absorption by the cells is low, leading to high blood glucose levels. Long-term complications involving the eyes, kidneys, nerves, and blood vessels result from this condition. Diabetes kills about 75,000 Americans a year. It is the top cause of kidney failure, limb amputations, and adult-onset blindness, as well as being a contributor to CVD.

TABLE 8.12 Blood Glucose Guidelines

Desirable	<100
Prediabetes	100–125
Diabetes	>126

Fasting blood glucose levels above 100 mg/dl are considered to be a sign of diabetes and should be brought to the attention of a physician (Table 8.12). Values between 100 and 125 mg/dL are considered to be borderline high whereas values above 125 mg/dL are high. Other signs and symptoms of diabetes include excessive urination, excessive thirst, unsatisfied hunger, weight loss, cessation of growth among the young, irritability, and drowsiness.

Type 1, or insulin-dependent, and type 2, non-insulin-dependent, are the two major forms of diabetes. Type 1 can occur at any age but may be referred to as juvenile diabetes because it is typically found in young people. Only about 10 percent of diabetes cases are type 1. Type 2 diabetes accounts for approximately 90 percent of all cases and more often occurs in people above 40, with the highest frequency in people above the age of 55. About 85 percent of type 2 diabetics were obese at the time of diagnosis; therefore, the term *diabesity* has been used to describe this condition (Nieman, 2011).

The difference between type 1 and type 2 diabetes is that in type 1, the pancreas produces very little or no insulin, whereas in type 2, the insulin production of the pancreas is adequate but the body cells are unable to use the insulin correctly.

A diet high in water-soluble fiber (found in fruits, vegetables, oats, and beans) and an aerobic exercise program can help prevent the onset of type 2 diabetes.

SECONDARY OR MINOR RISK FACTORS

Secondary risk factors for CVD are important to control but not to the same extent as smoking, blood pressure, obesity, diabetes, blood lipids, and physical activity. These minor risk factors include stress, gender, race, age, and heredity. Interestingly, some of these factors are under our control although others are not. Age, race, gender, and heredity cannot be altered; therefore, we are at the mercy of our biological makeup to some degree.

BOX 8.2

American Heart Association Diet and Lifestyle Goals and Recommendations for Cardiovascular Disease Reduction

Diet and Lifestyle Goals for Cardiovascular Disease Risk Reduction
- Consume an overall healthy diet.
- Aim for a healthy body weight.
- Aim for recommended levels of low-density lipoprotein (LDL) cholesterol, high-density lipoprotein (HDL) cholesterol, and triglycerides.
- Aim for a normal blood pressure.
- Aim for a normal blood glucose level.
- Be physically active.
- Avoid use of and exposure to tobacco products.

Diet and Lifestyle Recommendations for CVD Risk Reduction
- Balance calorie intake and physical activity to achieve or maintain a healthy body weight.
- Consume a diet rich in vegetables and fruits.
- Choose whole-grain, high-fiber foods.
- Consume fish, especially oily fish, at least twice a week.
- Limit your intake of saturated fat to <7% of energy, trans-fat to <1% of energy, and cholesterol to <300 mg per day by:
  - choosing lean meats and vegetable alternatives;
  - selecting fat-free (skim), 1%-fat, and low-fat dairy products; and
  - minimizing intake of partially hydrogenated fats.
- Minimize your intake of beverages and foods with added sugars.

- Choose and prepare foods with little or no salt.
- If you consume alcohol, do so in moderation.
- When you eat food that is prepared outside of the home, follow the AHA Diet and Lifestyle Recommendations.
- The following have unproven or uncertain effects on CVD risk: antioxidant supplements, soy protein, folate and other B vitamins, and phytochemicals.

Pediatric Dietary Strategies for Individuals Ages >2 Years: Recommendations to All Patients and Families
- Balance dietary calories with physical activity to maintain normal growth.
- 60 minutes of moderate to vigorous play or physical activity daily.
- Eat vegetables and fruits daily; limit juice intake.
- Use vegetable oils and soft margarines low in saturated fat and trans-fatty acids instead of butter or most other animal fats in the diet.
- Eat whole-grain breads and cereals rather than refined grain products.
- Reduce the intake of sugar-sweetened beverages and foods.
- Use nonfat (skim) or low-fat milk and dairy products daily.
- Eat more fish, especially oily fish, broiled or baked.
- Reduce salt intake, including salt from processed foods.

Sources: American Heart Association Nutrition Committee; Lichtenstein, A. H., Appel, L. J., Brands, M., Carnethon, M., Daniels, S., Franch, H. A., Franklin, B., Kris-Etherton, P., Harris, W. S., Howard, B., Karanja, N., Lefevre, M., Rudel, L., Sacks, F., Van Horn, L., Winston, M., Wylie-Rosett, J. (2006). Diet and lifestyle recommendations revision 2006: A scientific statement from the American Heart Association Nutrition Committee. *Circulation, 114*, 82–96; Gidding, S. S., Dennison, B. A., Birch, L. L., Daniels, S. R., Gillman, M. W., Lichtenstein, A. H., Rattay, K. T., Steinberger, J., Stettler, N., Van Horn, L., American Heart Association, & American Academy of Pediatrics. (2005). Dietary recommendations for children and adolescents: A guide for practitioners: Consensus statement from the American Heart Association. *Circulation, 112*, 2061–2075.

Stress

When individuals are subjected to stressful conditions, they experience an increase in catecholamines (stress hormones), which in turn elevate heart rate, blood pressure, and blood glucose levels. This is commonly referred to as the "fight or flight" syndrome because the body is preparing to either fight or flee. If the person takes action, either fights or flees, the higher level of catecholamines are metabolized and the body returns to its normal state. However, if a person is under constant stress due to a death of a relative or friend, loss of employment, marital troubles, or any other of a number of circumstances, the catecholamine levels stay elevated and so do blood pressure, heart rate, and blood glucose.

Individuals who are unable to relax have a constant stress applied to the cardiovascular system. Eventually, this strain could lead to CVD. Developing day-to-day coping skills and the ability to deal with work and social stressors are important ingredients to a healthy life. Exercise is one of the best ways to relieve the symptoms of stress. When an individual exercises, the body metabolizes excess catecholamines and the cardiovascular system is able to return to its normal state. For more information on stress management techniques, refer to Chapter 10.

Gender

CVD is the leading killer of both men and women. However, death rates are three times higher for men than for women during the early and middle decades of life (Figure 8.2). After age 55, this disparity drops dramatically. Moreover, when heart attacks occur in women, they are more deadly than for men: 39 percent of women who have heart attacks die within a year compared with 31 percent of men. After age 65 this disparity grows, with women who have heart attacks being twice as likely to die as men (American Heart Association, 2014).

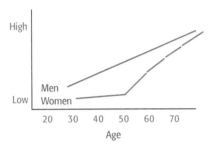

Levels of HDL-C are the protective factors causing younger women to be at lower risk for CVD. As mentioned previously in this chapter, HDL-C helps clear the arteries of disease-causing plaque, thus lowering CVD risk. Women, due to high estrogen levels, naturally produce about 20 percent more HDL-C than do men. After menopause estrogen levels decrease, causing a drop in HDL-C. Consequently, women experience a greater risk for CVD. Estrogen supplementation after menopause can help maintain HDL-C, however, with supplemental estrogen comes a higher risk for cancer. It is always advisable to visit with a physician concerning supplementation of estrogen.

Figure 8.2 • Cardiovascular risk by gender.

Heredity

Even though heredity plays a role in the development of CVD, the role is much less than most people think. People with a family history of CVD are more likely to develop disease than people with no family history, but it is not clear why this is the case. Most people think that it is obvious; genetics is the reason, but as to date, no gene has been identified as a carrier of CVD. The aforementioned old saying that we turn into our parents is probably true and may be the answer why heredity plays a role. Remember that most people inherit a lifestyle from their parents. If the parents are sedentary, then more than likely the children are, too. In addition, people develop a taste for the foods which they eat as youth. If the family meals consist of high-fat, high-calorie foods, these foods are the choice of the children as they grow into adults.

Persons with a family history of CVD need to closely monitor the other risk factors. Maybe more importantly, these people need to examine the lifestyle of their family members who have suffered from CVD and make lifestyle modifications to reduce CVD risk. In addition, people who have a parent suffered from a cardiovascular incident at a very early age (before age 40) should be very careful with their lifestyle choices and should keep close watch over their risk factors for developing CVD. For example, these people should closely watch their blood pressure and cholesterol levels.

Age

As we become older, our risk of CVD increases. Other factors such as less physical activity, obesity, and poor nutrition may be partly responsible for this increased risk with aging. Evidence demonstrates that a fit individual at age 50, 60, or even 70 is at lower risk for CVD than are unfit individuals of younger years. It is important to think physiological age instead of chronological age when determining CVD risk. Risk factor management and positive lifestyle habits are the best means for slowing down physiological aging.

Race

African American men and women are at greater risk for CVD. African Americans are almost one-third more likely to have high blood pressure compared with Americans of Caucasian ancestry. Mexican Americans are also more likely to have high blood pressure and suffer from other forms of CVD. Historically, Asian Americans have exhibited lower rates of CVD than do Caucasian Americans. However, recent data show that CVD is on the rise in this population, presumably owing to their adoption of the American lifestyle.

METABOLIC SYNDROME

Metabolic syndrome is a name given to a group of risk factors that significantly increase a persons risk for CVD. People with the metabolic syndrome are usually overweight or obese and have significantly increased risk for developing insulin resistance and type 2 diabetes, as well as early mortality. There are five risk factors associated with metabolic syndrome, and if a person has three of these factors they would be diagnosed with metabolic syndrome. Table 8.13 lists the risk factors for metabolic syndrome.

TABLE 8.13 Metabolic Syndrome

To diagnose Metabolic Syndrome a number of test will need to be performed. The results will be used to determine if three or more of the following signs exist.

1. Large waistline- greater than 35 in women; greater than 45 in men

2. High triglyceride level- greater than 150mg/dl

3. Low HDL cholesterol level- less than 50mg/dl for women; less than 40mg/dl in men

4. High blood pressure

5. Fasting glucose level above 100mg/dl

National Heart, Lung, and Blood Institute 2018 www.nhlbi.nih.gov/health

SUMMARY

Most major risk factors for heart disease are controllable. A person with a family history of heart disease is not doomed to develop the disease as well. Preventive medicine is the key to reducing the development of heart disease. It is evident that lifestyle habits largely determine susceptibility. Most physicians agree that eating a healthy diet low in fat and high in complex carbohydrates, exercising regularly, quitting smoking, maintaining proper body composition, and developing effective ways to handle stress do more to improve health than anything medicine could do. Heart disease is typically caused by a neglect in lifestyle, which can be reversed. What is required is a commitment to develop habits that contribute to total well-being.

References

American Heart Association. (2018). *Heart and Stroke Statistics 2018 At-a-Glance.* www.heart .org/HEARTORG/General/Heart-and-Stroke

Blair, S. N., Kohl, H. W., III, Barlow, C. E., Paffenbarger, R. S., Jr., Gibbons, L. W., & Macera, C. A. (1995). Changes in physical fitness and all-cause mortality. *Journal of the American Medical Association, 273*, 1093–1098.

Center for Disease Control and Prevention. (2018). www.cdc.gov

Crouse, S. F., O'Brien, B. C., Rohack, J. J., Lowe, R. C., Green, J. S., Tolson, H., & Reed J. L. (1995). Changes in serum lipids and apolipoproteins after exercise in men with high cholesterol: Influence of intensity. *Journal of Applied Physiology, 79*, 279–286.

Hartung, H. G. (1995). Physical activity and high density lipoprotein cholesterol. *Journal of Sports Medicine and Physical Fitness, 35,* 1–5.

Lee, I. M., Hsieh, C. C., & Paffenbarger, R. S., Jr. (1995). Exercise intensity and longevity in men. *Journal of the American Medical Association, 273,* 1179–1184.

National Heart, Lung, and Blood Institute. (2017). Metabolic Syndrome Risk Factors, www .nhlbi.nih.gov/health

National Heart, Lung, and Blood Institute. (1993). *The Fifth Report of the Joint National Committee on Detection, Evaluation, and Treatment of High Blood Pressure* (NIH Publication No. 93-1088). Hyattsville, MD: Author.

Neaton, J. D., & Wentworth, D. (1992). Serum cholesterol, blood pressure, cigarette smoking, and death from coronary heart disease. *Archives of Internal Medicine, 152,* 56–64.

Nieman, D. C. (2011). *Exercise testing and prescription* (7th ed.). New York, NY: McGraw-Hill.

Paffenbarger, R. A., & Hyde, R. T. (1984). Exercise in the prevention of coronary heart disease. *Preventive Medicine, 13,* 3–22.

Robergs, R. A., & Keteyian, S. J. (2010). *Fundamentals of exercise physiology* (4th ed.). New York, NY: McGraw-Hill.

Pronk, N. P. (1993). Short-term effects of exercise on plasma lipids and lipoproteins in humans. *Sports Medicine, 16,* 431–489.

Stone, N. J., Robinson, J., Lichtenstein, A. H., Merz, C. N. B., Lloyd-Jones, D. M., Blum, C. B., . . . Wilson, P. W. F. (2013). Guidelines for treatment of blood cholesterol to reduce atherosclerotic risk in adults. *Journal of the American College of Cardiology, 10,* 1016.

CHAPTER 8

PERSONAL GROWTH OPPORTUNITY 1

Risk Factors for Cardiovascular Disease

Your chances of suffering an early heart attack or stroke depend on a variety of factors, many of which are under your control. To help identify your risk factors, circle the response for each risk category that best describes you.

1. Gender
   - 0 Female
   - 2 Male

2. Heredity
   - 0 Neither parent suffered a heart attack or stroke before age 60.
   - 3 One parent suffered a heart attack or stroke before age 60.
   - 7 Both parents suffered a heart attack or stroke before age 60.

3. Smoking
   - 0 Never smoked
   - 1 Quit more than two years ago
   - 2 Quit less than two years ago
   - 8 Smoke less than one-half pack per day
   - 13 Smoke more than one-half pack per day
   - 15 Smoke more than one pack per day

4. Environmental Tobacco Smoke
   - 0 Do not live or work with smokers
   - 2 Exposed to ETS at work
   - 3 Live with smoker
   - 4 Both live and work with smokers

5. Blood Pressure
   The average of the last three readings:
   - 0 130/80 or below
   - 1 131/81 to 140/85
   - 5 141/86 to 150/90
   - 9 151/91 to 170/100
   - 13 Above 170/100

6. Total Cholesterol
   The average of the last three readings:
   - 0 Lower than 190
   - 1 190 to 210
   - 2 Don't know
   - 3 211 to 240
   - 4 241 to 270
   - 5 271 to 300
   - 6 Over 300

7. HDL Cholesterol
   The average of the last three readings:
   - 0 Over 65 mg/dL
   - 1 55 to 65
   - 2 Don't know
   - 3 45 to 54
   - 4 35 to 44
   - 5 25 to 34
   - 6 Lower than 25

8. Exercise
   - 0 Aerobic exercise three times per week
   - 1 Aerobic exercise once or twice per week
   - 2 Occasional exercise less than once per week
   - 7 Rarely exercise

9. Diabetes
   - 0 No personal or family history
   - 2 One parent with diabetes
   - 6 Two parents with diabetes
   - 9 Non-insulin-dependent diabetes (type 2)
   - 13 Insulin-dependent diabetes (type 1)

10. Weight
   - 0 Near ideal weight
   - 1 Six pounds or less above ideal weight
   - 3 Seven to 19 pounds above ideal weight
   - 5 Twenty to 40 pounds above ideal weight
   - 7 More than 40 pounds above ideal weight

11. Stress
   - 0 Relaxed most of the time
   - 1 Occasional stress and anger
   - 2 Frequently stressed and angry
   - 3 Usually stressed and angry

Scoring

Total your risk factor points. Refer to the list below to get an approximate rating of your risk of suffering an early heart attack or stroke.

Score	Estimated Risk
Less than 20	Low risk
20–29	Moderate risk
30–45	High risk
Over 45	Extremely high risk

CHAPTER 8

PERSONAL GROWTH OPPORTUNITY 2

How "Heart Healthy" Is Your Diet?

MEDFICTS: Dietary Assessment Questionnaire

In each food category for both group 1 and group 2 foods check one box from the "Weekly Consumption" column (number of servings eaten per week) and then check one box from the "Serving Size" column. If you check rarely/never, do not check a serving size box. See end of questionnaire for scoring.

Food Category	Weekly Consumption			Serving Size			Score
Meats ■ ■ Recommended amount per day: ≤6 oz (equal in size to 2 decks of playing cards). ■ Base your estimate on the food you consume most often. ■ Beef and lamb sections are trimmed to 1/8 inch fat.	Rarely/ never	3 or less	4 or more	Small < 6 oz/day 1 pt	Average 6 oz/day 2 pts	Large >6 oz/ day 3 pts	____ ____
1. 10 g or more total fat in 3-oz cooked portion **Beef.** Ground beef, ribs, steak (T-bone, flank, Porterhouse, tenderloin), chuck blade roast, brisket, meatloaf (w/ground beef), corned beef **Processed meats.** 1/4-lb burger or lg. sandwich, bacon, lunch meat, sausage/knockwurst, hot dogs, ham (bone-end), ground turkey **Other meats, Poultry, Seafood.** Pork chops (center loin), pork roast (Blade, Boston, sirloin), pork spareribs, ground pork, lamb chops, lamb (ribs), organ meats,* chicken w/skin, eel, mackerel, pompano	□	□ 3 pts	□ 7 pts	✕ □ 7 pts	□ 2 pts	□ 3 pts	____
2. Less than 10 g total fat in 3-oz cooked portion **Lean beef.** Round steak (eye of round, top round), sirloin,† tip & bottom round,† chuck arm pot roast,† top loin† **Low-fat processed meats.** Low-fat lunch meat, Canadian bacon, "lean" fast-food sandwich, boneless harn **Other meats, Poultry, Seafood.** Chicken, turkey (w/o skin)† most seafood,* lamb leg shank, pork tenderloin, sirloin top loin, veal cutlets, sirloin, shoulder, ground veal, venison, veal chops and ribs,† lamb (whole leg, loin, fore-shank, sirloin)†	□	□	□	✕ □	□	□‡ 6 pts	____

Food Category	Weekly Consumption			Serving Size			Score
Eggs ■ Weekly consumption is the number of times you eat eggs each week				Check the number of eggs eaten each time			
1. Whole eggs, yolks				≤1	2	≥3	
	☐	☐ 3 pts	☐ 7 pts	× ☐ 1 pt	☐ 2 pts	☐ 3 pts	——
2. Egg whites, egg substitutes (1/2 c)	☐	☐	☐	× ☐	☐	☐	——
Dairy ■							
Milk. Average serving 1 cup	☐	☐ 3 pts	☐ 7 pts	☐ × 1 pt	☐ 2 pts	☐ 3 pts	——
1. Whole milk, 2% milk, 2% buttermilk, yogurt (whole milk)							
2. Skim milk, 1% milk, skim buttermilk, yogurt (nonfat, 1% low-fat)	☐	☐	☐	× ☐	☐	☐	——
Cheese. Average serving 1 oz							
1. Cream cheese, cheddar, Monterey Jack, colby, swiss, American processed, blue cheese, regular cottage cheese (1/2 c), and ricotta (1/4 c)	☐	☐ 3 pts	☐ 7 pts	× ☐ 1 pt	☐ 2 pts	☐ 3 pts	——
2. Low-fat & fat-free cheeses, skim milk mozzarella, string cheese, low-fat, skim milk & fat-free cottage cheese (1/2 c) and ricotta (1/4 c)	☐	☐	☐	× ☐	☐	☐	——
Frozen Desserts ■ Average serving 1/2 c							
1. Ice cream, milk shakes	☐	1 ☐ 3 pts	☐ 7 pts	× ☐ 1 pt	☐ 2 pts	☐ 3 pts	——
2 Ice milk, frozen yogurt	☐	☐	☐	× ☐	☐	☐	——
Frying Foods ■ Average servings: see below. This section refers to method of preparation for vegetables and meat.							
1. French fries, fried vegetables (1/2 c), fried chicken, fish, meat (3 oz)	☐	☐ 3 pts	☐ 7 pts	× ☐ 1 pt	☐ 2 pts	☐ 3 pts	——
2. Vegetables, not deep fried (1/2 c), meat, poultry, or fish–prepared by baking, broiling, grilling, poaching, roasting, stewing: (3 oz)	☐	☐	☐	× ☐	☐	☐	——
In Baked Goods ■ 1 Average serving							
1. Doughnuts, biscuits, butter rolls, mulfins, croissants, sweet rolls, danish, cakes, pies, coffee cakes, cookies	☐	☐ 3 pts	☐ 7 pts	× ☐ 1 pt	☐ 2 pts	☐ 3 pts	——
2. Fruits bars, Low-fat cookies/cakes/pastries, angel food cake, homemade baked goods with vegetable oils, breads, bagels	☐	☐	☐	× ☐	☐	☐	——
Convenience Foods ■							
1. Canned, packaged, or frozen dinners: e.g., pizza (1 slice), macaroni & cheese (1 c), pot pie (1), cream soups (1 c), potato, rice & pasta dishes with cream/cheese sauces (1/2 c)	☐	☐ 3 pts	☐ 7 pts	× ☐ 1 pt	☐ 2 pts	☐ 3 pts	——
2. Diet/reduced-calorie or reduced-fat dinners (1), potato, rice & pasta dishes without cream/cheese sauces (1/2 c)	☐	☐	☐	× ☐	☐	☐	——

Food Category	Weekly Consumption			Serving Size			Score
Table Fats ■ Average serving: 1 tbsp							
1. Butter, stick margarine, regular salad dressing mayonnaise, sour cream (2 tbsp)	☐	☐ 3 pts	☐ 7 pts	×☐ 1 pt	☐ 2 pts	☐ 3 pts	____
2. Diet and tub margarine, low-fat & fat-free salad dressings, low-fat & fat-free mayonnaise	☐	☐	☐	×☐	☐	☐	____
Snacks ■							
1. Chips (potato, corn, taco), cheese puffs, snack mix, nuts (1 oz), regular crackers (1/2 oz), candy (milk chocolate, caramel, coconut) (about 1½ oz), regular popcorn (3 c)	☐	☐ 3 pts	☐ 7 pts	×☐ 1 pt	☐ 2 pts	☐ 3 pts	____
2. Pretzels, fat-free chips (1 oz), low-fat crackers (1/2 oz), fruit, fruit rols, licorice, hard candy (1 med piece), bread sticks (1–2 pc), air-popped or low-fat popcorn (3 c)	☐	☐	☐	×☐	☐	☐	____

*Organ meats, shrimp, abalone, and squid are low in fat but high in cholesterol.
†Only lean cuts with all visible fat trimmed. If not trimmed of all visible fat, score as if in group 1.
‡Score 6 pts if this box is checked.
§All parts not listed in group 1 have <10 g total fat.

Total from page 1 ____
Total from page 2 ____
Final Score ____

To score: For each food category, multiply points in weekly consumption box by points in serving size box and record total in score column. If group 2 foods checked, no points are scored (except for group 2 meats, large serving = 6 pts).

Example

☐	☐ 3 pts	☑ 7 pt	×☐ 1 pt	☐ 2 pts	☑ 3 pts	21

Add scores on page 1 and page 2 to get final score.

Key:
≥70	Need to make some dietary changes
40–70	Very good
<40	Excellent

Source: Kris-Etherton P., Eissenstat B, Jaax S, Srinath U, Scott L, Rader J, Pearson T. Validation for MEDFICTS, a dietary assessment instrument for evaluating adherence to total and saturated fat recommendations of the National Cholesterol Education Program Step 1 and Step 2 diets. J Am Diet Assoc 101:81–86, 2001.

Cancer, Diabetes, and Osteoporosis

© Cleomiu, 2014. Used under license from Shutterstock, Inc.

Specific Objectives

1. Explain the incidence and distribution of cancer.
2. List the various theories of the causes of cancer.
3. Identify the risk factors and warning signs for the various types of cancer.
4. Present guidelines for cancer prevention.
5. Exhibit a basic understanding of cancer treatment options.
6. Explain the incidence of diabetes and osteoporosis.
7. Identify the risk factors and warning signs for diabetes and osteoporosis.
8. Describe the role of proper diet and exercise in disease prevention.

Adapted from *Fitness for Life, Fourth Edition* by Bill Hyman, Gary Oden, David Bacharach, Tim Sebesta. Copyright © 2011 by Kendall Hunt Publishing Company. Reprinted by permission.

CANCER

Virtually everyone has been affected by cancer, either directly or indirectly. While cancer can strike anyone at any age, and is the second overall cause of death (behind cardio-vascular disease) and the leading disease killer of children, those most often affected are middle-aged or older adults. Seventy-seven percent of all cancers are diagnosed in persons 55 years and older. Lifetime risk is the probability that an individual will develop cancer or die from it in his/her lifetime. Women have slightly higher than a one in three lifetime risk of developing cancer, and in men, the lifetime risk is slightly less than one in two. While modern medical science provides a great deal of hope that cancer will be more preventable and curable in the future, it currently accounts for nearly 25 percent of all deaths, and cancer is now recognized as the leading cause of death for Americans below the age of 85 (American Cancer Society [ACS], 2013).

What Is Cancer?

Cancer is actually a term representing a group of diseases marked by uncontrolled growth and spread of abnormal cells. Cancer begins with one abnormal cell which has lost the mechanism of control for cell division and growth. It continues to keep dividing and form-ing more cells without control and order, and if the spread of these cells is not controlled, cancer can lead to death. As cancer cells continue to grow, they form a group of abnormal cells called a tumor, or neoplasm. There are two types of tumors. Benign tumors are not considered cancerous because they do not have the ability to spread and invade other healthy body tissue. They are not usually considered a threat to health unless their loca-tion causes them to interfere with basic physiologic functioning, such as a benign tumor placing pressure on part of the brain or blocking the esophagus. Benign tumors can usu-ally be removed if necessary and usually do not come back. A malignant tumor, or cancer-ous tumor, has the ability to invade nearby tissue and organs and spread to other sites in the body where secondary tumors are formed. If the cancer has not spread and remains localized, it is considered noninvasive and is referred to as cancer in-situ. If it has begun to move into surrounding tissue, it is referred to as invasive cancer. Cancerous cells can also spread through the body via the circulatory or the lymphatic system. This spreading of cancerous cells to other parts of the body is called metastasis and occurs because cancer cells break off from one another more readily than healthy cells.

Incidence of Cancer

The American Cancer Society (2018) estimates about 1.7 million new cancer cases and nearly 609,640 cancer deaths annually in the U.S. This represents nearly 1700 people per day who die of cancer, accounting for one of every four deaths. Over the last half of the 20th century, cancer deaths steadily rose, until a slow decline began in the 1990s. Due to this decline, the number of cancer survivors has increased showing that progress is being made against the disease (National Cancer Institute - NCI, 2017). There are 15.5 million cancer survivors in the U.S. today (ACS, 2017), some cancer-free and some still undergoing treatment. While survival rates for cancer vary greatly by type and stage of diagnosis, the five-year survival rate now stands at 69 percent, having increased 20 percentage points among whites and 24 percentage points among blacks over the past three decades. However, the overall five-year survival rate remains substantially lower for blacks than whites (63 percent versus 70 percent, respectively). Improvements in survival reflect improvements in treatment, as well as earlier diagnosis for some cancers (ACS, 2017). Cancer carries high economic costs as well. On the basis of growth and ag-ing of the U.S. population, medical expenditures for cancer in the year 2020 are projected to reach at least $158 billion (in 2010 dollars)—an increase of 27 percent over 2010, according to a National Institutes of Health analysis (Mariotto, Yabroff, Shao, Feuer, & Brown, 2011). This does not account for the cost of lost productivity due to premature death from cancer.

Causes of Cancer

While all causes of cancer are not identified or clearly understood, research has revealed several of the major factors that cause this disease. Cancer is caused by internal factors such as genetic makeup and immune function and external factors such as the environment and exposure to carcinogens (cancer-causing agents). Internal and external factors may also interact to promote carcinogenesis, but lifestyle factors are thought to be major contributors to cancer incidence. In fact, the ACS (2017) says that almost one-third of the cancer deaths in the U.S. are still caused by smoking (with the rapid increase in other forms of tobacco use, such as hookah/waterpipes, cigars, and e-cigarettes also cause for concern) and another third were related to poor diet, physical inactivity, and overweight and obesity. Additionally, many of the more-than-one-million skin cancer cases could be prevented by protection from the ultraviolet rays of the sun. The risk of developing several types of cancer can be assessed at the following website of the Siteman Cancer Center at the Washington University in St. Louis School of Medicine:

https://siteman.wustl.edu/prevention/ydr/

Genetic Factors. While the exact link between genetics and cancer remains unknown, some types of cancer do run in families. A family pattern appears to exist for cancers of the colon, stomach, prostate, breast, uterus, ovaries, and lungs. This pattern could be explained by shared environments (such as a polluted neighbourhood) and lifestyles (like smoking) among family members, or a shared characteristic like obesity (which may also be due to shared lifestyles). In some cases, however, the family pattern could be caused by an abnormal gene that is passed through generations. These conditions are called family cancer syndromes or inherited (hereditary) cancer syndromes. The cancer itself is not inherited, but the abnormal gene that can lead to the cancer. Only about 5 percent to 10 percent of all cancers are thought to result directly from gene defects (called mutations) inherited from a parent. Ongoing genetic research may answer many of the questions researchers have about these biological factors (ACS, 2017).

Environmental Factors. Some products found in our environment are carcinogenic. The most recent estimates from the ACS (2013) are that four percent of cancers are from occupational exposures to a carcinogen and two percent are from environmental pollutants (although many believe the number to be greater). This translates into 36,500 deaths each year. Certain workplaces, in which workers are exposed to materials on a regular and prolonged basis, may increase an individual's risk of cancer. Workers exposed to asbestos, for example, are known to be at risk for lung cancer. Other industrial settings that expose workers to vinyl chloride, arsenic, benzene, dyes, solvents, herbicides, pesticides, petrochemicals, and radiation may increase cancer risks. Those who work in these settings or experience frequent contact with these and other chemical compounds should take careful precautions to reduce their exposure.

Radiation is also a carcinogen. However, only high-frequency radiation, ionizing radiation, and ultraviolet radiation have been shown to cause cancer in humans. This includes x-rays, radon gas, and ultraviolet radiation, and while it is impossible to avoid all radiation, certain precautions can be taken to reduce exposure. Radon gas is a natural source of radiation found in certain geographical areas. It can increase the risk of lung cancer and is thought to be responsible for about two percent of cancer deaths.

Protecting Your Skin from the Sun

1. Wear protective clothing—a wide-brimmed hat is most effective in protecting the head, neck, and face from the sun's rays. Lightweight, long-sleeved clothing can protect the arms. Don't forget sunglasses to protect the eyes and the skin around the eyes.
2. Avoid prolonged sun exposure, especially during the peak hours of 10 a.m. to 3 p.m.
3. Seek the shade. If you are outdoors a lot, look for shelter from the sun's direct rays, and don't forget that rays reflected off water, snow, or even concrete can do damage.
4. Wear a sunscreen. The American Academy of Dermatology recommends that, regardless of skin type, a broad-spectrum (protects against UVA and UVB rays), water-resistant sunscreen with a sun protection factor (SPF) of at least 30 should be used year round. Apply liberally about 30 minutes before going out into the sun, and reapply the sunscreen about every two hours. Don't forget to protect the lips with an appropriate SPF 30 product. Lips are vulnerable to sun exposure because they do not contain melanin—a pigment in skin (and some other tissues) that provides some protection against sun damage.
5. Avoid tanning beds and sun lamps. These devices are categorized as definitely "carcinogenic to humans" by the International Agency for Research on Cancer.

Radon exposure is particularly dangerous when combined with cigarette smoking. Your local health department can help you determine the risk of radon exposure in your area. Medical and dental x-rays are other sources of radiation exposure but deliver the lowest possible dosage needed to create a quality image. These x-rays serve an important medical need, but it is a good idea to avoid unnecessary x-rays when possible.

Probably the most preventable type of cancer-causing radiation exposure is the ultraviolet rays of the sun, which are thought to cause almost all cases of basal and squamous cell carcinomas, and are a major cause of malignant melanomas. While basal and squamous cell cancers are highly curable, malignant melanomas are often deadly. The American Cancer Society estimates 9320 annual melanoma deaths (2018). Skin cancer is, however, one of the most preventable types of cancer, and the precautions found in Box 9.1 are recommended for the prevention of skin cancer. In addition to prevention, early detection is critical to the success of skin cancer treatment. Regular skin self-examination is recommended and is shown in Box 9.2.

Viral Causes. It is estimated that five percent of the cancers in the United States are caused by viruses, and 17 percent of new cancers worldwide are attributable to infection. These cancers are likely linked to immune suppression, chronic inflammation, or chronic stimulation. Some viruses may also disrupt cell cycle control, stimulating the replication of cancer cells.

Examples of virally caused cancers include cervical, vulvar, vaginal, penile, anal, and oropharyngeal (base of the tongue, tonsils, and back of throat), which have been linked to certain strains of the human papilloma virus (HPV), a sexually transmitted virus, and liver cancer, which has been linked to Hepatitis B and C. While most HPV-infected women do not develop cervical cancer, nearly 100 percent of women with cervical cancer show evidence of HPV infection. The HPV vaccine is a strong weapon in disease prevention. These safe, effective vaccines are available to protect females and males against some of the most common HPV types and the health problems that the virus can cause.

Lifestyle Causes. Many of the factors that contribute to cancer are highly preventable if an individual practices a healthy lifestyle. As suggested earlier, poor dietary choices, the decision to smoke and use other tobacco products, and failure to practice protection from the sun are significant lifestyle factors contributing to cancer cases and deaths. Excessive alcohol consumption is another. Clearly, wise choices can be made that have tremendous benefits in the prevention of many types of cancers.

Of all of the suspected causes of cancer, the one that carries the greatest risk is smoking. Tobacco use is responsible for 20 percent of all deaths in the U.S. (about 480,000 deaths in 2016) and debilitates many others with emphysema, chronic bronchitis, and other diseases. While cigarette smoking rates continue to decline, nearly 38 million adults in the U.S. still smoke cigarettes. That's more than 15 out of every 100 adults, and men continue to smoke more than women (17.5 percent to 13.5 percent respectively). Half of all Americans who continue to smoke will die from smoking-related illnesses

BOX 9.2

Monthly Self-Examination

The Skin Cancer Foundation recommends that everyone practice monthly head-to-toe self examination of their skin, so that they can find any new or changing lesions that might be cancerous or precancerous. Skin cancers found and removed early are almost always curable. Learn about the warnings signs of skin cancer and what to look for during a self examination. If you spot anything suspicious, see a doctor.

What you'll need: a bright light, a full-length mirror, a hand mirror, 2 chairs or stools, a blow dryer, body maps, and a pencil.

1  **2**  **3** 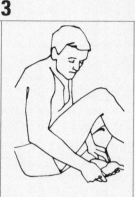 **4**

Examine your face, especially the nose, lips, mouth, and ears—front and back. Use one or both mirrors to get a clear view.

Thoroughly inspect your scalp, using a blow dryer and mirror to expose each section to view. Get a friend or family member to help, if you can.

Check your hands carefully: palms and backs, between the fingers and under the fingernails. Continue up the wrists to examine both front and back of your forearms.

Standing in front of the full-length mirror, begin at the elbows and scan all sides of your upper arms. Don't forget the underarms.

5 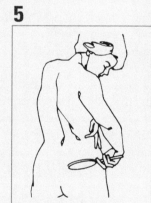 **6**  **7**  **8**

Next focus on the neck, chest, and torso. Women should lift breasts to view the underside.

Medical Reviewers
Perry Robins, MD
Ronald G. Wheeland, MD
Edna Atwater, RN
Noreen Heer Nicol, RN
Order this article as a brochure

With your back to the full-length mirror, use the hand mirror to inspect the back of your neck, shoulders, upper back, and part of the back of your upper arms you could not view in step 4.

Still using both mirrors, scan your lower back, buttocks, and backs of both legs.

Sit down; prop each leg in turn on the other stool or chair. Use the hand mirror to examine the genitals. Check front and sides of both legs, thigh to shin, ankles, tops of feet, between toes and under toenails. Examine soles of feet and heels.

© 2014 The Skin Cancer Foundation | 149 Madison Avenue Suite 901 New York, New York 10016 | (212) 725-5176
The Skin Cancer Foundation [EIN: 13-2948778] is a 501 (c)(3) nonprofit organization.

(Centers for Disease Control and Prevention -CDC, 2018). Cigarette smoke contains at least 43 carcinogens and is responsible for 87 percent of lung cancer and about one-third of all cancer deaths in the United States. It is responsible for at least 15 types of cancer, including cancer of the mouth, larynx, esophagus, kidney, bladder, pancreas, stomach, uterus, and cervix. Low-tar and light cigarette smokers have the same risk of lung cancer as full-tar cigarette smokers. Recently, more and more people have taken up cigar smoking, which has health consequences similar to those of cigarette smoking and spit tobacco. According to the CDC (2016), about 12.4 million Americans, or 5.2 percent of Americans 12 and older, smoke cigars. Cigar smoking causes increased risks for a number of lung disorders, including lung cancer. Cigar smokers are three to five times more likely to die from lung cancer than are nonsmokers. Overall cancer deaths for cigar smokers are 34 percent higher than for nonsmokers, coming mainly from an increase in cancer of the larynx, mouth, esophagus, lungs, and probably pancreas. Major cigar manufacturers in 2001 began placing warning labels on cigars sold in the United States to settle a lawsuit for failure to warn users about the dangers of cigar smoking. Spit tobacco is also a deadly carcinogen. More than 87 percent of oral cancer cases are directly linked to spit tobacco and cigarette use. Spit tobacco is harmful and is not considered a safe substitute for smoking cigarettes or cigars. Among long-term snuff users, the risk of cancer of the cheek and gums may be increased nearly 50-fold.

Another alarming trend in tobacco consumption is the increase in use of e-cigarettes. Use among middle and high school students has tripled since 2011, and young adults are also frequent users, as nearly 14 percent of those age 18-24 report past 30 day use. E-cigarette use is strongly associated with the use of other tobacco products among young adults, specifically the use of combustible tobacco products. Nearly 60 percent of e-cigarette users are also current users of combustible tobacco products. It is important to remember that there is no safe way to use tobacco, and e-cigarettes are not safe, as the dangers of nicotine exposure accompany their use as well. These products expose users to several chemicals known to have detrimental impact on health, and the aerosol from the products is not harmless, although it generally contains fewer toxins than combustible tobacco products (CDC, 2016).

In addition to cancer deaths, tobacco use is responsible for numerous deaths due to cardiovascular disease, stroke, and other lung diseases. In all, smoking is related to nearly half a million deaths each year in the United States. It has been identified as the leading behavioral cause of death and disability in the country. Not smoking or using tobacco is probably the best thing a person can do for good health, so if you are a non-smoker, do not start. If you do smoke or use tobacco products in any way, Box 9.3 contains additional information on quitting.

Alcoholic beverages cause cancer of the mouth, esophagus, and larynx, and when alcohol use is combined with tobacco use, the risk of these types of cancers is greatly increased. Alcohol is also clearly linked to an increased risk for breast cancer, and the risk increases with the amount of alcohol consumed. If you don't drink, don't start. If you do drink, moderation is critically important to good health. The ACS (2017) recommends that men limit alcohol consumption to no more than two drinks per day and women limit their consumption to no more than one drink per day.

In addition to smoking and alcohol consumption, dietary factors play a role in cancer risk. A diet that consists of high portions of plant foods and limited amounts of animal products is a great step to cancer risk reduction. A high-fat diet is considered a risk for cancer of the colon, rectum, prostate, and endometrium. The research on diet and breast cancer is inconclusive. A diet high in fiber, however, has been shown to provide protection against cancer of the gastrointestinal and respiratory tracts. Legumes, or beans and peas, may also protect against cancer. The ACS Guidelines on Nutrition and Physical Activity for Cancer Prevention are consistent with the ChooseMyPlate and

BOX 9.3

Tips for Smoking and Other Tobacco Use Cessation

If you smoke, quitting won't be easy, but it will be the greatest step that you can take toward good health. Remember, almost 50 million Americans are ex-smokers, so it can be done. The Texas Department of Health and Regulatory Services offers these guidelines for quitting tobacco:

No two smokers are alike, and your plan to free yourself of cigarettes will reflect you—and only you. By putting your commitment on paper, you take the driver's seat. You pick the strategies and tips that make sense to you and add new ones to fit your life. For most quitters, early withdrawal symptoms present the biggest hurdle. Nicotine is a powerful and extremely addictive drug, and if you do not make plans for handling withdrawal, you could easily slip into a relapse.

1. Consider medications to ease the symptoms of withdrawal.

Most quitters can benefit from using nicotine replacement therapy (NRT) or other medications. Studies show that your chances for success are doubled with the use of approved NRT or prescribed medications. Talk to your doctor about these medications. Together you can find the one that works for you:

- ❏ Nicotine patch (available by prescription and over the counter)
- ❏ Nicotine gum (available over the counter)
- ❏ Nicotine inhaler (available by prescription)
- ❏ Nicotine lozenge (available over the counter)
- ❏ Nicotine nasal spray (available by prescription)
- ❏ Buproprion SR (available by prescription)

Remember, withdrawal symptoms and cravings fade in about 20 minutes whether you smoke or not, and the first two weeks are often the most difficult. It's helpful to think of after-effects as "signals" of the start of a healthier life.

2. Seek out support and raise your odds of quitting for good.

Experts point out that successful quitters gain the support of family and friends and take advantage of counseling programs. Certainly, don't keep your intention to quit a secret. Tell your friends and family about your quit plans, invite friends who smoke to join you or wager a friendly bet with a coworker that you can stay smoke-free for a day, a week, a month, and so on. Find a friend who has been through it. Most former smokers are willing to help others. Telephone "quitlines" offer unbeatable convenience and flexibility. You don't have to leave home, find transportation, or arrange childcare. Trained counselors call on your schedule to help you form a quit plan that feels right for you. They share tips that help you overcome your barriers and offset cravings and otherwise provide critical support when you need it.

3. Keep in mind that most people try to quit again and again before they are successful.

In fact, you have an advantage if you tried to quit before. You can use what you learned and apply it to your "new and improved" attempt. Studies show that most relapses occur within the first three months after stopping, so prepare yourself for the difficult situations and temptations that lie ahead. Gather information and tips to help you create your new nonsmoking environment, avoid weight gain and triggers, and put new habits to use. For starters, visit the ACS's website at www.cancer.org

4. Remember to reward yourself for each day that you don't light up.

A reward of some kind, like buying a new CD, renting a movie, or calling a close friend, helps to remind yourself that what you're doing is important. And it is!

Every cigarette you don't smoke lengthens your life by about seven minutes.
After five years of quitting, you cut your risk of heart attack in half.

the Dietary Guidelines for Americans, as well as the other nutrition information found in Chapter 6. They are found at the following website: https://www.cancer.org/healthy/eat-healthy-get-active/acs-guidelines-nutrition-physical-activity-cancer-prevention/summary.html

ROLE OF EXERCISE IN CANCER PREVENTION

Another lifestyle factor that warrants attention in the discussion of cancer is exercise. Several studies have shown that exercise reduces the risks of certain forms of cancer, and there may be multiple mechanisms by which the risks are reduced. Exercise is critical in managing the amount of body fat one carries, and excess body fat increases the risk of cancer of the colon, breast, endometrium, and kidney, and adenocarcinoma of the esophagus. Obesity increases the risk of additional cancers, including cancers of the pancreas, gallbladder, thyroid, ovary, and cervix, as well as myeloma. Exercise also speeds the movement of food through the digestive tract, reducing the amount of time that the lining of the intestine is exposed to carcinogens that may build up, thereby reducing the risk of cancer of the colon. Exercise may also decrease the exposure of breast tissue to circulating estrogen, reducing the risk for breast cancer. Colon, breast, and other cancers may also be affected by exercise as it improves energy metabolism and reduces circulating concentrations of insulin. In addition to cancer prevention, exercise has been shown to be effective in the prevention of type 2 diabetes, which will be discussed later in this chapter. Type 2 diabetes has been associated with increased cancers of the liver, pancreas, uterine lining, colon, breast, and bladder. The specific link between diabetes and these types of cancer is speculative. Several of the other chapters in this book provide excellent guidelines for developing an exercise plan, which is important not only for overall fitness, but for disease prevention as well.

MAJOR TYPES OF CANCER

Most cancers are given their name on the basis of the location in the body where they originate. While there are too many types of cancer for all to be included in this discussion, the major types are addressed below.

Lung Cancer

Lung cancer has long been the deadliest cancer in men, and since 1987, has been the leading killer cancer for women as well. This is due to the increase in the number of women smokers. Lung cancer accounts for about 26 percent of cancer deaths (ACS, 2018). As mentioned earlier, cigarette smoking is by far the most important risk factor in the development of lung cancer, and environmental tobacco smoke (ETS) accounts for additional deaths in nonsmokers. Among the more than 7,000 chemicals that have been identified in ETS, at least 250 are known to be harmful. For example, hydrogen cyanide, carbon monoxide, ammonia, and at least 69 of the toxic chemicals in ETS cause cancer. Exposure to secondhand smoke (called passive smoking - inhaling the smoke in the air from a burning cigarette and that exhaled by the smoker) causes 7,333 annual deaths from lung cancer and another 33,951 annual deaths from heart disease (U.S. Department of Health and Human Services, 2017). Children exposed to secondhand smoke are at increased risk of sudden infant death syndrome, ear infections, colds, pneumonia, bronchitis, and more severe asthma. Being exposed to secondhand smoke slows the growth of children's lungs and can cause them to cough, wheeze, and feel breathless. There is no safe level of exposure to secondhand smoke. Other environmental causes of lung cancer include radiation exposure, radon, arsenic, benzene, and asbestos, as well as other potential industrial carcinogens. Exposure to various forms of air pollution may also increase risks. Symptoms of lung cancer include a persistent cough, voice change, blood-streaked sputum, chest pain, and recurring pneumonia and bronchitis (National Cancer Institute, 2013).

One of the reasons that lung cancer is so deadly is that early detection efforts have not yet been shown to reduce mortality. By the time a person is diagnosed with lung cancer, chances of its having spread are great, making treatment very difficult. In fact, the lung cancer five-year survival rate (17.7 percent) is lower than many other leading cancer sites, such as colon (64.4 percent), breast (89.7 percent) and prostate (98.9 percent). If detected prior to spreading, the five-year survival rate is 55 percent, but only 16 percent of cases are discovered that early (American Lung Association, 2016). Although surgery is the treatment of choice for localized cancers, radiation, chemotherapy, and biological therapies are also often used if the cancer has spread at the time of its discovery.

Breast Cancer

Breast cancer is the most common type of cancer found in women, estimated to cause about 41,400 deaths annually. It is rarely detected in men. It stood as the leading cancer killer in women for more than 40 years, but since 1987, has been second to lung cancer. Death rates have declined steadily since 1990, and since 1999, the incidence of breast cancer has declined as well (ACS, 2018). The decreasing incidence of breast cancer deaths can be attributed to increased awareness, advancing techniques in early detection, improved treatment methods, and reductions in the use of menopausal hormone therapy (MHT). The cause of breast cancer has yet to be pinpointed, but several risk factors have been identified.

The risk of breast cancer increases with age and is greater in those with a family history of breast cancer. Other risk factors include weight gain after the age of 18, being overweight or obese (for postmenopausal breast cancer), being physically inactive, alcohol consumption, and menopausal hormone therapy (combined estrogen and progestin). Reproductive factors that increase risk include a long menstrual history (menstrual periods that start early and/or end later in life), recent use of oral contraceptives, never having children, and having one's first child after age 30. Modifiable factors that are associated with a lower risk of breast cancer include breastfeeding, moderate or vigorous physical activity, and maintaining a healthy body weight. Two medications, tamoxifen and raloxifene, have been approved to reduce breast cancer risk in women at high risk. Raloxifene appears to have a lower risk of certain side effects, such as uterine cancer and blood clots; however, it is only approved for use in postmenopausal women (ACS, 2018).

Breast cancer typically produces no symptoms when the tumor is small and most treatable. Therefore, it is important for women to follow recommended screening guidelines to detect breast cancer at an early stage. Larger tumors may become evident as a breast mass, which is often painless. Less common symptoms include persistent changes to the breast, such as thickening, swelling, distortion, tenderness, skin irritation, redness, scaliness, or nipple abnormalities, such as ulceration, retraction, or spontaneous discharge. Breast pain is more likely to be caused by benign conditions and is not a common early symptom of breast cancer (ACS, 2013).

It is important for women to follow recommended screening guidelines because these can detect breast cancer at an early stage, even before symptoms begin. The most common symptom of breast cancer is a new lump or mass. A painless, hard mass that has irregular edges is more likely to be cancer, but breast cancers can be tender, soft, or rounded and even painful. For this reason, it is important to have your health care provider check any new breast mass, lump, or breast change. Other possible symptoms of breast cancer include: swelling of all or part of a breast (even if no distinct lump is felt), skin irritation or dimpling (sometimes looking like an orange peel), breast or nipple pain, nipple retraction (turning inward), redness, scaliness, or thickening of the nipple or breast skin, nipple discharge (other than breast milk) (ACS, 2017).

Breast cancer screening for women at average risk includes clinical breast exam and mammography. Mammography can often detect breast cancer at an early stage, when treatment is more effective and a cure is more likely (ACS, 2013). The recommended screening guidelines for several types of cancer are found at the following site: https://www.cancer.org/healthy/find-cancer-early/cancer-screening-guidelines/american-cancer-society-guidelines-for-the-early-detection-of-cancer.html. Monthly breast self-exams (BSE) are also recommended. The steps to performing this important examination are explained and illustrated in Box 9.4. Any abnormality noticed should be brought to the attention of a health care provider. As mentioned earlier, the declining death rates due to breast cancer may be attributed to better early detection methods, so these screenings should be taken seriously by all women, regardless of their risks.

Breast cancer is treated in a variety of ways depending on the medical condition of the patient. It may include a lumpectomy (removal of the tumor from the breast) or a mastectomy (removal of the breast). These generally include removal of the lymph nodes under the arm. Radiation, chemotherapy, or hormone therapy may also be used to treat breast cancer.

Prostate Cancer

Prostate cancer is the leading type of cancer found in men and is the second leading cancer killer of men. Aging increases the risk of prostate cancer, and African Americans have a greater incidence than do other races, with a death rate twice that of white men. Family history is positively related to prostate cancer. While the influence of dietary factors is not conclusive, recommended preventive steps include following a diet that is low in fat and full of fruits and vegetables. Following an active lifestyle and maintaining a healthy weight may also reduce risks. Other potential risks are under investigation. Early prostate cancer usually has no symptoms. Advanced prostate cancer is often indicated by urination abnormalities, including a weak or interrupted urine flow, inability to urinate or difficulty starting and stopping the urine flow, pain or burning with urination, the need to urinate frequently, especially at night, and blood in the urine. Advanced prostate cancer can spread to the bones causing pain in the hips, spine, ribs, or other areas.

Experts disagree concerning the value of prostate screening, but tests known as the prostate-specific antigen (PSA) test and a digital rectal exam (DRE) may detect prostate cancer at an earlier stage than if no screening is performed. Men are encouraged to discuss these screenings with their health care provider so that an informed decision about the screening can be made. Specific recommendations concerning prostate screening are found at the following website: https://www.cancer.org/cancer/prostate-cancer/early-detection/acs-recommendations.html Treatment for prostate cancer may include surgery, radiation, hormonal therapy, chemotherapy, or a combination of therapies. Since many prostate cancer cases are diagnosed while localized, the five-year survival rate is very good.

Colon and Rectal Cancer

Colorectal cancer is the third most common type of cancer, as well as the third most common killer cancer in both men and women, although the incidence is decreasing due to increased screening and polyp removal. Polyps are small fleshy tumors that grow on the inside lining of the colon. Most are benign, but some types may in time become malignant. The major risk factors for colorectal cancer are age, family, or personal history of colorectal cancer or polyps, or a personal history of inflammatory bowel disease. Other risk factors are obesity, physical inactivity, smoking, alcohol consumption, a diet high in red and processed meat, and possibly a low intake of fruit and vegetables.

TABLE 9.1 Screening Guidelines for the Early Detection of Cancer in Average-Risk Asymptomatic People

Cancer Site	Population	Test or Procedure	Frequency
Breast	Women, ages 20+	Breast self-examination (BSE)	It is acceptable for women to choose not to do BSE or to do BSE regularly (monthly) or irregularly. Beginning in their early 20s, women should be told about the benefits and limitations of BSE. Whether or not a woman ever performs BSE, the importance of prompt reporting of any new breast symptoms to a health professional should be emphasized. Women who choose to do BSE should receive instruction and have their technique reviewed on the occasion of a periodic health examination.
		Clinical breast examination (CBE)	For women in their 20s and 30s, it is recommended that CBE be part of a periodic health examination, preferably at least every three years. Asymptomatic women ages 40 and over should continue to receive a CBE as part of a periodic health examination, preferably annually.
		Mammography	Begin annual mammography at age 40.*
Cervix	Women, ages 21–65	Pap test & HPV DNA test	Cervical cancer screening should begin at age 21. For women ages 21–29, screening should be done every 3 years with conventional or liquid-based Pap tests. For women ages 30–65, screening should be done every 5 years with both the HPV test and the Pap test (preferred), or every 3 years with the Pap test alone (acceptable). Women ages 65+ who have had 23 consecutive negative Pap tests or 22 consecutive negative HPV and Pap tests within the past 10 years, with the most recent test occurring within 5 years, and women who have had a total hysterectomy should stop cervical cancer screening. Women should not be screened annually by any method at any age.
Colorectal	Men and women, ages 50+	Fecal occult blood test (FOBT) with at least 50% test sensitivity for cancer, or fecal immunochemical test (FIT) with at least 50% test sensitivity for cancer, or	Annual, starting at age 50. Testing at home with adherence to manufacturer's recommendation for collection techniques and number of samples is recommended. FOBT with the single stool sample collected on the clinician's fingertip during a digital rectal examination is not recommended. Guaiac-based toilet bowl FOBT tests also are not recommended, in comparison with gualac-based tests for the detection of occult blood. Immunochemical tests are more patient-friendly and are likely to be equal or better in sensitivity and specificity. There is no justification for repeating FOBT in response to an initial positive finding.
		Stool DNA test**, or	Interval uncertain, starting at age 50.
		Flexible sigmoidoscopy (FSIG), or	Every 5 years, starting at age 50. FSIG can be performed alone, or consideration can be given to combining FSIG performed every 5 years with a highly sensitive FOBT or FIT performed annually.
		Double contrast barium enema (DCBE), or	Every 5 years, starting at age 50.
		Colonoscopy	Every 10 years, starting at age 50.
		CT Colonography	Every 5 years, starting at age 50.
Endometrial	Women, at menopause		At the time of menopause, women at average risk should be informed about risks and symptoms of endometrial cancer and strongly encouraged to report any unexpected bleeding or spotting to their physicians.
Lung	Current or former smokers ages 59–74 in good health with at least a 30 pack-year history	Low-dose helical CT (LDCT)	Clinicians with access to high-volume, high-quality lung cancer screening and treatment centers should initiate a discussion about lung cancer screening with apparently healthy patients ages 55–74 who have at least a 30 pack-year smoking history, and who currently smoke or have quit within the past 15 years. A process of informed and shared decision making with a clinician related to the potential benefits, limitations, and harms associated with screening for lung cancer with LDCT should occur before any decision is made to initiate lung cancer screening. Smoking cessation counseling remains

(Continued)

TABLE 9.1 (Continued)

Cancer Site	Population	Test or Procedure	Frequency
			a high priority for clinical attention in discussions with current smokers, who should be informed of their continuing risk of lung cancer. Screening should not be viewed as an alternative to smoking cessation.
Prostate	Men, ages 50+	Digital rectal examination (DRE) and prostate-specific antigen test (PSA)	Men who have at least a 10-year life expectancy should have an opportunity to make an informed decision with their health care provider about whether to be screened for prostate cancer, after receiving information about the potential benefits, risks, and uncertainties associated with prostate cancer screening. Prostate cancer screening should not occur without an informed decision-making process.
Cancer-related checkup	Men and women, ages 20+	On the occasion of a periodic health examination, the cancer-related checkup should include examination for cancers of the thyroid, testicles, ovaries, lymph nodes, oral cavity, and skin, as well as health counseling about tobacco, sun exposure, diet and nutrition, risk factors, sexual practices, and environmental and occupational exposures.	

*Beginning at age 40, annual clinical breast examination should be performed prior to mammography.

**The stool DNA test approved for colorectal cancer screening in 2008 is no longer commercially available. New stool DNA tests are presently undergoing evaluation.

The symptoms include a change in bowel habits, rectal bleeding, blood in the stool, cramping in the lower abdomen, decreased appetite, and weight loss. Early detection methods currently available include regular rectal exams, as well as a fecal occult blood test (which tests the feces for hidden blood) or fecal immunochemical test, colonoscopy, double-contrast barium enema, and sigmoidoscopy (use of a lighted tube to inspect the rectum and colon). Screening is recommended to begin at age 50. These screenings are critically important to maintaining good health through disease prevention. The most common treatment for colorectal cancer is surgery, often combined with radiation or chemotherapy. Again, survival rates are significantly greater if the cancer is detected and treated at an early stage.

Skin Cancer

One of the most preventable types of cancer is skin cancer, but it remains the most commonly diagnosed cancer in the U.S. More than one million cases of basal cell and squamous cell carcinoma cancers (known as nonmelanoma skin cancers—NMSCs) occur each year, and most of these cases are curable, especially if caught early. The deadliest type of skin cancer is invasive melanoma, which accounts for about 1 percent of all skin cancer cases, but the great majority of skin cancer deaths, and its incidence has risen rapidly over the last 30 years.

Non-Hispanic whites have the highest incidence -26 per 100,000 -compared to 4 for Hispanics and 1 for blacks. Rates are higher for women than men before age 50, but by age 65, the rates for men are double those for women and by age 80 they are triple. This is due to differences in occupational and recreational exposure to ultraviolet radiation and possibly early detection practices and use of health care. Skin cancer may appear as a new growth on the skin, a change in the size, color or shape of a mole or other skin lesion, or a sore that does not heal. Carcinomas signs are flat, firm pale areas or small raised red or pink, translucent, shiny, waxy areas. They may bleed following minor injury. Other signs are a growing lump with a rough surface, or a slowly growing reddish, flat patch. Early detection of skin cancer may be practiced through regular skin self-examination (Box 9.2),

BOX 9.4

BREAST SELF EXAMINATION

ONCE A MONTH,
2-3 DAYS AFTER PERIODS

EXAMINE BREAST AND ARMPIT
WITH RAISED ARM

USE FINGERPADS WITH
MASSAGE OIL OR SHOWER GEL

UP AND DOWN

WEDGES

CIRCLES

EXAMINE BREASTS IN THE MIRROR
FOR LUMPS OR SKIN DIMPLING...

...CHANGE IN SKIN COLOR
OR TEXTURE...

...NIPPLE DEFORMATION,
COLOR CHANGE OR LEAKS OF ANY FLUID

EniaB/Shutterstock.com

and any of the indicators should be brought to the attention of a health care professional. The warning signs of melanoma are known as the ABCDEs. A is for asymmetry, or lack of matching between the sides of the growth. B is for border irregularity, which is ragged, notched, or blurred. C is for color, as there is no uniformity of color with shades of black, brown, or tan. D is for diameter, which is typically greater than 6 millimeters. E is for evolution, or a change in the moles appearance over time. Not all melanomas exhibit these signs.

The major risk factors for melanoma are a personal or family history of melanoma and the presence of numerous moles (over 50) or large, atypical moles. Exposure to ultraviolet (UV) radiation, from sunlight or use of indoor tanning, is a risk factor for all types of skin cancer. Indoor tanning is dangerous and review of research has resulted in these tanning devices being classified in the highest risk category of "carcinogenic to humans" by the International Agency for Research on Cancer (part of the World Health Organization) (U.S. Food and Drug Administration, 2017). Sun-sensitive individuals also carry a higher risk of skin cancer. Those who sunburn easily or have natural blond or red hair and those who have a history of excessive sun exposure (including sunburns) or skin cancer are at increased risk. Prevention of skin cancer is also quite clear–avoid overexposure to ultraviolet rays.

Testicular Cancer

Though not a major killer cancer, testicular cancer is one of the more common types of cancer found in young adult males. It accounts for only one percent of cancer deaths in males, but it is the most common type of cancer found in males age 15–34 (National Institutes of Health, 2010).

The cause of testicular cancer is unknown but men with undescended testicles appear to be at greatest risk. Other possible risk factors include family history, HIV infection, previous testicular cancer, and race—the risk for white men is about five times that of black men. Symptoms of testicular cancer include a lump or swelling in a testicle; pain or discomfort in a testicle or the scrotum; enlargement or heavy feeling of a testicle; sudden fluid collection in the scrotum; a dull ache in the lower abdomen, back, or groin; or a sudden collection of fluid in the scrotum. Testicular cancer is one of the most curable forms of cancer, and early detection gives the greatest chance of survival. Regular testicular self-examinations , shown in Box 9.5, may identify a lump or thickening, or unusual tenderness, which should immediately be brought to a physician's attention.

WARNING SIGNS AND PREVENTION

Since early detection is so important to the successful treatment of cancer, it is important to know what signs to look for. No one knows your body better than you do, so it is a good idea for everyone to be familiar with the warning signs of the various types of cancer. The signs and symptoms will depend on where the cancer is, how big it is, and how much it affects the organs or tissues. If a cancer has metastasized, signs or symptoms may appear in different parts of the body. While each type of cancer has its own specific warning signs, general signs of cancer could include the following:

Unexplained weight loss—most people with cancer will lose weight at some point.
Fever—fever is very common with cancer.
Fatigue—extreme tiredness that does not get better with rest could be an important sign.
Pain—pain may be a symptom of several types of cancer including bone, testicular, colon, and rectal cancer.
Skin changes—some cancers can cause darkened skin, yellowish skin/eyes, reddened skin, itching, and excessive hair growth.
Other symptoms of specific cancers include the following:
Change in bowel habits or bladder function—long-term diarrhea, constipation, or stool change or changes in bladder function may signal colon, bladder, or prostate cancer.
Sores that do not heal—a long-lasting sore on the skin or in the mouth could signal skin or oral cancer.

BOX 9.5

CHECK YOUR TESTICLES

CHECK YOUR TESTICLES AT LEAST ONCE A MONTH

PERFORM THE TEST IN THE SHOWER

SOAP YOURSELF UP

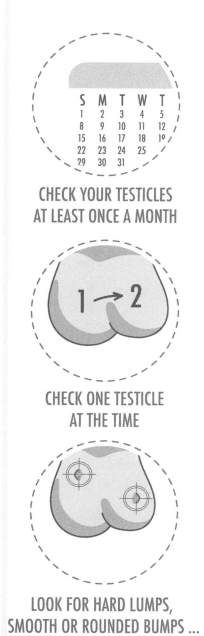

CHECK ONE TESTICLE AT THE TIME

GENTLY ROLL IT BETWEEN THE FINGERS

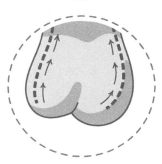

FEEL UP THE SPERMATIC CORDS ON THE BACK SIDE OF TESTICLES

LOOK FOR HARD LUMPS, SMOOTH OR ROUNDED BUMPS ...

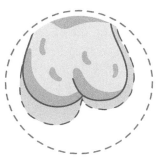

...CHANGES IN SIZE, SHAPE OR CONSISTENCY...

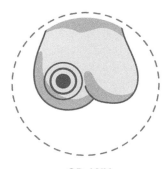

...OR ANY PAINFUL AREAS

EniaB/Shutterstock.com

White patches inside the mouth or on the tongue—these could signal precancerous conditions.

Unusual bleeding or discharge—blood in the sputum, stool, or urine or abnormal vaginal bleeding may signal cancer of the lung, colon, rectum, cervix, bladder, or kidney.

Thickening or lump in the breast or other part of the body—some cancers can be felt through the skin including testicular or breast cancer.

Indigestion or trouble swallowing—may signal digestive track cancer.

Recent change in wart or mole or any new skin change—these may signal a melanoma. Nagging cough or hoarseness—could signal lung or larynx cancer (ACS, 2014).

In addition to knowing the warning signs of cancer, it is recommended that all persons know and practice primary and secondary prevention. Primary prevention is taking behavioral steps that are intended to prevent cancer from ever occurring. Some of the major recommendations for primary prevention include:

1. Do not smoke cigarettes or use tobacco products.
2. Protect your skin from the sun.
3. Avoid alcohol. If you drink, drink in moderation.
4. Avoid unnecessary radiation.
5. Follow prudent dietary habits.
6. Maintain a healthy weight.
7. Minimize your exposure to occupational and environmental carcinogens.

Secondary prevention refers to steps that diagnose a cancer as early as possible after it has developed. For many types of cancer, the earlier it is detected, the better the chances of successful treatment and recovery. Regular screenings and exams for the early warning signs of cancer are beneficial for early detection. There are nine accessible screening sites where cancer may occur: breast, tongue, mouth, colon, rectum, cervix, prostate, testicles, and skin, with more than half of new cancer cases occurring at these sites. Again, refer to the ACS's Guidelines for the Early Detection of Cancer.

CANCER TREATMENT

Traditionally, cancer has been treated through one of three methods: chemotherapy, radiation, or surgery. Recently, several new treatments have been found to provide hope in the successful treatment of this disease.

Surgery

In cases where the cancer cells remain localized and have not spread or invaded surrounding tissue, surgical removal of the tumor is often the preferred treatment. This emphasizes the importance of early detection. If the tumor has already begun to metastasize, surgery may be unable to remove all of the cancer cells. Nearby tissue and lymph nodes may also be removed in an effort to eliminate other cancerous cells. Radiation or chemotherapy may be combined with surgery as additional precautions.

Radiation

This therapy involves targeting the cancerous cells with a stream of high-energy particles to destroy or damage cancer cells. It is very common, and is used in more than half of all cancer cases. It may be administered internally, through an implant, or externally, using a machine that directs a beam of radiation. Since cancer cells grow faster than healthy cells, the goal of radiotherapy is to kill or damage them so they cannot spread. Normal cells are sometimes affected by radiotherapy, but most people fully recover from the effects of this treatment. Careful administration of the radiation is used to minimize the damage to healthy cells.

Chemotherapy

The administration of drugs and chemotherapeutic agents may be used to kill cancer cells or prevent cell division, especially when the cancer has spread to various sites in the body. Since the drugs reach all parts of the body, damage to healthy cells may also occur. More than 100 drugs have been used in chemotherapy, and new agents, hopefully more effective with fewer side effects, are continually being explored.

Immunotherapy

Also known as biologic therapy, immunotherapy attempts to strengthen the body's immune system so that it becomes more efficient at eliminating cancer cells. This type of therapy is most often used along with another type of therapy. Immunotherapy can include targeting your own immune system to work better or boosting your immune system with man-made immune system proteins. While it still plays a small role in treating most cancers, research continues to progress in this promising area of cancer treatment.

Other new treatments that show promise for treating certain types of cancer are now being used and are becoming more widely available. Obviously, cancer is a serious disease and a major public health concern. However, with improved education and increased public awareness, advances in early detection techniques, and continued medical advances, progress in the fight against this disease continues. Hopefully, the impact of this disease on health and well-being will be lessened in the years to come.

DIABETES MELLITUS

Diabetes mellitus is a chronic metabolic disorder characterized either by a deficiency of insulin or a decreased ability of the body to utilize insulin. Insulin, a hormone secreted by the pancreas, is necessary for efficient metabolism of carbohydrates as it allows glucose (sugar) to enter body cells and be converted to energy. In healthy people, the body produces the needed amount of insulin to enable the glucose in the bloodstream to enter the cells, but the diabetic either produces too little insulin or their body cells do not respond to the insulin that is produced. Since the body can neither store nor utilize the glucose, elevated levels build up in the blood and urine. This condition of elevated blood glucose levels is known as hyperglycemia. This can lead to several long-term complications, including damage to the body's vital organs and possible contribution to heart disease, blindness, kidney failure, and the necessity of lower-extremity amputations not related to injury.

In 2015, 30.3 million (9.4 percent of the population) Americans had diabetes. About 23.1 million of these have been diagnosed, leaving over 7 million who do not know they have the disease. In 2015, 79,535 people died from diabetes, making it the seventh leading cause of death in the United States (American Diabetes Association, 2017).

Types of Diabetes

The major types of diabetes are type 1 and type 2. Type 1, previously known as juvenile diabetes, is the least common of the two types, accounting for 5 to 10 percent of cases. It can occur at any stage of life but most often appears in childhood or during the teen years. In the case of type 1 diabetes, the insulin-producing cells in the pancreas are destroyed, and the individual produces little or no insulin, and is therefore dependent on daily insulin injections to sustain life. The onset of symptoms is usually very sudden and the disease can progress very quickly. Symptoms include increased thirst and urination, weight loss, blurred vision, constant hunger, and extreme tiredness. If this disease goes undiagnosed or untreated, a life-threatening coma can result.

The other 90–95 percent of diabetics suffer from type 2 diabetes. As opposed to type 1 diabetes, this type of diabetes is most likely to occur after the age of 45. However, type 2 diabetes is increasingly being diagnosed in children and adolescents. About 80 percent of people diagnosed with this disease are overweight. Type 2 diabetics usually produce enough insulin, but their body cells have become resistant to the action of the insulin, thereby causing the same problem of an unhealthy buildup of glucose in the blood. The symptoms of type 2 diabetes are not as pronounced as those of type 1, and they typically develop more slowly. They include frequent infections, slow healing of sores, blurred vision, tingling and numbness in the hands and feet, and recurring skin, gum, or bladder infections, along with all of the type 1 symptoms.

Type 1 diabetes is more common in whites than in nonwhites. It occurs equally among males and females. Type 2, on the other hand, is more common among older people, especially older women who are overweight, and is more common among nonwhites. Native Americans have the highest rates of diabetes in the world (National Institute of Diabetes and Digestive and Kidney Disorders, 2012).

Gestational diabetes is diabetes which occurs only during pregnancy and it usually has no symptoms. If symptoms do occur they may be mild - being thirstier than normal or having to urinate more often. Gestational diabetes usually disappears when the pregnancy is over, but women who have had gestational diabetes have a greater risk of developing type 2 diabetes later in their lives. It occurs more frequently in African Americans, American Indians, Hispanic Americans, and women with a family history of diabetes.

Prediabetes is a condition in which blood glucose levels are higher than normal but not high enough for a diabetes diagnosis. The American Diabetes Association (2017) reports that in 2015 there were over 84 million people in the United States with prediabetes. Some damage to the body may be occurring during prediabetes. The good news is that preventive behaviors and management of blood glucose levels can delay or prevent type 2 diabetes from occurring.

Several factors have been identified as risks for diabetes. A risk factor assessment for diabetes can be found at the following website: http://www.diabetes.org/are-you-at-risk/diabetes-risk-test/?loc=atrisk-slabnav. The National Institutes of Health (2016) list the following as risk factors:

- A family history of diabetes
- Physical inactivity
- History of heart disease or stroke
- Depression
- Overweight or obesity
- Age greater than 45 years
- High blood pressure
- Low HDL (good) cholesterol or high level of triglycerides
- Previous diabetes during pregnancy or bearing a baby weighing more than 9 pounds
- Polycystic ovarian syndrome
- A condition called acanthosis nigricans, which causes dark thickened skin around the neck or armpits
- Certain ethnicities - African American, Alaska Native, American Indian, Asian American, Hispanic/Latino, Native Hawaiian, or Pacific Islander

Treatment of Diabetes

People with diabetes must be treated by a doctor who assists with the control of the disease and monitors potential health complications. Several factors should be considered as the diabetic and their physician engage in diabetes management. Diet, exercise, and monitoring blood sugar and the use of insulin or other antidiabetic agents are the three major strategies. While insulin is not a cure for diabetes, it is crucial to management of the severity of this disease and its complications. Daily injections of insulin are the basic therapy for type 1 diabetes, and those individuals must closely monitor their glucose levels to properly administer their medications. Individuals with type 2 diabetes may also require insulin injections or other medications, but careful regulation of diet and exercise habits are highly beneficial for this type.

Importance of Diet and Exercise in Diabetes Management

Acute and chronic benefits of exercise have been shown for individuals with type 1 and type 2 diabetes. Those with low physical fitness and little physical activity—including more time spent watching television—are at an increased risk of developing type 2 diabetes. On the other hand, engaging in regular physical activity is an important therapeutic intervention in diabetes management (Colberg, 2010). Regular physical activity improves the control of blood glucose in type 2 diabetes through increased insulin sensitivity and can reduce visceral (abdominal) fat—visceral fat accumulation is related to the development of insulin resistance, meaning that more insulin is required to keep blood glucose levels normal. Since overweight and obesity are prevalent in diabetes, weight loss is a primary goal in risk reduction and regular exercise can offer that benefit as well. Physical activity is also critical in the reduction of cardiovascular disease risk in diabetics. Regular exercise may increase well-being and cognitive function in diabetics and reduce depression that is common with diabetes (Kopp et al., 2012; Lysy, Da Costa, & Dasgupta, 2008).

In addition to the beneficial effects of regular exercise, diet plays a critical role in diabetes prevention and management. The Mayo Clinic (2017) provides the following recommendations for medical nutrition therapy (MNT) for those with diabetes or prediabetes. These recommendations are entirely consistent with the healthy eating plans found in Chapter 6.

Recommended Foods

Make your calories count with these nutritious foods:

- **Healthy carbohydrates.** During digestion, sugars (simple carbohydrates) and starches (complex carbohydrates) break down into blood glucose. Focus on the healthiest carbohydrates, such as fruits, vegetables, whole grains, legumes (beans, peas, and lentils), and low-fat dairy products.
- **Fiber-rich foods.** Dietary fiber includes all parts of plant foods that your body can't digest or absorb. Fiber moderates how your body digests and helps control blood sugar levels. Foods high in fiber include vegetables, fruits, nuts, legumes (beans, peas, and lentils), whole-wheat flour, and wheat bran.
- **Heart-healthy fish.** Eat heart-healthy fish at least twice a week. Fish can be a good alternative to high-fat meats. For example, cod, tuna, and halibut have less total fat, saturated fat, and cholesterol than do meat and poultry. Fish such as salmon, mackerel, tuna, sardines, and bluefish are rich in omega-3 fatty acids, which promote heart health by lowering blood fats called triglycerides. Avoid fried fish and fish with high levels of mercury, such as tilefish, swordfish, and king mackerel.
- **"Good" fats.** Foods containing monounsaturated and polyunsaturated fats can help lower your cholesterol levels. These include avocados, almonds, pecans, walnuts, olives, and canola, olive and peanut oils. But don't overdo it, as all fats are high in calories.

Foods to Avoid

Diabetes increases your risk of heart disease and stroke by accelerating the development of clogged and hardened arteries. Foods containing the following can work against your goal of a heart-healthy diet.

- **Saturated fats.** High-fat dairy products and animal proteins such as beef, hot dogs, sausage and bacon contain saturated fats.
- **Trans fats.** These types of fats are found in processed snacks, baked goods, shortening and stick margarines. Avoid these items.

- **Cholesterol.** Sources of cholesterol include high-fat dairy products and high-fat animal proteins, egg yolks, liver, and other organ meats. Aim for no more than 200 milligrams (mg) of cholesterol a day.
- **Sodium.** Aim for less than 2,300 mg of sodium a day. However, if you also have hypertension, you should aim for less than 1,500 mg of sodium a day.

OSTEOPOROSIS

Osteoporosis is a disease marked by a decrease in bone mass that progresses painlessly until a bone breaks. As bones lose their density, they become fragile and are more likely to fracture. Osteoporosis is a major cause of bone fractures in postmenopausal women and older persons in general. These bone fractures may in turn interfere with the ability to maintain functional abilities, including walking, and may cause prolonged disability.

After reaching its peak at about age 35, bone mass declines throughout the lifespan. During the course of a lifetime, women lose 30–50 percent of their bone mass while men lose 20–30 percent. Women are four times as likely as men to develop osteoporosis (National Osteoporosis Foundation, 2018).

Low bone density threatens to affect 60 percent of Americans age 50 and above—54 million in all. Ten million (8 million women and 2 million men) already have the disease, and 38 million have low bone density. Osteoporosis is responsible for two million broken bones (most commonly the hip, wrist, vertebrae, and pelvis) and the annual related costs is $19 billion. By 2025, osteoporosis is expected to be responsible for about three million fractures and $25.3 billion in costs annually. For those above 50 years of age, one in two women and one in four men suffer an osteoporosis-related fracture during their lifetime (National Osteoporosis Foundation, 2018). Some people are more susceptible to this condition and the resulting fractures. The risk factors that have been identified for osteoporosis include the following:

1. **Age**—Osteoporosis is clearly an age-related disease, with the risk increasing significantly with age as bones become thinner and weaker.
2. **Gender**—Women have about 30 percent less bone tissue than men, and their bone loss is accelerated, especially during the years following menopause.
3. **Race**—The greatest racial risk is for Caucasian and Asian women, but African American and Hispanic women are also at significant risk for developing osteoporosis.
4. **Bone structure and body weight**—Thin, small-boned women carry a greater risk of osteoporosis.
5. **Menopause/menstrual history**—Early menopause is one of the strongest predictors for the development of osteoporosis. Women who cease menstruation before menopause due to anorexia, bulimia, or excessive physical activity are also at risk for osteoporosis. Women can lose up to 20 percent of their bone density in the 5–7 years after menopause.
6. **Cigarette smoking**—Smoking has been identified as a risk factor for osteoporosis, as well as many other diseases. Heavy drinking can also reduce bone formation.
7. **Diet and exercise**—Inadequate calcium intake and getting little or no weight-bearing exercise increase the risk of osteoporosis. Immobilization and prolonged bed rest produce rapid bone loss.
8. **Family history**—Heredity may also play a role in the development of osteoporosis. Reduced bone mass may be a characteristic passed from mother to daughter.

Role of Diet and Exercise in Osteoporosis Prevention

Prevention of osteoporosis should focus on two essentials: increasing peak bone mass early in life and reducing bone loss in later years. While several factors impact these two preventive measures, diet and exercise are certainly two of the most controllable.

After much research, it is now clear that physical activity is essential for the development and maintenance of healthy bones. People who are physically active have greater density in bone mass, and the type of activity that produces the increased bone mass is called weight-bearing exercise. Weight-bearing exercises include walking, running, and racket sports, which are better at promoting bone density than non-weight-bearing activities like cycling or swimming. Weight training, obviously a weight-bearing activity, is an excellent avenue to the development of healthy bones. Other exercises that can help prevent falls (those designed to promote good posture, flexibility and balance), especially in the older population, are also important in the prevention and management of osteoporosis.

The most important dietary consideration appears to be the intake of calcium, which is the building block of bones. Adequate calcium intake throughout the lifespan creates a greater peak bone mass early in life and decreases age-related bone mass. About 85–90 percent of adult bone mass is acquired by age 18 in girls and 20 in boys, so building strong bones in childhood and adolescence is critically important. Peak bone mass is likely to be below optimal levels if calcium intake is not adequate, and many adults get only half or less of their daily calcium needs. The National Osteoporosis Foundation (2018) recommends that women age 50 and under and men age 70 and under consume 1,000 milligrams of calcium per day and that after age 50 for women and 70 for men, daily calcium intake increase to 1,200 milligrams. Pregnant and lactating women need even more. Calcium-rich foods should be incorporated into everyone's diet, especially those at risk for osteoporosis. These foods include dairy products (be sure to choose low-fat), nuts, seeds, and leafy green vegetables. A list of a few calcium-rich foods is found in Table 9.2. Vitamin D is also needed so that the body can absorb the calcium consumed. The body manufactures its own vitamin D through exposure to sunlight, and several foods are enriched with vitamin D.

TABLE 9.2 Foods Rich in Calcium

3.5 oz boiled shrimp	320 mg
1 cup nonfat milk	326 mg
1 cup yogurt	302 mg
1 cup whole milk	291 mg
1 oz Swiss cheese	272 mg
1 cup cooked spinach	244 mg
1 cup cooked broccoli	178 mg
1 oz almonds	75 mg
1 cup canned kidney beans	74 mg
1 tbsp Parmesan cheese	69 mg
1 medium orange	52 mg
1 slice whole-wheat bread	20 mg

Estrogen and Osteoporosis

Estrogen is another major factor in the prevention of osteoporosis, since it has a direct effect on bone by increasing density. Estrogen is a hormone that promotes the development of female secondary sex characteristics. The lowering of estrogen levels that results from the onset of menopause creates a risk for loss of bone density, and the earlier menopause takes place, the greater the risk. This is due to a longer period of time that the protective effect of estrogen is lost. Postmenopausal women may wish to discuss hormone replacement therapy with their physician, and anyone at risk of osteoporosis can discuss medical treatment and management options with their health care provider (National Osteoporosis Foundation, 2018).

References

American Cancer Society. (2017). Alcohol use and cancer. Retrieved from: https://www.cancer .org/cancer/cancer-causes/diet-physical-activity/alcohol-use-and-cancer.html

American Cancer Society. (2018). Cancer Facts & Figures 2018. Atlanta: American Cancer Society.

American Cancer Society. (2017). *Breast cancer signs and symptoms*. Retrieved from: https:// www.cancer.org/cancer/breast-cancer/about/breast-cancer-signs-and-symptoms.html

American Cancer Society. (2017). *Family cancer syndromes*. Retrieved from: https://www .cancer.org/cancer/cancer-causes/genetics/family-cancer-syndromes.html

American Cancer Society. (2014). *Signs and Symptoms of Cancer*. Retrieved from: https://www .cancer.org/cancer/cancer-basics/signs-and-symptoms-of-cancer.html

American Cancer Society. (2017). American Cancer Society Recommendations for the early detection of breast cancer. https://www.cancer.org/cancer/breast-cancer/screening-tests-and-early-detection/american-cancer-society-recommendations-for-the-early-detection-of-breast-cancer.html

American Cancer Society. (2016). Do I have testicular cancer? https://www.cancer.org/cancer/testicular-cancer/do-i-have-testicular-cancer.html

American Diabetes Association. (2018). Diabetes Basics. Retrieved from: http://www.diabetes.org/diabetes-basics/

American Diabetes Association. (2017). Statistics about diabetes. Retrieved from: http://www.diabetes.org/diabetes-basics/statistics/

American Lung Association. (2016). Lung cancer fact sheet. Retrieved from: http://www.lung.org/lung-health-and-diseases/lung-disease-lookup/lung-cancer/resource-library/lung-cancer-fact-sheet.html

Centers for Disease Control and Prevention. (2016). Cigars. Retrieved from: https://www.cdc.gov/tobacco/data_statistics/fact_sheets/tobacco_industry/cigars/index.htm

Centers for Disease Control and Prevention. (2018). Current cigarette smoking among adults in the United States. Retrieved from: https://www.cdc.gov/tobacco/data_statistics/fact_sheets/adult_data/cig_smoking/index.htm

Centers for Disease Control and Prevention. (2016). 2016 Surgeon General's Report: E-cigarette use among youth and young adults. Retrieved from: https://www.cdc.gov/tobacco/data_statistics/sgr/e-cigarettes/index.htm

Centers for Disease Control and Prevention. (2012). *HPV vaccine—Questions and answers.* Retrieved from http://www.cdc.gov/vaccines/vpd-vac/hpv/vac-faqs.htm

Colberg, S. R., Sigal, R. J., Fernhall, B., Regensteiner, J. G., Blissmer, B. J., Rubin, R. R., . . . Braun, B. (2010). Exercise and type 2 diabetes: American College of Sports Medicine and the American Diabetes Association: joint position statement. *Diabetes Care, 33*(12), 147–167.

Department of Health and Human Services. (2004). *The 2004 Surgeon General's report on bone health and osteoporosis.* Washington, DC: Author.

Hoyert, D. L., & Xu, J. Q. (2012). *Deaths: Preliminary data for 2011* (National Vital Statistics Report No. 6). Atlanta, GA: National Center for Health Statistics.

Kopp, M., Steinlechner, M., Ruedl, G., Ledochowski, L., Rumpold, G., & Taylor, A. H. (2012). Acute effects of brisk walking on affect and psychological well-being in individuals with type 2 diabetes. *Diabetes Research and Clinical Practice, 95*(1), 25–29.

Lysy, Z., Da Costa, D., & Dasgupta, K. (2008). The association of physical activity and depression in type 2 diabetes. *Diabetic Medicine, 25*(10), 1133–1141.

Mariotto, A. B., Yabroff, K. R., Shao, Y., Feuer, E. J., & Brown, M. L. (2011, January 19). Projections of the cost of cancer care in the United States: 2010-2020. *Journal of the National Cancer Institute, 103*, 2.

Mayo Clinic. (2017). Diabetes diet: Creating your healthy eating plan. Retrieved from: https://www.mayoclinic.org/diseases-conditions/diabetes/in-depth/diabetes-diet/art-20044295

Mayo Foundation for Medical Education and Research. (2011). *Diabetes management: How lifestyle, daily routine affect blood sugar.* Retrieved from http://www.mayoclinic.org/diseases-conditions/diabetes/in-depth/diabetes-management/ART-20047963

McCardle, W.D., Katch, F.I., and Katch, V.L. (2014). *Exercise physiology: Nutrition, energy,and human performance.* 8th edition. Baltimore: Lippincott, Williams, & Wilkins.

National Cancer Institute. (2014). Second-hand smoke exposure. Retrieved from: https://cancercontrol.cancer.gov/brp/tcrb/tobacco-second-hand.html

National Cancer Institute. (2017). Cancer Statistics. Retrieved from: https://www.cancer.gov/about-cancer/understanding/statistics

National Cancer Institute. (2011). *Testicular cancer.* Retrieved from http://www.cancer.gov/cancertopics/types/testicular

National Institute of Arthritis and Musculoskeletal and Skin Diseases. (2017). The Surgeon General's report on bone health and osteoporosis: What it means to you. Retrieved from: https://www.bones.nih.gov/health-info/bone/sgr/surgeon-generals-report

National Institute of Diabetes and Digestive and Kidney Disorders. (2012). *Am I at risk for type 2 diabetes?* (NIH Publication No 12-4805). Bethesda, MD: Author.

National Institute of Health. (2016) Risk factors for type 2 diabetes. Retrieved from: https://www.niddk.nih.gov/health-information/diabetes/overview/risk-factors-type-2-diabetes

National Institute of Health. (2013). *Are you at risk?* Retrieved from http://www.nof.org/articles/2

National Osteoporosis Foundation. (2018). Calcium/Vitamin D Retrieved from: https://www.nof.org/patients/treatment/calciumvitamin-d/

National Osteoporosis Foundation. (2018). Exercise to stay healthy. Retrieved from: https://www.nof.org/preventing-fractures/exercise-to-stay-healthy/

National Osteoporosis Foundation. (2018). Peak bone mass. Retrieved from: https://www.nof.org/preventing-fractures/nutrition-for-bone-health/peak-bone-mass/

National Osteoporosis Foundation. (2018). Treatment for osteoporosis. Retrieved from: https://www.nof.org/patients/treatment/

National Osteoporosis Foundation. (2018). What is osteoporosis and what causes it? Retrieved from: https://www.nof.org/patients/what-is-osteoporosis/

United States Department of Health and Human Services. (2014). *The Health Consequences of Smoking–50 Years of Progress. A Report of the Surgeon General.* Atlanta: Centers for Disease Control and Prevention, National Center for Chronic Disease Prevention and Health Promotion, Office on Smoking and Health.

United States Food and Drug Administration. (2017). Indoor tanning: the risk of ultraviolent rays. Retrieved from: https://www.fda.gov/ForConsumers/ConsumerUpdates/ucm186687.htm

Stress Management

© JHDT Stock Images LLC, 2014. Used under license from Shutterstock, Inc.

Specific Objectives

1. Define stress.
2. Explain how the body responds to stress.
3. Describe Selye's general adaptation syndrome.
4. Identify real and potential sources of stress.
5. Describe how various traits and personality characteristics can buffer the impact of stress.
6. Understand interventions for stress and how to use them.

College students speak often about being under stress. Academic pressures, finances, relationships, new freedoms and responsibilities, and apprehension about the future are a few of the major stressors that the typical college student may face. But what, exactly, is stress? Do we really want a stress-free life? Why do some individuals seem to hold up well in the face of intense stress, while others have difficulty dealing with seemingly minor issues? And perhaps most importantly, what are the best ways to deal with the stressors of life so that they do not negatively affect life and health? These are the questions that will be addressed in this chapter.

The American Psychological Association (2013) defines stress as "the pattern of specific and nonspecific responses an organism makes to stimulus events that disturb its equilibrium and tax or exceed its ability to cope." Simply put, it is the body's response to any demand placed on it. Those demands can come from a wide variety of sources (called stressors), and although there are certainly universal causes of stress, the major sources of stress in an individual's life at any given time vary from person to person. Stress can actually be a positive force, serving as a motivational tool and leading to improved performance. For example, if you know that an exam is important to your overall success in a course, you are more apt to study and come to class prepared. When managed properly, this type of stress is called eustress and is considered healthful and usually leads to positive outcomes and fulfillment. However, stress is often perceived as being a negative force. This type of stress is harmful and is called distress. Stress, both good and bad, is normal, and it follows the same general process in all people. Stress can also be acute or chronic. Acute stress, the most common form of stress, is short-term and stems from the demands and pressures of the recent past and anticipated demands and pressures of the near future. Chronic stress, a long-term form of stress, is a continuous state of arousal in which an individual perceives demands as greater than the inner and outer resources available for dealing with them (APA, 2013).

Dr. Hans Selye, a physician and endocrinologist, was one of the early pioneers in the research of stress and its impact on humans. His many works, including his books *The Stress of Life* and *Stress without Distress*, documented his detailed work in the field of how stress influences individual health. Through his research, he observed that individuals go through three stages in response to stress, which he called the general adaptation syndrome (GAS):

1. Alarm—In this stage, the body is first confronted with a stressor and exhibits a predictable physiological response in preparation for dealing with the immediate threat. The organs that are most important for responding to threats (the brain, heart, and skeletal muscles) receive greater amounts of glycogen and oxygen as a result of increased amounts of epinephrine (adrenaline) produced by the adrenal glands. The less important organs and systems for defense, like the digestive system and reproductive organs, receive less oxygen and glycogen. The heart rate and breathing rate increase, and muscles tense in preparation to provide defense against the stressor. This physical reaction to a stressor had previously been identified as the "fight or flight" syndrome by Harvard physiologist Walter Cannon. Cannon saw the body's physical changes in the face of stress as our initial preparation to "fight" against the stressor or to "flee" the perceived harm of the stressor.

2. Resistance—After the initial defenses are engaged, the body now prepares for the continued presence of the stressor. It attempts to return to normal functioning while remaining prepared to resist the stressor. Blood pressure increases, alertness is heightened, and remaining energy reserves are mobilized as the stressor continues to take its toll. During the resistance stage, the person either successfully copes with the stressor and returns to homeostasis (the constant, healthy, and natural state of balance in the body) or suffers the consequence of long-term negative stress. The

resistance stage cannot go on forever. If the stressor is not dealt with successfully, the third stage of the GAS is encountered.

3. Exhaustion—If adaptation tools are not present or successful in managing the stressor, the organism will eventually reach a state of exhaustion. The heart, adrenal glands, blood vessels, and other systems are unable to meet the demands placed on them in the resistance stage and begin to fail. The onset of serious illness is possible, and stress can even be a factor in some causes of death.

The Allostatic Load

The allostatic load is the term used to summarize the response of various systems of the human body when under stress. It is a complex phenomenon, but is represented by the load of stress that each individual carries over time—the "wear and tear" from whatever is bothering you—large or small, long term or short term. The allostatic systems include the cardiovascular, metabolic, immune, and parts of the nervous system. If one carries a heavy allostatic load, damage to these systems can occur. If adequate coping skills are not learned and applied to stressful situations, the allostatic load remains chronically high and is strongly suspected as a cause of illness.

Ill Health Effects of Stress

For years, most people have acknowledged that stress can make you sick. Studies on civil servants in stressful jobs, individuals who experience a family crisis like divorce or death in the family, and soldiers in war zones all give evidence that stressful events make us more prone to illness. However, breakthroughs in medical research have only recently begun to explain the physiological mechanism whereby stress actually produces illness. When a person is experiencing stress, the body mounts a chemical response. Through the autonomic (involuntary) nervous system, the brain sends a signal to the adrenal glands (located near the kidneys) and they increase their production of hormones including epinephrine (adrenaline), catecholamines, and most notably a hormone called cortisol. These hormones help us function by keeping us alert, increasing our heart rate and blood pressure, and preparing our energy reserves. But they are also known as stress hormones because they are preparing the body to deal with the stressor in one of two ways—to fight against it or to run from it (the "fight or flight" syndrome). Now the muscles are tensed, alertness is heightened, blood pressure rises, and the heart rate and breathing rate speeds up. As these systems are heightened in preparation to deal with the stressor, other systems, including the immune system, are suppressed because they are not vital at the time. These stress hormones remain in the bloodstream after the stressful situation has passed (explaining why it takes some time to calm down from a highly stressful experience) and can have negative effects on our health. Cortisol is known to speed the conversion of fats and proteins into carbohydrates so that they can be readily used as fuel as the body deals with the stressor, and while cortisol helps us get through the stressful situation, chronic stress can lead to continued production of cortisol and the other stress hormones. Abnormally high levels can lead to metabolic disturbances in the body, including suppression of the immune system, and can increase the susceptibility to a wide variety of ill health effects. Figure 10.1 illustrates how stress can impact body systems.

These ill health effects are still being identified, but research clearly points to a relationship between stress and heart disease, cancer, and stroke, the three leading killers of Americans. In addition, migraine headaches, skin disorders, ulcers, vulnerability to infections, metabolic disorders, and several other physical ailments can be caused or worsened by stress. Anxiety, paranoia, depression, suicide, and other emotional disorders may also be stress related. In fact, some estimate that 75–90 percent of physician visits and 80 percent of all major illness are related to stress.

Here are ways in which some key body systems react.

❶Nervous System

When stressed—physically or psychologically—the body suddenly shifts its energy resources to fighting off the perceived threat. In what is known as the "fight or flight" response, the sympathetic nervous system signals the adrenal glands to release adrenaline and cortisol. These hormones make the heart beat faster, raise blood pressure, change the digestive process, and boost glucose levels in the bloodstream. Once the crisis passes, body systems usually return to normal.

altanaka/Shutterstock.com

❷Musculoskeletal System

Under stress, muscles tense up. The contraction of muscles for extended periods can trigger tension headaches, migraines, and various musculoskeletal conditions.

❸Respiratory System

Stress can make you breathe harder and cause rapid breathing—or hyperventilation—which can bring on panic attacks in some people.

❹Cardiovascular System

Acute stress—stress that is momentary, such as being stuck in traffic—causes an increase in heart rate and stronger contractions of the heart muscle. Blood vessels that direct blood to the large muscles and to the heart dilate, increasing the amount of blood pumped to these parts of the body. Repeated episodes of acute stress can cause inflammation in the coronary arteries, thought to lead to heart attack.

❺Endocrine System

Adrenal glands

When the body is stressed, the brain sends signals from the hypothalamus, causing the adrenal cortex to produce cortisol and the adrenal medulla to produce epinephrine—sometimes called the "stress hormones."

Liver

When cortisol and epinephrine are released, the liver produces more glucose, a blood sugar that would give you the energy for "fight or flight" in an emergency.

❻Gastrointestinal System

Esophagus

Stress may prompt you to eat much more or much less than you usually do. If you eat more or different foods or increase your use of tobacco or alcohol, you may experience heartburn, or acid reflux.

Stomach

Your stomach can react with "butterflies" or even nausea or pain. You may vomit if the stress is severe enough.

Bowels

Stress can affect digestion and which nutrients your intestines absorb. It can also affect how quickly food moves through your body. You may find that you have either diarrhea or constipation.

❼Reproductive System

In men, excess amounts of cortisol, produced under stress, can affect the normal functioning of the reproductive system. Chronic stress can impair testosterone and sperm production and cause impotence.

In women stress can cause absent or irregular menstrual cycles or more-painful periods. It can also reduce sexual desire.

Figure 10.1 •
From http://www.stress.org/stress-effects/. Copyright © by American Institute of Stress. Reprinted by permission.

SIGNS OF STRESS

When we are stressed, our bodies begin emitting signs that homeostasis is being disrupted. If we are alert and aware of these symptoms, it is very likely that we can identify the source of the stress and address it in its early stages instead of letting it progress into additional problems. The initial signs of stress generally fall into one of two categories:

Physiological Signs of Stress

Headaches and muscle aches
Neck and back pain
Increased heart rate or heart palpitations
Increased blood pressure
Chest pains
Butterflies/upset stomach
Dry mouth
Loss of appetite
Increased urination
Rash or acne
Insomnia or disrupted sleep

Psychological Signs of Stress

Inability to concentrate
Irritability
Restlessness
Depressed mood
Impulsivity
Difficulty remembering things

These physiological and psychological signs of stress often manifest themselves as changes in the person's general behavior. Some behavioral changes that may result from stress include the following:

Emotional outbursts
Frequent crying
Angry outbursts
Lashing out at others
Isolation and withdrawal
Sexual dysfunction
Communication difficulties
Use of escape substances (alcohol and drugs)

Too Many Stressors?

The relationship between specific life events and the resulting health effects was significantly advanced in the 1960s by medial doctors Thomas Holmes and Richard Rahe, researchers at the University of Washington School of Medicine. They observed that many of their patients had experienced a set of life events likely to be viewed as distressful just before their illness. From that observation, they conducted research, which resulted in the "Social Readjustment Rating Scale." The conclusion of their research was that individuals who experience certain life events carry a higher likelihood of illness than do their counterparts who do not experience as many of these life events. The Undergraduate Stress Questionnaire, a life event assessment for college students, is available as Personal Growth Opportunity 10.1 at the end of this chapter for you to determine your likelihood of stress-related illness.

PERSONALITY AND STRESS

While the experience of the GAS is common to all, and a heavy allostatic load can negatively affect anyone, not everyone responds to stressors with the same intensity and reaction. Some individuals tend to withstand the storm of stressors quite well, whereas others cave in to even the smallest of stressors. Personality traits can make one more or less vulnerable to the ill health effects of stress.

Hardiness

A personality trait that can mediate the effects of stress in our lives is called hardiness. Hardiness may explain why some individuals tend to tolerate stress better than others. Hardiness has three central characteristics—commitment, challenge, and control—called the three Cs of hardiness.

- Commitment—a sense of dedication to life goals and aspirations. Hardy people understand that in life there will be troubles, but a deep sense of involvement and commitment can help maintain focus on major goals and help manage stress.
- Challenge—a view of new events and demands that sees them not as threats but as opportunities. New situations and new responsibilities are welcomed as changes in life as we grow, and personal improvement can result from these situations. Hardy people see challenging situations not as threats of failure, but as opportunities for growth.
- Control—the belief that an individual has influence over the course of life events. Hardy people look for ways to gain control over seemingly out-of-control situations, being proactive instead of reactive. It is not a strife for total control over every life event, but a feeling of the power to influence outcomes.

People with these characteristics are capable of sizing up stressful events and responding in more favorable ways than those with a low level of hardiness. They do not suffer the ill health consequences of stress as often. To assess your degree of hardiness, complete the Hardiness Scale in Personal Growth Opportunity 10.2 at the end of the chapter.

Social Connectedness

There is clear association between social support and reduced risk for mental as well as physical health problems. The resources provided by others that enable a person to feel valued, cared for, and part of a network of communication and mutual obligation create ones social support (Seeman, 2000, Stroebe, 2000). Social connectedness refers to the relationships that people have with others. Various research studies on diverse populations have shown social support to be related to less depression, lower serum cholesterol levels, less reoccurrence of heart disease among Type A personalities, less melanoma recurrences, healthier pregnancies, and improved academic performance. Involvement in campus activities and the social network of friends each play a significant role in the student's college experience. While the existence of social connections is critical, the style and degree of the connections is also important. To evaluate the value of your social connections, see Personal Growth Opportunity 10.3—Social Support—at the end of the chapter.

Humor and Stress

Learning to laugh at situations can bring a whole new outlook on an event initially perceived as stressful—in fact, laughter has been called "inner jogging" because it creates a physical response that some believe to be therapeutic in the management of stress. Laughter actually stimulates respiratory activity, increases heart rate and muscular activity, promotes oxygen exchange, and perhaps most importantly stimulates the production of endorphins and decreases the level of catecholamines. Endorphins are chemicals produced in the brain that act on the central and peripheral nervous systems to reduce pain. Following an episode of laughter, the relaxation response is experienced, in which blood pressure, heart rate, respiration rate, and muscular tension return to normal levels. Psychologically, laughter has been shown to buffer negative events and prevent them from becoming mood disturbances. Laughter is good, and anyone seeking to manage their stress in a productive way should seek wholesome opportunities for a good laugh.

In addition to humor and laughter, other personality characteristics can be beneficial as well. Looking out for the needs and interests of others (called altruism), volunteerism, expressing gratitude for the good things in one's life, seeking spiritual growth, and discussing problems with a caring friend can also bring a new perspective on some of our challenges.

Type A Personality

Not all personality traits help buffer stress—some make us more vulnerable. About 50 years ago, two cardiologists, Meyer Friedman and Ray Rosenman, identified a set of personality traits that they believed predisposed a person toward heart disease, which they called Type A personality. Their research identified these characteristics as aggressiveness, impatience, time urgency, being highly competitive, overbearing and controlling, and having free-floating hostility and deep-seated insecurity. On the other hand, Type B personalities exhibit different characteristics and experience far less heart disease. Their characteristics include a contemplative nature, greater relaxation, and less extreme competitiveness, aggressiveness, and time urgency. These differences are found in both men and women. Considerable subsequent research reinforces the findings that Type A individuals experience greater coronary vessel obstruction and more coronary heart disease and that they are also more likely to have a second heart attack than Type B persons. Interestingly, however, Type A persons are more likely to survive a heart attack than Type B persons. There is, on the other hand, some research that downplays the relationship between Type A personality and mortality and the duration of stay in coronary care hospital units. This illustrates how complex the study of stress, personality, and health really is. Some studies have separated out certain components of the Type A personality to determine if they alone increased disease risk. Those characteristics that have been found to be consistent in their association with heart disease include hostility, anger, and impatience and irritability. While the research may not be conclusive at this time, the recognition of these potentially dangerous personality traits and their modification certainly appears to be a significant issue in stress management for good health. To determine if you tend toward Type A or Type B personality, see Personal Growth Opportunity 10.4—The Type A Personality Quiz—at the end of this chapter. If you are a Type A individual, Box 10.1 provides suggestions for some helpful attitude changes.

BOX 10.1

Attitude Changes for the Type A Personality

Focus on one thing at a time, and perform that task to your greatest ability.
Listen quietly, be patient with others, and learn from them.
Allow others to perform tasks their way.
Identify a relaxation technique that you can use daily.
Try to work some flex time into your schedule.
Take a little time to be alone and reflect on your thoughts.
Prioritize your activities. Consider eliminating some of the less important and less valuable commitments that you have made with your life.
See life as a journey, not a destination or a task to be accomplished.
Place yourself in situations where you must wait. You may learn that it is not that bad.

STRESS AND THE COLLEGE STUDENT

While college students are susceptible to any life event that they may find stressful, studies have identified the major sources of stress for the college student. According to the American College Health Association (2017), over 57 percent of college students reported feeling more-than-average stress or tremendous stress over the past year. Over 75 percent reported having at least one issue in their life that was traumatic or very difficult to handle, with academics being the most reported issue. Finances, intimate relationships, and family problems were the next most traumatic experiences, followed by sleep difficulties, other social relationships, personal appearance, and career-related issues. Another study identified that daily hassles were reported more often than major life events, with intrapersonal sources of stress being the most frequently reported stressor (Ross, Niebling, & Heckert, 1999). Overload stress is also common among college students. Within the past year, over 87 percent of students reported feeling overwhelmed by all they had to do, and over 84 percent reported feeling exhausted (not from physical activity) (American College Health Association, 2017).

College stressors generally fall into four broad categories:

1. Environmental stressors—These include living conditions and surroundings including traffic, the weather, the condition/location of housing, and exposure to high noise levels.
2. Physiological stressors—These are primarily lifestyle-related sources of stress such as a sedentary lifestyle and poor nutritional habits, inadequate sleep, and physical illness or injury.
3. Social stressors—These stressors include difficult relationships with friends, roommates, and family, problems at work, financial difficulties, and academic challenges.
4. Psychological stressors—These are thoughts and perceptions that can cause stress, including feelings of inferiority, fears of rejection, negative thinking, and allowing a minor stressor to balloon out of control (called catastrophizing).

These categories of stress are sometimes identified as external or internal. External stress includes the life events that one identifies as stressful, as well as physical and environmental conditions. For example, an abusive relationship, financial difficulties, problems at work, or a death in the family would be considered external stressors. Internal stress can come in the form of a physical illness or injury, but is more often a negative view or mind-set regarding a situation or circumstance. Intense worry about life situations is an example of an internal stressor. While control over all external events may not be possible, each person does get to decide what mind-set they will take toward external stressors. The avenues for coping with external and internal stressors are different and are discussed in the section Developing a Plan for Coping with Stress.

Posttraumatic Stress Disorder

One of the most serious types of stress is posttraumatic stress disorder (PTSD). The American Psychological Association (2014) defines PTSD as an anxiety problem that develops in some people after extremely traumatic events, such as combat, crime, an accident, or natural disaster. People with PTSD may relive the event via intrusive memories, flashbacks, and nightmares; avoid anything that reminds them of the trauma; and have anxious feelings they didn't have before that are so intense their lives are disrupted. PTSD received its first public attention in relation to war veterans, but any traumatic event can trigger this disorder. While it is natural to have some stress symptoms after a traumatic event, they often fade after a few weeks. This is known as acute stress disorder (ASD). PTSD symptoms last more than a few weeks and become an ongoing problem, and some people with PTSD don't show symptoms for weeks or months.

This is not a rare disorder. It is estimated that PTSD affects about 7.7 million Americans (National Institute of Mental Health [NIMH], 2014). It is more common in women than in men, and there is some indication that susceptibility may run in families. It can occur at any age and can also be triggered by a dangerous or harmful experience to a friend or family member. Experiencing unexpected death of a loved one may also serve as a trigger.

Numerous factors likely interact to result in PTSD. Risk factors may include experiencing a dangerous or traumatic event, a history of mental illness, getting hurt or seeing people get hurt, experiencing feelings of horror, helplessness, or extreme fear, having no postevent support system, or dealing with another postevent stressor like injury, loss of job, or loss of a loved one.

On the other hand, certain resilience factors may reduce the risk of PTSD. These factors include having strong support groups (preevent and postevent), having good coping skills to get through the event, being able to act effectively in spite of feeling fear, and feeling good about one's actions in the face of danger.

There are a number of potential symptoms of PTSD. The NIMH (2014) groups the signs and symptoms into three categories:

- Reexperiencing symptoms—This includes having flashbacks and bad dreams of frightening thoughts and can cause problems with a person's everyday routines. Certain situations, objects, or even words may be the trigger for reexperiencing, or it may emerge from the person's own thoughts and feelings.
- Avoidance symptoms—This includes emotional numbness, feelings of depression, worry, or guilt, loss of interest in enjoyable events, trouble remembering the traumatic event, or physically staying away from places, events, or objects that could serve as reminders of the event.
- Hyperarousal symptoms—This includes feeling tense and "edgy," being easily startled, sleep difficulties, and angry outbursts. As opposed to being brought on by a trigger, these symptoms are usually constant. They can result in stress and anger and can also interfere with daily tasks.

PTSD is identified when a person has symptoms for at least one month and can be clinically diagnosed by a qualified mental health professional. Treatments for PTSD include several types of psychotherapy (talk therapy) and approved medications. If you or someone you know experiences the symptoms of PTSD, seek help from your campus counseling center or a qualified mental health professional.

Minorities and Stress

Minority students may experience unique stressors and may be particularly vulnerable to stress. Stress is one factor that may contribute to health disparities. Health disparities refer to differences between groups of people which can affect how frequently a disease affects a group, how many people get sick, or how often the disease causes death. Chronic stressors associated with health disparities include perceived discrimination, neighborhood stress, daily stress, family stress, acculturative (cultural changes) stress, environmental stress, and maternal stress (Duric et al., 2010). Minority stress is a term used to refer to chronically high stress levels faced by members of minority groups. They often include poor social support, low socioeconomic status, prejudice, and discrimination (American Psychological Association, 2013).

Armstead, Lawler, Gorden, Cross, and Gibbons (1989) found that perceived racist feelings toward minorities were related to higher resting blood pressure. This prompted the researchers to suggest that racism in our society may be a serious health concern for all minority classes and has led to considerable additional research on race and stress.

It is now widely recognized that minority status can significantly shape how students experience campus life. Minority stress has the greatest negative impact on satisfaction with campus social life and psychological health and has the potential to undermine the health and wellness of minority students. In and out of the classroom, the lack of role models and mentors as well as cultural differences in how we respond to others can contribute to minority student stress. Everyone should be sensitive to individual differences and how our treatment of one another contributes to the overall campus environment for all students. All students should be encouraged to seek out campus support services, and minority student services can play a crucial role in making the campus life and educational experience a positive one for minority students.

DEVELOPING A PLAN FOR COPING WITH STRESS

When the signs of stress appear, immediate intervention is paramount in the process of returning to homeostasis. Numerous approaches to stress management are available, and while each individual has to discover what works for them, there are some basic principles that are highly effective for overall stress management.

1. Alter or Eliminate

This is the most direct approach to stress management—changing the situation that is causing the majority of your stress. It involves attacking the stressor itself and eliminating or moderating the source of the stress. If the heavy traffic and wasted time of a commute is creating a difficult transition to school, one might consider a physical move to be closer to campus and social activities. If finances are the major source of stress, getting a part-time job that does not impede progress toward academic goals could help. For the student who constantly feels as they are in a state of disarray, organizational skills can be helpful. And for the large majority of college students who can never find time to get everything accomplished, implementing some time-management skills may solve much of the problem. Box 10.2 provides some practical suggestions for time management for the college student.

Sometimes, we are confronted with a decision that we know is in our best interest, yet difficult to make. A specific life event may need to be changed in order to prevent the stress of the event from taking a negative toll. For example, if our best efforts to get along with a difficult roommate have not resulted in a peaceful living arrangement, then a new roommate might be in order. If work interferes with academics, then cutting back on work hours might be necessary. Overinvolvement in a campus organization may be stealing time away from academics, and one might be faced with restricting participation in an organization that has great value to them. While each person must decide for themselves what actions are in their best interest, try not to lose sight of the big picture and keep your most important goals as the highest priority in your activities and lifestyles.

2. Change Your Perception

As hard as it may be to admit, sometimes the best solution to handling stress is to change our mental approach to life's situations. The old approach of counting to ten and taking some deep breaths may in fact be useful in today's stressful and fast-paced life. Slowing down and viewing life's challenges in a new perspective can often help us see that our situation is not nearly as bad as we have perceived it. An individual's general outlook on life may influence a person toward suffering from stress-related effects. Catastrophizing is the practice of allowing your mind to exaggerate the intensity of a perceived stressor, sometimes referred to as making a mountain out of a mole hill. It creates a negative outlook, which allows the stressor to intensify.

BOX 10.2

Time Management Tips

Many college students are poor time managers, and poor time management can lead to increased stress and poor academic performance. The following suggestions are designed to get you started on making the most of the hours in your day.

Set long-term and short-term goals. Each student should take inventory at the beginning of each semester to determine their long-range objective. Is the degree track that you are on adequately preparing you for that end? If you are unsure about your future aspirations, speak to an academic advisor or career counselor at your school. Once a goal is determined, realize that you are in a very important stage of life in the pursuit of that goal, and resolve not to waver from your quest. Then, break the long-term goal into shorter goals. They may include a specific grade point average, or a target grade in a difficult course, or a good grade on a term paper. Visit with your teachers to determine a reasonable goal for their class and projects. Put your goals in writing and share them with your support group—you will be more committed to managing your time and following through with your efforts. Reward yourself for accomplishing the goal.

Get organized. Get rid of unneeded clutter. Clean out and organize your study space. Put everything in its proper place instead of leaving it sprawled out across the dorm room or apartment. Designate a spot for items that are easily misplaced—keys, glasses, purses or wallets, cell phones—and keep those things in the same place all of the time. Lots of time is wasted looking for that special item, and often it occurs when we are in a hurry, causing us to be even more time crunched. Also, many people find that making and working from a list of things to do helps them stay focused on using time wisely.

Prioritize. Simply put, some tasks are more important than others, and knowing the difference can help us manage our time. Make lists of things that need to be done, and number them in order of importance. Due dates for projects and the grade value of assignments make a great place to begin prioritizing your academic tasks. Focus on the highest priority activities one at a time, and stay intent on them until they are complete.

Don't procrastinate. Often, assignments are given at the beginning of a semester only to be due at the end. Weeks pass with no progress, creating time urgency at the end ("crunch time"), resulting in inferior work. Set progress dates for major projects, and stick to them. Use "crunch time" for fine tuning the project. Also, learning to say no to distracting commitments, especially when trying to meet deadlines, can help you stay on task.

Eliminate interruptions. When studying, get away from the phone or the flow of traffic where you are likely to be interrupted. Turn off the television and cell phone, and close the door and ask others not to interrupt you when you are working. Libraries still make great places to read, write, and study.

Maximize your time for productivity. Most of us know when we are most productive. Are you a morning or an evening person? Schedule your most important tasks for times that you know are your most industrious. Most of us also have small pockets of spare time in our day that we could use to do simple tasks like make your daily list, return short phone calls, balance the checkbook, or clean out a wallet or purse, or maybe even review a reading assignment.

Identify time wasters. Most people also know when they are least productive, and have activities in their lives that waste time. Television and video games are good sources of entertainment, but too much time in these activities results in lost productivity. Engage in these activities on a limited basis, and set a time limit for them. Set a timer when you start, allowing a reasonable time for them, and when the timer goes off, put them away.

While it may be easier said than done, turning to the characteristics of humor, altruism, and optimism can help change perspectives. How many times have you experienced an unpleasant event, only to be able to have a good laugh about it later? Altruism is the characteristic of serving and doing good deeds in the interest of another person. Optimism is the ability to keep the positive attitude that all things will eventually work for the good, even in the face of difficult times. Some people can find the silver lining in every cloud. Each of these attitudes toward stress has been shown to be valuable in developing a productive stress-management plan.

3. Relax

A number of relaxation techniques have been identified as effective ways to help the body return to homeostasis. Again, while each person must find what helps them relax, some may be interested in developing a new, specific relaxation technique. Relaxation techniques do not address the source of the stress, but do assist the individual in gaining control over the physical symptoms of stress.

Positive imagery—Using mental imagery to deal with stressful situations is a simple method for creating a positive as opposed to a negative mind-set. If you have ever had to give a speech in a class and had anxiety or negative thoughts before the task, positive imagery might be helpful for you. Used often in the field of sports and athletics, this technique teaches the individual to create a mental picture of a highly successful outcome of a specific task or event. Before making the speech, envision yourself having exactly the right words, being highly articulate, and delivering a speech with a convincing method. (And don't forget to practice the speech as well.) Getting rid of negative, self-limiting thoughts can free you to perform at a higher level.

Progressive muscle relaxation (PMR)—Pioneered in the 1930s by physiologist and psychologist Edmund Jacobsen, this technique uses a precise method to teach individuals to achieve muscular relaxation. Some psychologists consider this to be one of the most reliable and effective procedures for achieving relaxation. It works on the concept that emotional tension brings about physical, muscular tension and can result in headaches and muscle aches. As the individual is trained to relax the muscles, much of the emotional tension is relaxed as well—in other words, physical relaxation brings a mental calmness. Focusing on a specific muscle or muscle group, the muscle is intentionally tensed for a few seconds, followed by a release of the tension and focus on the deep relaxed state of the muscle. Each muscle of the body is in turn tensed and relaxed, until the individual learns to experience total physical relaxation. Anyone interested in PMR can practice the technique until they find it helpful in alleviating muscular stress. This technique, combined with deep breathing, is encouraged by the American Lung Association for those who are trying to quit smoking in dealing with the stress of their behavior change. A guideline for practicing PMR is provided in Personal Growth Opportunity 10.5.

Deep breathing—Since stressful experiences can result in shallow, labored breathing, one approach to battling the symptoms of stress is to regain a deeper and more efficient breathing pattern. With deep breathing, like PMR, the individual learns to breath using a slow and deep pattern of inhalation, breathing in through the nose and out through the mouth. Many find deep breathing a welcome release from the stress of the day.

Biofeedback—Biofeedback uses various devices to measure the reaction of certain body processes while under stress. The individual can observe their body's physiological responses to stress and can be taught to use specific techniques to exercise control over those responses. Common biofeedback indicators include measures of muscular tension, heart rate, skin temperature, and perspiration rate. The person can watch a screen or meter that shows the response, then practice their relaxation techniques and watch the relief of the stress as they relax. This process is typically used in a clinical setting and teaches the stressed person how to induce the relaxation response. The subject then practices using the same relaxation techniques in daily-living situations that they find to be stressful.

Social support systems—Benefiting from the understanding and support of others is the basis behind the numerous support groups that exists for various life situations. Establishing a meaningful connection with other people has been shown to help people deal with the stressors of everyday life as well as the catastrophic types of stressors that some people face during difficult times. Disease support groups are quite popular, and many participants report that these groups are critical in sustaining their efforts and energies during stressful times. In addition, studies reveal that married people tend to live longer than single people, and while there are several possible reasons for this, many researchers believe the presence of social support from a significant other is the most important factor. For college students, establishing meaningful connections with peers can help in dealing with life changes. Making new friends, sharing common interests with classmates in your academic department, and getting involved in campus organizations are not only socially fulfilling, but they can help with stress management as well.

4. Maintain Healthy Lifestyles

One's overall level of health is probably the most important component of a total stress-management program. Avoiding tobacco products, the responsible use of alcohol, having regular physical exams and check-ups, and seeking appropriate medical care when needed can contribute to a high level of physical well-being that makes a person more stress resistant. Many of the other chapters of this text, while focusing on physical fitness, also serve as stress management approaches. Maintaining a regular exercise routine, eating a balanced diet, and getting plenty of rest and sleep are three habits that develop the physical foundation to manage stress.

An emphasis on sleep and rest is well-directed to college students. Many college students dismiss the importance of getting regular sleep and rest as part of an overall healthy lifestyle. In fact, only 12 percent report that they get enough sleep to feel rested in the morning six or seven days per week, and ninety percent report a problem with sleepiness during daytime activities (American College Health Association, 2017). While the exact purpose of sleep remains unknown, researchers have determined that sleep plays a number of important roles, including the removal of toxins from the brain that build up during waking hours, and controlling the risk for high blood pressure, stroke, diabetes, obesity, depression, cardiovascular disease, infections, and even certain types of cancer. Brain function, including how nerve cells communicate with each other, is impacted by sleep patterns. There are two types of sleep–REM (rapid eye movement) and non-REM–and usually 4-6 sleep cycles per night, cycling between the stages. There are three stages of non-REM sleep and all types are experienced several times during a night's sleep. In Stage One non-REM sleep, sleep is light as the transition from wakefulness to sleep takes place. It is a short stage as muscles relax (and may twitch) and breathing, eye-movement, heart rate and even brain waves slow. In Stage Two non-REM sleep, muscle relaxation, breathing and heart rate continue to slow in preparation for deeper sleep. Brain waves slow down (but with small bursts of electrical activity) and body temperature drops. More cycles are spent in Stage Two non-REM sleep than in other stages of sleep. Stage Three non-REM sleep brings the deeper sleep that is needed to feel refreshed. These are periods of longer sleep that take place in the first half of the sleep period. Brain waves, breathing, and heart rate are slowest in this stage, and muscle relaxation is at its greatest. Awakening from this stage of sleep may be difficult. Finally, REM sleep is the period of sleep in which heart rate, blood pressure and brain activity are similar to wakefulness and breathing becomes irregular and more rapid. It takes place about 90 minutes after falling asleep. Eyes move rapidly side-to-side and most dreaming takes place in this stage. Muscles in the arms and legs become temporarily paralyzed so that dreams are not acted out. With age, less time is spent in REM sleep (National Institute of Neurological Disorders and Stroke, 2017).

Sleep deprivation and disorders have gained attention as a significant health problem for Americans. According to the Sleep Health Index (National Sleep Foundation, 2014), 45 percent of Americans reported that poor or insufficient sleep affected their daily lives at least once in the past week, and those who report poor quality sleep also report poor quality health, and the American Sleep Association (2018) reports that 50-70 million Americans have a sleep disorder. The American Academy of Sleep Medicine (2018) categorizes sleep disorders as follows.

Insomnias – the inability to fall asleep or stay asleep.

Hypersomnias – excessive sleepiness, with the possibility of falling asleep at dangerous or inconvenient times.

Sleep-Related Breathing Disorders – difficulty breathing during sleep.

Circadian Rhythm Sleep-Wake Disorders – sleep times are out of rhythm and normal sleep times are not followed.

Parasomnias – the experience of unwanted events or experiences while falling asleep, sleeping, or waking up.

Sleep Movement Disorders – movement during or prior to sleep making it difficult to fall or stay asleep, or to attain restful sleep.

BOX 10.3

Trouble Sleeping? Try these . . .

Over 90 percent of people experience some degree of insomnia at some point in their lives, and studies indicate that insomnia affects one in three adults every year in the United States. Lack of sleep can result in irritability, loss of attention, poor academic performance, and increased incidence of accidents. The "correct" amount of sleep is still unknown, and most likely varies from person to person, but the seven-to-nine-hour rule is still a good one to follow. If you feel well rested, you are getting enough sleep. If you are tired and drowsy a lot, it is highly possible that you are not getting enough sleep. If you are having trouble sleeping, try some of these suggestions:

Establish a regular sleep schedule. Set a regular bedtime and wake up time and don't change it on the weekends. This pattern tends to set the body's clock and promote a more restful sleep.

Avoid daytime napping. This disrupts the regular sleep schedule.

Avoid tobacco, caffeine, and alcohol. Nicotine and caffeine are stimulant drugs which can disturb sleep, and tobacco also interferes with sleep due to its effects on the lungs, heart, sinuses, and cardiovascular circulation. Alcohol may cause some people to fall asleep quicker, but it tends to result in fragmented and un-refreshing sleep.

Use your established stress management techniques. Three out of four people who suffer significant insomnia are experiencing a specific stressful event in their lives.

Get daily exercise, but time it right. Exercise too close to bed time may cause some people to not feel tired and ready for sleep due to increased metabolism.

Designate your bed for sleep only. Don't use it for reading, watching television, or studying.

If noise from distracting sources bothers you, consider using some form of "white noise" such as the hum of the motor of a small fan.

Try relaxing with a warm bath at least one hour before bedtime, and perform low key activities (reading, listening to music, or relaxation routines) just prior to bedtime.

Don't over-focus on watching the clock, but if you don't fall asleep in 15–30 minutes, get out of bed and don't return until you are feeling drowsy.

Finally, don't panic about a poor night's sleep. Occasional sleep disruptions are part of life, and getting upset or worrying about it can only make it worse.

Some of the more specific and common types of sleep disorders include (Mayo Clinic, 2016):

- Insomnia – difficulty falling asleep or staying asleep throughout the night.
- Sleep apnea – the experience of abnormal patterns in breathing while you are asleep.
- Restless legs syndrome (RLS) – a type of sleep movement disorder. Restless legs syndrome, also called Willis-Ekbom disease, causes an uncomfortable sensation and an urge to move the legs while you try to fall asleep.
- Narcolepsy – characterized by extreme sleepiness during the day and falling asleep suddenly during the day.

Sleep disorders can be diagnosed in many ways, including polysomnography, or a sleep study. This diagnostic sleep test records sleeping heart rate, blood oxygen levels, brain waves, breathing, and eye and leg movements in order to diagnose the disorder. Once properly diagnosed, most sleep disorders can be effectively treated.

While sleep needs vary from person to person, most adults need 7-9 hours of restful sleep per night. If you have trouble sleeping, see Box 10.3 for some helpful suggestions.

5. Get Outside Support or Help

If your best attempts at stress management don't seem to resolve your feelings, seeking professional assistance is in order. Contact your division of student services or campus counseling center to get help. A trained professional who deals with stress and the college student on a regular basis is likely to have some valuable plans for you.

References

American Academy of Sleep Medicine. (2018). *Sleep Disorder Categories.* Retrieved from: http://www.sleepeducation.org/sleep-disorders-by-category

American College Health Association. (2013). *National College Health Assessment-National College Health Assessment II: Reference Group Executive Summary Spring 2017.* Hanover, MD: American College Health Association; 2017.

American Psychological Association. (2013). *Glossary of psychological terms.* Retrieved from http://www.apa.org/research/action/glossary.aspx#s

American Psychological Association. (2014). *Post traumatic stress disorder.* Retrieved from http://www.apa.org/topics/ptsd/index.aspx

American Sleep Association. (2018). *Sleep and Sleep Disorder Statistics.* Retrieved from: https://www.sleepassociation.org/sleep/sleep-statistics/

Armstead, C. A., Lawler, K. A., Gorden, G., Cross, J., & Gibbons, J. (1989). Relationship of racial stressors to blood pressure responses and anger expression in black college students. *Health Psychology, 8,* 554.

Cannon, W. (1932). *The wisdom of the body.* New York, NY: W. W. Norton.

Conrad, C. D. (2011). *The handbook of stress: Neuropsychological effects on the brain.* Hoboken, NJ: Wiley.

Contrada, R. J., & Baum, A. (Eds.). (2011). *The handbook of stress science.* New York, NY: Springer.

Djuric, Z., Bird, C. E., Furumoto-Dawson, A., Rauscher, G. H., Ruffin, M. T., Stowe, R. P., . . . Masi, C. (2010). *Biomarkers of psychological stress in health disparities research* (NIH Public Access). Retrieved from http://www.ncbi.nlm.nih.gov/pmc/articles/PMC2841407/

Jacobsen, E. (1938). *Progressive relaxation* (2nd ed.). Chicago, IL: University of Chicago Press.

Mayo Clinic. (2016). Sleep Disorders. Retrieved from: https://www.mayoclinic.org/diseases-conditions/sleep-disorders/symptoms-causes/syc-20354018

Mayo Clinic. (2014). Polysomnography (Sleep Study). Retrieved from: https://www.mayoclinic.org/tests-procedures/polysomnography/about/pac-20394877

McEwen, B. S. (1998). Protective and damaging effects of stress mediators. *New England Journal of Medicine, 338,* 171–179.

Molpin, E. (2004). *Perceived stress levels and sources of stress among colleges students.* Retrieved from http://faculty.weber.edu/molpin/dissabstract.html

Monat, A., Lazarus, R. S., & Reevy, G. (2007). *The Praeger handbook on stress and coping, Volume 1.* Westport, CT: Guilford.

National Institute of Mental Health. (2014). *Post traumatic stress disorder.* Retrieved from http://www.nimh.nih.gov/health/topics/post-traumatic-stress-disorder-ptsd/index.shtml

National Institute of Neurological Disorders and Stroke. (2017). *Brain Basics: Understanding sleep.* NIH Publication No. 17-3440c

National Sleep Foundation. (2014). Lack of sleep is affecting Americans. Retrieved from: https://sleepfoundation.org/media-center/press-release/lack-sleep-affecting-americans-finds-the-national-sleep-foundation

Paffenbarger, R., & Olsen, E. (1996). *Lifefit.* Champaign, IL: Human Kinetics.

Ross, S. E., Niebling, B. C., & Heckert, T. M. (1999). Sources of stress among college students. *College Student Journal, 33,* 2.

Seaward, B. L. (2012). *Managing stress: Principles and strategies for health and well-being* (7th ed.). Sudbury, MA: Jones and Bartlett.

Seeman, T. E. (2000). Health promoting effects of friends and family on health outcomes in older adults. *American Journal of Health Promotion, 55,* 362–70.

Selye, H. (1956). *The stress of life.* New York, NY: McGraw-Hill.

Selye, H. (1974). *Stress without distress.* Hagerstown, MD: Lippincott, Williams and Wilkins.

Stroebe, W. Moderators of the stress-health relationship. In: Stroebe, W. *Social psychology and health.* Philadelphia, PA: Open University Press; 2000:236–73

Thiots, P. A. (2010). Stress and health: Major findings and policy implications. *Journal of Health and Social Behavior. 51*(1).

CHAPTER 10

PERSONAL GROWTH OPPORTUNITY 1

Undergraduate Stress Questionnaire

(Stressful events in descending order of severity)

Please check the appropriate stressors in your life that have affected you during the past semester.

_____ 1. Death (family member or friend)
_____ 2. Had a lot of tests
_____ 3. It's finals week
_____ 4. Applying to graduate school
_____ 5. Victim of a crime
_____ 6. Assignments in all classes due the same day
_____ 7. Breaking up with boy/girlfriend
_____ 8. Found out boy/girlfriend cheated on you
_____ 9. Lots of deadlines to meet
_____ 10. Property stolen
_____ 11. You have a hard upcoming week
_____ 12. Went into a test unprepared
_____ 13. Lost something (especially wallet)
_____ 14. Death of a pet
_____ 15. Did worse than expected on test
_____ 16. Had an interview
_____ 17. Had projects, research papers clue
_____ 18. Did badly on a test
_____ 19. Parents getting divorce
_____ 20. Dependent on other people
_____ 21. Having roommate conflicts
_____ 22. Car/bike broke down, flat tire
_____ 23. Got a traffic ticket
_____ 24. Missed your period and waiting
_____ 25. Thoughts about future
_____ 28. Lack of money
_____ 27. Dealt with incompetence at the Register's Office
_____ 28. Thought about unfinished work
_____ 29. No sleep
_____ 30. Sick, Injury
_____ 31. Had a class presentation
_____ 32. Applying for a job
_____ 33. Fought with boy/girlfriend
_____ 34. Working while in school
_____ 35. Arguments, conflicts of values with friends
_____ 36. Bothered by having no social support of family
_____ 37. Performed poorly at a task
_____ 38. Can't finish everything you needed to do
_____ 39. Heard bad news
_____ 40. Had confrontation with an authority figure

___ 41. Maintaining a long-distance boy/girlfriend
___ 42. Crammed for a test
___ 43. Feel unorganized
___ 44. Trying to decide on major
___ 45. Feel isolated
___ 46. Parents controlling with money
___ 47. Couldn't find a parking space
___ 48. Noise disturbed you while trying to study
___ 49. Someone borrowed something without permission
___ 50. Had to ask for money
___ 51. Ran out of toner while printing
___ 52. Erratic schedule
___ 53. Can't understand your professor
___ 54. Trying to get into your major or college
___ 55. Registration for classes
___ 56. Stayed up late writing a paper
___ 57. Someone you expected to call did not
___ 58. Someone broke a promise
___ 59. Can't concentrate
___ 60. Someone did a "pet peeve" of yours
___ 61. Living with boy/girlfriend
___ 62. Felt need for transportation
___ 63. Bad haircut today
___ 64. Job requirements changed
___ 65. No time to eat
___ 68. Felt some peer pressure
___ 67. You have a hangover
___ 68. Problems with your computer
___ 69. Problem getting home from bar when drunk
___ 70. Used a fake ID
___ 71. No sex in a while
___ 72. Someone cut ahead of you in line
___ 73. Checkbook didn't balance
___ 74. Visit from a relative and entertaining them
___ 75. Decision to have sex on your mind
___ 76. Spoke with a professor
___ 77. Change of environment (new doctor, dentist, etc.)
___ 78. Exposed to upsetting TV show, book, or movie
___ 79. Got to class late
___ 80. Holiday
___ 81. Sat through a boring class
___ 82. Favorite sporting team lost

Source: Crandall, C.S., Preisler, J.J., & Aussprung, J. (1992). Measuring life event stress in the lives of college students: The undergraduate stress questionnaire. <u>Journal of Behavioral Medicine</u>, 15, 627–662.

Experiencing these events can have a significant negative impact, physically and mentally. However, your well-being will depend on how you employ psychological resources to cope with these stresses. We're available to help with the development of optimal coping skills.

For further information, please call (918) 631-2200.

CHAPTER 10

PERSONAL GROWTH OPPORTUNITY 2

How Hardy Are You?

Below are twelve items that appear in the hardiness questionnaire. Evaluating hardiness requires more than this quick test, but this exercise should give you some idea of how hardy you are. Write down how much you agree or disagree with the following statements.

0 = strongly disagree, 1 = mildly disagree, 2 = mildly agree, 3 = strongly agree

____ A. Trying my best at work makes a difference.
____ B. Trusting to fate is sometimes all I can do in a relationship.
____ C. I often wake up eager to start on the day's project.
____ D. Thinking of myself as a free person leads to great frustration and difficulty.
____ E. I would be willing to sacrifice financial security in my work if something really challenging came along.
____ F. It bothers me when I have to deviate from the routine or schedule I've set for myself.
____ G. An average citizen can have an impact on politics.
____ H. Without the right breaks, it is hard to be successful in my field.
____ I. I know why I am doing what I am doing at work.
____ J. Getting close to people puts me at risk of being obligated to them.
____ K. Encountering new situations is an important priority in my life.
____ L. I really don't mind when I have nothing to do.

Scoring

These questions measure control, commitment, and challenge. For half the questions a high score indicates hardiness; for the other half, a low score does. To calculate your scores, fill in the numbers of your responses as specified on the lines on the next page. Then subtract the totals in the second line from those in the first and write in the results on the bottom line. Add your scores on commitment, control, and challenge together on the bottom line to get a score for total hardiness. A total score of 10–18 shows a hardy personality; 0–9, moderate hardiness; below 0, low hardiness.

$$\underline{\quad\quad} \quad + \quad \underline{\quad\quad}$$

A + G = _____

minus:

$$\underline{\quad\quad} \quad + \quad \underline{\quad\quad}$$

B + H = _____

$$\underline{\hspace{4cm}}$$

Control   +

$$\underline{\quad\quad} \quad + \quad \underline{\quad\quad}$$

C + I = _____

minus:

$$\underline{\quad\quad} \quad + \quad \underline{\quad\quad}$$

D + J = _____

$$\underline{\hspace{4cm}}$$

Commitment   +

$$\underline{\quad\quad} \quad + \quad \underline{\quad\quad}$$

E + K = _____

minus:

$$\underline{\quad\quad} \quad + \quad \underline{\quad\quad}$$

F + L = _____

$$\underline{\hspace{4cm}}$$

Challenge   = _____

Total Hardiness Score _____

CHAPTER 10

PERSONAL GROWTH OPPORTUNITY 3

Social Support

Part I. Assessing Your Level of Social Support

To determine whether your social network measures up, select whether each of the following statements is true or false for you.

	True	False
1. If I needed an emergency loan of $100, there is someone I could get it from.	___	___
2. There is someone who takes pride in my accomplishments.	___	___
3. I often meet or talk with family or friends.	___	___
4. Most people I know think highly of me.	___	___
5. If I needed an early morning ride to the airport, there's no one I would feel comfortable asking to take me.	___	___
6. I feel there is no one with whom I can share my most private worries and fears.	___	___
7. Most of my friends are more successful making changes in their lives than I am.	___	___
8. I would have a hard time finding someone to go with me on a day trip to the beach or country.	___	___

Your Score ___

Scoring

If you marked four or more statements true, you should have enough support to protect your health. If your score is 3 or less, refer to your textbook for suggestions on how to build up your social network.

Part II. Social Support Profile

Learn more about your network of social support by completing a social support profile. For each type of support listed below, list the people who most often provide that type of support for you. Check the category box if that person reciprocates by coming to you for the same type of support.

Type of Support	Emotional: Someone you can trust with your most intimate thoughts and fears	Social: Someone with whom you can hang out and share life experiences	Informational: Someone you can ask for advice on major decisions	Practical: Someone who will help you out in a pinch
Partner □				
Relative □				
Friend □				
Neighbor □				
Coworker or boss □				
Therapist or clergy □				

Internet Activity

The Internet can be a valuable resource for building up your social support network. Think about your hobbies and areas of interest. With the Internet, you can get in touch with organizations and people who share your interests. For example, from Yahoo's recreation and sports listings (http://dir.yahoo.com/recreation/sports), in-line skaters can learn about equipment and technique as well as local clubs and skating events. If you are interested in human rights, Amnesty International's home page (http://www.amnesty .org/) can put you in touch with a local chapter of the organization. Whatever your interests, odds are that you can find applicable Web pages, bulletin boards, chat rooms, and other Internet resources.

Choose a topic, and use a search engine to locate online resources. Describe what you find: What sites are available? What sorts of information can you obtain? Are there opportunities for you to interact online with people who share your area of interest? Did you find any organizations or groups operating in your area?

Area of interest:

Resources located:

CHAPTER 10

PERSONAL GROWTH OPPORTUNITY 4

Type A Personality Quiz

This scale, based on the one by Friedman and Rosenman, will give you an estimate of your Type A tendencies. Directions: Answer the following questions by indicating the response that most often applies to you.

Yes	No	Statement
____	____	1. I always feel rushed.
____	____	2. I find it hard to relax.
____	____	3. I attempt to do more and more in less and less time.
____	____	4. I often find myself doing more than one thing at a time.
____	____	5. When people take too long to make a point, I finish the sentence for them.
____	____	6. Waiting in line for anything drives me crazy.
____	____	7. I am always on time or early.
____	____	8. In a conversation, I often clench my fist and pound home important points.
____	____	9. I often use explosive outbursts to accentuate key points.
____	____	10. I am competitive at everything.
____	____	11. I tend to evaluate my success by translating things into numbers.
____	____	12. Friends tell me I have more energy than most people.
____	____	13. I always move, walk, and eat quickly.
____	____	14. I bring work home often.
____	____	15. I tend to get bored on vacation.
____	____	16. I feel guilty when I am not being "productive".
____	____	17. I tend to refocus other people's conversations on things that interest me.
____	____	18. I hurry others along in their conversations.
____	____	19. It is agonizing to be stuck behind someone driving too slowly.
____	____	20. I find it intolerable to let others do something I can do faster.

Scoring

Add up the number of items for which you checked yes. The greater the number of yes items, the more likely it is that you are a Type A personality.

CHAPTER 10

PERSONAL GROWTH OPPORTUNITY 5

Progressive Muscle Relaxation

Preparation

Generate about 70–80 percent of the total possible tension in a muscle or muscle group to avoid cramping or injury.

Spend twice as much time relaxing each muscle as you spend tensing each muscle.

Do not skip any body parts unless that muscle or muscle group is injured.

Do not skip around in the sequence of body parts to be tensed and relaxed.

Lie supine on a comfortable mat or carpeted floor, take a few deep breaths in through your nose and out through your mouth. You may now proceed with a normal, relaxed breathing pattern throughout the rest of the exercise.

Close your eyes and prepare for a total body relaxation experience.

Relaxation

Curl your toes so your feet and calves are tense. Focus on the feeling of tension. Relax your feet and calves, quickly letting go of the tension. Concentrate on the difference between the feelings of tension and relaxation. Curl your toes and tense the calves and feet once again, this time slightly tighter. Now relax and feel the difference.

Point your feet back toward your face this time. Study the tension. Relax and focus on the muscles of your lower legs and feet. Relax the tension in the lower legs and feet and concentrate on the difference between the feelings of relaxation and tension. Try to relax your entire body.

Push both heels against the ground. Hold them and feel the tension in the back of your hips and thighs. Relax and feel the tension slowly diminish until you feel no more tension at all. Focus on the relaxed feeling in your calves, thighs, and hips. Feel the heaviness in your legs as you relax further. Take a nice, deep breath, in through your nose and out through your mouth.

Now tense the buttocks by raising the hips ever so slightly off the floor. Hold the tensed position for a few seconds. Relax, again focusing on the difference in the feelings. Repeat the tensing of the buttocks, and add the tensing of as many leg muscles as possible. Relax all muscles of the lower body, feeling the tension moving out of your limbs and noticing how heavy the lower body has become.

Next, suck in your stomach and tense the abdominal muscles. Remember to continue a relaxed breathing pattern. Relax the abdominal muscles. Repeat the tensing and relaxing of the abdominal muscles, concentrating on the feeling that results from the relaxation.

Take a moment to relax the entire body, breathing in through your nose and out through your mouth. Take a few of these deep, relaxing breaths. Feel the warmth of the body as it moves tension away. Feel the heaviness that comes with relaxed muscles.

Now inhale deeply, and study the resulting tension in your chest. Exhale, letting your chest collapse naturally and freely. Now continue to breathe normally and feel the relaxation grow every time you exhale. Inhale deeply once again, feeling the tightness in the chest. Exhale and relax, allowing the relaxed feeling to spread through the chest to the muscles of your back as you breathe normally.

Place your arms at your sides and tightly clench your fists. Relax. Clench your fists again, trying to keep your entire body relaxed except for your fists. Make sure you are not tensing any other body part, like the shoulders, back, or toes, or clenching your teeth. Now relax the fists, again focusing on the feeling of relaxation.

Now tense the shoulders by shrugging them upward, as high as possible. Drop your shoulders to their normal position, and feel the relaxation. Shrug the shoulders again, moving them forward and back a bit. Focus on the tensed feeling. Now relax them and concentrate on the contrast between the tensed and relaxed feelings. Allow the relaxation to move into your back and down your arms. Settle into a comfortable position and feel the relaxation taking over your entire body.

Now tend to the muscles in your neck and face. Tighten the neck muscles, clench your jaw, and scowl the muscles of the face. Relax all of those muscles. Tighten each of those muscle groups again, concentrating on the tense feeling. Relax and concentrate on the feelings in the neck, face, and jaw. Take a deep breath, in through the nose, and exhale slowly out the mouth. Concentrate on the relaxed feeling of the muscles of the entire body.

The final step is to tense as many of the muscles of the entire body as possible. Tense the entire body at one time. Relax all of the muscles of the body once, and concentrate on total body relaxation. Repeat the total body tension and relaxation, enjoying the feeling of an entirely relaxed body. Feel the tension dissipate and the relaxation taking over. Feel the warmness, the deepest level of relaxation yet. Your desire to move should be minimal, as you enjoy the relief from all muscle tension.

Now open your eyes, and gradually adjust to your surroundings. Resist the urge to move, and if any tension creeps back into your body, allow yourself to relax it away. When you wish to get up, count backward from ten. Sit up slowly, and then stand up slowly. You should feel calm, relaxed, and refreshed.

Your Personal Program

© wavebreakmedia, 2014. Used under license from Shutterstock, Inc.

Specific Objectives

1. Summarize the components of wellness and the components of physical fitness.
2. Understand the benefits of being a willing participant in lifetime wellness and fitness activities.
3. Explain lifestyle factors important for improving health and longevity.
4. Identify the various principles of training and conditioning.
5. Recognize the roles of warm-up and cooldown for an activity program.
6. Review the components of physical fitness.
7. Describe the characteristics of a safe and effective exercise prescription.
8. Understand how motivational techniques can assist in compliance with an activity program.
9. List safety precautions that will aid in successful initiation and maintenance of an activity program.

Adapted from *Fitness for Life, Fourth Edition* by Bill Hyman, Gary Oden, David Bacharach, Tim Sebesta. Copyright © 2011 by Kendall Hunt Publishing Company. Reprinted by permission.

OVERVIEW

The desired outcome the authors wish for this book is that you will develop your personal wellness program. This chapter will review topics discussed in previous chapters in order to provide more guidelines on how to make wellness a part of your lifestyle. In the Motivational Techniques section, toward the end of this chapter, fitness/wellness apps (which are free) are excellent informational and motivational tools that can keep your program fresh and fun. It is our hope that you use the presented information to decrease you risk of chronic lifestyle disease and to enhance your wellness for a lifetime.

COMPONENTS OF WELLNESS

Recall from Chapter 1 that the overall goal of wellness is not just physical fitness, but the fulfillment of several dimensions of our lives. Wellness includes five distinct components (Figure 11.1). Social health addresses the development and maintenance of personal relationships, establishing a network of family and friends, and having feelings of comfort in social settings. The foundation of strong emotional health depends on stress management and the appropriate expression of our feelings. Although it is very normal to experience some highs and lows, the avoidance of drastic swings in emotions is important to mental health. Spiritual health means different things to different people. Regardless of religious feelings or beliefs, spiritual health is a function of personal values. Having a true sense of purpose and direction in life, understanding human nature, maintaining sensitivity and respect for others, and having appreciation for the beauty of life are all a part of sound spiritual health. Intellectual health addresses the mind and a perpetual love of learning. Reading, interacting with others, and attending lectures are all excellent methods to maintain intellectual health. Physical health involves taking good care of the body and its systems to ensure that they remain disease free and capable of functioning at a high level of efficiency. As we have suggested throughout this text, physical health contributes significantly to total health and well-being. Physical health has perhaps the most widespread impact on overall health and can be accomplished in so many different ways. Improved quality of life and a longer life are the common results, making it difficult to dispute the positives of physical activity.

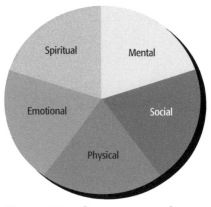

Figure 11.1 • Components of wellness.

HEALTH BENEFITS OF PHYSICAL ACTIVITY

The twentieth century brought about tremendous strides in the understanding of health and wellness, not only through advances in the medical field, but in a more thorough understanding of how our lifestyles influence our health status. A review of the last one hundred years also reveals how lifestyles have changed and how those changes have affected overall health. Certainly, the physical demands of daily life have lessened as our occupations now rely far more on automation than physical effort in the majority of professions in our country. However, just because we no longer have a need for physical activity in most occupational settings does not mean that we do not need to remain physically active to maintain our health. Risks to our society have turned from infectious diseases (polio, rubella, tuberculosis, influenza, etc.) to chronic diseases (obesity, hypertension, heart disease, stroke, cancer, emphysema, etc.). This transition took the better part of the century and only in the last few decades have we begun to recognize the relationship between physical activity and causes of death.

Being healthy and physically fit is a personal choice. It has been suggested that about two-thirds of all deaths in the United States are a result of chronic disease and 80 percent of those deaths could be prevented via lifestyle changes. In most cases, we have the ability to choose a healthy or an unhealthy diet, to be active or inactive, and to take or avoid certain risks. All of our daily choices influence our health. The "Be Active Your Way" program has a website that you might find useful. It includes a 14-page document provided by the government, with four components from getting started to being active for life: http://www.health.gov/paguidelines/pdf/adultguide.pdf. Among the benefits are risk reductions in diabetes, hypertension, heart disease, stroke, and colon cancer. Along with reduced risk for most chronic diseases comes positive increases in bone density, reduced symptoms of depression and anxiety, and a delay of the aging process through maintenance of metabolically active muscle tissue.

FACTORS IMPORTANT FOR HEALTH AND LONGEVITY

Physical activity by itself cannot guarantee good health—other factors undoubtedly play a role in overall health. However, numerous research studies have consistently shown that higher levels of physical activity are associated with decreased risks of coronary heart disease, cerebrovascular disease, hypertension, osteoporosis, type 2 diabetes mellitus, colon cancer, and possibly breast cancer. The 2008 *Physical Activity Guidelines for Americans Summary* (Appendix A) comes from the original 250+-page document entitled, *Healthy People 2020*, covering all aspects of health and well-being for Americans. It was developed by leading experts in the field and compiled by the Health and Human Services (HHS) department. From the Surgeon General's Report of 1996 to the present, we are on an accelerated course of obesity, diabetes, hypertension, stroke, and heart disease. But that can all change with an individual commitment to being active on a daily basis. The American College of Sports Medicine has initiated a program entitled *Exercise Is Medicine*; the program is worldwide, not just for the United States, and the basic recommendations are really quite simple.

Do moderately intense cardio 30 minutes/day, 5 days/week

OR

Do vigorously intense cardio 20 minutes/day, 3 days/week

AND

Do 8–10 strength-training exercises, 8–12 repetitions of each exercise twice each week.

Moderate-intensity physical activity means working hard enough to raise your heart rate and break a sweat, yet still being able to carry on a conversation. It should be noted that to lose weight or maintain weight loss, 60 to 90 minutes of physical activity may be necessary. The 30-minute recommendation is for the average healthy adult to maintain health and reduce the risk for chronic disease, not to use to lose unwanted fat mass. Encouraging everyone to do 20–30 minutes or more of vigorous physical activity every day parallels the Surgeon General's Report, which indicates that a minimum caloric expenditure of 1,000 weight-adjusted calories per week reduces the risk of most chronic diseases and premature death. Table 11.1 reflects the value of some fitness activities and ranges of caloric expenditures.

No single factor has been shown to influence health more than physical activity.

TABLE 11.1 Fitness Ranking

Activity	Cardiorespiratory Endurance	Upper Body Strength	Lower Body Strength	Flexibility	Calories Burned/min
Aerobic dance	High	Moderate	Moderate	Moderate	5–10
Basketball	Moderate	Moderate	Moderate	Moderate	5–10
Bowling	None	Low	Low	Low	2–4
Canoeing	Low	Moderate	Low	Moderate	4–10
Cycling	High	Low	High	Moderate	5–15
Golf (walking)	Low	Low	Moderate	Moderate	2–4
Jogging	High	Moderate	High	Moderate	5–15
Karate	Moderate	High	High	High	5–10
Racquet sports	Moderate	Moderate	Moderate	Moderate	5–10
Running	Very high	Moderate	Moderate	Moderate	10–15
Skating (ice)	Moderate	Low	Moderate	Moderate	5–10
Skating (in-line)	High	Low	High	Moderate	5–15
Skiing (Alpine)	Moderate	Moderate	High	Moderate	5–10
Skiing (Nordic)	Very high	High	High	Moderate	5–15
Soccer	High	Moderate	Moderate	Moderate	5–15
Volleyball	Moderate	Moderate	Moderate	Moderate	5–10
Walking	Moderate	Low	Moderate	Low	3–4
Waterskiing	Low	Moderate	Moderate	Moderate	4–8
Weight lifting	Low	Very high	Very high	Moderate	4–6

PRINCIPLES OF TRAINING AND CONDITIONING

Taking charge of planning and implementing a fitness program that matches your personal goals is not hard. These five steps can get you on your way right now.

Step 1: Set specific, measureable goals. Doran (1981) presented a simple "SMART" strategy for goal setting. SMART goals are **S**pecific, **M**easureable, **A**chievable, **R**ealistic, and **T**imely.

Step 2: Apply key training principles. These include the following:

1. **Overload and progression**—Whatever system we want to change for the better, we need to provide a mild stress or overload that stimulates the system to adapt. The key is to provide an overload great enough to cause change without causing injury. Once we get accustomed to this new load, we must progress to a slightly greater load until we have reached our goal(s).

2. **Specificity**—To obtain optimal adaptations, we must stress the system of interest. To improve flexibility of the shoulders, for example, we have to do specific stretches for the muscles crossing the shoulder joint. To increase arm strength, we should do resistance training for arm muscles. To improve aerobic capacity, we must engage in activities that increase heart rate and oxygen demands at the muscle level.

3. **Reversibility**—As we have stated previously, we lose what we fail to use. This holds true for muscular strength and endurance, aerobic capacity, flexibility, and so on. However, there is a positive regarding reversibility. It is easier to regain a level of fitness once you have been there before; for example, suppose you are sedentary and decide to attain a high level of fitness, and it takes 16 weeks to attain this fitness level and then you become sedentary again and lose all the gains for your 16 weeks of

workouts. If you decide to reach your previous high level of fitness, it will not take as long. In fact, the second time may take only 12 weeks as compared with the 16 weeks it took the first time.

4. **Individual differences**—People differ in their responses to various forms of overload training. What might be an appropriate routine for one person would be excessive for another.

Step 3: Select activities. Regardless of a person's fitness level, each of the five components (body composition, muscular strength, muscular endurance, flexibility, and cardiovascular endurance) should be addressed. Not all areas need to be emphasized, but *everyone* should engage in some type of aerobic activity.

Step 4: Pay attention to the **FITT** principle in determining how **F**requent, how **I**ntense, what **T**ype, and how much **T**ime you spend on an activity. Follow the guidelines from the HHS or ACSM to help you achieve your goals for health and fitness.

The Center for Disease Control (CDC) is also run by the government and supports efforts to improve overall health in multiple areas. The website for physical activity can be found at http://www.cdc.gov/physicalactivity/everyone/guidelines/index.html

The President's Council on Physical Fitness and Sports has resources available to the public. This website is located at http://www.fitness.gov/council_pubs.htm

Different recommendations on minutes per day or days per week appear because they are intended for different groups and may be age specific or relevant to overweight or obese individuals. Tools for success and video clips to help you with various aspects of fitness, such as aerobic exercise, stretching, and strength training, can be found at this web link: http://www.myexerciseplan.com/assessment/

The recommendation for frequency of most aerobic activities is 3–6 days per week and, for strength training, 2–5 days/week. Figure 11.2 reflects the potential benefits versus risk of injury for increased frequency of exercise. Improvements in strength or aerobic fitness will then plateau or diminish after five days in comparison with the increased risk of injury. You may also note that the greatest gains are realized by simply becoming active just a few days each week.

Safety Precautions

After applying the basic FITT principles of exercise, it is critically important to consider safety issues. First, establish your goals and select appropriate activities to meet those goals. Then your focus should turn to safety. Here is a checklist to help you exercise safely.

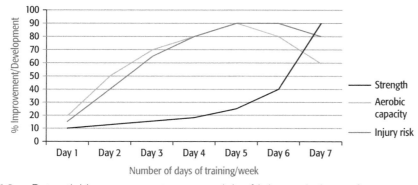

Figure 11.2 • Potential improvements versus risk of injury relative to frequency of activity.

TABLE 11.2 Safe Exercise Tips for Expectant Mothers

1. Consult your physician.
2. Do not exercise to fatigue.
3. Avoid activities that bounce, twist, and jar the body.
4. Avoid high-risk activities that might challenge balance.
5. Do not complete exercises while lying on your back.
6. Avoid exercise in hot, humid environments.
7. Avoid intensities that exceed 70 percent maximal heart rate.
8. Avoid starting exercise in the 1st or 3rd trimester.
9. Drink plenty of fluids before, during, and after exercise.

1. Wear proper clothing and footwear. Typically, loose or stretchy, comfortable clothing that allows freedom of movement is ideal. Footwear should match the activity, but in any case, shoes that are supportive of the main arch of the foot are important.

2. Be prepared for weather conditions. Acclimating to environmental conditions is the key. Acclimation can occur in 4–7 days of gradual and continued exposure. In hot weather, *consume fluids* with electrolytes before, during, and after activity. This will reduce your risk of heat illness. To conserve heat loss in cold weather, wear a hat, gloves, warm socks, and dry footwear. Dress in layers, and avoid cotton clothing. Cotton clothing, when wet, actually draws heat away from the body.

3. Include time for a proper warm-up and cooldown 5–10 minutes before engaging in strenuous activity, which allows blood to be shifted to the muscles. These few minutes will help prevent you from experiencing early fatigue or delayed soreness. Cooldown is the perfect time to focus on stretching. If you have a goal of increasing flexibility, cooldown is the optimal time to improve range of motion.

4. Follow the mantra, "Train don't strain" versus "No pain, no gain." Pain is clearly a sign that something is wrong. If you feel pain, stop and evaluate it. Seek medical assistance, if needed, but don't simply ignore pain.

5. Take personal health status into consideration. Very few medical conditions would prevent you from physical activity; however, many conditions do require some modification of intensity or type of activity. Women bring such common issues to the task of exercising safely: menstruation and pregnancy. Recent medical research has confirmed that exercise has no harmful effects on menstruation. In fact, exercise may lessen the mood swings associated with hormonal fluctuations during the premenstrual period. Guidelines for exercise during pregnancy are found in Table 11.2. The key to exercising during pregnancy is to reach a moderate level of fitness before getting pregnant and then maintaining that level of fitness throughout the pregnancy. Whatever your issue(s), consider them when choosing to be active, but don't use them as an excuse not to be active.

6. Exercise in safe, well-lit areas. Use common sense, and avoid dangerous areas and/or situations that are out of your control.

7. Avoid exercising alone. If you choose to exercise alone, be sure someone else knows the general direction you have gone, how long you expect to be gone, and whenever possible, have a working cell phone with you in case of emergency.

MOTIVATIONAL TECHNIQUES FOR LONG-TERM ADHERENCE

Motivation is often a factor in getting people engaged in routine physical activity. Teague, Mackenzie, and Rosenthal (2007) listed common barriers to activity and solutions to overcoming these barriers. Some of these are provided in Table 11.3.

Regardless of the activity a person chooses to engage in, the basic principles of training and conditioning apply. First and foremost, activities should be fun. Activities must deliver a level of enjoyment for them to be continued. Allow your exercise time to

TABLE 11.3 Activity Barrier and Possible Solutions to This Barrier

Activity Barrier	Possible Solutions to This Barrier
Exercising alone	Ask people to join you. Involve people you care about in your activity goals so they can help motivate you. Join a walking group or an active club.
Too busy	Look for short intervals in your day and do something active in them. Doing more activity in your daily routine will help you get going. Look for half-hour time slots, and dedicate one of those each day to being active.
Not athletic	Engage in less-skilled activities, such as walking, cycling, or doing simple calisthenics. Take lessons to learn a new skill. Get a friend to teach you something new.
No willpower	Find a workout partner. Set a time and place to meet. If someone is counting on you to be there, you'll make a stronger attempt to comply. Give your workout partner $20 per month, and each time you don't show up to work out, s/he gets to keep $5. If you don't miss a day, s/he has to give you back your $20.
No energy	Find a way to give activity a chance. Over time, exercise will make you more energetic and you'll have more energy for all the things you do.
Travel too much	Make accommodations in exercise routines to allow you to be active even if you're away from home. Therabands or jump ropes are easy to pack.
Fear of injury	Follow guidelines of safety, warm-up, and cooldown, and select appropriate activities. If you do so, you can minimize any risk of injury you might have.
Weather	Have backup activities if weather prevents you from following your plan.

also be a social time, enjoying various activities with family and friends. Enjoyment provides the best motivation for a lifetime of activity. Box 11.1 provides a few suggestions for making physical activity a fun thing to do.

There are a number of fitness apps that can be used for motivation as well as a resource for diversifying your exercise routine. There are many apps to choose from; however, here are a few of the most popular:

1. Hot5
   Hot5 contains pages and pages of 5-minute video workouts that are very easy to follow. From abs to core to yoga and everything in between, Hot5 will have a workout video that should fit your need.
2. RunKeeper
   RunKeeper allows you to track all of your exercise activities by using the GPS system in your phone.
3. Zombies, Run!
   Zombies, Run! mixes games and stories into your exercise as you complete missions in a world laden with zombies.
4. Fitbit Coach
   Fitbit Coach gives you access to unlimited video workouts and audio coaching.
5. Nike Training Club
   Nike Training Club provides everything needed to develop your personal fitness plan.

> **BOX 11.1**
>
> **Invitations to Activity**
>
> 1. Exercise with a friend.
> 2. Plan exercise time into your daily schedule.
> 3. Include a variety of activities.
> 4. Set short-term goals.
> 5. Reward yourself for goals achieved.
> 6. Keep a log of your activities.
> 7. Do not get angry if you miss an activity or fail to achieve a goal.

Once activity becomes a part of your lifestyle, it will be hard for you to imagine life without it. But before that time, you must consider activity a priority. This will help you continue a good habit. We hope that this book has encouraged you to develop or continue an active lifestyle. It's great to be fit, and the exhilarating feeling that physical activity generates can be addictive.

PLANNING YOUR FITNESS PROGRAM

Now that you have evaluated your overall health status through the various laboratory assessments in this textbook, it is time to create a health/fitness plan. Your plan should start with goals, followed by strategies for maintaining and/or improving your status in each health/fitness parameter. Your next step is to complete parts I and II of the Personal Program Lab and Worksheet located at the end of this chapter.

References

American College of Sports Medicine. (1993). Position stand on physical activity, physical fitness, and hypertension. *Medicine and Science in Sport and Exercise, 10*, i–x.

Arnheim, D. D., & Prentice, W. E. (1993). *Principles of athletic training* (8th ed.) St. Louis, MO: Mosby-Year Book.

Centers for Disease Control and Prevention. (2004). *Leading causes of death, 1900–1998.* Retrieved from http://www.cdc.gov/nchs/statab/lead1900_1998.pdf

Centers for Disease Control and Prevention. (1996). *Physical activity and health: A report of the surgeon general.* Washington, DC: U.S. Government Printing Office.

Doran, G. T. (1981). There's a S.M.A.R.T. way to write management goals and objectives. *Management Review, 70*(11)(AMA FORUM), 35–36.

McArdle, W. D., Katch, F. I., & Katch, V. L. (2001). *Exercise physiology: Energy, nutrition, and human performance* (5th ed.). Baltimore, MD: Lippincott, Williams & Wilkins.

National Center for Health Statistics. (2005). *Health, United States, 2005.* Hyattsville, MD: U.S. Government Printing Office.

Teague, M. L., Mackenzie, S. C., & Rosenthal, D. M. (2007). Fitness: Physical activity for life. In M. L. Teague, S. C. Mackenzie, & D. M. Rosenthal (Eds.), *Your health today: Choices in a changing society* (pp. 195–224). New York, NY: McGraw-Hill.

U.S. Centers for Disease Control and Prevention & American College of Sports Medicine. (1993). Summary statement: Workshop on physical activity and public health. *Sports Medicine Bulletin, 28*, 7.

U.S. Department of Health and Human Services. (2000, November). *Healthy People 2010: Understanding and improving health* (2nd ed.). Washington, DC: U.S. Government Printing Office.

Wolf, L., Amey, M., & McGrath, M. (1995). Exercise in pregnancy. In J. Torg & R. Shepard (Ed.), *Current therapy in sports medicine.* St. Louis, MO: Mosby-Year Book, 211–212.

CHAPTER 11

PERSONAL GROWTH OPPORTUNITY 1

Personal Program Lab and Worksheet

Part I—Your Lab Assessments

HEALTH/FITNESS PARAMETER	LAB SCORE	SATISFIED? (Y/N)
Cardiorespiratory Endurance		
Body Composition		
Flexibility		
Muscular Strength and Endurance		
Nutrition		
Cardiovascular Disease Risk		
Smoking		
Cancer Risk		
Diabetes Risk		
Stress Inventory		

Part II—Plan of Action

For each of the health/fitness parameters, briefly describe how you plan to maintain and/or change your current status.

Cardiorespiratory Endurance _____

_____

_____

Body Composition _____

_____

_____

Flexibility _____

_____

_____

Muscular Strength and Endurance _____

_____

_____

Nutrition _____

_____

_____

Cardiovascular Disease Risk _____

_____

_____

Smoking _____

_____

_____

Cancer Risk _____

_____

_____

Diabetes Risk _____

_____

_____

Stress Inventory _____

_____

_____

TOPIC AREA: DIABETES

Goal

Reduce the disease burden of diabetes mellitus (DM) and improve the quality of life for all persons who have, or are at risk for, DM.

Overview

DM occurs when the body cannot produce enough insulin or cannot respond appropriately to insulin. Insulin is a hormone that the body needs to absorb and use glucose (sugar) as fuel for the body's cells. Without a properly functioning insulin signaling system, blood glucose levels become elevated and other metabolic abnormalities occur, leading to the development of serious, disabling complications.

Many forms of diabetes exist. The 3 common types of DM are:

Type 2 diabetes, which results from a combination of resistance to the action of insulin and insufficient insulin production

Type 1 diabetes, which results when the body loses its ability to produce insulin

Gestational diabetes, a common complication of pregnancy. Gestational diabetes can lead to perinatal complications in mother and child and substantially increases the likelihood of cesarean section. Gestational diabetes is also a risk factor for the mother and, later in life, the child's subsequent development of type 2 diabetes after the affected pregnancy.

Effective therapy can prevent or delay diabetic complications. However, about 28 percent of Americans with DM are undiagnosed, and another 86 million American adults have blood glucose levels that greatly increase their risk of developing type 2 DM in the next several years. Diabetes complications tend to be more common and more severe among people whose diabetes is poorly controlled, which makes DM an immense and complex public health challenge. Preventive care practices are essential to better health outcomes for people with diabetes.

Why Is Diabetes Important?

DM affects an estimated 29.1 million people in the United States and is the 7th leading cause of death. Diagnosed DM:

Increases the all-cause mortality rate 1.8 times compared to persons without diagnosed diabetes

Increases the risk of heart attack by 1.8 times

Is the leading cause of kidney failure, lower limb amputations, and adult-onset blindness

In addition to these human costs, the estimated total financial cost of DM in the United States in 2012 was $245 billion, which includes the costs of medical care, disability, and premature death.

The number of DM cases continues to increase both in the United States and throughout the world. Due to the steady rise in the number of persons with DM, and possibly earlier onset of type 2 DM, there is growing concern about:

The possibility of substantial increases in prevalence of diabetes-related complications in part due to the rise in rates of obesity

The possibility that the increase in the number of persons with DM and the complexity of their care might overwhelm existing health care systems

The need to take advantage of recent discoveries on the individual and societal benefits of improved diabetes management and prevention by bringing life-saving discoveries into wider practice

The clear need to complement improved diabetes management strategies with efforts in primary prevention among those at risk for developing type 2 DM

TOPIC AREA: HEART DISEASE AND STROKE

Goal

Improve cardiovascular health and quality of life through prevention, detection, and treatment of risk factors for heart attack and stroke; early identification and treatment of heart attacks and strokes; prevention of repeat cardiovascular events; and reduction in deaths from cardiovascular disease.

Overview

Heart disease is the leading cause of death in the United States. Stroke is the fifth leading cause of death in the United States. Together, heart disease and stroke, along with other cardiovascular disease, are among the most widespread and costly health problems facing the Nation today, accounting approximately $320 billion in health care expenditures and related expenses annually. Fortunately, they are also among the most preventable.

The leading modifiable (controllable) risk factors for heart disease and stroke are:

High blood pressure
High cholesterol
Cigarette smoking
Diabetes
Unhealthy diet and physical inactivity
Overweight and obesity

Over time, these risk factors cause changes in the heart and blood vessels that can lead to heart attacks, heart failure, and strokes. It is critical to address risk factors early in life to prevent these devastating events and other potential complications of chronic cardiovascular disease.

Controlling risk factors for heart disease and stroke remains a challenge. High blood pressure, cigarette smoking, and high blood cholesterol are still major contributors to the national epidemic of cardiovascular disease. High blood pressure affects approximately 1 in 3 adults in the United States, and only about half of them have it under control. High sodium intake can increase blood pressure and the risk for heart disease and stroke, yet about 90% of American adults exceed their daily recommendation for sodium intake.

The risk of Americans developing and dying from cardiovascular disease would be substantially reduced if major improvements were made across the U.S. population in diet and physical activity, control of high blood pressure and cholesterol, smoking cessation, and appropriate aspirin use.

Why Are Heart Disease and Stroke Important?

Currently more than 1 in 3 adults (85.6 million) live with 1 or more types of cardiovascular disease. In addition to being the first and fifth leading causes of death, heart disease and stroke result in serious illness and disability, decreased quality of life, and hundreds of billions of dollars in economic loss every year.

The burden of cardiovascular disease is disproportionately distributed across the population. There are significant disparities in the following based on gender, age, race/ethnicity, geographic area, and socioeconomic status:

Prevalence of risk factors
Access to treatment
Appropriate and timely treatment
Treatment outcomes
Mortality

TOPIC AREA: NUTRITION AND WEIGHT STATUS

Goal

Promote health and reduce chronic disease risk through the consumption of healthful diets and achievement and maintenance of healthy body weights.

Overview

The Nutrition and Weight Status objectives for Healthy People 2020 reflect strong science supporting the health benefits of eating a healthful diet and maintaining a healthy body weight. The objectives also emphasize that efforts to change diet and weight should address individual behaviors, as well as the policies and environments that support these behaviors in settings such as schools, worksites, health care organizations, and communities.

The goal of promoting healthful diets and healthy weight encompasses increasing household food security and eliminating hunger.

Americans with a healthful diet:

Consume a variety of nutrient-dense foods within and across the food groups, especially whole grains, fruits, vegetables, low-fat or fat-free milk or milk products, and lean meats and other protein sources.
Limit the intake of saturated and trans-fats, cholesterol, added sugars, sodium (salt), and alcohol.
Limit caloric intake to meet caloric needs.

All Americans should avoid unhealthy weight gain, and those whose weight is too high may also need to lose weight.

Why Are Nutrition and Weight Status Important?

Diet and body weight are related to health status. Good nutrition is important to the growth and development of children. A healthful diet also helps Americans reduce their risks for many health conditions, including:

Overweight and obesity
Malnutrition
Iron-deficiency anemia

Heart disease
High blood pressure
Dyslipidemia (poor lipid profiles)
Type 2 diabetes
Osteoporosis
Oral disease
Constipation
Diverticular disease
Some cancers

Individuals who are at a healthy weight are less likely to:

Develop chronic disease risk factors, such as high blood pressure and dyslipidemia.
Develop chronic diseases, such as type 2 diabetes, heart disease, osteoarthritis, and some cancers.
Experience complications during pregnancy.
Die at an earlier age

TOPIC AREA: PHYSICAL ACTIVITY

Goal

Improve health, fitness, and quality of life through daily physical activity.

Overview

Released in 2008, the Physical Activity Guidelines for Americans (PAG) is the first-ever publication of national guidelines for physical activity. The Physical Activity objectives for Healthy People 2020 reflect the strong state of the science supporting the health benefits of regular physical activity among youth and adults, as identified in the PAG. Regular physical activity includes participation in moderate- and vigorous-intensity physical activities and muscle-strengthening activities.

More than 80% of adults do not meet the guidelines for both aerobic and muscle-strengthening activities. Similarly, more than 80% of adolescents do not do enough aerobic physical activity to meet the guidelines for youth. Working together to meet Healthy People 2020 targets via a multidisciplinary approach is critical to increasing the levels of physical activity and improving health in the United States.

The Physical Activity objectives for Healthy People 2020 highlight how physical activity levels are positively affected by:

Structural environments, such as the availability of sidewalks, bike lanes, trails, and parks
Legislative policies that improve access to facilities that support physical activity

New to Healthy People 2020 are objectives related to policies targeting younger children through:

Physical activity in childcare settings
Behavioral interventions to reduce television viewing and computer usage
Recess and physical education in the Nation's public and private elementary schools

Why Is Physical Activity Important?

Regular physical activity can improve the health and quality of life of Americans of all ages, regardless of the presence of a chronic disease or disability. Among adults and older adults, physical activity can lower the risk of:

Early death
Coronary heart disease
Stroke
High blood pressure
Type 2 diabetes
Breast and colon cancer
Falls
Depression

Among children and adolescents, physical activity can:

Improve bone health
Improve cardiorespiratory and muscular fitness
Decrease levels of body fat
Reduce symptoms of depression
Improve cognitive skills
Improve ability to concentrate and pay attention

For people who are inactive, even small increases in physical activity are associated with health benefits.

TOPIC AREA: TOBACCO USE

Goal

Reduce illness, disability, and death related to tobacco use and secondhand smoke exposure.

Overview

Scientific knowledge about the health effects of tobacco use has increased greatly since the first Surgeon General's report on tobacco was released in 1964. Since the publication of that report, more than 20 million Americans have died because of smoking.

Tobacco use causes:

Cancer (oropharynx, larynx, esophagus, trachea, bronchus, lung, acute myeloid leukemia, stomach, liver, pancreas, kidney and ureter, cervix, bladder, and colorectal)
Heart disease and stroke
Lung diseases (emphysema, bronchitis, chronic airway obstruction, chronic obstructive pulmonary disease, and pneumonia)
Reproductive effects (ectopic pregnancy, premature birth, low birth weight, stillbirth, reduced fertility in women, and erectile dysfunction; and birth defects, including cleft-lip and/or cleft palate)
Other effects (Type 2 diabetes, age-related macular degeneration, rheumatoid arthritis, blindness, cataracts, hip fractures, impaired immune function, periodontitis, and overall diminished health)

The harmful effects of tobacco do not end with the user. There is no risk-free level of exposure to secondhand smoke. Since 1964, 2.5 million deaths have occurred among nonsmokers who died from diseases caused by secondhand smoke exposure. Secondhand smoke causes heart disease, lung cancer, and stroke in adults, and can cause a number of health problems in infants and children, including:

More severe asthma attacks
Respiratory infections
Ear infections
Sudden infant death syndrome (SIDS)

In addition, smokeless tobacco causes a number of serious oral health problems, including cancer of the mouth and gums, periodontitis, and tooth loss.

Why Is Preventing Tobacco Use Important?

Tobacco use is the largest preventable cause of death and disease in the United States.[4] Each year, approximately 480,000 Americans die from tobacco-related illnesses. Further, more than 16 million Americans suffer from at least one disease caused by smoking.

Smoking-related illness in the United States costs more than $300 billion each year, including nearly $170 billion for direct medical care for adults and more than $156 billion in lost productivity

Healthy People 2020 [Internet]. Washington, DC: U.S. Department of Health and Human Services, Office of Disease Prevention and Health Promotion. Cited March 26, 2018. Available from: https://www.healthypeople.gov/

Being physically active is one of the most important steps that Americans of all ages can take to improve their health. The *2008 Physical Activity Guidelines for Americans* provides science-based guidance to help Americans aged 6 and older improve their health through appropriate physical activity.

The U.S. Department of Health and Human Services (HHS) issues the *Physical Activity Guidelines for Americans*. The content of the *Physical Activity Guidelines* complements the *Dietary Guidelines for Americans*, a joint effort of HHS and the U.S. Department of Agriculture (USDA). Together, the two documents provide guidance on the importance of being physically active and eating a healthy diet to promote good health and reduce the risk of chronic diseases.

The primary audiences for the *Physical Activity Guidelines* are policymakers and health professionals. These Guidelines are designed to provide information and guidance on the types and amounts of physical activity that provide substantial health benefits. This information may also be useful to interested members of the public. The main idea behind the Guidelines is that regular physical activity over months and years can produce long-term health benefits. Realizing these benefits requires physical activity each week.

REGULAR PHYSICAL ACTIVITY CAN PRODUCE LONG-TERM HEALTH BENEFITS

The steps used to develop the *Physical Activity Guidelines for Americans* were similar to those used for the *Dietary Guidelines for Americans*. In 2007, HHS Secretary Mike Leavitt appointed an external scientific advisory committee, called the Physical Activity Guidelines Advisory Committee. The Advisory Committee conducted an extensive analysis of the scientific information on physical activity and health. The *Physical Activity Guidelines Advisory Committee Report, 2008* and meeting summaries are available at http://www.health.gov/PAGuidelines/

HHS primarily used the Advisory Committee's report, but also considered comments from the public and Government agencies when writing the Guidelines. The Guidelines will be widely promoted through various communications strategies, such as materials for the public, websites, and partnerships with organizations that promote physical activity.

The *Physical Activity Guidelines for Americans* describes the major research findings on the health benefits of physical activity:

- Regular physical activity reduces the risk of many adverse health outcomes.
- Some physical activity is better than none.
- For most health outcomes, additional benefits occur as the amount of physical activity increases through higher intensity, greater frequency, and/or longer duration.
- Most health benefits occur with at least 150 minutes (2 hours and 30 minutes) a week of moderate intensity physical activity, such as brisk walking. Additional benefits occur with more physical activity.
- Both aerobic (endurance) and muscle-strengthening (resistance) physical activity are beneficial.

- Health benefits occur for children and adolescents, young and middle-aged adults, older adults, and those in every studied racial and ethnic group.
- The health benefits of physical activity occur for people with disabilities.
- The benefits of physical activity far outweigh the possibility of adverse outcomes.

Here are the key Guidelines included in the *Physical Activity Guidelines for Americans.*

Key Guidelines for Children and Adolescents

- Children and adolescents should do 60 minutes (1 hour) or more of physical activity daily.
  - **Aerobic:** Most of the 60 or more minutes a day should be either moderate- or vigorous-intensity aerobic physical activity, and should include vigorous-intensity physical activity at least 3 days a week.
  - **Muscle-strengthening:** As part of their 60 or more minutes of daily physical activity, children and adolescents should include muscle-strengthening physical activity on at least 3 days of the week.
  - **Bone-strengthening:** As part of their 60 or more minutes of daily physical activity, children and adolescents should include bone-strengthening physical activity on at least 3 days of the week.
- It is important to encourage young people to participate in physical activities that are appropriate for their age, that are enjoyable, and that offer variety.

Key Guidelines for Adults

- All adults should avoid inactivity. Some physical activity is better than none, and adults who participate in any amount of physical activity gain some health benefits.
- For substantial health benefits, adults should do at least 150 minutes (2 hours and 30 minutes) a week of moderate-intensity, or 75 minutes (1 hour and 15 minutes) a week of vigorous-intensity aerobic physical activity, or an equivalent combination of moderate- and vigorous-intensity aerobic activity. Aerobic activity should be performed in episodes of at least 10 minutes, and preferably, it should be spread throughout the week.
- For additional and more extensive health benefits, adults should increase their aerobic physical activity to 300 minutes (5 hours) a week of moderate-intensity, or 150 minutes a week of vigorous-intensity aerobic physical activity, or an equivalent combination of moderate- and vigorous-intensity activity. Additional health benefits are gained by engaging in physical activity beyond this amount.

- Adults should also do muscle-strengthening activities that are moderate or high intensity and involve all major muscle groups on two or more days a week, as these activities provide additional health benefits.

Key Guidelines for Older Adults

The Key Guidelines for Adults also apply to older adults. In addition, the following Guidelines are just for older adults:

- When older adults cannot do 150 minutes of moderate-intensity aerobic activity a week because of chronic conditions, they should be as physically active as their abilities and conditions allow.

- Older adults should do exercises that maintain or improve balance if they are at risk of falling.
- Older adults should determine their level of effort for physical activity relative to their level of fitness.
- Older adults with chronic conditions should understand whether and how their conditions affect their ability to do regular physical activity safely.

Key Guidelines for Safe Physical Activity

To do physical activity safely and reduce the risk of injuries and other adverse events, people should:

- Understand the risks and yet be confident that physical activity is safe for almost everyone.
- Choose to do types of physical activity that are appropriate for their current fitness level and health goals, because some activities are safer than others.
- Increase physical activity gradually over time whenever more activity is necessary to meet guidelines or health goals. Inactive people should "start low and go slow" by gradually increasing how often and how long activities are done.
- Protect themselves by using appropriate gear and sports equipment, looking for safe environments, following rules and policies, and making sensible choices about when, where, and how to be active.
- Be under the care of a health-care provider if they have chronic conditions or symptoms. People with chronic conditions and symptoms should consult their health-care provider about the types and amounts of activity appropriate for them.

Key Guidelines for Women during Pregnancy and the Postpartum Period

- Healthy women who are not already highly active or doing vigorous-intensity activity should get at least 150 minutes of moderate-intensity aerobic activity a week during pregnancy and the postpartum period. Preferably, this activity should be spread throughout the week.
- Pregnant women who habitually engage in vigorous-intensity aerobic activity or who are highly active can continue physical activity during pregnancy and the postpartum period, provided that they remain healthy and discuss with their health-care provider how and when activity should be adjusted over time.

Key Guidelines for Adults with Disabilities

- Adults with disabilities, who are able to, should get at least 150 minutes a week of moderate-intensity, or 75 minutes a week of vigorous-intensity aerobic activity, or an equivalent combination of moderate- and vigorous-intensity aerobic activity. Aerobic activity should be performed in episodes of at least 10 minutes, and preferably, it should be spread throughout the week.
- Adults with disabilities, who are able to, should also do muscle-strengthening activities of moderate or high intensity that involve all major muscle groups on 2 or more days a week, as these activities provide additional health benefits.
- When adults with disabilities are not able to meet the Guidelines, they should engage in regular physical activity according to their abilities and should avoid inactivity.
- Adults with disabilities should consult their health-care provider about the amounts and types of physical activity that are appropriate for their abilities.

Key Messages for People with Chronic Medical Conditions

- Adults with chronic conditions obtain important health benefits from regular physical activity.
- When adults with chronic conditions do activity according to their abilities, physical activity is safe.
- Adults with chronic conditions should be under the care of a health-care provider. People with chronic conditions and symptoms should consult their health-care provider about the types and amounts of activity appropriate for them.

The PA Guidelines link is https://health.gov/PAGuidelines/

YES	NO	
_____	_____	**1.** Has your doctor ever said that you have a heart condition and that you should only do physical activity recommended by a doctor?
_____	_____	**2.** Do you feel pain in your chest when you do physical activity?
_____	_____	**3.** In the past month, have you had chest pain when you were not doing physical activity?
_____	_____	**4.** Do you lose your balance because of dizziness or do you ever lose consciousness?
_____	_____	**5.** Do you have a bone or joint problem that could be made worse by a change in your physical activity?
_____	_____	**6.** Is your doctor currently prescribing drugs (for example, water pills) for your blood pressure or heart condition?
_____	_____	**7.** Do you know of any other reason why you should not do physical activity?

If you answered

YES to one or more questions

Talk with your doctor by phone or in person BEFORE you start becoming much more physically active or BEFORE you have a fitness appraisal. Tell your doctor about the PAR-Q and which questions you answered YES.

- You may be able to do any activity you want—as long as you start slow and build up gradually. Or, you may need to restrict your activities to those which are safe for you. Talk with your doctor about the kinds of activities you wish to participate in and follow his/her advice.
- Find out which community programs are safe and helpful for you.

NO to all questions

If you answered NO honestly to all PAR-Q questions, you can be reasonably sure that you can:

- start becoming much more physically active—begin slowly and build up gradually. This is the safest and easiest way to go.
- take part in a fitness appraisal—this is an excellent way to determine your basic fitness so that you can plan the best way for you to live actively.

DELAY BECOMING MUCH MORE ACTIVE

- if you are not feeling well because of temporary illness such as a cold or a fever—wait until you feel better; or
- if you are or may be pregnant—talk to your doctor before you start becoming active.

I have read, understood, and completed this questionnaire. Any questions I had were answered to my full satisfaction.

_____   _____

Signature   Date

Buffalo Wild Wings
https://www.buffalowildwings.com/en/food/nutrition/

Chipotle Mexican Grill
https://www.chipotle.com/nutrition-calculator

Panda Express Chinese Kitchen
https://www.pandaexpress.com/menu

Wendy's
https://www.wendys.com/nutrition-and-health

KFC
http://www.kfc.com/nutrition/

McDonald's
https://www.mcdonalds.com/us/en-us/about-our-food/nutrition-calculator.html

Burger King
https://www.bk.com/menu

Papa John's
http://www.papas-nutritional-calculator.com/

Subway
http://www.subway.com/en-us/menunutrition/nutrition

Long John Silver's
https://www.ljsilvers.com/menu

Taco Bell
https://www.tacobell.com/nutrition/info

Whataburger
http://whataburger.com/food/nutrition

Domino's Pizza
https://www.dominos.com/en/pages/content/nutritional/nutrition.jsp

Jack in the Box
http://www.jackinthebox.com/food

McAlister's Deli
https://www.mcalistersdeli.com/nutrition

Index

Note: Page numbers followed by b, f and t indicates boxes, figures and tables respectively.

A

AABA. *See* American Anorexia/Bulimia Association, Inc.
Abdominal crunch test, 89, 91
Abdominal strength, 10
ACHA. *See* American College Health Association
ACSM. *See* American College of Sports Medicine
Active isolated stretching (AIS), 61, 62
Acute muscle soreness, 5
Acute stress, 202
Acute stress disorder (ASD), 208
Adenosine triphosphate (ATP), 20
ADP. *See* Air displacement plethysmography
Adrenal glands, 204
Aerobic exercise, 143
  acute and chronic adaptations to, 22
  components of
    duration, 25
    frequency, 23
    intensity, 23–25
    mode, 23
Aerobic processes, 20
Age, 168
  osteoporosis, 196
Agility, 8
Air displacement plethysmography (ADP), use of, 44–45
AIS. *See* Active isolated stretching
ALA (alpha-linolenic acid), 108
Alcohol consumption, 122–123, 182
Allostatic load, 203
Allyl sulfides, 122
Alter or eliminate approach, 210
Altruism, 207, 211
American Anorexia/Bulimia Association, Inc. (AABA), 151
American Cancer Society, 137, 178
American College Health Association (ACHA), 3–4, 208
American College of Sports Medicine (ACSM), 22, 23, 29, 78, 229
American Heart Association, 108, 164, 165t
  diet and lifestyle goals and recommendations for cardiovascular disease reduction, 167b

American Psychological Association, 202
Anabolic steroids, 82
ANAD. *See* National Association of Anorexia Nervosa and Associated Disorders
Anaerobic exercise, 141, 143
Anaerobic processes, 20
Android obesity, 47, 136
Anemia, 114
Anencephaly, 111
Angina pectoris, 154–155, 155t
Anorexia athletica, 149
Anorexia nervosa, 148
Anorexia Nervosa and Related Eating Disorders, Inc. (ANRED), 150–151
Antioxidants, 121
Apparatus work Pilates, 63
Appetite, exercise and, 144
Apple-shaped body. *See* Android obesity
Asana, 64
ASD. *See* Acute stress disorder
Atherosclerosis, 155
ATP. *See* Adenosine triphosphate
Avoidance symptoms, 209

B

Balance, 8
Ballistic bar stretch, 72f
Ballistic stretching, 61
Basal cell cancers, 180
"Be Active Your Way" program, 229
Bench jump test, 89
Benign tumors, 178
BIA. *See* Bioelectrical impedance analysis
Binge-eating disorder, 149b
Binge-purge syndrome, 148
Bioelectrical impedance analysis (BIA), 43
Biofeedback techniques, 212
Biologic therapy. *See* Immunotherapy
Biotin, 112t
Blood lipids, 162
  dietary adjustments, 164
  effects of exercise on, 163t
  levels, 136
Blood pressure, 9–10, 155, 160t
  lowered, 21
BMI. *See* Body mass index

Bod-Pod®, 44–45
Body composition, 8, 9
  assessing, 42–48
  ideal body weight, 48–49
  overview, 40
  overweight
    and obesity, problems with, 42
    overfat versus, 40–41
Body fat distribution, 135–136
Body mass index (BMI), 45–47
Bone mineral loss, 22
Breast cancer, 185–186, 189b
Breast self-exams (BSE), 186
Breath, natural rhythm of, 63–64
Breslow, Lester, 5
Bridge stretch, 70f
BSE. *See* Breast self-exams
Bulimia nervosa, 148

C

Calcium, 115t
  foods rich in, 197t
Califano, Joseph, 2
Caloric intake and expenditure, 10
Cancer, 137
  causes of, 179–183
    environmental factors, 179–180
    genetic factors, 179
    lifestyle, 180, 182–183
    viral, 180
  incidence of, 178–179
  major types of
    breast, 185–186, 189b
    colon and rectal, 186, 188
    lung, 184–185
    prostate, 186
    skin, 188–190
    testicular, 190, 191b
  overview, 178
  risk for, 10
  role of exercise in, 184
  treatment
    chemotherapy, 192–193
    immunotherapy, 193
    radiation, 192
    surgery, 192
  warning signs and prevention, 190–192